JOURNAL FOR THE STUDY OF THE NEW TESTAMENT
SUPPLEMENT SERIES
161

GENDER, CULTURE, THEORY
5

Editor
J. Cheryl Exum

Sheffield Academic Press

Courting Betrayal

Jesus as Victim
in the Gospel of John

Helen C. Orchard

Journal for the Study of the New Testament
Supplement Series 161

Gender, Culture, Theory 5

Copyright © 1998 Sheffield Academic Press

Published by
Sheffield Academic Press Ltd
Mansion House
19 Kingfield Road
Sheffield S11 9AS
England

Typeset by Sheffield Academic Press
and
Printed on acid-free paper in Great Britain
by Bookcraft Ltd
Midsomer Norton, Bath

British Library Cataloguing in Publication Data

A catalogue record for this book is available
from the British Library

ISBN 1-85075-892-1
ISBN 1-85075-884-0 pa

In Memory of

Martin Peter Hobbs

19 May 1966–26 May 1995

ὅτι ἐκ τοῦ πληρώματος αὐτοῦ ἡμεῖς πάντες ἐλάβομεν
καὶ χάριν ἀντὶ χάριτος

CONTENTS

PREFACE

This book had its origin as a thesis submitted for the degree of PhD at the University of Sheffield in September 1995. I was a student in the Biblical Studies Department at Sheffield between 1984 and 1995 and, without doubt, the knowledge and skills acquired during that time have had the most profound impact on my life. I would like, therefore, to express my appreciation to a Department which is internationally respected as a centre of innovative and rigorous scholarship. I owe a debt of gratitude to my tutor, Professor David Clines, whose teaching and writing has been an inspiration to me, and to my examiners, Professor Cheryl Exum and Professor Ann Loades, for their insightful comments. In particular, I would like to thank Professor Exum for her interest in the work and for accepting it for publication in the Gender, Culture, Theory series. I am grateful to Professor John Rogerson for his support, both in and out of the Department, and to Dr Mark Stibbe and Dr Loveday Alexander who read and commented on the work in its early stages. Thanks are due to my parents who, despite their better judgment, allowed me to go my own way in taking a degree in a subject as esoteric as Biblical Studies in the first place. It has been a decision I have never regretted.

I wish to record my appreciation to the following people who provided varying degrees of financial assistance during my first three years of postgraduate study: Mark Birchall, Roger Firman, Nick Hunt, Grace and Peter Lander, Brenda and Lewis Orchard, Ann Warren and Ulric Wilson. I would also like to thank my former employer, Weston Park Hospital, for permitting me to take an invaluable two months study leave in the summer of 1995, and Clive Newman who covered for me during that period.

Among the long suffering friends who bore with me while I was writing the PhD are Louise Ashley, Leslie Hill, Susan Hobbs, Nick Hunt, Paul Lewis, Caroline Orchard, Stuart Orchard, Guy Rotherham, Fiona Simpson, Julie Turner and Ulric Wilson. Thanks especially to Lorna Campbell for her encouragement and confidence in me during the time

I was turning the thesis into a book. Finally and considerably, thanks to Jane Howcroft—intellectual sparring partner and valued confidante during this long journey.

Helen Orchard
11 January 1998

Abbreviations

AAR	American Academy of Religion
AB	Anchor Bible
AnBib	Analecta biblica
ANCL	A. Roberts (ed.), *Ante-Nicene Christian Library*
AusBR	*Australian Biblical Review*
AV	Authorized Version
BAGD	Walter Baur, William F. Arndt, F. William Ginrich and Frederick W. Danker, *A Greek–English Lexicon of the New Testament and Other Early Christian Literature* (Chicago: University of Chicago Press, 2nd edn, 1958)
BETL	Bibliotheca ephemeridum theologicarum lovaniensium
Bib Int	*Biblical Interpretation*
Bib	*Biblica*
BibRes	*Biblical Research*
BSac	*Bibliotheca Sacra*
BTB	*Biblical Theology Bulletin*
CBQ	*Catholic Biblical Quarterly*
ChS	*Chicago Studies*
ConBNT	Coniectanea biblica, New Testament
CurTM	*Currents in Theology and Mission*
EvQ	*Evangelical Quarterly*
ExpTim	*Expository Times*
HBT	*Horizons in Biblical Theology*
HeyJ	*Heythrop Journal*
HNT	Handbuch zum Neuen Testament
HTKNT	Herders theologischer Kommentar zum Neuen Testament
HUT	Hermeneutische Untersuchungen zur Theologie
ICC	International Critical Commentary
Int	*Interpretation*
JBL	*Journal of Biblical Literature*
JSNT	*Journal for the Study of the New Testament*
JSNTSup	*JSNT* Supplement Series
JSOT	*Journal for the Study of the Old Testament*
JSOTSup	*JSOT* Supplement Series
JTheolSA	*Journal of Theology for Southern Africa*
JTS	*Journal of Theological Studies*

LCL	Loeb Classical Library
LNPNF	P. Schaff (ed.), *Library of the Nicene and Post-Nicene Fathers*
LTP	*Laval Théologique Philosophique*
NCB	New Century Bible
Neot	*Neotestamentica*
NIDNTT	Colin Brown (ed.), *The New International Dictionary of New Testament Theology* (3 vols.; Exeter: Paternoster Press, 1975)
NIGTC	New International Greek Testament Commentary
NIV	New International Version
NovT	*Novum Testamentum*
NovTSup	*Novum Testamentum* Supplement Series
NTS	*New Testament Studies*
NTTS	New Testament Tools and Studies
RB	*Revue Biblique*
RelSRev	*Religious Studies Review*
RevExp	*Review and Expositor*
RL	*Religion in Life*
RSV	Revised Standard Version
SBL	Society of Biblical Literature
SBLDS	Society of Biblical Literature Dissertation Series
SJLA	Studies in Judaism in Late Antiquity
SJT	*Scottish Journal of Theology*
SNTW	Studies of the New Testament and its World
SR	*Studies in Religion/Sciences religieuses*
Str-B	H. Strack & P. Billerbeck, *Kommentar zum Neuen Testament*
TDNT	Gerhard Kittel and Gerhard Friedrich (eds.), *Theological Dictionary of the New Testament* (trans. Geoffrey W. Bromiley; 10 vols.; Grand Rapids: Eerdmans, 1964–)
TE	*The Theological Educator*
TJT	*Toronto Journal of Theology*
TS	*Theological Studies*
USQR	*Union Seminary Quarterly Review*
VT	*Vetus Testamentum*
VTSup	*Vetus Testamentum* Supplement Series
WBC	Word Biblical Commentary
WUNT	Wissenschaftliche Untersuchungen zum Neuen Testament
ZNW	*Zeitschrift für die neutestamentliche Wissenschaft*

1

The Disconcerting Gospel

Introduction

The Gospel of John is an unsettling text. There is there a tendency among many scholars to sanitize and spiritualize it, usually in an attempt to render its portrayal of Jesus slightly more palatable. It has been 'embraced by the arms of Christian piety'[1] to a far greater extent than the Synoptics, with much of its offensiveness being 're-interpreted' or simply stripped away. Some admit quite openly that they have been 'repelled'[2] by the Fourth Gospel; others see it as the 'maverick'[3] or 'problem' gospel;[4] or at least admit that there is *something* about it that makes it 'fascinating'.[5]

There are some fairly obvious aspects of the Gospel which the reader might feel uncomfortable about. A common anxiety is the perception that blatant anti-Jewish sentiment pervades the narrative[6] as well as the

---

1.   G.C. Nicholson, *Death as Departure: The Johannine Descent–Ascent Schema* (SBLDS, 63; Chico, CA: Scholars Press, 1983), p. 1.

2.   P.S. Minear, *John: The Martyr's Gospel* (New York: Pilgrim Press, 1984), p. ix.

3.   R. Kysar, *John: The Maverick Gospel* (Atlanta: John Knox Press, 1976).

4.   This is the title of the first chapter of A.T. Hanson's *The Prophetic Gospel: A Study of John and the Old Testament* (Edinburgh: T. & T. Clark, 1991).

5.   M.J.J. Menken, 'The Christology of the Fourth Gospel: A Survey of Recent Research', in M.C. de Boer (ed.), *From Jesus to John: Essays on Jesus and New Testament Christology in Honour of Marinus de Jonge* (JSNTSup, 84; Sheffield: JSOT Press, 1993), pp. 292-320 (292).

6.   Michael Goulder comments: 'Even a simple reader feels that John does not love "the Jews"; that his book is motivated by a great hatred of them' ('Nicodemus', *SJT* 44 [1991], p. 168). Judith Hellig concludes that 'the Gospel of John reaches the highest development of philosophic incorporation of the anti-Jewish midrash' ('The Negative Image of the Jew and its New Testament Roots', *JTheolSA* 64 [1988], pp. 39-48 [44]). Samuel Sandmel notes that traditionally John has been seen as 'the most anti-Semitic, or at least the most overtly anti-Semitic of all the Gospels' (*Anti-Semitism in the New Testament?* [Philadelphia: Fortress Press, 1978], p. 101). He

overriding sectarian attitude of an evangelist who is capable of 'harsh-ness'[7] or even 'hot hatred'[8] towards those outside the community. Other concerns are the perceived theological manipulation of the original 'facts', which exposes the Gospel's dubious historicity,[9] the 'obnoxious theological verbiage',[10] or simply the general 'sense of alienation and superiority'.[11] The most significant bequest of the Gospel, however, must surely be its portrayal of a Jesus who is radically different from his

attempts to explain this in terms of the Gospel's *Sitz im Leben*, but concludes: 'one may accordingly explain the historical circumstances but one cannot deny the exis-tence of a written compilation of clearly expressed anti-Jewish statements' (p. 119).

Recent discussion on the identity and role of the Jews in John can be found in M. Davies, *Rhetoric and Reference in the Fourth Gospel* (JSNTSup, 69; Sheffield: JSOT Press, 1992), pp. 290-312. Davies notes that, based on what is known about Judaism during the first two centuries CE, the Fourth Gospel's portrayal of the Jews is little short of a 'gross caricature' (p. 17). Similarly, J.D.G. Dunn warns of the dangers of misreading John's treatment of the Jews by failing to appreciate the complexity of that treatment and failing to give enough attention to the historical context. He concludes, 'it is highly questionable whether the Fourth Evangelist himself can fairly be indicted for either anti-Judaism or anti-Semitism' ('The Question of Anti-Semitism in the New Testament Writings of the Period', in J.D.G. Dunn [ed.], *Jews and Christians: The Parting of the Ways A.D. 70 to 135* [WUNT, 66; Tübingen: J.C.B Mohr (Paul Siebeck), 1992], pp. 177-11 [203]). J. McHugh, writing in the same volume, takes a similar line. Although he sees 'a powerful and deep stream of apologetic directed towards those of the Jewish faith', he feels that 'hostility' is too strong a word to use to describe it ('In him Was Life', in Dunn [ed.], *Jews and Christians*, pp. 123-58 [158]). Colin Hickling sees a tension between the evangelist's universalist theme, the traditional understanding of the rejection of Jesus by some Jews and his church's harsh experience of Judaism ('Attitudes to Judaism in the Fourth Gospel', in M. de Jonge [ed.], *L'Evangile de Jean: Sources, Rédaction, Théologie* [BETL, 44; Leuven: Leuven University Press/Uitgeverij Peeter, 1977], pp. 347-54).

7.   M. Hengel, *The Johannine Question* (trans. J. Bowden; London: SCM Press, 1989), p. 44.

8.   W. Bauer, *Das Johannesevangelium* (HNT, 6; Tübingen: J.C.B. Mohr [Paul Siebeck], 3rd edn, 1933), p. 248.

9.   Examples of those who see a creative theological overlay to the Gospel— history serving theology rather than theology interpreting historical fact—include E.C. Hoskyns, *The Fourth Gospel* (ed. F.N. Davey; London: Faber & Faber, 2nd edn, 1947); S.S. Smalley, *John: Evangelist and Interpreter* (Exeter: Paternoster Press, 1978); and L. Morris, *The Gospel According to John: The English Text with Introduction, Exposition and Notes* (Grand Rapids: Eerdmans, 1971).

10.   Minear, *John: The Martyr's Gospel*, p. x.

11.   R.E. Brown, *The Community of the Beloved Disciple* (London: Geoffrey Chapman, 1979), p. 89.

Synoptic counterpart.[12] And not just different, but *strange*.[13] In fact, not just strange, but not all that *nice* in parts. The truth is that John's Gospel does not hold much appeal for those attracted to the 'St Francis of Assisi type'.[14] The Synoptic accounts present the reader with a popular Galilean rabbi, who performs frequent miracles and healings and speaks to the crowds flocking to hear him in the language of everyday life. By contrast, the Johannine Jesus is a more detached figure, who keeps his '"professional" distance' from the other characters,[15] and 'feels indignation, not pity, when needy people come to him'.[16] His oratorical style is not as easily accessible as that of the Synoptic Jesus.[17] Complicated theological concepts are expounded in long monologues to audiences who rarely understand him, and are often less than appreciative.[18] What this Jesus lacks is the generally amenable disposition that

12. J.D.G. Dunn sees the Synoptics providing a portrait of Jesus, whereas John is more like an impressionist painting (*The Evidence for Jesus: The Impact of Scholarship on our Understanding of how Christianity Began* [London: SCM Press, 1985], p. 43).

13. In his review of Ernst Käsemann's *The Testament of Jesus*, Wayne Meeks makes the following statement: 'Käsemann succeeds in making us face up to the strangeness of the Johannine Christology, and that is a significant accomplishment. But a more precise definition of that strangeness is called for' (Review of *The Testament of Jesus, by Ernst Käsemann*', in *USQR* 24 [1969], pp. 414-20 [419]). Unfortunately, it has proved impossible to obtain a copy of this article. The quotation has therefore been taken from M.M. Thompson, *The Humanity of Jesus in the Fourth Gospel* (Philadelphia: Fortress Press, 1988), p. 6.

14. See J.D. Salinger for a tirade against those unable to love or understand any son of God who throws tables around and says a human being is more valuable than a soft, helpless Easter chick. They invariably attempt to merge Jesus with St Francis and Heidi's grandfather to make him more 'lovable' (*Franny and Zooey* [repr.; New York: Penguin Books, 1980 (1964)], p. 130).

15. J.A. du Rand, 'The Characterization of Jesus as Depicted in the Narrative of the Fourth Gospel', *Neot* 19 (1985), pp. 18-36 (18, also 29, 30). Du Rand concludes that he remains 'a mysterious figure' (p. 33).

16. H. Windisch, 'John's Narrative Style', in M.W.G. Stibbe (ed.), *The Gospel of John as Literature: An Anthology of Twentieth-Century Perspectives* (NTTS, 17; Leiden: E.J. Brill, 1993), pp. 25-64 (60).

17. For a brief discussion of differences between the Synoptic and Johannine Christ see S. Barton, 'The Believer, the Historian and the Fourth Gospel', *Theology* 96 (1993), pp. 289-302.

18. D. Moody Smith comments, 'the richness, colour, specificity, concreteness, and variety which characterize the teaching of Jesus in the Synoptic Gospels are by and large absent from John' ('The Presentation of Jesus in the Fourth Gospel', *Int* 31 [1977], pp. 367-78 [370]).

makes the Synoptic character attractive to the modern reader. He is just not '*our man Jesus*, friend of the common folk'.

The fourth evangelist has also been accused of having minimal concern with some of the physical details of Jesus' life which would perhaps make him seem a little more human. It is certainly true that several Synoptic stories of a distinctly physical nature are missing from John's account: Jesus' birth and baptism, the wilderness temptation and the agony in Gethsemane. This gives the impression that the Synoptics are more solidly anchored in this world and perhaps it is unsurprising that, when compared with them, the Fourth Gospel has been subjected to accusations of docetism during its interpretative history. However, while the content and style of John's Gospel may seem to encourage the reader to focus on matters other than Jesus' corporeal existence, a close reading of the narrative reveals that it is not devoid of material concerning his physical experiences. The real issue is one of knowing where to look. Scholars have commented on some of the more obvious texts— Jesus is weary (4.6), Jesus is thirsty (19.28)—often claiming that the inclusion of these in the Gospel provides poor evidence for a thoroughly human Jesus,[19] but there is a mass of less obvious material. This study suggests that much of this can be found by focusing on a specific motif—violence—and goes on to explore the way in which the motif is manifested in John's Gospel. This is not an area which has been explored by scholars, and it would probably not be thought of as an automatic pointer to Jesus' tangibility.[20] The Gospel's 'spiritual' reputation has tended to obfuscate some of the more unsavoury details of the

---

19. So C.K. Barrett, following Käsemann, sees Jn 4.6 as an 'unskilful' attempt by the evangelist to emphasize Jesus' humanity (*Gospel According to St John: An Introduction with Commentary and Notes on the Greek Text* [London: SPCK, 2nd edn, 1978], p. 231). Likewise Jesus is seen to thirst on the cross because it is required to fulfil Scripture rather than out of a desperate physical need. This is indicated by Alfred Loisy's comment: 'one has to suppose that Christ is really thirsty; but the evangelist attributes to him above all the consciousness of a prophecy coming true' (*Le Quatrième Evangile* [Paris, Alphonse Picard et Fils, 1903], pp. 880-81. Quotation translated by L.E. Orchard).

20. Rene Girard does discuss the role of violence in the Gospels in relation to Jesus' identity as a scapegoat. In the Fourth Gospel Jesus is 'the Paraclete, par excellence, in the struggle against the representation of persecution. Every defence and rehabilitation of victims is based on the Passion's power of revelation' (*The Scapegoat* [trans. Y. Freccero; Baltimore: The Johns Hopkins University Press, 1986], pp. 206-12 [208]).

narrative and the less pleasant characteristics of its protagonist. This study suggests that it is the dynamics of violence that makes the Fourth Gospel disconcerting; and that the 'strangeness' of Jesus is linked to his identity as a victim.

The Remit of this Study

The next three chapters will discuss the various contexts in which this piece of research has been carried out; however, it is necessary in this introductory chapter to clarify the main issue of interest and to mention areas that lie outside of its remit. The preceding section has already started to touch on some christological issues, but it needs to be made clear at the outset that this study is not an investigation into the Christology of John's Gospel. The approach employed to discuss Jesus as a victim is primarily literary, not theological. The exegesis is therefore focused on Jesus as a character within the narrative world of the Fourth Gospel. Nevertheless, it is necessary to make some brief comments on Christology because the literary investigation is strengthened by the presupposition of a 'low', rather than a 'high' Christology. It could be argued that Jesus' identity as a victim can be divorced from his christological status—after all, whether he is god or man in the Gospel, he still experiences the same acts of victimization. While it is true that his fate remains the same whatever his ontological nature, the issue is not quite that simple. It becomes clear that the extent of Jesus' victimization is influenced by Christology if we briefly consider what it means to be a victim.

Being a credible victim requires the assumption of a level of vulnerability that is instinctively difficult to reconcile with divinity. This is because the experience of true victimization implies such a loss of autonomy and control on the part of the victim that he or she is placed utterly at the mercy of the victimizer.[21] There is therefore an incompatibility between the power inherent in the nature of divinity, and the total absence of power (and not simply its surrender) experienced by the victim. A 'low' Christology, which accepts the full humanity of Jesus in

---

21. It should be noted that I am not talking about victims in the cultic sense, but rather in the sociological sense. Sacrificial victims can, of course, be human or animal and this too involves the loss of liberty culminating in the loss of the victim's life. To discuss cultic implications at this point would confuse the argument. There is a limited treatment of the issue in Chapter 9.

the Fourth Gospel, is therefore necessary for him to be considered a victim. While this may seem to be a rather precarious argument at this point, the reader should note that it is further substantiated in Chapter 2, where the importance of a human Jesus will become obvious; and Chapter 6, where the term 'victim' will be explored.

Johannine Christology

The preceding paragraph renders it necessary to include a paragraph on the Christology of the Fourth Gospel. This has been an area of significant debate among Johannine scholars and it is possible only to give a brief overview here.

Discussion concerning the person of the Johannine Jesus and his ontological nature has generally concentrated on whether the evangelist presents us with a character who is a credible human being. Those who believe he does not, adopt, to a greater or lesser extent, the sort of high Christology propounded by Ernst Käsemann. Käsemann's position is best summarized by his oft-quoted statement that the Johannine Jesus is 'a god striding on the earth'.[22] That John's Gospel presents us with a high Christology has been the dominant view of traditional scholarship[23] and even on a brief trawl through Johannine literature it is not difficult to produce an interesting crop of 'neo-Docetic' sentiments.[24] Jesus is

22. E. Käsemann, *The Testament of Jesus: A Study of the Gospel of John in the Light of Chapter 17* (trans. G. Krodel; Philadelphia: Fortress Press, 1968), p. 73. Käsemann builds on the work of F.C. Baur, W. Wrede, G.P. Wetter and E. Hirsch, all of whom reject John's picture of Jesus as being that of a credible human. See Thompson for description and analysis (*Humanity of Jesus*, p. 4).

23. Robin Scroggs, for one, notes this, commenting: 'High Christology! Jesus Christ is completely divine, is God. This is the judgement universally held of the thought of the Gospel of John' (*Christology in Paul and John* [Proclamation Commentaries; Philadelphia: Fortress Press, 1988], p. 63). Similarly, Richard Cassidy writes: 'It is hardly an exaggeration to say that the entire Gospel of John is permeated with the sovereignty of Jesus. Jesus possesses sovereign standing from the first moment that he is present within John's Gospel...[this] concept of sovereignty...is closely related to the widely recognized concept of John's high Christology' (*John's Gospel in New Perspective: Christology and the Realities of Roman Power* [Maryknoll, NY: Orbis Books, 1992], p. 29).

24. Such as the following by C.F. Evans: 'One may legitimately ask with respect to this gospel as a whole whether its Christ ever really has his feet firmly on the earth' ('The Passion of John' in *Explorations in Theology* [9 vols.; London: SCM Press, 1977], II, p. 50-66 [62]). A.T. Hanson expresses similar sentiments: 'the Jesus

viewed as an exalted figure who is in control of the course of events, playing out his soteriological role in his own way, in his own time. He is omniscient, authoritative, beyond suffering and generally devoid of 'human' characteristics. He is, without doubt, a *divine* figure.

The opposing view, which emphasizes the humanity of Jesus in the Gospel, has been traditionally upheld by Rudolf Bultmann. Bultmann's focus is on the Word *made flesh*:

> Jesus is the Revealer who appears not as *man-in-general*, i.e. not simply as a bearer of human *nature*, but as a *definite human being in history*: Jesus of Nazareth. His humanity is genuine humanity.[25]

Moreover, Jesus is a human being 'in whom *nothing unusual is perceptible* except his bold assertion that in him God encounters men'.[26] Bultmann and Käsemann represent the opposite ends of the christological spectrum with many scholars falling somewhere between these two points.[27] Two scholars who have argued against the prevailing view of high Christology in recent times are Marianne Meye Thompson and Margaret Davies. Thompson discusses the humanity of Jesus in detail, arguing that the Fourth Gospel clearly sees Jesus as fully human, but that this does not mean that he was 'nothing but a man'. She does not see the humanity and divinity of Jesus as mutually exclusive options, concluding that:

of the Fourth Gospel cannot possibly be a historical representation: he is a divine figure, the eternal Word appearing as a man but retaining all the attributes of God except invisibility and omnipresence' (*The Prophetic Gospel*, p. 269). Hans Windisch sees the Johannine Jesus as '*the new Christ-type, detached from the earth and from history...a divine Christ from heaven*' ('John's Narrative Style', p. 62, emphasis original).

   25. R. Bultmann, *Theology of the New Testament* (trans. K. Grobel; London: SCM Press, 1983), II, p. 41, emphasis original.

   26. Bultmann, *Theology of the New Testament*, II, p. 50, emphasis added.

   27. A brief discussion of Käsemann versus Bultmann and the other more recent major players in this field can be found in M.J.J. Menken, 'The Christology of the Fourth Gospel', pp. 292-320. See also Scroggs for a full exploration of Jesus' 'earthly credentials' (*Christology in Paul and John*, p. 78). The commentaries generally focus their christological investigations around the titles used of Jesus in the Fourth Gospel: Son of God, Messiah, Logos and Son of Man. So, Barrett, *Gospel According to St John*, pp. 70-75; G.R. Beasley-Murray, *John* (WBC, 36; Waco, TX: Word Books, 1987), pp. lxxxi-lxxxiv and D.A. Carson, *The Gospel According to John* (Leicester: IVP, 1991), pp. 95-96. See also J.F. O'Grady, ('The Human Jesus in the Fourth Gospel', *BTB* 14 [1984], pp. 63-66) for this approach.

> although Jesus shares his humanity in common with all other human
> beings, that humanity does not finally limit or define him; nevertheless,
> his uniqueness or *unlikeness* does not efface his humanity. It is that
> *unlikeness* which is disconcerting.[28]

Davies argues against both ancient and modern docetic and subordina-
tionist views of the Johannine Jesus. Jesus is not 'God merely appearing
to be a man', but 'a man wholly dedicated to the mission God sent him
to fulfil.'[29] Moreover, as a human being Jesus is made of flesh, is vulnerable and is mortal.[30]

This introductory chapter has begun to explore some of the major
concerns of the book. It has started by suggesting that there is something
disconcerting about John's Gospel and that this is linked to its presentation of Jesus. It has gone on to suggest that there is a motif of violence
in the Gospel which can be used to interpret this presentation of Jesus,
identifying him as a victim. For this interpretation to be understandable,
it is necessary to accept the full humanity of Jesus in the Fourth Gospel,
adopting a low Christology. This runs counter to traditional scholarship,
but has been convincingly argued in recent monographs and is an
acceptable position to take. It is, in fact, probably the case that it is the
belief in a high Christology that has prevented scholars from discerning
the amount of material relating to violence in John's Gospel.

28. Thompson, *Humanity of Jesus*, p. 128. See pp. 117-28 for her full concluding
argument.
  29. Davies, *Rhetoric and Reference*, p. 43.
  30. Davies, *Rhetoric and Reference*, p. 16.

2

The Theological Context

Liberation Theology's Picture of Jesus

Liberation theology is by its very nature a pluralistic discipline. Numerous approaches have been born during the last few decades as communities search for new ways of confronting the physical and religious oppression they experience. The midwives for these theologies have been poverty, colonialism, state violence, sexism, racism, political injustice, homophobia, or any other situation in which humanity is demeaned and deformed.[1] What they have in common is their recognition of the specific context in which they function, the purpose they fulfil and the goals to which they aspire. They do not arise out of mere intellectual curiosity and do not exist in a political vacuum. For example, a feminist theology would see itself as part of the practical struggle of women and women-identified men against sexism and towards the realization of a fully inclusive humanity. These are immediate and concrete concerns that aim not simply to understand the history of texts or theological concepts, but to *use* the Bible in order to liberate. The very nature of the goals held by liberation theologies necessitates an engagement in the life and world-view of the people. There is a functional and experiential dimension here—to be at all meaningful, a theology must spring from, and be directly relevant to its community. This is particularly the case when liberation theologies turn their attention to the person of Christ. Jon Sobrino explains that 'the need for a "new" Christology is felt in a "new" situation, where people clearly feel the meaninglessness of the existing situation and glimpse the

---

1.   The sources of oppression are limitless but can be classified as deriving from one or more of the following: institutions, enemies, victims, or the system. See the work of Robert Elias for a thorough treatment of the subject (*The Politics of Victimization: Victims, Victimology and Human Rights* [Oxford: Oxford University Press, 1986], pp. 209-15).

direction in which new meaningfulness might be found'.[2] This, then, is no 'ivory tower' occupation. Its proponents must be prepared to take sides and to state openly that this is what they have done. Leonardo Boff expresses the point well:

> Theologians do not live in the clouds. They are social actors with a particular place in society... Their findings are also addressed to a particular audience... The themes and emphases of a given Christology flow from what seems relevant to the theologian on the basis of his or her social standpoint. In that sense we must maintain that no Christology is or can be neutral. Every Christology is partisan and committed.[3]

Boff's comment confronts us immediately with an obvious characteristic of this type of theology. Its overt engagement with the community reveals that it is inescapably subjective in nature. It is now generally recognized that *no* theology is objective, or 'neutral', since every theologian incorporates his or her own value system and experiences into the interpretative process. However, this is a particularly obvious feature (and in the past has been the cause for criticism) of liberation theologies. In fact, theologians working from this perspective rarely attempt to conceal it, often acknowledging their preconceptions and setting out much of their agenda alongside the results of their hermeneutics. Hence the feminist Sheila Collins writes:

> We openly acknowledge the self-interest involved in our critiques of present systems. We know that our theologizing and philosophizing will have political implications, and in admitting our biases from the outset, perhaps we are one step ahead in the search for a just order.[4]

It has already been indicated that the reason that subjectivity is such a conspicuous feature of liberation theologies is that it is experiential in nature and, moreover, that the experiences are so extreme. The suffering

---

2. J. Sobrino, *Christology at the Crossroads: A Latin American Approach* (trans. J. Drury; London: SCM Press, 1978), p. 347.

3. L. Boff, *Jesus Christ, Liberator: A Critical Christology for our Time* (trans. P. Hughes; Maryknoll, NY: Orbis Books, 1978), p. 265.

4. S. Collins, 'A Feminist Reading of History', in A. Kee (ed.), *The Scope of Political Theology* (London: SCM Press, 1978), pp. 79-83 (80-81). For other examples, see the prologue to L. Russell (ed.), *Feminist Interpretation of the Bible* (Oxford: Basil Blackwell, 1985). Perhaps the simplest and most profound instance of the practice of this experiential hermeneutics by the *pueblo oprimido* can be seen in Ernesto Cardenal's *Love in Practice: The Gospel in Solentiname* (trans. D.D. Walsh; London: Search Press, 1977).

of the community plays a crucial role in its formulation, with oppression functioning as a key interpreter of Scripture, shaping the understanding of God and Jesus. Rebecca Chopp elaborates, claiming that the difference between liberation theologies and other modern theologies is found in the paradigm shift caused by the questions asked by the former. The fundamental question asked by liberation theologies is that of *massive public suffering*.

> Suffering, according to liberation theology, is the representative experience of being human for the masses of nonpersons on the fringes or outside of modern history. Such suffering ruptures our ideologies and illusions about progress and security, revealing to us that for the majority of our fellow human beings 'progress' and 'history' consist of a long, dark night of tragic terror. Liberation theology stands within this rupture of suffering and does the traditional work of theology—it speaks of God.[5]

The suffering community finds a point of contact with the gospel through the suffering Jesus and reinterprets his experience in the light of its own. If they are victims, so too is he. This is portrayed strikingly through the picture of Jesus common among poor and persecuted communities in South America. Writing about the image of Jesus among these people, Georges Casalis sees a saviour who suffers *in extremis*—the abject Lord:

> In most instances he appears as one on the point of death—his eyes rolled up in their sockets, his face turned down to earth, and his whole body exhibiting the havoc wreaked upon it by the blows of his torturers.[6]

Casalis claims that these representations arouse a morbid fascination for the people: 'it is blood and death that is loved the most'.[7] Questioning why this is the case, why the people choose this type of image, he comes to the following conclusion:

> When the faithful people pray before these images or venerate them, when their spirit is seared all through life by a pedagogy of submission and passivity, *evidently it is their own destiny that they encounter here*—and worship, and accept with masochistic resignation.[8]

5. R. Chopp, *The Praxis of Suffering: An Interpretation of Liberation and Political Theologies* (Maryknoll, NY: Orbis Books, 1986), p. 151.

6. G. Casalis, 'Jesus: Neither Abject Lord nor Heavenly Monarch', in J.M. Bonino (ed.), *Faces of Jesus: Latin American Christologies* (trans. R.R. Barr; Maryknoll, NY: Orbis Books, 1977), p. 72.

7. Casalis, 'Neither Abject Lord', p. 74.

8. Casalis, 'Neither Abject Lord', p. 73, emphasis added. W.F. Warren suggests

This picture of Jesus is the most accessible in the eyes of the people because he is the one who speaks to their condition. They worship him because he is one of them. Their experience mirrors his and they are victims together. Moreover, because of the extremes at which the oppressed live their lives, it is imperative that their Christology speaks directly to these situations. Sobrino asserts:

> We live in the presence of so much death. There is the reality of definitive, physical death and of the death that people experience in the toils of oppression, injustice and sinfulness. *Any consideration of God that ignores such a basic dictum of life is idealistic, if not downright alienating.*[9]

Perhaps this begins to address the question of why victims commonly choose a messiah who is also a victim as their representative, rather than a liberator with all the trappings of power. A meaningful Christology must offer an identification of the figure of Jesus with the believer's experience of life in this world. Authentic liberation is not granted to an oppressed people from 'the authorities on high', nor even by one who deigns to represent the people, assuming their mantle. It is fought for by the oppressed themselves and achieved from within their ranks. True liberation of the oppressed necessitates that the liberator too be oppressed. The liberator must be identifiable as a member of the community, being seen by outsiders as 'one of them', participating in their suffering and identifying with their experiences. If the gospel really is to be 'good news' to the poor and if it is to release captives and liberate the oppressed (Lk. 4.18), then the saviour it presents must be one of them. It is as Bonhoeffer exclaimed: 'only the suffering God can help'.[10]

---

that this picture of Jesus developed out of the Spanish view of Christ which was the bequest of the conquistadors. The Spanish Christ was 'a suffering figure who had emerged from the centuries of suffering by the Spanish people'. Moreover, he 'taught by example how to suffer with resignation the injustice of this world' ('Christology, Culture and Reconciliation in Latin America', *TE* 44 [1991], pp. 5-14 [6]). Warren notes that this picture has been modified in recent years by Protestant theology, which embraces a more active Christ who aids the oppressed in overcoming their suffering.

9.   Sobrino, *Christology at the Crossroads*, p. 196, emphasis added.

10.   'God lets himself be pushed out of the world on to the cross. He is weak and powerless in the world, and that is precisely the way, *the only way*, in which he is with us and helps us' (D. Bonhoeffer, *Letters and Papers from Prison* [ed. E. Bethge; trans. R. Fuller *et al.*; London: SCM Press, 1967], pp. 196-97, emphasis added).

Case Study: A Feminist Christology
As a means of exploring these issues further, the following section works
through some of the questions raised by using feminist theology as an
example.

It can be argued that, to be accessible to women, whose experience of
life is one of marginalization and discrimination through sexism, a male
saviour must reveal a non-compliance with patriarchal power structures
and have suffered comparable marginalization himself in his earthly life.
As with the Latin American examples quoted above, the experiential
dimension is immediately invoked:

> Only a Jesus who is relevant and applicable to human experience, and
> particularly to women's experience, can possibly *save*. Any understanding
> of Jesus' person which removes him from the scene of human living and
> suffering is no longer able to mediate the salvation Christians have always
> found in him.[11]

Again, it may seem that an emphasis on suffering and victimization
would be a negative starting point for a Christology. In particular, as far
as feminists are concerned, it could be claimed that it is unhelpful and
undesirable to classify women primarily in terms of their experience of
violence, or to assume that simply being female implies that a person
should be labelled a victim in any sense. In defence of this approach, it
should be reiterated that it is in the very *nature* of liberation theologies
that they adopt a negative starting point. We have already seen that they
arise from the oppression of a group of people—conceived through
violence and born from situations of death. The identification and
examination of the circumstances of suffering mark the beginning of the
liberative process. It is often the case that unmasking the cause of
powerlessness reveals a source of transformative power.

But is it acceptable to claim that women *per se* are victims? Not only
is it acceptable, but it is necessary to describe womankind in general as
'victimized'. Certainly not all women are subjected to physical violence
at the hands of men, but in a global context women suffer the violence
of sexism and patriarchally structured societies. Even 'privileged' white,
middle-class, Western women experience marginalization and abuse on
account of their gender. The recognition of the victimization of women

11. G.R. Lilburne, 'Christology: In Dialogue with Feminism', *Horizons* 11
(1984), pp. 7-27 (13).

does not imply an acceptance of the situation. It does not function to trap them, asserting that as victims they are bound by weakness and passivity. It merely reveals the reality of the world that women experience. Violent abuse of a female as a 'non-person' is the most extreme expression of patriarchal evil and hence this is the depth that an effective feminist Christology must reach.

Of course Jesus was *not* a woman and no amount of feminist wishing will change that fact. He does not actually need to be a woman to descend to a comparable nadir through his harassment, humiliation, mutilation and death at the hands of vicious men. Jesus' liberating potential does not lie in his sharing the same personal identity with the oppressed—be it gender, colour or class—but from sharing a similar experience.[12] Girard asserts that 'Christ is the God of victims primarily because he shares their lot until the end'.[13] Thus victimization is a point of contact between womankind and this male saviour because it is through Jesus' suffering that his life parallels theirs. The hatred by society and the pain of alienation, rejection and physical abuse suffered by Jesus is analogous to women's experience of the full force of a sexist society that permits their degradation. In a very real way, therefore, *vox victimarum vox Dei*.[14]

Situating the Exegesis

How can these concerns be related to what is found in the Gospels? Soteriology is a primary concern of liberation theologies and is commonly developed through reflection on the 'liberating praxis' of the

12. The reverse of this statement must also be true. The ability to imitate Christ is not confined by gender, colour or class. This can be used with positive or negative effect. It was used in a positive sense as an argument for women's ordination. For a more negative usage, where identification with the suffering Jesus resulted in an increase in the suffering of women, see Ann Loades (*Searching for Lost Coins: Explorations in Christianity and Feminism* [London: SPCK, 1987], pp. 39-57). Writing principally on Simone Weil, Loades identifies a strand of tradition in which the 'imitation of Christ' is sought through women becoming victims themselves — 'they can be "*in persona Christi*" all too successfully if the Christ they imitate is the dead or dying Christ, rather than the Christ of the resurrection' (p. 43).

13. R. Girard, *Job the Victim of his People* (trans. Y. Freccero; London: Athlone Press, 1987), p. 157.

14. 'The cries of the victims are the voice of God', states Matthew Lamb (*Solidarity with Victims: Toward a Theology of Social Transformation* [New York: Crossroad, 1982], p. 23).

Synoptic Jesus and the implementation of the kingdom of God.[15] Feminist approaches[16] have frequently focused on the attitude and actions of Jesus towards women and a number have concluded that 'Jesus was a feminist'.[17] They reveal the 'inclusive' nature of Jesus' ministry and the community described in the Synoptics.[18] Thus in the construction of her Christology, Rosemary Radford Ruether[19] identifies an appropriate image for Jesus from the Synoptic stories: he is neither an imperial nor an androgynous figure, but the prophetic, iconoclastic Christ who overturns existing societal orders and represents a new kind of humanity. He is a paradigm of liberated humanity, modelling what it means to be authentically human and, through this, revealing how to relate to the poor and oppressed. This approach is particularly appropriate for the Synoptic Jesus, who, throughout his ministry, deliberately seeks out society's outcasts to bring them the message of the inclusive kingdom. The same cannot be said of the Fourth Gospel. Its form, language, emphases and even content differ radically from those of the first three.

15. Such as the previously mentioned works of Sobrino and Boff as well as J.L. Segundo, *Jesus of Nazareth Yesterday and Today*. II. *The Historical Jesus of the Synoptics* (trans. J. Drury; Maryknoll, NY: Orbis Books; London: Sheed & Ward, 1985). See also George Pixley for a focus on the political impact of the coming of the kingdom (*God's Kingdom* [trans. D.E. Walsh; London: SCM Press, 1981], pp. 64-87).

16. I am referring here specifically to feminist biblical interpretation of the Gospels, not to the much broader discipline of feminist theology. For a general introduction see the varied collection of styles and approaches by the writers in A. Loades (ed.), *Feminist Theology: A Reader* (London: SPCK, 1990). Despite noting that feminist hermeneutics is 'of very recent vintage', Elisabeth Schüssler Fiorenza is able to identify ten different interpretative strategies, ranging from the revisionist to her own critical feminist rhetorical model (*But she Said: Feminist Practices of Biblical Interpretation* [Boston: Beacon Press, 1992], pp. 20-50 [20]).

17. L. Swidler, 'Jesus Was a Feminist', *Catholic World* 212 (1971), pp. 177-83.

18. Examples of this approach include E. Moltmann-Wendel, *The Women around Jesus* (London: SCM Press, 1982); B. Witherington, *Women in the Ministry of Jesus* (Cambridge: Cambridge University Press, 1984); F.J. Moloney, *Woman: First among the Faithful* (London: Darton, Longman & Todd, 1984); B. Grenier, 'Jesus and Women', *St. Mark's Review* 119 (1984), pp. 13-21. For a discussion specific to John's Gospel see S.M. Schneiders, 'Women in the Fourth Gospel and the Role of Women in the Contemporary Church', *BTB* 12 (1982), pp. 35-45.

19. R. Radford Ruether, *To Change the World: Christology and Cultural Criticism* (London: SCM Press, 1981), p. 53. See also detailed discussion in M.H. Snyder, *The Christology of Rosemary Radford Ruether: A Critical Introduction* (Mystic, CT: Twenty-Third Publications, 1988).

Likewise, as has already been mentioned, the character of Jesus in John is so unlike that of the Synoptics that it is sometimes difficult to recognize him as the same man. The 'liberating praxis' of Jesus is not as clearly evident in John and an alternative approach is required to construct it from this Gospel. Liberation theologians usually attempt to construct Christologies from biblical material that is seen to be relevant—where Jesus displays inclusive behaviour towards the poor or women. Recognizing the importance of a saviour who participates in and reflects the experiences of the marginalized, the starting point for this study is the oppression of Jesus himself in John's Gospel. It will investigate *his* experience of harassment, highlighting occasions when he is victimized and the effect that this has on him as a character. This is a 'bottom up' approach, which takes the suffering of a man (rather than the apotheosis of a 'god') as its point of reference. It is not the creation of a new humanity that is of primary relevance to this undertaking (as is the concern of the Synoptics) but the way in which Jesus suffers at the hands of the old humanity: not his liberating praxis but his own experience of oppression.

Violence and the Ethos of John's Gospel

The approach outlined above is appropriate for John's Gospel precisely because, as already mentioned in Chapter 1, violence and the subject of Jesus' death are so prominent throughout the narrative. Compared with the Synoptics, John depicts markedly more violence directed against Jesus from all sections of his community. For much of his ministry, the Synoptic Jesus enjoys the support of the crowd as a popular hero, so much so that the religious authorities are afraid that arresting him will cause a riot (Mk 9.12; Mt. 21.46; Lk. 20.19). His numerous parables and miracles attract a large contingent of followers and, with the exception of Lk. 4.28-30, his audience do not oppose him until the very end of the narrative when they call for his crucifixion. Conversely, in the Fourth Gospel, Jesus never has a high level of support from the people; the crowd are always divided and frequently hostile. Direct threats to his life occur not just on one occasion, but continually throughout the narrative. The subject of his death is not deferred until its chronological position in the narrative, but surfaces time and time again during the course of the story. It is raised as early as John 2 (having been hinted at twice in Jn 1) and is mentioned or alluded to constantly. The Gospel is written from the perspective of the hour of death, with the oppression and victimization of its protagonist being one of its central features.

The following few pages pull together the relevant references on violence and make an attempt at categorization. The tables below reveal the sheer volume of this material. The violence is not hidden, abuse of Jesus is not discreet; yet this theme appears to be a feature of the evangelist's work that has not previously attracted the attention and imagination of Johannine exegetes. Some of the statements indicating violence and oppression are as startling as the text's infamous theological assertions, although the former are frequently overshadowed by the latter in scholarship. A systematic collection and evaluation of this material has not been made and it is one of the functions of this study to do so. The categorization of the verses relevant to the victimization of and general opposition to Jesus will form the subject material for Chapters 5 to 9. In addition, a further table which sets out the comments of Jesus himself about the violence and oppression that he suffers is included in Chapter 6.

Textual References to Violence

Tables 1-3: *Examples of Direct Violence Against Jesus*

1. *Severe Physical Violence: Actual or Intended*

Verse	Perpetrator	Action
7.30	Jerusalemites	attempted arrest
7.32	officers	deployed to arrest
7.44	the crowd	desire and possible attempt to seize Jesus
8.20	Pharisees	possible attempt at arrest
8.59	the Jews	attempted stoning
10.31	the Jews	attempted stoning
10.39	the Jews	attempted seizure
18.12	soldiers/officers	successful arrest and binding
18.22	officers	physical abuse (struck)
19.1	Pilate	physcal abuse (scourged)
19.2	soldiers	physical abuse (crown of thorns)
19.3	soldiers	physical and mental abuse (taunted and beaten)
19.17	soldiers	Jesus forced to carry the cross
19.18	soldiers	execution
19.34	soldiers	physical abuse (body stabbed)

Courting Betrayal

2. Harassment: Direct Physical

Verse	Perpetrator	Action
5.13	crowd	oppress Jesus/cause him to withdraw
6.15	people	threat of being taken by force and made king
10.24	the Jews	surround Jesus as he walks in the temple
19.24	soldiers	Jesus stripped and his clothes gambled for

3. Harassment: Direct Verbal

Verse	Perpetrator	Action
7.20	crowd	accusation of demon possession
8.6	Pharisees	attempt to trick Jesus
8.41	Pharisees	accusation of illegitimacy
8.48	the Jews	accusation of being a Samaritan and possessed
8.52	the Jews	accusation of demon possession
10.33	the Jews	accusation of blasphemy
18.40	the Jews	rejection in favour of Barabbas
19.6	chief priests	authorities shout 'crucify' at Jesus
19.15	crowd	people shout 'crucify' at Jesus

Tables 4-5: *Examples of Indirect Opposition and Threats to Jesus*

4. Statements of Opposition and Discrimination

Verse	Perpetrator	Action/statement
1.10	world	does not receive him
1.11	his own	reject him
1.46	Nathanael	prejudice against Jesus' birthplace
4.43	(indirectly Jesus)	implied prejudice from birthplace
5.16	the Jews	report of persecution
6.41	the Jews	murmur againts Jesus
7.12	crowd	accusation of being a deceiver
7.41	crowd	discrimination against birthplace
7.52	Pharisees	discrimination against birthplace
9.16	Pharisees	accusation of sabbath breaking
9.22	the Jews	agreement to oust followers
9.24	Pharisees	accusation of being a sinner
10.20	the Jews	accusation of possession and mania
11.36	the Jews	criticism for failure to heal
11.57	chief priests	instruction to people to inform on Jesus
12.42	Pharisees	threat of expulsion silences followers
18.5	Judas	betrayal to authorities
18.25	Peter	denial of association
18.27	Peter	denial of association
19.7	the Jews	attempted sentencing for blasphemy

5. *Reported Death Threats*

Verse	Perpetrator	Action/Statement
5.18	the Jews	report of intention to kill Jesus
7.1	the Jews	report of intention to kill Jesus
11.8	the Jews	note of intention to stone Jesus
11.50	Caiaphas	legitimization of death
11.53	Pharisees	deliberate plot to kill Jesus reported
18.14	Caiaphas	report of Caiaphas' advice on Jesus death
18.31	Pharisees	noted intention of Jews to have Jesus killed

3

The Literary Context

A Word on Method

The following chapter will set out the methodological ground rules that have been adhered to in this study, taking into account some basic considerations that should be made when carrying out research in John's Gospel. Following this, a brief discussion of the structure and plot of the Gospel will be made in order to set out the framework that has been used to organize this work.

Johannine criticism over the last decade has tended to polarize into two camps: the literary and the historical critical schools. The new breed of literary critics that emerged in the eighties was characterized by a suspicion of historical–critical methods and their usefulness for the future study of John. The general starting point for this work was seen to be the literary competence of the Gospel as it stands in its final form. Introducing his book *Jesus: Stranger from Heaven and Son of God*, Marinus de Jonge summarized the position well:

> Behind the present studies lies the assumption that the Fourth Gospel is a meaningful whole, highly complicated in structure, with many paradoxes and many tensions in thought and syntax, but yet asking to be taken seriously as a (more or less finished) literary product in which consistent lines of thought can be detected.[1]

This was subsequently the assumption adopted by Alan Culpepper in his seminal Johannine study *Anatomy of the Fourth Gospel*, which rejected the traditional stance of using the Gospel as a means of understanding its creators.[2] Accepting Murray Krieger's metaphor of the text as a

1.   M. de Jonge, *Jesus, Stranger from Heaven and Son of God: Jesus Christ and the Christians in Johannine Perspective* (trans. J.E. Steely; Missoula, MT: Scholars Press, 1977), p. vii.
2.   R.A. Culpepper, *Anatomy of the Fourth Gospel: A Study in Literary Design* (Philadelphia: Fortress Press, 1983), p. 3.

mirror placing meaning on the side of the reader, rather than a window through which the critic can catch glimpses of the community,[3] Culpepper examined the text primarily as one would a novel. This approach yielded many new insights about the Gospel, illuminating characterization, literary form, symbolism and structure.[4] However, its rejection of the importance of the Gospel's origin is now viewed by some to be a limiting feature. De Boer sees Culpepper's approach as being not simply ahistorical, but *anti*historical in its bias and agenda.[5] Stibbe points to its weakness in obscuring 'the value of the gospel as narrative history and as community narrative.'[6] A further concern, which is of wider import than Johannine, or even biblical studies, has been the accusation that the narrative critical approach to the text serves in reality to rob it of its meaning—its 'point'. The proponents of the discipline do not see this as a problem, since the narrative is an autonomous entity whose meaning is located within its own structure and sequence. Thus Hans Frei can claim:

3.   M. Krieger, *A Window to Criticism: Shakespeare's Sonnets and Modern Poetics* (Princeton, NJ: Princeton University Press, 1964). Krieger identifies the approaches of pre-New Criticism and New Criticism to the function of poetic language. The former views language as a window with meaning coming *through* it, the latter sees it as a set of mirrors with meaning locked *in* it. In fact, Krieger sees both a mirror and a window, the poem 'trapping us *in* the looking glass and taking us *through* it'. This takes us through the poem's closed context back to history and existence (p. 3).

Ironically, John Painter uses the image of a mirror to do that to which Culpepper was opposed. He comments: 'while the Gospels were written to proclaim Jesus, indirectly they give us insight into the life of the communities for which they were written. This indirect insight can be referred to as a *reflection*, a mirror image. From the reflections an attempt can be made to reconstruct the history of the communities that shaped the tradition' ('The Farewell Discourses and the History of Johannine Christianity', *NTS* 27 [1981], pp. 525-43 [526, emphasis original]).

4.   Although, as Stephen Moore points out, *Anatomy of the Fourth Gospel* proved to be something of a misnomer for a work which was not an anatomical dissection at all; rather a physical examination: '"Let's have a good look at you", is what Dr Culpepper intends to say to John—not "Let's open you up and have a look"' ('How Jesus' Risen Body Became a Cadaver', in E.S. Malbon and E.V. McKnight [eds.], *The New Literary Criticism and the New Testament* [JSNTSup, 109; Sheffield: Sheffield Academic Press, 1994], pp. 269-82 [274]).

5.   M.C. de Boer, 'Narrative Criticism, Historical Criticism and the Gospel of John', *JSNT* 47 (1992), pp. 35-48 (37).

6.   M.W.G. Stibbe, *John as Storyteller: Narrative Criticism and the Fourth Gospel* (Cambridge: Cambridge University Press, 1992), p. 11.

34   *Courting Betrayal*

> Especially in narrative, novelistic, or history-like form, where meaning is
> most nearly inseparable from the words—from the descriptive shape of
> the story as a pattern of enactment, there is neither need for nor use in
> looking for meaning in a more profound stratum underneath the struc-
> ture (a separable 'subject matter') or in a separable author's 'intention', or
> in a combination of such behind-the-scenes projections.[7]

In her analysis of Frei's work, Lynn Poland identifies the hermeneutical
problem that this poses: 'the New Critics' stress on the literary work's
discontinuity with the full range of human experience and value make it
difficult to describe how literature actually *does*, in fact, extend and
transform our perceptions'.[8] The point is that if the active role of the
reader is to be given any weight, then the reader's historical situation
must be addressed. This is presumably as true for a text's original or
intended readership as it is for present day readers. Concordance with this
view can be found in the work of the literary critic Ross Chambers,
who discerns that what has been lacking in criticism and theory[9] is
'recognition of the significance of situational phenomena—of the social
fact that narrative mediates human relationships and derives its "meaning" from them'.[10] Implicitly for Poland, in dialogue with the biblical
'New Critics', and explicitly for Chambers, in dialogue with the
structuralists, it would seem that the limitation of the 'a-contextual', autonomous text is the absence of a 'point'. Chambers illustrates this by
using the example of a 'faggot' joke to demonstrate the importance of
context in determining the meaning of a story. This, of course, will de-
pend on whether the joke is told by gay people among themselves, by
straight people among themselves, by a straight to a gay person, or vice
versa. As Chambers explains, 'the significance of the story is determined
less by its actual content than by the point of its being told... That is
why, when one looks hard at stories, it becomes extremely difficult to

7. H.W. Frei, *The Eclipse of Biblical Narrative: A Study in Eighteenth and Nineteenth Century Hermeneutics*, (New Haven: Yale University Press, 1974), p. 281.
8. L.M. Poland, *Literary Criticism and Biblical Hermeneutics: A Critique of Formalist
Approaches* (AAR Academy Series, 48; Chico, CA: Scholars Press, 1985), p. 132,
emphasis added.
9. With reference to Seymour Chatman's *Story and Discourse: Narrative Structure
in Fiction and Film* (Ithaca, NY: Cornell University Press, repr. 1989 [1978]) in
particular, and structuralism in general.
10. R. Chambers, *Story and Situation: Narrative Seduction and the Power of Fiction*
(Theory and History of Literature, 12; Minneapolis: University of Minnesota;
Manchester: Manchester University Press, 1984), p. 4.

distinguish them from their *telling*.'[11] In his recent work on hermeneutics, Grant Osborne discusses in detail the issue of meaning, which is no less of a problem for current day narrative critics than it was for Hans Frei, believing as they do that there is *no* 'first-order system' that unlocks the meaning of texts. Indeed, Osborne claims that the discipline still holds that all works are 'aesthetic productions that are open to one extent or another... to the reader's "freeplay" on the playground of the text, and polyvalence ... is the necessary result'.[12]

What, then, do these concerns about the robustness of literary critical approaches to texts in general and the Bible in particular, leave us by way of a methodology for exploring issues in John from a generally literary critical perspective? Are we to heed the grim warning of Scot McKnight, that:

> literary theorists may stand in awe of the ice 'floating on' the water and they may describe its aesthetic shape and its evocative powers, but sooner or later their ship will awaken to a crashing 'Titanic-like' revelation of the fact that what they were staring at was in fact an iceberg, with much more below the surface than above.[13]

The desire to say anything creative or interesting about the Gospel outweighs this risk, providing the impetus for proceeding... but with caution. Riley advises: 'if the narrative approach is to be critically grounded and avoid the subjectivity to which it is sometimes prey, context may provide the key to the process... *an essential context is the community*

11. Chambers, *Story and Situation*, p. 3.

12. G.R. Osborne, *The Hermeneutical Spiral: A Comprehensive Introduction to Biblical Interpretation* (Downers Grove, IL: IVP, 1991), pp. 395-96. This is not the only weakness of narrative criticism according to Osborne, who documents the following eight tendencies that the would-be narrative critic should beware of :
   — a dehistoricizing tendency
   — setting aside the author
   — a denial of intended or referential meaning
   — reductionist and disjunctive thinking
   — the imposition of modern literary categories upon ancient genres
   — a preoccupation with obscure theories
   — ignoring the understanding of the early church
   — a rejection of the sources behind the books (pp. 164-68).

13. S. McKnight, *Interpreting the Synoptic Gospels* (Grand Rapids: Baker Book House, 1988), p. 128.

dynamic of which the text is the tangible evidence'.[14] Likewise, Teresa Okure contends: 'the need to relate the Gospel evidence (the literary dimension) to the social context (the audience-dimension) is called for by...John's Gospel itself'.[15] It could therefore be claimed that research in the Gospel of John which completely ignores the circumstances of the birth of the text and the community that produced it does so at its peril. As W. Randolph Tate observes: 'texts reflect their culture, and to read them apart from that culture is to invite a basic level of misunderstanding'.[16] Even a cursory consideration of a document's original authors and readers will guard against the treatment of the narrative as disembodied fiction. A consideration of the text's *Sitz im Leben* can enhance our understanding of both the life of the original community and the contents of the text itself. The Fourth Gospel is undoubtedly a text with character and a personality which, if nothing else, singles it out as different from the Synoptics. This personality is inextricably linked to the nature of the Johannine community. It is both derived from it and reflects it. It follows that study of the text and study of the community cannot feasibly be carried out in complete isolation from each other and that a recognition of their common traits will enrich our comprehension of the Johannine *Weltanschauung*.

The hermeneutical value of the social function of the Gospel is therefore accepted as important for this study and will be discussed in the next chapter. In fact, it will be seen that it gives further substance to the motif of violence under investigation. The starting point will be the examination of a few of the attempts to use the text as a 'window' through which the community can be seen and reconstructed. Although these activities have their limitations, they are legitimate and useful in their goal of situating the text. But in addition to this, our glimpses of the community can serve to alter the perspective from which we survey

14. W. Riley, 'Situating Biblical Narrative: Poetics and the Transmission of Community Values', *Proceedings of the Irish Biblical Association* 9 (1985), pp. 38-52 (38), emphasis original.

15. T. Okure, *The Johannine Approach to Mission: A Contextual Study of John 4.1-42* (WUNT, 2.31; Tübingen: J.C.B. Mohr, 1988), p. 228.

16. W.R. Tate, *Biblical Interpretation: An Integrated Approach* (Peabody, MA: Hendrickson, 1991), p. 4. James Dunn goes further. His concern seems to be manipulation, rather than a simple misunderstanding: 'a text freed ("liberated"!) from its native context is a text much more readily abused and subjected to the reader's will' (*The Partings of the Ways: Between Christianity and Judaism and their Significance for the Character of Christianity* [London: SCM Press, 1991], p. 16).

the text, bringing previously unnoticed aspects into fuller view. De Boer is in support of this approach, believing that narrative and historical-critical approaches are not mutually exclusive. Both use the same author–text–reader model of communication and both have the text at the centre. In defence of those who pay some attention to the text's origins, he states:

> ...the history of Johannine Christianity and of the gospel's composition is not brought *to* the text by critics bent on its fragmentation or on its marginalization for the actual interpretative task. This history is in fact imbedded, or encoded, within the text itself and any imaginative reconstruction of this history must find its impetus and its foundation and certainly its confirmation in the evidence that is produced by that text— the *extant, finished* form of that text.[17]

Tate also speaks on behalf of the integrated, rather than exclusive hermeneutical approach. Outlining the basic positions of author-centred, text-centred and reader-centred interpretative methods, he proposes that: 'the locus of meaning is not to be found exclusively in either world or in a marriage of any two of the worlds, but in the interplay between all three worlds'.[18]

Finally, it could be argued that it is politically unacceptable to ignore the original context of a document. Treating a text merely as a linguistic object can sometimes smack of exploitation. This is more obviously the case with texts that have been written within the context of some kind of struggle, where to disregard the context is to disregard the pain of the writer and his or her readers. It would be akin to discussing, for example, the works of Toni Morisson or Alan Paton without recognizing the political environment within which they were written. This is particularly pertinent for this book, as the subject matter is victimization, which, it is argued, is a shared characteristic of the Johannine Jesus and the Johannine community. It is this aspect of the historical context of the Gospel that will be the focus of the next chapter. Prior to this, however, it is necessary to engage in some text-centred discussion that will elucidate the exegesis in Chapters 5–10 of the book.

17. de Boer, 'Narrative Criticism', p. 43.
18. Tate, *Biblical Interpretation*, p. xx.

On Plots and Patterns

It is not within the remit of this study to attempt to redefine such basic literary categories as narrative structure, story and plot. Suffice to say that the traditional understanding of these concepts, derived from Aristotle and elucidated by, among others, E.M. Forster, will be adopted here. Forster's definitions run as follows: A story is 'a narrative of events arranged in their time sequence'. A plot is 'also a narrative of events, the emphasis falling on causality'.[19] Plots require two things of their readers: intelligence and memory. The reason for this is the part played by mystery, or curiosity about the outcome of a story, which serves to lure the reader ever deeper into its domain. So vital is this function, that Leyland Ryken can claim that 'stories succeed *only* as they generate such curiosity'.[20] The mechanism through which suspense is created and maintained, and hence the usual pattern of organization of a plot, is conflict. Ryken outlines four different manifestations of conflict that can contribute towards plot development: physical, character, inner psychological and moral–spiritual. The plot is organized around the progress of the conflict towards the point of resolution. Culpepper, for instance, sees the plot of John's gospel as being 'propelled' by the conflict between belief and unbelief, supported by the overriding use of the verb πιστεύω.[21]

19. E.M. Forster, *Aspects of the Novel* (ed. O. Stallybrass; Harmondsworth: Penguin Books, repr. 1985 [1927]), p. 87. Forster then proceeds with his oft-quoted example: 'The king died and then the queen died' is a story, in contrast to 'The king died and then the queen died of grief', which qualifies as a plot, due to the addition of causation. Seymour Chatman points out that, in practice, it is difficult to see the first sentence as a plotless story, as the reader will generally provide the causal link between the king and queen's deaths automatically. The reason for this is that we are 'inherently disposed to turn raw sensation into perception'. Causation is 'inferred through ordinary presumptions about the world, including the purposive character of speech' (*Story and Discourse*, p. 46). A useful definition of plot is also provided by M.H. Abrams: 'The plot in a dramatic or narrative work is the structure of its actions, as these are rendered and ordered toward achieving particular emotional and artistic effects' (*A Glossary of Literary Terms* [Chicago: Holt, Rinehart & Winston, 5th edn, 1988], p. 139).

20. L. Ryken, *Words of Delight: A Literary Introduction to the Bible* (Grand Rapids: Baker Book House, 1987), p. 62, emphasis added.

21. Culpepper, *Anatomy of the Fourth Gospel*, p. 97.

Closely related to the plot of a story, but not to be confused with it, is its structure. Mark Stibbe explains that 'whilst plot is the organizing principle which gives order and meaning to separate events, structure is the architectural end-product of this arrangement of parts into a whole'.[22] However, the difference between these two terms is not simply a shift in perspective—from 'zoom' to 'wide-angle'. The boundaries, contours and decoration of the architectural end-product are constructed such that the structure itself resonates the interpretative significance of the plot, setting and theme so that, as O'Connor reflected, 'the whole story is the meaning'.[23] Viewed this way, structure is not easily distinguishable from what Forster labelled a story's pattern. Pattern is the aesthetic aspect of the work, nourished primarily by the plot, but also by other elements such as characters, words and scenes.[24] The pattern (and hence the architectural end-product), may look symmetrical, like an hourglass, or represent converging and diverging lines, like a grand chain, but what is *good* about it, claims Forster, is 'the suitability of the pattern to the author's mood'.[25]

John's Literary Devices

The following section will examine the architectural end-product, the organizing principle and the aesthetic pattern of John's Gospel. Although they are, to a great extent, interdependent, it is possible that attempting to analyse them separately and from the perspective of this study will yield some interesting insights.

22. Stibbe, *John as Storyteller*, p. 26. Structure is the 'end-product of emplotment', emplotment being Paul Ricoeur's configurational act which creates a meaningful ensemble of interrelationships (p. 27).

23. 'Some people have the notion that you read the story and then climb out of it into the meaning, but for the fiction writer himself the whole story is the meaning, because it is an experience not an abstraction.' Although O'Connor is writing about the nature of fiction writing here, her comments are particularly pertinent for biblical studies (*Mystery and Manners* [ed. S. Fitzgerald and R. Fitzgerald; London: Faber & Faber, 1972], p. 73).

24. Forster, *Aspects of the Novel*, p. 136.

25. Forster, *Aspects of the Novel*, p. 136.

Structure

The traditional view of the structure of John's Gospel has been that it is bipartite in nature.[26] The Prologue is followed by what Brown terms the 'Book of Signs', characterized by seven signs and seven discourses. At the end of John 12 there is a division and the 'Book of Glory' commences, encompassing the ministry to the disciples, the passion and resurrection. The Gospel ends with the epilogue of chapter 21. More recent studies of the structure of the whole Gospel have included tri-partite structures, for example that of Charles Giblin, which splits the main body of the gospel into three parts, based on grounds of geography, temporal sequence and relationships between Jesus and his adversaries as follows:

I: 1.19-4.54   Thematic motif: Jesus' contact with all sorts
                  of persons (no hostility)
II: 5.1-10.42   Thematic motif: Controversy; widespread
                  opposition (marked hostility)
III: 11.1-20.29   Thematic motif: Jesus' love for his friends;
                  opposition specifically from Jewish leaders[27]

Two other important studies, carried out in the 1980s, were those of George Mlakuzhyil and Marc Girard. Mlakuzhyil focuses on the christocentric purpose of the Fourth Gospel to suggest a literary structure that consists of two closely linked principal parts: the Book of Jesus' Signs (2.1-12.50) and the Book of Jesus' Hour (11.1-20.29). These are flanked by a christocentric introduction (1.1-2.11) and a christocentric conclusion (20.30-31).[28] Girard, on the other hand, sees the seven signs of the Gospel forming a concentric pattern as follows:

26. R.E. Brown, *The Gospel According to John* (AB; 29, 29A; 2 vols.; repr; Garden City, NY: Doubleday, 1966), I, pp. cxxxviii; C.H. Dodd, *The Interpretation of the Fourth Gospel* (Cambridge: Cambridge University Press, 1953), p. 289.

27. C.H. Giblin, 'The Tripartite Narrative Structure of John's Gospel', *Bib* 71 (1990), pp. 449-68. D.A. Carson also proposes a tripartite-based structure, which sees the prologue and epilogue encasing the following three major sections:

I: 1.19-10.42   Jesus' self-disclosure in word and deed.
II: 11.1-12.50   Transition: Life and death, king and suffering servant.
III: 13.1-20.31   Jesus' self-disclosure in his cross and exaltation.

(*Gospel According to John* [Leicester: IVP, 1991], pp. 105-8)

28. G. Mlakuzhyil *The Christocentric Literary Structure of the Fourth Gospel* (AnBib, 117; Rome: Editrice Pontificio Istituto Biblico, 1987), pp. 137-68.

A: L'eau changée en vin (2.1-12)
  B: Guérison d'un moribond (4.43-54)
    C: Guérison d'un infirme (5.1-18)
      D: Multiplication des pains (6.1-15)
    C': Guérison d'un infirme (9.1-6)
  B': Réanimation d'un mort (11.1-44)
A': Le vinaigre, l'eau et le sang (19.17-37)

The central climactic sign in this arrangement is the feeding of the five thousand, which emphasizes the central position of the eucharist in the Gospel.[29]

It could legitimately be questioned whether there is anything to gain from reanalysing the structure of the Fourth Gospel. However, as Moody Smith comments: 'The exegesis of any text must take account of its position and role in the document of which it is a part. Thus our exegesis of Johannine texts must keep the structure of the Fourth Gospel in view.'[30] My exegesis will highlight examples of the victimization of the protagonist and it is therefore relevant to demonstrate the extent to which violence and the victimization of the protagonist are woven into the fabric of the narrative as a whole. It should be clear, however, that it is the subject matter that informs the construction of the framework and consequently the reverse is not necessarily the case.

My aim, then, is functional. It is not to propose a substitute to the bipartite or tripartite structures, but to suggest a framework that will facilitate an understanding of the text for the purposes of this study. Charles Giblin reminds us that 'analysis of the literary structure of a given work should avoid the assumption that only a single structure would prove to be possible'.[31] The motivation for Giblin's structure is to render the plot-line 'clearer and theologically more rewarding'[32] and to aid the

---

29. M. Girard, 'La composition structurelle des sept 'signes' dans le quatrième évangile', *SR* 9/3 (1980), pp. 315-24. Matthias Rissi also divides up the Gospel into seven units, using a geographical theory based primarily on journeys made by Jesus ('Der Aufbau des vierten Evangeliums', *NTS* 29 [1983], pp. 48-54, discussed by Robert Kysar in 'The Gospel of John in Current Research', *RSR* 9/4 [1983], pp. 314-23 [318]).

30. D. Moody Smith, *John* (Proclamation Commentaries; Philadelphia: Fortress Press, 1986), p. 19.

31. Giblin, 'Tripartite Narrative Structure', p. 449.

32. Giblin, 'Tripartite Narrative Structure', p. 450.

reader's 'perception of unity, coherence and definable theological em-phasis'[33]—objectives worthy of emulation. Figure 1 sets out an under-standing of the structure of John's Gospel that I have devised for use in this study. It is essentially a tripartite structure, with a prologue, a link passage and an epilogue, and the following section functions as a com-mentary on this arrangement.

Part One documents Jesus' relationship with the community. Its boundaries are two prophecies which embrace the corporate aspect of his death. Both are uttered by significantly representative figures; John, the Prophet sent from God, and Caiaphas, the High Priest. The former introduces Jesus as the lamb of God who takes away the sin of the world (1.29). The latter refers to Jesus as the one man who must die for the nation, expanded by the evangelist to have global significance (11.50-51). The action contained within Part One can be analysed from two perspectives. The first focuses on the physical action—chaotic and vio-lent incidents in which Jesus is physically threatened. This material is discussed in Chapter 5. The second is concerned with the emotional realm of Jesus as the protagonist. By this is meant the expression of Jesus' understanding of the violence that befalls and still awaits him, which will be explored in detail in Chapter 6. In the middle of Part One there is a turning point signified by another prophecy about Jesus' death, this time uttered by himself. It is a statement that links his few remain-ing followers to his execution. The twelve are those whom Jesus has chosen himself, yet within their number is a devil—the instrument through which Jesus will be delivered to his death. (6.70-71). Prior to this point, the physical disturbances surrounding Jesus have been intim-idating, but as far as inflicting actual bodily harm is concerned, they have been confusing rather than deliberately menacing. For example, the feeding miracle results in public chaos and a physical threat to Jesus (6.15), but it is not specifically an intention to maim, but rather a dis-ordered attempt to force him into adopting a particular role. Likewise, the speeches of Jesus prior to the prophecy of betrayal display suspicion about the community's relationship with him. Throughout John 1–5 he speaks in veiled terminology of his death and the Jews' part in it; of 'this temple' being destroyed (2.19), of not being 'received' by them (3.11, 32; 5.43), of being 'lifted up' (3.14), of not being honoured (5.23). During this section of the narrative Jesus does not *directly* accuse the community of trying to kill him. The readers, of course, know that the

33. Giblin, 'Tripartite Narrative Structure', p. 467.

Prologue: 1.1-18

↓

Part 1. *Relationship with the Community: 1.20–11.54*

Prophecy at start of Jesus' ministry (1.29)
ἴδε ὁ ἀμνὸς τοῦ θεοῦ ὁ αἴρων τὴν ἁμαρτίαν τοῦ κόσμου

Physical aspects	⇐*chaos*	*Emotional aspects*
1. Temple Incident (2.13-22)		1. Temple Prophecy (2.16-20)
2. Healing at Bethesda (5.1-18)		2. Veiled terminology (3–5)
3. Feeding miracle (6.1-20)	*suspicion*⇒	3. Feeding discourse (6.22-65)

Prophecy of Betrayal (6.70)
καὶ ἐξ ὑμῶν εἷς διάβολός ἐστιν...

Physical aspects	⇐*violence*	*Emotional aspects*
4. Feast of Tabernacles (7.1-52)		1. Temple Prophecy (2.16-20)
5. Children of Abraham (8.1-59)		2. Veiled terminology (3–5)
6. Feast of Dedication (10.22-39)	*anxiety*⇒	3. Feeding discourse (6.22-65)

Plot/Prophecy at end of Jesus' ministry (11.50)
συμφέρει ὑμῖν ἵνα εἷς ἄνθρωπος ἀποθάνη ὑπὲρ τοῦ λαοῦ

↓

Link Passage. *Announcement of the Hour: 11.55–12.50*

Looking forwards		*Looking backwards*
Anointing (11.55–12.11)	καὶ ἐδόξασα⇒	Cause of unbelief (12.37-43)
Entry into Jerusalem (12.12-19)	⇐καὶ πάλιν δοξάσω	Summary of claims (12.44-50)

↓

Part 2. *Relationship with Disciples: 13.1–17.26*

1. Humiliation: footwashing, dismissal of betrayer, prediction of denial (13.1-38)
2. Departure: sending of counsellor, warning of sorrow (14.1-31)
3. Instruction to believers: the vine, command to love (15.1-17)
4. Hatred of the world, prediction of persecution (15.18–16.4)
5. Explanation of departure: sending of counsellor, warning of sorrow (16.5-33)
6. Summoning of the hour: prayer for disciples, prayer for believers (17.1-26)

↓

Part 3. *Relationship with Death: 18.1–20.29*

1. Arrest (18.1-11)
2. Trial (18.12–19.16)
3. Crucifixion (19.17-37)
4. Burial (19.38-42)
5. Resurrection (20.1-18)
6. Appearances (20.19-29)

↓

Epilogue: 20.30–21.25

Figure 1: Structure of John's Gospel

Jews intend this, as the evangelist has already told them in 5.18 (and an astute reader would have deduced it from John 1). It is legitimate, therefore, to see a measure of ambiguity and uncertainty concerning the violence manifested before the betrayal prophecy.

After Jesus' prophecy, there is little doubt surrounding his relationship with the community. Not only does the evangelist remind us in 7.1 that Jews are seeking to kill him, but Jesus immediately begins to use strong language about hatred and openly accuses the people of wanting to murder him (7.7, 19; 8.37, 40). There is no ambiguity about the physical threat to his person either—the people try again and again to arrest him and to stone him (7.30, 44; 8.20, 59; 10.31, 39). It is during this section that Jesus must come to terms with his impending death and this is something that it tackled through the shepherd discourse (10.1-18) and the raising of Lazarus (11.1-44). It would appear, then, that following this prophecy of betrayal, the violence moves more clearly onto the surface of the narrative.

John 11.55–12.50 forms a link between Parts One and Two. It projects the reader forward towards Jesus' death as he prepares for it with the anointing and moves into the correct location (12.1-19). It also provides an opportunity for the evangelist to take a backward glance at Jesus' public ministry and give an explanation as to why he was rejected (12.37-50). In the middle of this there is a speech by Jesus in which he indicates that the hour has come... but not quite yet (vv. 23, 35) and rhetorically questions himself about whether there is a possibility of escape ('And what shall I say? Father, save me from this hour?', v. 27). The Father's reply to Jesus' call for the glorification of his name is also both retrospective and prospective: 'I have glorified it, and I will glorify it again' (καὶ ἐδόξασα καὶ πάλιν δοξάσω [v. 28]).

For the purposes of this study, the farewell discourse clearly forms Part Two of the Gospel. It explores Jesus' relationship with his followers through the footwashing (13.1-20), and the explanation of how the disciples form part of the family that consists of Jesus, the Father and the Counsellor (chs. 14–16). In addition, the consequences of this relationship are set out: sacrificial love for each other and vilification and death at the hands of a world that hates them (15.12-27). Part Two functions primarily as an interval from the real 'action' of the narrative, providing an opportunity for the evangelist to clarify points of theology through the monologues made by Jesus.

The action recommences at the beginning of Part Three with the arrest of Jesus (18.1-14). The final stage of Jesus' journey towards his death begins and is played out in a fairly straightforward manner. A brief account of the arrest is followed by a lengthy and elaborate trial. The crucifixion and death of Jesus are also brief, set out almost mechanistically. The burial, resurrection and appearances follow, concentrating on the new relationship between the resurrected Jesus and his followers.

Plot

Alan Culpepper sees evidence of deliberate manipulation of the plot in John through the organization of the sequence of events and the contrived nature of much of the dialogue. This points to the 'careful crafting of a unified sequence and a logic of causality'.[34] As with structure, it would be inappropriate to claim that there is only one representation of plot germane to the Fourth Gospel. There is therefore no point in disputing an interpretation that claims that the plot 'revolves around Jesus' mission to reveal the Father and authorize the children of God'.[35] Again, the aim is rather to offer an additional, rather than alternative, understanding—to ask what hermeneutic significance this intentional shaping of the narrative holds for a study that focuses on Jesus as a victim. Taking Ryken's cue, it is necessary to examine the curiosity generated by the narrative through the conflict that it contains.

At the heart of the conflict manifest in John is the incompatibility between the words (λόγος) and the world (κόσμος). This is evident from the prologue (1.9-18), through the tale of Jesus' ministry (7.6-8; 8.23; 12.25; 12.44-50), the farewell discourse (15.18-25; 16.20; 17.14), the trial (18.36), and even the epilogue—the world cannot circumscribe all that Jesus is or has done (21.25). Suspense for John's readers is not maintained through curiosity over *what* is going to happen, but *how*. Jesus will be rejected, we know this from the outset. This story is about the way in which the rejection will be played out. We even know the

34. Culpepper, *Anatomy of the Fourth Gospel*, p. 87.

35. Culpepper, *Anatomy of the Fourth Gospel*, p. 88. Similarly J.A. du Rand states, 'the unifying plot... is really the witness to the identity of Jesus. He is the bearer of the divine glory as the incarnate Son of God' ('Plot and Point of View in the Gospel of John', in J.H. Petzger and P.J. Hartin [eds.], *A South African Perspective on the New Testament: Essays by South African New Testament Scholars Presented to Bruce Manning Metzger during his Visit to South Africa in 1985* [Leiden: E.J. Brill, 1986], pp. 149-69 [167-68]).

result of the struggle—the darkness will not overcome the light (1.5). Far from ruining the ending, this heightens the intrigue, as the task of the plot will be to reveal the true meaning of the triumph of the λόγος against the violence and evil that the world inflicts on it. The development of the plot draws the reader into the mode and extent of Jesus' rejection. Verbally abused and physically persecuted, he proceeds towards his inevitable death and the reader must understand the significance of this outcome. Thus the plot revolves around the rejection and physical destruction of the protagonist and the subversion of his 'failure' (in the world's eyes) into an eventual victory over death and liberation for the chosen.

Pattern

After discussing both structure and plot, it might be seen as somewhat self-indulgent to suggest an exposition of pattern as well. It is not, after all, a concept that lends itself to academic rigour and, probably for this reason, is not one generally employed by literary or biblical critics. My motive in including this final section is purely creative interest. Again, it contributes to the understanding of the text from the point of view of Jesus as a man pursued by and consumed by violence.

If Forster can see the shape of an hourglass or a chain in a text, what shape could appropriately be used to interpret John's Gospel? I would suggest that, as far as our theme is concerned, a helix is a good fit. A spiral consists of a single thread that travels round and round on itself until it reaches the centre, which is both its beginning and its end. This is the case with John's story, where the protagonist is propelled continually towards the centre of the helix, where death awaits him. The ever decreasing circles display the inevitability of the central point— there is no escape, no alternative ending. Violence intensifies as death approaches, but it has always been there and its thread can be traced to the very beginning. Joseph Clancy, writing on a different literary form (early Welsh poetry), captures this sense of circularity well, explaining of this genre; 'the normal lyric employs what I have elsewhere called "radial" structure, circling about, repeating, and elaborating the central theme. It is all "middle", we might say.'[36] Similarly, John is all 'end', the central theme being literally the end—the death of Jesus. It is

---

36. J.P. Clancy, *The Earliest Welsh Poetry* (London: Macmillan, 1970), p. 5.

for this reason that the Fourth Gospel can be described as 'neither-passion-narrative-with introduction nor aretalogy-with-sequel, but *one continuous passion narrative*'.[37]

This analysis of the structure, plot and pattern of John's Gospel reveals the meaningful artistry of a writer with an agenda, rather than just a tale to tell. It assists the task of highlighting aspects relevant to the perspective of this study—the victimization suffered by Jesus. The structure suggested will form the framework for the examination of relevant passages in Chapters 5–10, the architectural end-product contributing to the interpretative significance of the work.

---

37. R.T. Fortna, 'Christology in the Fourth Gospel: Redaction-Critical Perspectives', *NTS* 21 (1975), pp. 489-504 (504).

4

The Historical Context

I have argued in the previous chapter that the social context of the
Gospel has hermeneutical value and that consideration of the community that produced the text will enhance our understanding of the motif
of violence. Jeffrey Trumbower claims that: 'ideas in the Fourth Gospel
must be understood in terms of their function within the sociological
reality of the Johannine sect *insofar as that reality may be plausibly reconstructed*'.[1] There is nothing new about this concept; it is a decade since
Bruce Malina investigated the social system revealed in and presupposed
by John in order to illuminate some of the text's distinctive features.[2]
While it is recognized that such attempts at reconstruction are fraught
with difficulty and frequently open to criticism, I hope, nevertheless, that
this chapter will be viewed as contributing to the main argument of the
book, providing insight into the understanding of the Johannine Jesus as
a victim. It should be noted that, although the first section of the chapter
discusses attempts to reconstruct the history and development of the
community—an activity seen as necessarily speculative in itself[3]—my

1.	J.A. Trumbower, *Born from Above: The Anthropology of the Gospel of John*
(HUT, 29; Tübingen: J.C.B. Mohr, 1992), p. 83, emphasis added.

2.	B. Malina, 'The Gospel of John in Sociolinguistic Perspective', in H.C.
Waetjen (ed.), *Protocol of the Forty Eighth Colloquy, 11 March 1984: Centre for
Hermeneutical Studies in Hellenistic and Modern Culture, Graduate Theological Union and
University of California, Berkeley* (Berkeley, CA: The Centre for Hermeneutical Stud-
ies, 1985). See also Jerome Neyrey's *An Ideology of Revolt: John's Christology in Social-
Science Perspective* (Philadelphia: Fortress Press, 1988). Neyrey perceives a high Christology in the Fourth Gospel, which he examines using traditional critical methods.
He then utilizes the methods of cultural anthropologist Mary Douglas to assess how
this Christology 'replicates the social cosmology of the Johannine group and functions as an ideology for it', arguing that high Christology is a 'code for revolt' against
the synagogue and other formal structures (p. 209).

3.	J. Painter notes that it is essential to recognize the hypothetical nature of all
reconstructions, but adds that this is not an excuse for avoiding reconstruction (*The*

concern is even vaguer than this. I am interested in how these generally accepted ideas about the community's experience are subsequently reflected in their 'mindset'. This, I suggest, can be discerned from the contents of the text and is relevant to my theme.

Prospecting for the Johannine Community

What can be understood about the nature and circumstances of the community that produced the Gospel of John? When answering this question, scholars commonly focus on the rupture between Judaism and early Christianity, and indeed the following section will examine the impact that this might have had on the Johannine community. The works of J. Louis Martyn[4] and Raymond Brown[5] have been formative in this area and, despite the reservations now held by many scholars about the results of their investigations, they are still widely accepted as being valuable and merit summarizing.

Martyn's thesis is constructed from the events related in John 9, discerning within them evidence of a social crisis facing the group that produced the text. The miracle and inquisition of the blind man and his parents reflect the interaction between the synagogue and the community. The narrative functions as 'a witness to Jesus' powerful presence in actual events experienced by the Johannine church'.[6] It addresses the social situation of its readership, the characters fulfilling the dual role of individuals within the text and representatives of different social groups within the evangelist's environment. Martyn focuses particularly on the threat contained in Jn 9.22, where believers face being put out of the synagogue (ἀποσυνάγωγος) if they confess Christ. This, he believes, transports the narrative forward in time, incorporating the reformulated *Shemone Esre* of the Jamnia Academy, published around 85 CE. Expulsion from the synagogue would not have been a threat in Jesus' time,

Quest for the Messiah: The History, Literature and Theology of the Johannine Community [Edinburgh: T. & T. Clark, 2nd edn, 1993], p. 68, n. 104).

4. J.L. Martyn, *History and Theology in the Fourth Gospel* (Nashville: Abingdon Press, 2nd edn, 1979); 'Glimpses into the History of the Johannine Community', in M. de Jonge (ed.), *L'Evangile de Jean: Sources, Rédaction, Théologie* (BETL, 44; Leuven: Leuven University Press/Uitgeverij Peeters, 1977), pp. 150-75; and *The Gospel of John in Christian History: Essays for Interpreters* (New York: Paulist Press, 1979).

5. Brown, *The Community of the Beloved Disciple*.

6. Martyn, *History and Theology*, p. 30.

but would have been a very real threat to Johannine Christians. A
formal decision taken by the authorities in Jamnia to rid the synagogue
of Jewish Christians meant the inclusion of the ברכת המינים, the *birkhat
ha-minim,* into the series of benedictions used in community worship.
The reciting of this twelfth benediction against the heretics was a means
of routing out Christians and expelling them. Martyn constructs a series
of stages in the relationship between the synagogue and the Johannine
church from the text. Excommunication being insufficient to curtail the
activities of the Jewish Christians, more drastic measures were necessary.
Thus in 16.2b Martyn sees evidence of the death penalty for those accused of leading their own people astray. 'There are reasons for seeking
to kill Jesus during his earthly lifetime, and there are reasons for seeking
to kill him now, in John's own day.'[7]

Raymond Brown prefaces his investigation into the development of
the Johannine gospel and community by asserting that: 'the deeds and
words of Jesus are included in the Gospels because the evangelist sees
that they are (or have been) useful to members of his community. From
that we gain general knowledge about the life situation of the community.'[8] The form and content of the Gospel are influenced by the
writer's desire to reflect and address the needs of its readers. Brown
traces the development of the community through the Gospel, beginning with small groups of Jews, among them followers of John the
Baptist, anti-temple factions and converted Samaritans. The move towards a high Christology (seen in the Gospel after Jn 4) caused sharp
conflict with the synagogue and excommunication prior to the Gospel
actually being written in 90 CE. In no stage of the pre-Gospel history

----

7.   Martyn, *History and Theology,* p. 70. Excommunication and martyrdom are
seen by Martyn to be the two major traumas that mark the development of the
Johannine community during the 'middle period'. The Johannine evangelists were
now not only socially dislocated and alienated, but were also subject to the possibility of being 'snatched away' out of life (cf. 10.28-29; 15, 18) ('Glimpses into the
History', pp. 160-4). Minear agrees that the Gospel was set within the context of a
realistic fear of martyrdom. He comments that it is difficult to understand the reluc-
tance of many scholars to recognize this in the light of Jn 16.2 and the subsequent
stoning of Stephen and Paul at the hands of the religious authorities. 'To minimize
the brutal truth of [16.3] is to minimize the hatreds exemplified in the death of Jesus
as well as the pressures on his disciples to fall away' (Minear, *John: The Martyr's
Gospel,* p. 28).
8.   Brown, *Community of the Beloved Disciple,* p. 18.

does Brown see evidence of internal struggle among the community, but there are plenty of battles with outsiders which, he claims, give rise to the sense of 'us against them'.[9] Seven representative categories of adversaries are identified to whom the evangelist addresses himself within the narrative. These include the world, the Jews, the adherents of John the Baptist and a collection of other Christians who, according to the evangelist, have inadequate faith. One might indeed think that this sort of outlook would win the Gospel the label of 'an in-group manifesto meant as a triumph over outsiders',[10] but Brown will not go quite this far, conceding only that there is much that was sectarian in the community's nature and that it developed a generally hostile attitude towards the world. In the end, the community disintegrated due to its basic Gnostic tendency.

The basic principles of much of the reconstructive work of Martyn and Brown have prevailed in Johannine scholarship into the 1990s.[11] Disputes remain over the details, particularly surrounding the theory of the Eighteen Benedictions.[12] David Rensberger, for example, judges it

9. Brown, *Community of the Beloved Disciple*, p. 56.

10. Brown, *Community of the Beloved Disciple*, p. 62.

11. For example, in his work on the Fourth Gospel, John Ashton follows Martyn's basic structure for the community's history, although he modifies it in places (*Understanding the Fourth Gospel* [Oxford: Clarendon Press, 1991], pp. 166-74). Similarly, John Painter accepts Brown's reconstruction as 'generally convincing' in *The Quest for the Messiah*, the first edition of which came out in 1991 (p. 67). Robert Kysar, writing in 1993, also summarizes Martyn and Brown as the most widely endorsed and most convincing hypothesis ('Anti-Semitism and the Gospel of John', in C.A. Evans and D.A. Hagner [eds.], *Anti-Semitism and Early Christianity: Issues of Polemic and Faith* [Philadelphia: Fortress Press, 1993], pp. 113-27 [119]).

12. So Lawrence Schiffman, who asserts that the function of the Twelfth Benediction was to ensure that those who were *minim* did not serve as precentors—'It cannot be overemphasized that, while the benediction against the *minim* sought to exclude Jewish Christians from active participation in the synagogue service, it in no way implied expulsion from the Jewish people' ('At the Crossroads: Tannaitic Perspectives on the Jewish–Christian Schism', in E.P. Sanders [ed.], with A.I. Baumgarten and A. Mendelson, *Jewish and Christian Self-Definition*, II [2 vols.; London: SCM Press, 1981], pp. 115-56 [152]).

Martin Hengel notes 'the "expulsion" of Christians from the synagogue... took place in a lengthy and painful process which began even before Paul with the martyrdom of Stephen' (*The Johannine Question*, pp. 114-15). He therefore does not attribute the same importance to the Twelfth Benediction, seeing it simply as 'the ultimate consequence of a development full of combat and suffering' (p. 115).

doubtful that the ברכת המינים was actually the means for excluding Johannine Christians from the synagogue, but points out that this does *not* mean that they did not face expulsion. On the contrary, it seems to him 'incontrovertible' on the basis of Jn 9.22, 12.42 and 16.2 that this was the experience of the community.[13] Wayne Meeks argues that the ברכת המינים has been a red herring in Johannine research, which raises more questions than it answers.[14] 'All we have to assume', he states, 'is that the *archontes* of the Jewish community in John's location had simply made up their minds to get rid of these trouble-making followers of a false Messiah'.[15] Margaret Davies judges it unlikely that Jews in the first century CE excluded people from the synagogue at all. She argues that to accept the Fourth Gospel's references to exclusion as a reflection of the practices of the time an unacceptable number of assumptions must be made. 'It is more likely', she claims, 'that the Evangelist is not reflecting the practice of contemporary Jews at all, but is extrapolating from Scripture in order to justify the fact that the Christian community has nothing to do with the Jewish community'.[16]

A major contribution on this subject has also been made by James Dunn.[17] Dunn sees the Fourth Gospel reflecting a crisis between the Johannine sect and the dominant form of Judaism in the late first century CE. By the time the Gospel was written, this form of Judaism no longer regarded it as acceptable for Jews to confess Jesus as Messiah.

Stephen Katz also sees Martyn's claims as unacceptable because he accepts uncritically that Samuel the Small's revision of the malediction includes the two terms found in the Genizah fragment—*notzrim* and *minim*. Katz sees the benediction functioning as a filter and a self imposed ban as well as raising the awareness of other Jews that the *minim* were a threat and should be treated as apostates ('Issues in the Separation of Judaism and Christianity after 70 CE: A Reconsideration', *JBL* 103 [1984], pp. 43-76 [71]).

13. D.K. Rensberger, *Overcoming the World: Politics and Community in the Gospel of John* (London: SPCK, 1989), p. 26.

14. W. Meeks, 'Breaking Away: Three New Testament Pictures of Christianity's Separation from the Jewish Communities', in J. Neusner and E.S. Frerichs (eds.), *To See ourselves as others See us: Christians, Jews, 'Others' in Late Antiquity* (Chico, CA: Scholars Press, 1985), pp. 93-115 (102).

15. Meeks, 'Breaking Away', p. 103.

16. Davies, *Rhetoric and Reference*, p. 299. See pp. 291-301 for the whole argument.

17. J.D.G. Dunn, *The Partings of the Ways: Between Christianity and Judaism and their Significance for the Character of Christianity* (London: SCM Press, 1991).

This belief was enforced among local synagogues, as seen in Jn 9.22.[18] The confrontation between the two groups was caused by the forceful expression of the Christian claims about Jesus and the attempt by rabbinic Judaism to draw in tightly the boundaries of Jewish belief. At this point, Dunn contends, the Evangelist was still operating within the context of Judaism, involved in a contest for the hearts and minds of the Jewish people. His usage of the term 'the Jews' should not be seen as a distancing of the Johannine community from the Jews, but rather as an acknowledgment of a dispute over the pre-70 Jewish heritage. In summary:

> while the parting of the ways between Christianity and the Judaism of the Yavnean rabbis seems already an accomplished fact, John, in his own perspective at least, was still fighting a factional battle within Judaism rather than launching his arrows from without.[19]

No doubt, this debate will continue to run and run, as the so-called 'parting of the ways' benefits from an increased level of scholarly attention. However, despite the efforts of biblical critics, it remains clear that, without additional textual evidence, further clarity on the development of the Johannine community will be difficult to glean without a high level of speculation and assumption. Clues about the life and experiences of the community can be sought in the Gospel, but there are few certainties.[20] Indeed, Mark Stibbe concludes that the *only* real certainty is that the Gospel reflects a severe controversy with Judaism:

---

18. Dunn sees this as a direct reference to the ברכת המינים, or something like it, such as a local equivalent (*The Partings of the Ways*, p. 222).

19. Dunn, *The Partings of the Ways*, p. 159. Judith Lieu, however, is sceptical about Dunn's conclusion, commenting: 'the "Jews" of the Fourth Gospel hardly see the Johannine Christians as their fellows, and he may be over optimistic in thinking John had not yet been disowned by the Jewish people' (review of *The Partings of the Ways*, by J.D.G. Dunn, in *JTS* 44 [1993], pp. 668-70 [669]).

20. Perhaps it is for this reason that more recent works on this subject have focused on tracing aspects of theological development in the Gospel as it relates to the community's experience, rather than attempting to reconstruct history. See the reviews of works by Minear, Burge and Rensberger in K. Quast, 'Re-examining the Johannine Community', *TJT* 5 (1989), pp. 293-95. See also D. Moody Smith for general discussion on the subject in 'The Life Setting of the Gospel of John', *RevExp* 85 (1988), pp. 433-44.

As for the exact date of the controversy, the exact mechanism for its obvious destabilizing consequences, such details cannot be described with complete confidence. All we can say is that John's story of Jesus is at the same time a story of a community in crisis, and that John the storyteller uses the narrative and literary devices at his disposal to address the pressing social needs of his day.[21]

The Roman Context

The previous section discussed the Johannine community with reference to its original religious context, Judaism. The recent work of Richard Cassidy has explored the impact of the Roman environment on the Fourth Gospel in some detail and this merits some attention here.[22] Cassidy's thesis is that the Gospel 'generally responds to the phenomena of Roman claims and Roman persecution with extraordinary effectiveness'.[23] In order to make this claim, he must locate and date the Gospel appropriately, and this is done by setting it within the general confines of the Roman empire sometime after the early 80s CE.[24] Cassidy's work may be viewed as interesting rather than wholly convincing,[25] but it does afford us a glimpse of another facet of the community's oppression—oppression that does not come from within its own religious context but is officially sanctioned by the ruling power of the day.

21. Stibbe, *John as Storyteller*, p. 61. In the same vein, Painter cautions against becoming preoccupied with identifying the Johannine situation with the ברכת המינים, arguing that it is simply the best known relevant factor external to the Gospel which may prove illuminating. 'What is important', he concludes, 'is the situation of conflict with Formative Judaism whenever or wherever it happened' (*Quest for the Messiah*, p. 73).

22. See Cassidy, *John's Gospel in New Perspective: Christology and the Realities of Roman Power* (New York: Orbis Books, 1992).

23. Cassidy, *John's Gospel in New Perspective*, p. 5. Note that he does not claim that the evangelist *consciously* responded to aspects of Roman rule when writing the text.

24. See pp. 3-4 of *John's Gospel in New Perspective* for the argument on these points. Cassidy claims that developments highly relevant to John's account occurred during the reigns of Domitian (81-96) and Trajan (98-117).

25. J. Edgar Bruns sees Cassidy's thesis as having some verisimilitude, but concludes 'there is simply not enough in the Fourth Gospel to suggest that the Roman Empire was *the* enemy' (review of *John's Gospel in New Perspective: Christology and the Realities of Roman Power*, by Richard Cassidy, in *CBQ* 56 (1994), pp. 134-35 [135, emphasis original]). My study simply suggests that the Roman Empire was *another* enemy.

The principal source drawn upon to explore the position of Christians during this time is the correspondence between Pliny the Younger, pro-consul of Bithynia-Pontus, and the emperor Trajan. These letters, designated 10.96 and 10.97 in Pliny's *Epistulae*,[26] have the significance of being the earliest and fullest pagan communication about the Christian movement.[27] It is clear from Pliny's letter that his policy at the time was to execute Christians who refused to renounce their faith.[28] Unfortunately, this had led to a proliferation of accusations against individuals and the situation seemed in danger of becoming out of hand. Consequently, Pliny sought clarification of the correct course of action from Trajan. In particular, Pliny wished to know whether it was 'the name itself' (*nomen ipsum*) that was punishable, or just criminal activity associated with the name. Trajan's response was brief but unequivocal:

> You have followed the right course of procedure, my dear Pliny, in your examination of the cases of persons charged with being Christians... If they are brought before you and the charge against them is proved, they must be punished.[29]

Cassidy claims that Pliny would certainly have followed the emperor's instruction and, moreover, that governors of other provinces adjacent to

26. Fully reproduced in B. Radice (ed. and trans.), *The Letters of the Younger Pliny* (repr.; Harmondsworth: Penguin Books, 1985 [1963]). See p. 293 for Pliny's letter to Trajan (10.96) and p. 295 for Trajan's reply (10.97).

27. So claims A.N. Sherwin-White in *The Letters of Pliny: A Historical and Social Commentary* (Oxford: Clarendon Press, 1966), p. 693. Sherwin-White discusses their setting in detail and sees their main value lying in their evidence about the causes and legal forms of Christian persecution (pp. 693-94).

28. 'For the moment this is the line I have taken with all persons brought before me on the charge of being Christians. I have asked them in person if they are Christians, and if they admit it, I repeat the question a second and third time, with a warning of the punishment awaiting them. It they persist, I order them to be led away for execution' (Radice, *Letters of the Younger Pliny*, p. 293).

29. Radice, *Letters of the Younger Pliny*, p. 295. Stephen Benko suggests that Trajan's reply indicates the *nomen ipsum* constituted the crime because he 'tacitly assumed that Christianity automatically and inevitably led to wrongdoing' (*Pagan Rome and the Early Christians* [London: B.T. Batsford, 1984], p. 13). Trajan does, however, state that Christians should not be 'hunted out' and that pardon is possible for those who repent. W.H.C. Frend notes that, despite the ambiguities of their situation, with the implication that sleeping dogs should be allowed to lie, Christians were nevertheless considered 'a danger to the state' (*Martyrdom and Persecution in the Early Church: A Study of a Conflict from the Maccabees to Donatus* [Oxford: Basil Blackwell, 1965], pp. 220-21).

Bithynia-Pontus may have taken similar action,[30] heightening the risk to Christians.

Clearly there are uncertainties surrounding Cassidy's thesis; however, it is worth recognizing that the context of John's Gospel need not be constrained by our understanding of its relationship with Judaism. The Gospel may also reflect a relationship with wider society that further contributed towards the community's oppression. This should be borne in mind when examining the text for material concerning persecution.

Common Themes: Text and Community

While there are limits to our ability to understand the life of the Johannine community in much detail, it is possible to identify general (and more or less undisputed) aspects of the community's experience that are reflected within the text. I am referring primarily to experiences such as persecution, alienation and ostracization and the threat of violence. If the text can be used to understand the experiences of the community that produced it, then the reverse also follows—the self-image of the community can be used to hermeneutical advantage when facing the text.[31]

Scholars who have followed this line of investigation have often taken a sociolinguistic approach. Wayne Meeks, for example, makes a plea for attention to the system of myths woven into the text and the social

30. Cassidy, *John's Gospel in New Perspective*, p. 26.

31. Note the caution of Judith Lieu on this practice. Lieu questions the validity of seeing theology as a response to a historical situation. 'This is not to deny that John does reflect the community's own circumstances; it is to question whether those circumstances can be "read off" directly from distinctively Johannine passages' (*The Second and Third Epistles of John* [SNTW; Edinburgh: T. & T. Clark, 1986], p. 214). It is undeniable that certainties gained from 'reading off' the text are simply not available to us, but insights may still be gained. David Aune successfully demonstrates this in his thesis on realized eschatology. He argues that the characteristics of the Johannine community can be delineated by using the text, which is the end product of their worship and piety. Moreover, that the Christology of the Fourth Gospel is the primary means of expressing the values and ideals of the community. Consequently, 'the Johannine Jesus becomes comprehensible as a projection (or retrojection) of the religious needs and experiences of the Johannine community' (*The Cultic Setting of Realized Eschatology in Early Christianity* [NovTSup, 28; Leiden: E.J. Brill, 1972], p. 77; see pp. 73-84 for the main argument).

function that they served, using the ascent–descent theme as a case study. He claims there was 'a continuing dialectic between the group's historical experience and the symbolic world which served both to explain that experience and to motivate and form the reaction of group members to the experience'.[32] Bruce Malina explores the evidence for an antilanguage in John, discerned by the development and use of new words in preference to old ones, and the tendency to 'overlexicalize' by using a large range of lexical items to cover the same area—clearly the case in the Fourth Gospel.[33] The function the antilanguage performs is as follows:

> Like language itself, antilanguage is the bearer of social reality, but of an alternative social reality that runs counter to the social reality at large. Thus antilanguage serves to maintain inner solidarity under pressure. The pressure, of course, stems from the surrounding broader society…in which they are to a large extent still embedded.[34]

It is clear that the experience of the community was characterized by severe hostility from its surrounding environment, rejection by its spiritual parent and physical threat, possibly death. The text bears continual witness to this, both explicit and implicit in its references to persecution and rich in the imagery of violence and death. The all-pervasive nature of this material can be seen from the tables that document it in Chapter 2. From the very beginning of the Gospel the victimization of the community can be glimpsed. The Prologue provides the introduction to the key themes important throughout the rest of the narrative, functioning as it does as 'a microcosm of the fourth gospel *in toto*'.[35] That the first encounter between the Logos and humanity is recorded negatively is deeply significant. The world did not know him, his people rejected him, but the Johannine community received him (1.10-12). The community are set apart from the world—they are τέκνα θεοῦ (children of God), different from those born by the will of the flesh and the will of man. Their self-image is immediately characterized by their dissociation from the world. They too are misunderstood and spurned and they are unique in recognizing the identity and significance of the Logos. The themes of rejection and separation are woven into the rest of the

32. W. Meeks, 'The Man from Heaven in Johannine Sectarianism', *JBL* 91 (1972), pp. 144-72 (145).
33. Malina, 'The Gospel of John in Sociolinguistic Perspective', p. 12.
34. Malina, 'The Gospel of John in Sociolinguistic Perspective', pp. 13-14.
35. Smalley, *John: Evangelist and Interpreter*, p. 93.

narrative through its style, language and metaphors and form part of John's symbolic world. The reader does not have to look hard to find evidence of this,[36] and the conclusion drawn by Warren Carter is the obvious one: 'the repeated expression of that symbolic world by such variety suggests the intensity of the community's trauma and pain.'[37] Carter sees the Prologue as part of the community's attempt to assert its identity, legitimize its claims and interpret its experiences.

If the life of the community is reflected through the Prologue, where else can it be seen in the Gospel? As previously mentioned, Wayne Meeks finds it through examination of the ascent–descent theme in passages such as the Nicodemus discourse (3.12-14), the 'gallows humour'[38] of the ὑψόω terminology and the above–below claims made in 8.23. This motif is closely linked to the Johannine Christians' experience of separation from the synagogue and reflects the dualistic way in which it perceived itself: 'a small group of believers isolated over against "the world" that belongs intrinsically to "the things below", i.e. to darkness and the devil'.[39] Meeks reaches the conclusion that the community's social identity, which the narrative serves to reinforce, is in fact 'largely negative'.[40]

John Painter trawls the narrative for examples of rejection stories which also mirror the community's experience.[41] John 5.1-18 provides the pattern for rejection. Painter sees it as a traditional miracle story that

36. For example 3.18-21; 7.7; 15.18-19 and see the tables in Chapter 2 of this book.
37. W. Carter, 'The Prologue and John's Gospel: Function, Symbol and the Definitive Word', *JSNT* 39 (1990), pp. 35-58 (50).
38. Meeks, 'Man from Heaven', p. 155.
39. Meeks, 'Man from Heaven', p. 161.
40. Meeks, 'Man from Heaven', p. 163.
41. J. Painter, 'Quest and Rejection Stories in John', *JSNT* 36 (1989), pp. 17-46. Painter builds on Robert Tannehill's concept of objection stories found in the gospel of Mark and identifies four elements of each story:
    1. cause of the objection
    2. expression of the objection
    3. response to the objection
    4. final rejection of Jesus.
The stories occur in ch. 5–12 and emphasize the unreasonable nature of the rejection. Thus Painter concludes; 'time and again rejection occurs on a basis that should have led to belief. Thus we do not have an historical presentation of the events leading up to the decision to kill Jesus. Rather we have that decision made again and again and each time as if no previous decision had been made' (p. 39).

has been reworked by the evangelist into a rejection story. The element of conflict has been added after the miracle by the addition of the words: 'Now that day was the Sabbath' (v. 9b). Jesus is forced to justify his actions. This intensifies the conflict and leads to the accusations of his being a law-breaker and blasphemer (5.18). Painter surmises that the reason the evangelist chooses the language and form of a rejection story to relate this event is not to attempt to persuade those who have rejected Jesus to accept him, but rather 'to confirm the resolve of the Johannine community in facing the rejection that Jesus had faced before them'.[42] In other words, it has a direct social function.

The farewell discourses are fruitful material for a deeper understanding of the Johannine church. The situation of the readers is dealt with directly as Jesus warns his disciples of what is to come.[43] He includes the prediction that the believers will be expelled from the synagogue and suffer death (16.2). Rodney Whitacre sees in this final discourse the reason why conflict is such an all-pervasive theme in John's work. The function of the polemic in the story is to speak to the life situation of its audience; that of expulsion from the synagogue.

> It is of the greatest significance that we…find a connection explicitly drawn between what Jesus suffers and what his disciples will suffer (15.18-21). The author consciously intends that his readers find parallels between the conflicts they are experiencing and those which Jesus experienced.[44]

The Gospel is addressed to those suffering persecution from their mother community, the Jews.[45] However, despite their extreme isolation they are not orphans (ὀρφανούς, 14.18), as the evangelist reminds them that Jesus has sent the Holy Spirit to comfort and counsel them.

---

42. Painter, 'Quest and Rejection Stories', p. 35.

43. Specifically in 15.18-16.11; 16.19-24 and 17.20-26.

44. R.A. Whitacre, *Johannine Polemic: The Role of Tradition and Theology* (SBLDS, 67; Chico, CA: Scholars Press, 1982), p. 6.

45. Cassidy argues that Roman persecution should also be considered: 'it is not possible to establish definitively from presently existing data that some of John's readers were proximate to Roman persecution… However, for the sake of conceiving the maximum impact that Jesus' farewell addresses would have had in such circumstances, let it be assumed that at least some in John's audience were reading or hearing these chapters within a situation in which denunciations, Roman trials and sentences of death were immediate realities' (*John's Gospel in New Perspective*, p. 62).

Lindars also discusses the importance of these passages to the community, claiming that they indicate the evangelist felt the situation was becoming critical and that there was 'a real risk of violent, even fanatical, conflict'.[46]

Another theme prominent in the farewell discourse is love and hate. Fernando Segovia explores the social significance of the love and hatred of Jesus exhibited by individuals and groups in the Fourth Gospel. Segovia explores references to love and hate in the farewell discourses, as well as in John 1–4 and 5–12, to see what light they shed on the situation of the Johannine believers.[47] Love for Jesus is strongly connected to belief—to love him is to believe in him. In the farewell discourses this language is used to distinguish between two distinct groups in bitter dispute with one another. The public expression of love for Jesus, as practised by Jesus' disciples and the Johannine community, entails expulsion from the synagogue. Hatred of Jesus, as displayed by the parent synagogue, results in attempts to kill Jesus and his second generation followers.[48] The result of the intense battle between these two groups is the estrangement of the community, alienation from the world and rejection of its values—in short, the development of a sectarian attitude. Martin Hengel echoes this when he comments on the way in which the commandment to love one another refers solely to the disciples (13.34; 15.12, 17) and the fact that the departing Christ prays not for the world but only for the community of disciples (17.8).[49]

Elisabeth Schüssler Fiorenza sees similar messages in the language of love and the act of the footwashing in John 13.[50] The footwashing is a paradigmatic act of altruistic love that marks the Johannine community out as alternative.[51] However, the love of the disciples is focused

46. B. Lindars, 'The Persecution of Christians in John 15.18–16.4a', in W. Horbury and B. McNeil (eds.), *Suffering and Martyrdom in the New Testament: Studies Presented to G.M. Styler by the Cambridge New Testament Seminar* (Cambridge: Cambridge University Press, 1981), pp. 48-69 (67).

47. F.F. Segovia, 'The Love and Hatred of Jesus in Johannine Sectarianism', *CBQ* 43 (1981), pp. 258-72.

48. Segovia, 'Love and Hatred', p. 270.

49. Hengel, *The Johannine Question*, p. 44.

50. E. Schüssler Fiorenza, *In Memory of Her: A Feminist Theological Reconstruction of Christian Origins* (London: SCM Press, 1983).

51. Schüssler Fiorenza points out that, while in the Pastorals it is the enrolled widows who are required to perform this duty for the 'saints', in John *all* disciples

inwards. The witness that they give to the world is by the praxis of *agape*
but it seems to be directed towards each other with the world viewing
from the outside. This love is at its greatest when it is demonstrated
sacrificially by believers for their friends (15.13), as this shows that they
are not part of the world themselves but stand against it. The core of
discipleship is love and service, which must be lived as 'a public witness
which indicts the hate and death-dealing powers of "the world"' [52]
Schüssler Fiorenza does not go so far as to call the community introversionist, but the idea is implicit—the world will recognize the Johannine disciples of Jesus because of their love for each other and hatred of
every one else!

A general picture of some of the experiences of the Johannine community has begun to emerge from these approaches to language and
metaphor in the Gospel. A more thorough analysis of the social and
political existence of the community has been undertaken by David
Rensberger.[53] Accepting Martyn's basic proposal of expulsion from the
synagogue as a central feature of the community's traumatic existence,
he describes some of the consequences of this crisis:

> The Christians who were expelled would have been cut off from much
> that had given identity and structure to their lives. Expulsion would have
> meant social ostracism and thus the loss of relationship with family and
> friends, and perhaps economic dislocation as well. It would certainly have
> meant religious dislocation.[54]

As we have already seen, the effect that this threatening environment
has on the community is that it turns in on itself and becomes alienated
from the outside world.[55] Rensberger discusses whether or not the
group can be classified as a sect, concluding that it is a sectarian group
with an introversionist nature, although he perceives that it may have

are to follow Jesus' example of love and service towards each other (*In Memory of Her*, p. 324).

52. Schüssler Fiorenza, *In Memory of Her*, p. 323.
53. Rensberger, *Overcoming the World*.
54. Rensberger, *Overcoming the World*, pp. 26-27.
55. Ashton is in agreement: 'Finding itself alone and confronting persecution [the Johannine group] had two choices: It could either look for support elsewhere or huddle self-protectively in a small knot. Perhaps it did both these things, but the evidence is stronger for the latter' (*Understanding the Fourth Gospel*, p. 173).

some missionary concern.[56] An overriding attribute appears to be para-noia, fed by the insularity of the community's world-view. The 'general sense of alienation and superiority',[57] mentioned at the beginning of Chapter 1 as one of the unnerving aspects of the Gospel, can be applied without reservation to the community that produced it. This is hardly surprising, since the community has produced a text that shares its own characteristics—the resemblance is by no means accidental. The peculiarities of John's narrative and the idiosyncrasies of its protagonist function as a means of communication. This position is implicit, for example, in the work of Robert Karris. Writing about the contact between Jesus and 'the marginalized'[58] in the Fourth Gospel, Karris sees these stories as having a twofold purpose: first, they demonstrate to the Johannine community *the nature of their Messiah Jesus* and secondly they serve as *paradigms of behaviour* for the persecuted members of the community.[59] The interplay between the text and the community means, however, that the *reverse* is also the case—the nature of the community is reflected in the picture of their Messiah; and the

56. Rensberger, *Overcoming the World*, p. 27. Rensberger compares Johannine Christianity to the model of sectarianism developed by Bryan Wilson, according to which it would be classified as an introversionist sect that sees the world as irre-deemably evil and seeks to renounce it. Wilson identifies eight basic supernaturalist responses to the dilemma of salvation from evil. The introversionist response is evidenced in a social movement by 'the establishment of a separated community preoccupied with its own holiness and its means of insulation from the wider society... The community itself becomes the source and seat of all salvation' (*Magic and the Millennium: A Sociological Study of Religious Movements of Protest among Tribal and Third-World Peoples* [London: Heinemann, 1973], pp. 18-30 [24]).

W.R. Domeris uses Ernst Troeltsch's profile of a sect to look at the social profile of the Johannine community. He sees features such as the absence of an emphasis on sacraments; the lack of bureaucracy and hierarchy; and the importance of personal experience as being important indicators in the Gospel. 'Clearly there is a good case for viewing the Johannine community as a sect with a particularly strong sense of equality among its members', he concludes ('Christology and Community: A Study of the Social Matrix of the Fourth Gospel', *JTheolSA* 64 [1988], pp. 49-56 [53]).

57. Brown, *Community of the Beloved Disciple*, p. 89.

58. By which is meant the economically, physically and geographically marginal-ized; women and those marginalized through ignorance.

59. R.J. Karris, *The Marginalized in John's Gospel* (Zacchaeus Studies, New Testament; Collegeville, MN: Liturgical Press, 1990), pp. 105-106.

behaviour of the community serves as a paradigm for the stories within the narrative. Moreover, David Aune claims that 'the character and function of Jesus is *identical* with the character and function of the followers of Jesus'.[60] In fact, the characterization of the life of the Johannine Jesus is 'explicitly correlated' by the evangelist to the experience of the community.[61] There is a certain degree of circularity here: the text is used to communicate with and, importantly, to legitimize the behaviour of a group which created it 'in its own image' in the first place. This is what is implied by Brown's comment that 'the Johannine Christians are those who understand Jesus best, for *like him* they are rejected, persecuted and not of this world'.[62] The Johannine Christians have created as their representative a Jesus who *like them* is rejected, persecuted and not of this world. It is a natural enough tendency, and one that is continually played out with every new hermeneutical endeavour to find a topical and relevant messiah. Thus John Parr, writing about Latin American liberation theology, points out: 'not only are liberation theologians trying to relate Jesus to their own situations, they are also trying to relate their own situations to the Jesus of the Gospels'.[63] It follows that the little that can be surmised about the disposition of the Johannine community is invaluable for further understanding the nature and behaviour of the Johannine Jesus—their mark will be stamped on his identity. At the very least we can expect that Jesus, like his creators, will be rejected by his own religious community and expelled from the synagogue, alienated from members of his family, accused of being insane, persecuted and continually threatened with death. The environment in which he operates will be a violent and dangerous one and his encounters will be grim. It would not be surprising if he was characterized by a somewhat sectarian attitude—superior, exclusive, obsessive and even paranoid at times. Nor would it be surprising if these attributes rendered him a little *strange* or not very *nice*, jarring the sensibilities of the modern reader. This Jesus has no time

60. Aune, *Cultic Setting of Realized Eschatology*, p. 78, emphasis added.
61. Aune, *Cultic Setting of Realized Eschatology*, p. 78.
62. Brown, *Community of the Beloved Disciple*, p. 89, emphasis added.
63. J. Parr, 'Jesus and the Liberation of the Poor: Biblical Interpretation in the Writings of Some Latin American Theologians of Liberation' (PhD dissertation, University of Sheffield, 1989), p. 87.

for musing about the lilies of the Synoptic field. He is living through the brutal and chaotic experiences of what was happening to a victimized community and, as Kott aptly observed, 'in periods of madness, mad gods and their even madder prophets always appear'.[64]

64. J. Kott, *The Eating of the Gods: An Interpretation of Greek Tragedy* (trans. B. Taborski and E.J. Czerwinski; London: Eyre Methuen, 1974), p. 230.

5

Relationship with the Community I: Scenes of Violence

Having documented in Chapter 2 the references in John's Gospel that contain examples of violence and oppression inflicted on Jesus, this chapter will be used to examine some of them in more detail. The material to be discussed is primarily contained within six events that happen during Jesus' public ministry. The scenes generally begin as attempts to educate the crowd regarding Jesus' mission and identity but, as his words become increasingly controversial, they erupt into chaotic situations that seriously threaten his personal safety. This material charts the practical and physical dimensions of Jesus' relationship with the community in John 1–12.

Chaos in the Temple (2.13-22)

The incident in the temple is the first piece of violent action that occurs in the Gospel. It strikes the reader as an unexpected and startling event, particularly since it appears early on in the narrative. The previous pericope has seen Jesus participating in a domestic scene at Cana, responding to the practical, though somewhat peripheral, need of some friends. Immediately following this, and without any warning, the reader is confronted with an incident that takes place in the religious heart of the community in which Jesus appears to display behaviour that can best be described as 'berserk'. While this is undoubtedly an act of hostility committed *by* Jesus rather than *against* him, it adds significant detail to his identity as a victim, as well as framing the context in which the opposition of the Jews will develop.

John's account of the incident is longer and more theologically intense than its Synoptic counterpart. The details are elaborate: in addition to the basic facts of the event, where an outraged Jesus overturns tables and drives animals out of the temple, John provides the reader with

information about the three types of animals being sold and two additional acts of deliberate aggression by Jesus. The extra information
underscores the violence of Jesus' actions. The Synoptic Jesus carries out
an act of 'cleansing'[1] in a mechanical manner, and it is related primarily
because it fulfils Isaiah's 'house of prayer/den of robbers' prophecy (Isa.
56.7). It is a two-dimensional episode that lacks the vital element present
in the Fourth Gospel's account: emotion. John has Jesus finding
(εὗρεν[2]) the animal sellers in the temple, spontaneously constructing a
weapon of vandalism[3] and, like a man possessed, attacking everything in
his path.[4] Four active verbs are used to convey the scene:

> and making (ποιήσας) a whip of cords, he drove them out (ἐξέβαλεν)
> …of the temple;
> and he poured out (ἐξέχεεν) the coins of the money-changers and over-
> turned (ἀνέτρεψεν) their tables

(v. 15)

The fact that this incident occurs at the beginning of Jesus' public ministry instead of at the end, as in the Synoptics, is noteworthy.[5] Jesus'

---

1.   See E.P. Sanders for the argument that Jesus' action is not a cleansing. 'Jesus
predicted (or threatened) the destruction of the temple and carried out an action
symbolic of its destruction by demonstrating against the performance of sacrifices.
He did not wish to purify the temple, either of dishonest trading or of trading in
contrast to "pure" worship' (*Jesus and Judaism* [London: SCM Press, 1985], p. 75).

2.   The meaning here is 'to come upon accidentally, without seeking' (BAGD,
p. 325). This would make Jesus' actions a sudden response to the situation—more
akin to an outburst than the purposeful, seemingly planned, action of the Synoptic
character.

3.   Contrast B.F. Westcott's assertion that the whip is a 'symbol of authority'
and not a 'weapon of offence' (*The Gospel According to St John* [London: John
Murray, 1898], p. 41). It is difficult to see how a whip, purposefully used to harm
people and animals, could be anything *but* a weapon of offence.

4.   Note Carson's attempt to tone down Jesus' behaviour: 'Jesus' physical action
was forceful but not cruel; one does not easily drive out cattle and sheep without a
whip of cords' (*Gospel According to John*, p. 179). Given that Jesus was 'consumed by
zeal' this argument appears unjustified. The point of constructing a whip is so that it
can be used to whip things and Jesus uses it not only on the animals but on people as
well—he drives them *all* (πάντας) out of the temple. Beasley-Murray comments on
the inclusion in 𝔓. 66 and 𝔓. 75 of the prefix ὡς to φραγέλλιον—'a kind of whip',
which looks like an early attempt to tone down the action of Jesus (*John*, p. 38).

5.   Although see Carson (*Gospel According to John*, pp. 177-78) and L. Morris
(*The Gospel According to John: The English Text with Introduction, Exposition and Notes*

behaviour cannot be interpreted as a reaction to harassment by the Jewish authorities; rather, it is a belligerent act of disorder that functions as an indictment of the temple and its sacrificial system. The scene conveys both the opposition of Jesus to the old religious order, and a foreshadowing of the violence to be inflicted on him through the establishment of the new. Here he is overtly the destroyer, but he is also, less ostensibly, the object of destruction—'he who wields the scourge will himself be scourged and the temple of his body will be destroyed'.[6] The vocabulary used to describe Jesus' attack functions as an ironic prolepsis of the acts to be committed against him. He will be consumed (καταφάγεταί),[7] destroyed (λύσατε) and, as John explains, he will die (implied by the comment that he will be raised from the dead; ἠγέρθη ἐκ νεκρῶν). Theologically, Jesus is symbolized as both the new temple and the new sacrifice in this passage. He drives out the sacrificial animals of the old order to make way for the new sacrificial lamb at the very time when the ritual slaughter is taking place—Passover—prefiguring his own bloody slaughter in two years' time.

The quotation of the phrase ὁ ζῆλος τοῦ οἴκου σου καταφάγεταί με ('Zeal for thy house will consume me', v. 17), from Ps. 69.9, identifies the experience of Jesus with the plight of a severely oppressed man. It is quoted again in Jn 15.25 and 19.29, being one of the evangelist's *testimonia*, prophesying and illuminating the gospel events and the character of Jesus.[8] The psalm describes a man attacked, insulted and dishonoured—an outcast (Ps. 69.8; cf. Jn 1.11). Not only does the text decry the sacrificial system several times,[9] in accordance with Jesus' subsequent words, but it uses strong language of an innocent man close to despair through victimization:

[Grand Rapids: Eerdmans, 1971], pp. 188-91) for arguments that there were two temple incidents and that John chooses to report the first one.

6.   F. Kermode, 'John', in R. Alter and F. Kermode (eds.), *The Literary Guide to the Bible* (London: Collins, 1987), pp. 440-66 (450).

7.   Beasley-Murray comments: '"will consume", not in a psychological sense, but more drastically "*will destroy*"' (*John*, p. 38).

8.   Hanson notes that Ps. 69 was generally very popular with the New Testament writers (*Prophetic Gospel*, p. 212).

9.   'Let their own table before them become a snare; let their sacrificial feasts become a trap' (v. 22) and 'I will praise the name of God with a song; I will magnify him with thanksgiving. This will please the Lord more than an ox or a bull with horns and hoofs' (vv. 30-31).

> More in number than the hairs of my head
> are those who hate me without cause;
> mighty are those who would destroy me,
> those who attack me with lies (Ps. 69.4).

The text makes it clear in Jn 2.19-21 that it is Jesus' body that will be the object of destruction. The Jews challenge Jesus' disruptive actions in 2.18 with a request for a sign to indicate his authority, but Jesus' response is to refer them to the ultimate sign of the Gospel: his own death. His words are phrased in the imperative: λύσατε τὸν ναὸν τοῦτον, functioning as a command that identifies those who will fulfil it: *you* destroy my body. This has different import from its Synoptic counterpart, where Jesus claims he will tear down the temple *himself*.[10] The evangelist does not leave the meaning of the text in doubt, revealing Jesus' body as the shrine (v. 21) to be destroyed. Jesus implicitly names his opponents and defines their task. It is now clear what form the 'rejection by his own' (1.11) will take.

As the first example of an act of violence in the narrative, the temple incident is a significant starting point for the negative relationship between Jesus and the Jewish authorities. It results in a dispute that creates an atmosphere of tension between the two, formulating a framework within which to view their subsequently opposing roles. Jesus is deliberately provocative, carrying out an act that is incomprehensible to followers and opponents alike, designed to invite the wrath of the Jews. Despite this, he is represented as the innocent party by the evangelist, who justifies his actions theologically. He is to become the victim of religious leaders who will be responsible for his death.

Healing and Controversy at Bethesda (5.1-18)

The next scene that brings Jesus into direct confrontation with the Jewish authorities is the public healing of a paralytic on the sabbath. The structure of this section can be subdivided into two parts: the miracle itself (vv. 1-9) and the consequences of the miracle (vv. 10-18). There

10. Mt. 26.61, 27.40; Mk 14.58, 15.29. Sanders comments, 'The change is necessary for the evangelist's explanation that the temple is Jesus' body. Jesus could not have said that he would destroy his own body' (*Jesus and Judaism*, p. 73). The change is, however, more fundamental than this as it shifts the identity of the destroyer/destroyed. In the Synoptics it is the temple that will ultimately be the object of destruction, but in John, Jesus is identified as the victim.

then follows Jesus' third discourse (v. 19-47), which elaborates on his authority to act in the name of the Father. For our purposes, the crucial verses for interpretation are vv. 13 and 16-18, as these provide material indicating the nature and extent of the conflict at Bethesda.

At first glance, Jesus appears to perform a relatively straightforward healing miracle. However, the reader is forced to reassess the circumstances on learning in v. 9b that it was carried out on the sabbath.[11] A situation of confrontation quickly arises as the healed man is apprehended by the Jews for violating the sabbath.[12] The paralytic deflects their interest away from himself by shifting the blame[13] onto 'the man who healed me' (v. 11). When interrogated about who this is, however, the paralytic reveals that he does not know because Jesus had already slipped away (ἐξένευσεν). The reason for his sudden departure is clearly stated: ὄχλου ὄντος ἐν τῷ τόπῳ ('as there was a crowd in the place', v. 13). The miracle has attracted a large crowd, whose presence, it is implied, is intimidating to Jesus. Throngs of excited people, coupled with the arrival of the authorities to question the paralytic, have created an environment that Jesus feels the need to escape from in a hurry.[14] His early departure is undesirable and unintentional, as the evangelist indicates that Jesus has been unable to complete his work with this man. He has not been able to speak to him or reveal his identity, but has escaped from a situation that was becoming too heated. It is not until

---

11. J.L. Staley notes that the reader has to re-evaluate both the significance of the miracle and the characters involved ('Stumbling in the Dark, Reaching for the Light: Reading Character in John 5 and 9', *Semeia* 53 [1991], p. 55-80 [60]).

12. So Jer. 17.21-22. See also H.L. Strack and P. Billerbeck on the 39 works forbidden on the sabbath, of which removal of a bed was included (*Kommentar zum Neuen Testament aus Talmud und Midrasch*, II [4 vols.; Munich: C.H. Becksche Verlagsbuchhandlung/Oskar Beck, 1924], pp. 454-61).

13. Carson comments: 'he is simply "ducking" the authorities' (*Gospel According to John*, p. 245).

14. Stibbe sees this as part of the Johannine motif of withdrawals from places of hostility and unbelief that enhance the portrayal of Jesus' elusive presence ('The Elusive Christ: A New Reading of the Fourth Gospel', *JSNT* 44 [1991], pp. 19-38 [22]). Carson claims that Jesus was 'acting in accordance with what became a consistent policy', as if he deliberately planned to leave early of his own accord (*Gospel According to John*, p. 245). In fact, the reverse is the case. His behaviour is only consistent because he is continually forced to flee to avoid being arrested or stoned.

later on[15] that Jesus can return to seek out the man and deliver his warning: μηκέτι ἁμάρτανε (v. 14).

Having discovered Jesus' identity, the healed man ignores his warning and informs the authorities who was really responsible for breaking the sabbath. The character of the paralytic is commonly seen to be passive and timid,[16] rather than deliberately negative. However, his behaviour indicates otherwise. He does not wait for the authorities to return to question him again (as a timid character might), but departs specifically to tell the Jews who Jesus is. This is treachery for the purpose of self-preservation. The paralytic has lived on the margins of society for 38 years, doubtless considered to be a sinner by the Jews on account of his disability. His healing is an opportunity for integration back into the community and he has no intention of jeopardizing this by exposing himself to the accusation of sabbath-breaking by the authorities. This, then, is a betrayal[17] of Jesus and it is a betrayal that has serious consequences. John concludes that the justification for persecuting Jesus has its origin in this event:

> And this was why the Jews persecuted (ἐδίωκον) Jesus,
> because he did this on the sabbath (5.16).

It is not clear how Jesus has specifically transgressed the sabbath, since what he has actually done is incited another to break it by carrying a pallet.[18] Possibly John is referring generally to Jesus' attitude to the sabbath law.[19] What is important is that, from the perspective of his

---

15. μετὰ ταῦτα in v. 14 could be seen to imply that the crowd had dispersed and the authorities left but we do not know how much later on it was.

16. Martyn, *History and Theology*, pp. 71-72. Brown sees him as unimaginative and obtuse but not treacherous, culpable rather of 'persistent naïveté' (*Gospel According to John*, I, p. 209). 'Guilty of dullness rather than treachery', declares Carson (*Gospel According to John*, p. 246). Note, however, Stibbe: 'there is a hint of disloyalty in him' (*John*, p. 75). So too Kysar: 'the man attempts to escape any guilt by passing the blame onto the man who healed him, thus implicating Jesus... He has no sense of gratitude' (*John*, p. 77).

17. The cripple is Judas in the making. As he departs (ἀπέρχομαι) to inform the authorities of Jesus' identity, so Judas will go out (ἐξέρχομαι) to inform the authorities of Jesus' whereabouts (13.30).

18. Bruce claims that this is *worse* than breaking it oneself (*Gospel of John*, p. 126), although he does not substantiate this claim.

19. So Barrett, *Gospel According to St John*, p. 255.

oppressors, this action legitimizes persecution of Jesus.[20] Although it can be presumed that the authorities make a direct accusation to Jesus regarding his activities, this is not recorded by the evangelist, who instead focuses on the response that he makes: 'My Father is working still, and I am working' (v. 17). This claim elicits even greater animosity from the Jews, who sought all the more to kill him (διὰ τοῦτο οὖν μᾶλλον[21] ἐζήτουν αὐτὸν οἱ Ἰουδαῖοι ἀποκτεῖναι). The evangelist explains that this is because they perceived that he had added to his sin of sabbath-breaking the blasphemy of making himself equal with God (v. 18). He is now deserving of death—they heard him blaspheming and it was their duty to condemn and execute him: 'the machinery of justice had started to turn, and there could be no looking back'.[22]

The reader now understands the origin of and reason for Jesus' persecution and has been introduced to the christological issue of the relationship with the Father as the root of the antithesis between Jesus and his opponents.[23] The term used to describe the action of the Pharisees in this passage is διώκω, which commonly means 'persecute' or 'pursue with hostile intent'.[24] This is the sense in which it occurs in the Septuagint, particularly in psalms of individual lament[25] where the psalmist pleads for deliverance from his attackers. In the New Testament it occurs thirty times, especially in the Gospels, Acts and Paul, with the

---

20. Kysar goes so far as to claim: 'the healed man is responsible for the fact that the authorities persecuted Jesus' (*John*, p. 78).

21. The phrase 'all the more' may be explained by the inclusion of καὶ εζητουν αυτον αποκτειναι in v. 16 of some manuscripts, notably A, Θ, Ψ. See K. Aland *et al.* (eds.), *Novum Testamentum Graece* (Nestle–Aland; Stuttgart: Deutsche Bibelstiftung, 26th edn, 1979), p. 261.

22. A.E. Harvey, *Jesus on Trial: A Study in the Fourth Gospel* (London: SPCK, 1976), p. 52. Dorothy Lee also comments that John 5 is seen as beginning a new section in the Gospel: 'It sets in motion the motif of the opposition of the "Jews" which will run through the ensuing chapters, culminating in the "sign" at Bethany and the plot to kill Jesus' (*The Symbolic Narratives of the Fourth Gospel: The Interplay of Form and Meaning* [JSNTSup, 95; Sheffield: JSOT Press, 1994], p. 99).

23. Culpepper contends that the Jews have now received their 'script' for the rest of the story. The remainder of the chapter is Jesus' response to this script, exploring from his perspective why the Jews reject him. 'The plot line of the prologue has begun to unfold—Jesus comes to his own and his own people do not receive him' (*Anatomy of the Fourth Gospel*, p. 127).

24. BAGD, p. 210.

25. For example, Pss. 7.2, 31.15, 35.3, 71.11. See A. Oepke, 'διώκω', *TDNT*, II, p. 229-30.

meaning of religious persecution.[26] It conveys forceful opposition to the victim, who is hunted out by a group of aggressors. Within the context of John's Gospel, hints of this sort of persecution can be seen throughout the narrative. Continual pressure, harassment and ill-treatment are suffered by Jesus. Groups of opponents plague him throughout his travels, verbally abusing him and inciting the crowds around him to physical violence.[27] Their activity includes plots and tricks (8.6),[28] a restriction on free movement (7.1; 11.8) and a general denial of privacy. The implication is not that Jesus was continually 'shadowed', but the narrative implies that whenever mention is made of a crowd following Jesus (such as in 6.2), this does not consist solely of a throng of enthusiastic and interested simple folk,[29] but includes a contingent of 'persecutors' who are energetically seeking ways to harm him. The statement that the Jews were, even at this stage, seeking to kill Jesus adds to the picture of general persecution and harassment. There is a more sinister, calculated plot against Jesus than merely the intention to disrupt his ministry and make life dangerous for him. The group of Jews mentioned here are unidentified 'authorities' who are committed to Jesus' death, although they are not directly connected to the official plot of the authorities (11.49-53).[30] They are his regular attackers. They examine his words for blasphemy and scrutinize his deeds for legal transgressions (9.16), searching for further reasons to legitimize violence against him. The evangelist makes it clear that by the time Jesus has performed his third miracle he has emerged as a controversial figure who has aroused the hatred of a cross section of the population. Plans by the Jews to murder him, or assist the multitude in doing so, are already formulating. An occasion of healing has become the legitimization for death.

26. G. Ebel, 'Persecution, Tribulation, Affliction', *NIDNTT*, II, p. 806. The term is essentially an active one—its alternative meaning is to 'zealously follow', to 'run after' and in a metaphorical sense it can imply striving after Christian objectives (Rom. 12.13; 1 Pet. 3.11).

27. For example 7.44; 8.59 and see the tables in Chapter 3 of this study.

28. 'This they said to test him, that they might have some charge to bring against him' (τοῦτο δὲ ἔλεγον πειράζοντες αὐτόν, ἵνα ἔχωσιν κατηγορεῖν αὐτοῦ).

29. The impression that one might get from the Synoptic accounts.

30. See U.C. von Wahlde for a description of the this use of Ἰουδαῖος ('The Johannine Jews: A Critical Survey', *NTS* 28 [1982], pp. 33-60 [47]). Von Wahlde concludes that, with the exception of 6.41, 52, Ἰουδαῖος is used to refer to the authorities rather than the common people.

Fleeing the Five Thousand (6.1-15)

Closely following the Bethesda miracle is the next 'sign' in Jesus' public ministry, the outcome of which is a chaos that necessitates his fleeing his audience. The location has moved from Jerusalem to the Sea of Galilee,[31] and the evangelist notes that the Passover is approaching. The temporal marker brings with it the theme of the sacrificial slaughter of the Passover lambs. The feeding miracle and associated discourse (6.22-59) are commonly interpreted as having eucharistic undertones and it is subsequently asserted that it is the flesh of this sacrifice, given for the life of the world (v. 51), that must be consumed by the disciples. Many of these issues will be discussed in Chapter 6, where the contents of the discourse will be examined in detail. The following short section will concentrate on the course of events that culminates in a threatening situation for Jesus. However, prior to this a word needs to be said about the characterization of Jesus in this passage.

There are two verses within this pericope that have exerted disproportionate hermeneutical influence over the passage, serving to fuel the conviction of commentators that the Johannine Christ is a sovereign, omniscient being in accordance with the Gospel's high Christology. Clear indication of this feature of his character is commonly seen in vv. 6 and 15, where Jesus appears to know what is going to happen next, displaying his 'miraculous foreknowledge'.[32] Working systematically through the story will bring these comments by the evangelist back into perspective. Following his success in healing the cripple at Bethesda (and others, as indicated by v. 2), Jesus' fame has spread to the extent that he has been followed by a great crowd.[33] The question of feeding the

31. Lee claims that Jn 6 is a deliberate insertion of Galilean material into a narrative that otherwise represents a devolving of conflict on Jerusalem. 'As the conflict between Jesus and the "Jews" escalates in Jerusalem (John 5, 7–8), Galilee is drawn into the net. It too is seen as part of the tide of hostility which finally engulfs Jesus' (*Symbolic Narratives*, pp. 128-29).

32. Lee, *Symbolic Narratives*, p. 133. See also Westcott: 'internal, absolute knowledge' (*Gospel According to St John*, p. 96), and Robert Kysar: 'the absolute knowledge of Christ' (*John* [Augsburg Commentary on the New Testament; Minneapolis: Augsburg, 1986], p. 91).

33. The evangelist clearly states that the crowd have a 'signs faith', being seduced by Jesus' acts rather than believing in his words. The inadequacy of this faith has already been indicated in 2.23-25. People believe when they see his miracles but

crowd is a practical matter for the Johannine Jesus, who does not appear
to be motivated by compassion.[34] He asks his disciple Philip where they
can buy enough bread to feed the growing multitude, but before
Philip's answer is given, the narrator includes an explanatory aside for
the reader: 'This he said to test him, for he himself knew what he would
do' (v. 6). Rather than viewing this verse as a pointer of Jesus' omniscience and a means of protecting his supremacy,[35] it fits better as a
device that creates suspense within the narrative and indicates *forward
thinking* rather than *foreknowledge*. Jesus has a plan—he has already
decided what course of action he is going to take. The suspense is created by the narrator informing us of this fact. Like Philip and Andrew,
the reader does not know the solution to the problem of how to satisfy
so many people with insufficient resources. There is a solution, indicates
John, and Jesus knows what it is. The interest of the reader is thus
secured and the question framed: What will happen next? Unfortunately
there is little suspense for most readers as this is a well-worn tale. However, what actually does happen would only start to dawn on a reader
unfamiliar with the story perhaps as late as v. 11. Five thousand people
have sat down and Jesus has distributed the food. Suspicion that something preternatural has taken place is aroused by the phrase ὅσον ἤθελον
(v. 11). For five thousand people to have had as much as they wished,
some kind of multiplication must have taken place. This is confirmed in
vv. 12-13: there are twelve baskets of fragments as evidence of the
miracle.

It is at this point that Jesus' plan begins to go awry. The crowd,
greatly impressed by his performance, become excited at the prospect of
having discovered a figure with supernatural powers, enthusiastically
hailing him as 'the prophet who is to come into the world' (v. 14). The
situation intensifies to such a level that the people transform into a
threatening mob, intent on overpowering him in order to thrust leadership upon him. That Jesus 'perceives' (γνοὺς) this danger is, again, less

---

Jesus does not trust them as he knows 'what is in man' (αὐτὸς γὰρ ἐγίνωσκεν τί ἦν
ἐν τῷ ἀνθρώπῳ, v. 25b).

34. Compare Mk 6.34; Mt. 15.32.

35. In other words, the evangelist has had to include it lest the reader should
think that Jesus is not sure how to handle this situation and is asking for advice. So
Carson: 'John adds this comment to forestall any reader from thinking that Jesus was
stumped, surprised by the miracle that was eventually performed' (*Gospel According to
John*, p. 269).

an example of omniscience[36] than of simple observation. He is faced with a turbulent mass of five thousand over-excited people who are not minded to pack up and go home peaceably. He reads their mood and anticipates that they are going to seize him. The word employed by the evangelist, ἁρπάζειν, is a violent and physical one, used, for example, to mean kidnapping.[37] The situation is so volatile that Jesus is unable to contain it. He makes no attempt to calm the people, reason with them, or educate them about the true meaning of the miracle.[38] His response is simply to flee his would-be captors. The word ἀνεχώρησεν is usually translated as 'he withdrew' or 'departed',[39] but the term can also mean 'to take refuge'[40]—a more appropriate rendering given the threatening context. The mob are on the verge of seizing him when he flees to the mountain and hides there alone. It is only when it is dark[41] and they have dispersed that he risks rejoining his disciples.

Jesus' behaviour seems contradictory in this pericope. He uses super-natural means to attend to the physical needs of the crowd, but when his own physical safety is threatened, there is no indication that he has

36. As claimed by Barrett (*Gospel According to St John*, p. 278), and supported by Barnabas Lindars (*The Gospel of John* [NCB; London: Oliphants, 1972], p. 244). Carson hedges his bets: Jesus' knowledge could be either supernatural or merely insightful (*Gospel According to John*, p. 271). Kysar comments that it 'may be a kind of supernatural knowledge on the part of Jesus' (*John*, p. 93).

37. So, Barrett, quoting Herodotus 1.2 and Mt. 11.12 (*Gospel According to St John*, p. 278). For associated meanings see BAGD, p. 109.

38. Rudolf Bultmann claims that the reason this explanation does not directly follow the sign is due to the nature of the text's sources: 'of course, the Evangelist could have introduced the discussion of vv. 26ff. immediately after the feeding of the multitude' (*The Gospel of John: A Commentary* [trans. G.R. Beasley-Murray; Oxford: Basil Blackwell, 1971 (1964)], p. 214). On reading the text, it becomes obvious that John has painted a scene in which it would have been practically impossible for Jesus to begin a reasoned discourse with the people.

39. RSV and AV respectively. Du Rand also interprets Jesus' action in this way, assuming some sort of control on his part: 'He knows exactly when to withdraw from the crowds when they have reached misconceptions about him (cf 6.15; 8.59; 10.39-40)' ('The Characterization of Jesus', p. 29). An alternative to his reading of these texts would be that Jesus fails to communicate his message effectively, is unable to fulfil the expectations of his listeners and consequently finds himself in a dangerous situation from which he has to escape.

40. BAGD, p. 63.

41. 'When evening came', v. 16.

used, or has been able to use, such powers to protect himself.[42] Rather than appearing as an awesome prophet or mesmeric orator who has control over his listeners, he is shown to *lose* control and is forced to take defensive action.[43] As was the case in Bethesda, Jesus is unable to finish his work. He is not able to teach the crowd and to correct their misunderstanding of the nature of his kingship. It is not being asserted here that the crowd have deliberately violent intentions towards him— this is obviously not the case at this stage. He is the victim of messianic adulation rather than malevolence. The end result of their action is nevertheless a chaos that is personally threatening to Jesus.

The Threat at Tabernacles (7.1-52)

The Feast of Tabernacles is the occasion for a rapid intensification of the risk to Jesus' safety.[44] A string of violent intentions, emotions and actions runs through the narrative, being brought to a crisis point three times. The main area of interest to be discussed for the purposes of this study is the way in which the death threat to Jesus is developed and explored by the evangelist. For this purpose, the structure set out in Figure 2 overleaf will be used to divide up the pericope.

---

42. Hengel notes that Jesus' inability to manage this sort of situation drew comment from the ancients. Euripides' *Bacchae* and the Homeric hymn to Dionysus show how 'a real god in disguise' should deal with this sort of threatening circumstance (*The Johannine Question*, p. 70). Celsus drew express attention to Jesus' failure in this area, Origen's only defence being that just because Jesus did not liberate himself, it did not mean he *could* not (*Contra Celsus* 2.34).

43. However ἀναχωρέω is translated, it is undoubtedly a defensive action.

44. It is frequently asserted that Jn 7 and 8 form a single unit of events happening at Tabernacles, with 7.53–8.11 a later insertion into the section. So Beasley-Murray, *John*, p. 100; Lindars, *Gospel of John*, pp. 277-80; Dodd, *Interpretation*, pp. 345-7. In addition, Dodd claims that the evangelist employs a dramatic technique during these chapters of repeated references to attempted violence to Jesus. These references are designed to 'keep alive in the mind of the reader a sense of the atmosphere of intense hostility in which the dialogues are conducted', but he claims that they need not be considered as a record of separate and successive outbreaks (C.H. Dodd, *Historical Tradition in the Fourth Gospel* [repr.; Cambridge: Cambridge University Press, 1979 (1963)], p. 97). This appears to complicate unnecessarily the hermeneutical task. For our purposes the two chapters will be discussed as separate but consecutive units, in which the events described by the evangelist are treated as literal (within the narrative) rather than symbolic.

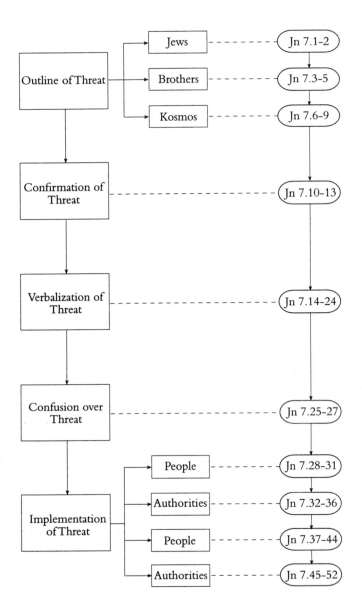

Figure 2: Development of the Death Threat in John 7

1. *Vulnerability to the Threat: Extent of the Rejection of Jesus*

Reading the Gospel as a continuous narrative, ignoring the artificial chapter and verse divisions, it becomes clear that the end of the feeding discourse and the beginning of the Tabernacles material comprise a small section that outlines the extent of the rejection of Jesus. In the space of fifteen verses (6.66–7.9), the evangelist describes five powerfully negative reactions to Jesus. It is easy to miss the full force of these because the reader's attention fixes onto Peter's positive response, which happens in the midst of it: 'you are the Holy One of God' (v. 69). The context of this acclamation is, however, death and rejection. Death is hinted at in 6.71 (παραδιδόναι), 7.6 and 8 (καιρός). Rejection of Jesus occurs at the hands of the following groups of people:

1. many of his disciples, who desert him (6.66);
2. one of his closest followers, who will betray him (6.70-71);
3. the Jews, who are seeking to kill him (7.1);
4. his brothers, who do not believe in him (7.3-4);
5. the world, which hates him (7.7).

These groups collectively encompass his friends, family and community. The narrative has therefore now established in the fullest sense how his own have not received him (οἱ ἴδιοι αὐτὸν οὐ παρέλαβον, 1.11). These statements play an important role in shaping the expectations the reader has concerning the events about to unfold. When the time finally comes for Jesus to go up to Jerusalem, we know that he has experienced rejection on all fronts. He is reluctant to put in an appearance and is in a very vulnerable position. Jerusalem is a dangerous place for Jesus and he has few supporters and many enemies. We rightly have a sense of foreboding about what will happen.

2. *Outline of the Threat to Jesus*

Verses 1-9 set the scene, outlining the extent of the threat to Jesus. His movement is now restricted because the Jews are seeking to kill him (v. 1). Barrett suggests that he 'could not' travel or 'was not free' to travel to Judea, and puzzles over the historical legitimacy of the narrative. His concern is that this text implies Jesus had previously been working in obscurity—something obviously untrue.[45] An alternative

---

45. Barrett, *Gospel According to St John*, p. 309. Lindars notes that the Curetonian and Old Latin, W and a few other Greek MSS, as well as Chrysostom and Augustine all read 'did not have the ability to go about' (ειχεν εξουσιαν in Nestle–Aland,

interpretation would be to translate the verse simply as he did not *wish* to go to Judea, the reason obviously being that he is aware of the danger. The last occasion that Jesus visited Jerusalem for a feast was a traumatic one in which he provoked the wrath of the Jews by commanding a paralytic to break the sabbath and 'making himself equal with God' (5.1-18). Readers of the narrative already know that the Jews intend to kill Jesus and he is undoubtedly aware that he is a wanted man. The evangelist is able to state this as a basic fact about Jesus' life.

The ensuing quarrel between Jesus and his brothers[46] raises several interesting questions. The most important of these is the motive of the brothers in suggesting that Jesus attends the feast in Jerusalem. It is reasonable to surmise that they are aware of the hazardous possibilities of a trip to the temple—we should not assume they are ignorant of this, after all, it is a fact that is obviously influencing Jesus' behaviour. We know from 7.13 and 25 that the Judeans are aware the authorities want to kill Jesus and 7.1 can be seen to imply that this was also known in Galilee. If this is the case, their advice to him to go to Judea and deliberately attract public interest is no mere folly[47] but suggests more sinister intentions. The brothers' request is generally seen to be evidence of unbelief, or at least a misunderstanding of Jesus' mission that aims to force his hand in claiming earthly messianic power and widespread recognition.[48] Morris thinks that they are particularly naïve, having 'no

Novum Testamentum Graece, p. 269). Lindars adds, 'The well attested *would not* is an early improvement to correct the impression that Jesus was not in control of events' (*Gospel of John*, p. 281). Kysar suggests that John used the stronger 'could not go' to impress on the reader the dangers of going to Jerusalem (*John*, pp. 115-16). Carson simply notes 'the reason for this geographical restriction was his desire to avoid Judea, *because the Jews were there waiting to take his life*' (*Gospel According to John*, p. 305, emphasis original).

46. Generally assumed to be his blood brothers, rather than half-brothers or 'spiritual brothers'. So, Kysar, *John*, p. 116; Trumbower, *Born from Above*, p. 86.

47. As suggested by Bultmann, *Gospel of John*, p. 290.

48. Hoskyns, *Fourth Gospel*, p. 311; Barrett, *Gospel According to John*, p. 311; F.F. Bruce, *The Gospel of John* (Basingstoke: Pickering & Inglis, 1983), p. 170; Sanders, *Gospel According to St John*, p. 202. Lindars sees them as hostile, with their words being a taunt to Jesus, suggesting that a new display of power is now needed to recover the ground lost after the feeding miracle (*Gospel of John*, p. 282). Likewise Beasley-Murray, who sees their advice as concurrent with the 'Tempter's' voice (*John*, pp. 106-107), and P.F. Ellis, *The Genius of John: A Composition-Critical Commentary on the Fourth Gospel* (Collegeville, MN: Liturgical Press, 1984), p. 142.

idea that Jesus' mission...must be unpopular'.[49] However, the same request made by shrewd men could be interpreted as a trap designed to *curtail* rather than enhance his ministry. The brothers are insistent that he appear in public:

> Leave here and go to Judaea,
> that your disciples may see the works you are doing.
> For no man works in secret if he seeks to be known openly.
> If you do these things, show yourself to the world. (vv. 3-4)

Following their advice would undoubtedly lead to arrest for Jesus—indeed to death at the hands of the authorities. Their motive must therefore surely be that they *intend* him to be apprehended by the authorities. They are not merely unbelievers but sly opponents, who wish him harm. There are two primary indicators that support this interpretation. The first is the fact that the evangelist clearly notes the brothers are unbelievers. They possess the kind of inadequate 'signs' faith[50] that the evangelist comments on in 2.23, but do not truly believe. Given that they do not believe, their motivation *cannot* be to assist Jesus in gaining more supporters and encouraging others to believe. Unbelief is aligned with hatred for Jesus—'their unbelief epitomizes the rejection of the revelation and the saturation of humanity in darkness'.[51] The second indication is the vehemence with which Jesus rejects them and their advice. He does not bother to educate them about the nature of his mission, explaining that belief should not be founded on signs (see 4.48). Instead he retaliates with strong words, identifying his brothers with those who are evil and hate him. For ὁ καιρὸς ὁ ἐμὸς οὔπω πάρεστιν ...ὅτι ὁ ἐμὸς καιρὸς οὔπω πεπλήρωται (vv. 6, 8) we can read 'my death is not yet imminent'.[52] Jesus exposes their motive for suggesting he appears openly: their suggestion will hasten his death and that time has not yet arrived. Their καιρός is always here because they are of the world and with it, they live 'in death',[53] hating the one who testifies to

---

49. Morris, *Gospel According to John*, p. 396.

50. So Carson, *Gospel According to John*, p. 307. Also indicated by Culpepper, *Anatomy of the Fourth Gospel*, p. 138.

51. Kysar, *John*, p. 117.

52. J.P. Miranda, *Being and the Messiah: The Message of St John* (trans. J. Eagleson; Maryknoll, NY: Orbis Books, 1977), p. 103; Barrett, *Gospel According to St John*, p. 313; Brown, *Gospel According to John*, I, p. 306.

53. Bultmann, *Gospel of John*, p. 293.

its evil nature. So saying, Jesus opts to remain behind in Galilee (vv. 8-9), where he is safer.[54]

3. *Confirmation of the Threat to Jesus*
Once his brothers have left, Jesus travels to Jerusalem in secret (v. 10).[55] The evangelist wastes no time in confirming the danger that he is exposed to.[56] The Jews[57] are actively searching for him with 'menacing seriousness'[58] and harassing the people by demanding to know his whereabouts. The enmity of the Pharisees towards those sympathizing with Jesus becomes evident later on in the passage (vv. 47-49) but we know that the multitude are already intimidated—'for fear of the Jews no one spoke openly of him' (v. 13). The crowd themselves are divided, some seeing him as a good man (ἀγαθός), while others accuse him of leading the people astray. That the penalty for 'leading Israel astray' was stoning[59] indicates that this section of the crowd had already condemned Jesus and would see him executed.

4. *Verbalization of the Threat by Jesus*
Much to the reader's surprise, having had depicted the hostile environment and his clandestine arrival in the city, Jesus is suddenly projected

---

54. Presumably, although ironically the people there have already tried to mob him (6.15), murmured and disputed at his words (6.41, 52) and deserted him (6.66).

55. Ellis claims that Jesus goes up to Jerusalem when he wants to, acting 'with complete freedom and independence...no human being dictates his actions' (*Genius of John*, p. 143). This is directly contrary to 7.1 where Jesus is clearly not able to exercise complete freedom. Similarly, Kysar explains the apparent contradiction of Jesus saying he will not go to the feast and then going, by seeing it as 'another example of Jesus' refusal to fulfil a human request, only later to do so' (*John*, p. 118). The most obvious reason for Jesus telling his brothers that he would not go is that he did not want to travel with them, or even for them to know that he was going, because this would have increased the risk of being exposed to the authorities.

56. Dodd reviews the statements by the evangelist that emphasize that Jesus was in danger of his life in Jn 7–8 (*Interpretation*, p. 347).

57. Clearly distinguished here from the crowd (ὁ ὄχλος) and hence indicating the authorities. So Carson, *Gospel According to John*, p. 309.

58. Lindars, *Gospel of John*, p. 285

59. Lev. 24.16; also *b. Sanh.* 43a, 'he is going forth to be stoned because he has...enticed Israel to apostasy'.

back into the public arena in v. 14 as he begins to teach in the temple.[60] The reader has been fully primed to expect trouble and can hardly be surprised to hear Jesus exclaiming: 'Why do you seek to kill me?' He confronts his audience directly with their threat to his life, but they protest their innocence and ignorance. Jesus' actions appear reckless. He is aware of the volatile nature of this milieu yet has placed himself in this position voluntarily. It can be assumed that he faces the crowd alone— there is no mention of the disciples and the fact that he has travelled to Jerusalem secretly indicates that he had gone up without his entourage. He has therefore intentionally made himself vulnerable, soliciting adversity. The people initially respond to Jesus' accusation of harassment with incredulity, telling him that he is mad and paranoid: 'You have a demon. Who is seeking to kill you?' (v. 20).[61] The crowd's denial does not mean that they support him, merely that they do not understand his fears. Jesus pursues the matter accusing them this time of being angry with him (ἐμοὶ χολᾶτε, v. 23).

5. *Confusion Concerning the Threat to Jesus*
Following Jesus' accusations, there is a degree of confusion among the crowd. Jesus has appeared openly and is making outrageous claims, yet remains unapprehended. The Jerusalemites reject the possibility that the authorities have accepted Jesus as the Christ on account of their knowledge of his origin (v. 27)—another point of obvious Johannine irony.

6. *Implementation of the Threat to Jesus*
The climax of the scene approaches. Jesus' response to the queries about his origin finally ignites the crowd, provoking swift and violent action as they attempt to seize him (πιάσαι, v. 30).[62] The reason for the crowd's failure to catch Jesus is frequently credited to his supernatural powers. So Barrett claims that it is 'a miraculous deliverance of Jesus from the hands of his assailants'.[63] Others see the 'hour' as having a protective function in this situation: 'it is as if a spell lay on his opponents: no one can lay

60. The temple was 'not a site that fostered privacy', notes Carson (*Gospel According to John*, p. 311).
61. This accusation is tantamount to saying that he is insane. See Kysar, *John*, p. 121; Lindars, *Gospel of John*, p. 290. Compare also their judgement at 10.20—he is demon possessed and raving mad.
62. Indicates 'seizure with hostile intent' (BAGD, p. 657).
63. Barrett, *Gospel According to St John*, p. 323.

hands on him, for his hour has not yet come'[64] and 'it came to nothing, for in the purpose of God the hour...had not yet arrived'.[65] The end result of this interpretative slant is to minimize the violence of the situation by focusing on the 'miraculous' nature of the escape rather than the jeopardy that Jesus is in in the first place. This picture of the mysterious, untouchable Christ walking through a crowd that has frozen in a still frame deadens the vitality of the narrative. It is not acceptable to claim that the crowd *could* not seize him, but rather to note that they *did* not. The evangelist has retrospectively provided a theological interpretation as to why Jesus managed to escape a situation of extreme personal danger.[66] The terminology used by the evangelist to describe what happens is adequately forceful: καὶ οὐδεὶς ἐπέβαλεν ἐπ' αὐτὸν τὴν χεῖρα ('but no one laid hands on him', 7.30b). The phrase used indicates a violent physical attempt to seize someone by force[67] and presumably the intention is to put him immediately to death.[68] John's interpretation also serves to remind us that the moment of death has only been deferred and not completely averted—Jesus is a man living under a constant threat.

The impromptu attempt by the people to dispose of Jesus alerts the attention of the authorities, who proceed with official measures to apprehend him. No doubt the Pharisees have spies among the people who inform them of what is going on (cf. 11.57). Temple guards (ὑπηρέται)[69] are dispatched to arrest him, but the outcome is not recorded. It could be assumed that, since they are dispatched in the middle of the feast but do not return to their masters until the last day, an initial attempt at arrest is intended at 7.32. This would accord well with Jesus' subsequent words: 'I shall be with you a little longer'— particularly appropriate considering the intensifying antipathy towards

---

64. Bultmann, *Gospel of John*, p. 302.

65. Bruce, *Gospel of John*, p. 179. Morris echoes this sentiment (*Gospel According to John*, p. 414). Similarly Kysar: 'The mob cannot succeed...because of the divine determination of Jesus' hour' (*John*, p. 125).

66. Thus a practical interpretation would be that the crowd did not capture Jesus because, in the chaos of the situation he had acted quickly and managed to flee. Therefore, because he had managed to flee, his hour had not yet arrived.

67. BAGD, p. 131.

68. So Ellis, *Genius of John*, p. 145.

69. Barrett claims that only the chief priests had ὑπηρέται at their disposal, hence the arrest can be seen to have had the highest orders (*Gospel According to St John*, p. 324).

him. The Jews interpret the words with scorn as being those of a cow-
ard; will he flee to the Diaspora and teach the *Greeks*? They might well
expect him to flee, recognizing the intimidation he has experienced
from his own people, but they are incredulous at the concept of his
teaching the heathen.

The final day of the feast sees Jesus teaching openly once more and
provoking heated debate among the people. Controversy concerning his
origin again spurs the crowd into hostile action and similar terminology
is used for the second attempted lynching.[70] It is reasonable to assume
that this is not an official attempt at arrest and we are left wondering
what action the temple guards have taken on this occasion. The hench-
men of the Pharisees are castigated for returning empty handed to their
masters, with the sheepish excuse 'no one ever spoke like this man'
(v. 46).

The events of John 7 have shifted the narrative action onto an intensified level. Prior to Tabernacles the reader is aware that the Jews want
to kill Jesus (5.18), but they have made no definite move to implement
this threat. Throughout the feast the threat develops, with the opposing
forces of the people and the authorities combining against him. Arrest
and death become an imminent possibility. The reader recognizes that it
is likely Jesus will now face danger whenever he appears in public.
Additionally, there are groups among the population who are prepared
actively to seek him out and catch him.

The Dispute over Parentage (8.12-59)

The negative intensity of Jesus' interaction with the Jews is retained in
John 8. Once more there is a pattern of accusation, confusion and
attempted implementation of the death threat against him. It is the
content of the accusations made by both Jesus and the Jews which is
developed during this discourse, the primary focus being Jesus' authority
and parentage over and against the ancestry of the Jews. The reader is
aware that the implementation of the threat is continually hovering
beneath the surface and at several points during this pericope it breaks
though.

---

70. 'Some of them wanted to arrest him, but no one laid hands on him' (7.44).

The section can be subdivided as follows:

1. Claim by Jesus and accusation by Pharisees regarding his authority, resulting in presumed attempted *implementation* of threat (8.12-20);
2. *Confusion* and *accusation* regarding Jesus' fate (8.21-29);
3. Positive response of some Jews to Jesus (8.30);
4. Series of *accusations* and *counter-accusations* regarding ancestry during which hostility escalates (8.31-58);[71]
5. Attempted *implementation* of threat (8.59).

We can make the assumption that there is a further attempt at arrest following Jesus' teaching in the treasury (8.20), as the formula used by the evangelist here matches the previous occasions in John 7 where he was threatened.[72] It certainly keeps at the forefront of the reader's mind the real possibility of physical danger to Jesus and sets an appropriate tone for the main body of the discourse.

There follows a short section in which Jesus makes several accusations regarding the nature of the Jews ('you are from below...) and their part in his death ('when you have lifted up...). There is a good deal of misunderstanding on the part of his audience, however; the end result is that many 'believe' in him (8.30). It soon becomes evident that Jesus is not satisfied with this outcome since his response is in the offensive. Some scholars see v. 31 as a gloss since it is obvious that those who 'believed in him' quickly become his opponents.[73] However, the fickle nature of the belief of the Jews has been a feature of the Gospel since 2.23-25 and the reader may well already suspect that these 'believers'

71. M.W.G. Stibbe sees a pattern of statement, followed by misunderstanding, followed by explanation occurring five times during this section (*John* [Readings; Sheffield: JSOT Press, 1993], p. 98).

72. The verse reads: 'but no one arrested him, because his hour had not yet come'. Beasley-Murray comments 'that no one seized Jesus at this point indicates a desire to do so' (*John*, p. 130).

73. Writing on v. 31, Carson notes that 'the opening clause seems innocuous, until it becomes apparent in the ensuing verses that *the Jews who had believed him*... turn out to be, in Jesus' view, slaves to sin (v. 34), indifferent to Jesus' word (v. 37), children of the devil (v. 44), liars (v. 55), and guilty of mob tactics, including the attempted murder of the one in whom they have professed to believe (v. 59)' (*Gospel According to John*, pp. 346-48). An explanation is therefore necessary for Carson and he details five options, settling on the Johannine theme of 'fickle faith'. Brown sees this verse as a gloss (*Gospel According to John*, I, p. 354). Likewise Lindars, *Gospel of John*, p. 323.

have a deficient faith. Accusations and counter-accusations are exchanged as the atmosphere becomes increasingly hostile and the environment increasingly dangerous for Jesus. He accuses them overtly twice and indirectly once of seeking to murder him. Their claim to be descendants of Abraham is rejected by him on the grounds that their attitude towards the truth (8.40) does not mirror that of Abraham. Their response to the word that Jesus brings is violence, revealing their true parentage: 'You seek to kill me, because my word finds no place in you' (v. 37). In return, the Jews cast aspersions on *his* parentage, alluding to the dubious circumstances of his birth. Beasley-Murray notes that from the time of Origen it has been thought that this verse is an attack on the suspicious nature of Jesus' birth.[74] Barrett states that rumours about his illegitimacy were probably already circulating[75] and Jesus' audience certainly do not hesitate to make this accusation, implying that he was born of fornication (ἐκ πορνείας, v. 41). In his defence, Jesus asserts that his true origin is from the Father, whereas theirs is from the devil, whom he labels a murderer and liar.[76] Hostility between Jesus and his opponents is expressed in extreme terms: they accuse him of being a bastard, he then claims that they are murderers and liars, set to destroy him. The abuse continues in vv. 48-58 with the Jews hailing him a demon-possessed Samaritan[77] (a far cry from the accolade he received in 6.14 as 'the prophet'). Jesus' audience interpret his teaching on Abraham literally and cannot comprehend it, viewing his words as those of a madman.

---

74. Beasley-Murray, *John*, p. 135. Celsus accuses Jesus of having 'invented his birth from a virgin' when actually he was illegitimate and Mary was turned out by Joseph for adultery (Origen, *Contra Celsus* 1.28). Trumbower sees a link between v. 41 and v. 44, which has its background in the myth that Cain was fathered by 'some entity' other than Adam, for example the evil angel Sammael. The Jews are therefore spiritual descendants of Cain and/or the Devil (*Born from Above*, pp. 91-92).

75. Barrett, *Gospel According to St John*, p. 334.

76. The characterization of the devil as a murderer and liar is probably an allusion to Gen. 2–3, where the serpent was seen as the cause of Adam and Eve's fall and his influence was behind the murder of Abel (Ellis, *Genius of John*, p. 155). The whole exchange is somewhat reminiscent of a group of children in the playground taunting each other by abusing each other's parents.

77. Undoubtedly intended as an insult, since Samaritans were viewed as an apostate race and treated as outcasts (cf. 4.10). Carson notes that for a Jew to question the paternity of other Jews was so despicable that only demon possession could explain it (*Gospel According to John*, p. 355).

They are incredulous at his statements, demanding, τίνα σεαυτὸν ποιεῖς ('who do you claim to be?', 8.53).[78] This dispute continues, with both parties failing to make a connection between their different levels of meaning. Jesus speaks from his spiritual perspective and the Jews interpret from their earthly one, until the climactic assertion of v. 58: 'Truly, truly, I say to you, before Abraham was, I am'. It is now clear to the Jews that Jesus' claim is to pre-existence and pre-eminence.[79] The Jews, outraged, attempt to stone him for blasphemy.[80] The situation has degenerated from one in which Jesus instructs believers in the liberating powers of the truth (v. 31), to a turbulent, vicious quarrel. The recriminations culminate in an outburst of brutality. The self-proclaimed 'sons of Abraham', those who had previously believed in him, do indeed turn murderous. The intensity of the situation is denoted by Jesus' subsequent action: he must hide to escape death ('Ιησοῦς δὲ ἐκρύβη καὶ ἐξῆλθεν ἐκ τοῦ ἱεροῦ, v. 59b).[81] The word ἐκρύβη, translated 'hid himself',[82] is interpreted by some commentators as indicating a supernatural disappearance, whether by active or passive means.[83] This is conjecture on the part of interpreters, fuelling the tenet

78. Popular translation: 'Who do you think you are?' So, the NIV translation.

79. They understood his words as a blasphemous claim to deity (Carson, *Gospel According to John*, p. 358). Dodd claims, 'he belongs to a different order of being... he stands outside the range of temporal relations' (*Interpretation*, p. 261).

80. Stoning was the prescribed punishment for blasphemy. See Lev. 24.16 as well as *m. Sanh.* 7.1, 4. Trumbower notes the midrashic tradition that claims Abel was killed by Cain with a stone (*Targ. Ps.-J.* Gen. 4.8; *Gen. R.* 22.8 and *PRE* 21). He adds, 'it may therefore be significant that Cain's children pick up stones with which to kill Jesus' (*Born from Above*, p. 91).

81. Lindars comments: 'the spontaneous attempt to lynch Jesus expresses with dramatic force the Jews' reaction to the electrifying effect of his brief words' (*Gospel of John*, p. 336).

82. Both Stibbe and Ellis comment that Jesus' action recalls the introduction to the events at Tabernacles where Jesus travels up to the feast ἐν κρυπτῷ (7.10, 'secretly' or 'in hiding') (Ellis, *Genius of John*, p. 156; Stibbe, *John*, p. 96). Contrary to the suggestion of his brothers—a few public signs by way of a recruitment drive—Jesus' appearance and his words have resulted in an increase in the antipathy towards him. As he arrived in secret, so he must leave in secret.

83. Barrett, *Gospel According to St John*, p. 352; J.R. Michaels also thinks it is 'mysterious' (*John* [San Francisco: Harper & Row, 1984], p. 177). Morris goes so far as to state; 'It is not so much that Jesus by superior cleverness was able to conceal Himself from them. It was rather that *He was concealed by Another*' (*Gospel According to John*, p. 474, emphasis added).

that Jesus is somehow immune from harm and in control of his circumstances, thus 'adversaries are powerless against him until he wills his
own death at the appointed time'.[84] It is difficult to deny, however, that
the narrative portrays Jesus as having *lost* control of the proceedings and
consequently being forced to flee to avoid instant death at the hands of
the mob. Anarchy has broken out and as the crowd pick up their
weapons, Jesus absconds, hiding and then fleeing the area of danger.

An escalation in hostility from the attempted arrests of ch. 7 is evident
in this section. This crowd have no intention of waiting for an official
trial by the religious authorities, but will kill him with their own hands,
such is their hatred for him. One reason for the deterioration in the
relationship between Jesus and the crowd is that during the discourse he
is subject to a systematic dehumanization by his audience. This can be
traced through the conflict concerning the origin and ancestors of both
parties and the boundaries of racial purity that are subsequently established. Jesus' claims are perceived to be so reprehensible to his listeners
that he cannot possibly be considered to be part of their community. By
the time 8.48 is reached the dehumanizing process is at its climax: Jesus
is accused of being a demon-possessed Samaritan. Note that he is not
just a Samaritan (an outcast) or demon possessed (insane or evil) but *both
together*—a 'non-human' as far as the Jews are concerned. The theory of
human aggression is clear about the link between dehumanization and
violence:

> Victims are denied human qualities, so that it's not a 'real person', not
> 'someone like me', who is hurt or killed. The result is that the aggressors
> don't feel guilty when they think of attacking their victims, and thus they
> don't restrain themselves.[85]

And so the crowd do not restrain themselves. They see Jesus as an alien
(which is, ironically, both what he is and how he characterizes himself)
and as an alien he is dispensable. What follows is the first occurrence in
the Gospel of the attempted murder of Jesus, rather than just his attempted arrest.

84. Barrett, *Gospel According to St John*, p. 352.
85. L. Berkowitz, *Aggression: Its Causes, Consequences, and Control* (New York:
McGraw–Hill, 1993), p. 119. Berkowitz provides historical examples of the dehumanization process, the most obvious one being the Jews by the Nazis, but also
conflicts between Turks and Greeks, Israelis and Arabs, who repeatedly characterize
each others as brutes and monsters. Experiments demonstrate that devaluation of the
opponent lowers inhibitions against aggression.

Confrontation at the Feast of Dedication (10.22-39)

The final scene of disorder and confrontation between Jesus and the Jews during his public ministry occurs when he appears at the temple during the Feast of Dedication. The passage contains the now familiar elements of confusion (v. 24), accusation (vv. 32, 35-38), counter-accusation (v. 33) and attempted implementation (vv. 31, 39) of the death threat to Jesus. This time, however, the initial debate over Jesus' identity is not genuine confusion, but is aimed at eliciting a clear statement from Jesus that will legitimize his arrest. Jesus is not the initiator, but a group of Jews[86] have sought him out to confront him in order to clarify the nature of his claims. By this stage in the narrative Jesus is unable to appear in the temple without experiencing harassment, even while engaging in a seemingly harmless activity—strolling in the court—rather than provoking opposition by teaching publicly. He is presumably alone, without his disciples, in Solomon's portico when a group of Jews begin to pester him:

> So the Jews gathered round him and said to him,
> 'How long will you keep us in suspense?
> If you are the Christ, tell us plainly.' (v. 24).

There can be little question that their approach is antagonistic.[87] The text barely disguises the frustration present in the demand 'tell us plainly'. The use of παρρησία provides a verbal link back to 7.4,[88]

---

86. We already know that this term most often indicates opponents to Jesus. See Kysar, *John*, p. 165; Ellis, *Genius of John*, p. 172; Barrett: 'the enemies of Jesus', *Gospel According to St John*, p. 380.

87. Although Kysar sees the request as implying an 'honest inquiry' (*John*, p. 166). Carson debates whether the Jews' question actually means 'how long will you keep us in suspense?' and therefore that they are not necessarily adversaries, or, more negatively, 'how long are you going to annoy us?' (*Gospel According to John*, p. 392). Presumably the latter follows Pernot, who notes that it is an expression of familiarity which is conserved in modern Greek. Pernot translates the meaning as: 'Jusqu'à quand vas-tu nous tracasser de la sorte?' (Quoted in A. Pallis, *Notes on St John and the Apocalypse* [Oxford: Oxford University Press, undated], p. 23). Ellis claims that 'the vehemence of the question...suggest[s] that John means his readers to see Jesus in a menacing situation' (*Genius of John*, p. 172).

88. Mark Stibbe also perceives a link, though sees it functioning to emphasize

where Jesus' brothers urge him to be known openly. It is made clear at this point that being 'known openly' would place Jesus in a vulnerable position and is associated with the threat of death. Here also the request of the Jews demands an exposure from Jesus that will make him vulnerable to arrest and execution.[89] In addition, the verb κυκλόω means to 'encircle, mostly with hostile intent'[90] and by this point in the narrative the reader surely expects that any such gathering of Jews will represent threatening behaviour rather than mere curiosity. The aim of this group is to attempt to pressure Jesus into providing a clear statement about his status that can subsequently be used against him.

Jesus will not oblige his interrogators straight away, pointing instead to the works that witness to his identity and insisting that these opponents *cannot* believe him as they are not of the elect. He finishes, however, with a rejoinder that is clear enough for even them to understand: 'I and the Father are one' (10.30). Whether the precise meaning of this claim to 'oneness' is moral[91] or ontological[92] the reaction of the Jews indicates that his words are outrageous enough to justify immediate death for blasphemy in their eyes. Faced once more with the prospect of a lynching, Jesus does not flee the crowd but attempts to defend himself with an appeal to his good works (ἔργα καλὰ, v. 32). His words, ironically, are again reminiscent of the exchange with his brothers in 7.3-6. The brothers urged him to carry out his works in public, ostensibly to win support, although in reality the aim was to place him in danger. Now, in a situation of grave danger, Jesus cites his public works in an attempt to demonstrate his authenticity and win support,[93] but the response of the Jews is a rejection of the validity of these works.[94] His

the elusiveness of Jesus' movements (he will not move about openly) and his language (he does not speak plainly) (*John*, p. 118).

89. In the sense that the Jews intend for Jesus to incriminate himself. An unambiguous 'yes' would furnish them with ammunition for a further attack.

90. BAGD, p. 456.

91. In other words, the will of the Father is that of the Son. So, Barrett, *Gospel According to St John*, p. 382, and Kysar, *John*, p. 167.

92. So Ellis, *Genius of John*, p. 184.

93. This is hardly a serious attempt to win support from any of his listeners, rather an attempt to temporarily divert the threat of stoning. It could potentially be seen as a goad that has the effect of a delaying tactic. Thus Jesus sneers, 'I've shown you *good* works, for which of *these* do you want to *kill* me?'

94. For further ironies contained within 10.32 see Paul Duke: 'It is an irony of simply incongruity. Jesus presents two images: here are my good works—noble,

question delays the lynching long enough for the Jews to be able to state their accusation: 'you, being a man, make yourself God' (v. 33). But the arguments that Jesus marshals in his defence—scriptural quotes and evidence of his actions—are useless since he is unable to avoid their condemnation, compelled as he is to reveal the truth of his unity with the Father. Inevitably, the discourse quickly reaches the point where his words again ignite the crowd and they respond with violence against him. The mob rush to seize him, but Jesus is wise to their intentions and reacts swiftly. The language is physical and tangible—ἐξῆλθεν ἐκ τῆς χειρὸς αὐτῶν ('he escaped from their hands', v. 39)—as he escapes[95] for the final time from the grasp of his would-be murderers.[96]

Concluding Comment: Scenes of Violence

The six scenes discussed above have been viewed from the perspective of Jesus as a character who is subject to a series of violent attacks at the hands of the Jews. They demonstrate a steady progression in the opposition to and oppression of Jesus by all sections of his community. They do not comprise all of the relevant material on the subject within John 1–12—that there are a number of other instances where an indication is given that Jesus is harassed or at risk is evidenced from the tables of Textual References to Violence in Chapter 2.[97] Much of this

beautiful (*kala*) works, works clearly from the Father; and there are the stones in your hands. "For which of these works...do you stone me?"' (*Irony in the Fourth Gospel* [Atlanta: John Knox Press, 1985], pp. 46-47).

95. There is no indication here of a miraculous escape, contra Barrett, *Gospel According to St John*, p. 386.

96. Why the Jews do not continue with their original plan of stoning Jesus and now make an attempt to arrest him instead is an interesting question. It could be posited that his words have cooled the mood of the crowd to the extent that they are able to act more rationally, deciding that it will be preferable to dispose of this troublemaker by legal means rather than by a lynching.

97. An example of this material can be seen in Jn 4.44. John 4 relates the story of Jesus' encounter with a Samaritan woman and her people from Sychar. The response to Jesus from this racial group, pariahs themselves in the eyes of orthodox Judaism (4.9), is acceptance and belief (vv. 39-42). Directly following this pericope the evangelist records Jesus' testimony of his rejection by others: προφήτης ἐν τῇ ἰδίᾳ πατρίδι τιμὴν οὐκ ἔχει (v. 44). Thus the evangelist reminds the reader that, despite acceptance by a group of social outcasts, rejection is the overall reaction to Jesus by 'his own', as the prologue warned. The reader cannot hear of Jesus' success without it being tempered by the baseline message of the gospel: repudiation.

additional material, however, consists of details about short incidents or comments about, for example, an area where it was not safe to travel. They serve mainly to enlighten the reader about the implications of Jesus' actions or circumstances, providing mounting evidence for the hostility amassing against Jesus and the unsafe environment in which he operated. It is the six major incidents that develop the theme of the victimization and violent rejection of Jesus as his personal safety becomes more precarious with each public appearance.

As suggested in the section on the structure of the Gospel in Chapter 3, the scenes fall into two groups. The first three are characterized primarily by confusion. The temple incident commences by posing the question: 'who is the victim?' It is Jesus who perpetrates this episode of chaos, but the reader quickly learns that this act merely prefigures the destruction he is to experience himself. At the healing and feeding miracles, the threat to Jesus is a by-product of the resultant public disorder at each event, rather than the deliberate intention of the crowd to harm him. Nevertheless, there is a definite indication of physical intimidation on both occasions.

It is following the prophecy of betrayal in 6.70, which forms part of the pericopae establishing the all-encompassing rejection of Jesus, that his relationship with the community rapidly deteriorates. The second three scenes contain much material of a malevolent nature: public encounters between Jesus and the Jews that become violently chaotic, with the crowd displaying numerous deliberate attempts at physical attack. There is no disguising the victimization of Jesus in these scenes and, as a theme, it makes a major contribution to the plot development of the narrative. Jeffrey Staley, who refers to this section (7.1-10.42) as the 'third ministry tour' makes the following comment:

> false accusations, attempts to arrest Jesus, and allusions to violent death recur with greater frequency and greater emotional intensity than they recur in any preceding or subsequent unit. References to excommunication and blasphemy, madness and demon possession, illegitimate birth and Samaritan ancestry, lying, deception, moral blindness and sinfulness, arresting, stoning and killing show that antagonism to Jesus' teaching has reached its zenith.[98]

That Jesus suffers physical and verbal harassment during his public ministry, particularly in the latter sections, was perhaps never in question,

---

98. J.L. Staley, *The Print's First Kiss: A Rhetorical Investigation of the Implied Reader in the Fourth Gospel* (SBLDS, 82; Atlanta: Scholars Press, 1988), p. 66.

but this chapter has aimed to show the extent to which this has posed a genuine threat to his freedom and safety. The narrative reveals that, although Jesus certainly has some supernatural powers, they do not enable him to control all aspects of his environment. He may be able to walk on water, but he cannot stem the wave of violence welling up against him. The Johannine Jesus displays an unquestionably *human* vulnerability to the expressions of hatred and opposition by the Jews, exhibiting reactions which are often better described as fugitive than sovereignly elusive.

6

Relationship with the Community II:
The Victim's Self-Cognizance

Whatever the precise terminology employed, discussion concerning the 'self-cognizance', 'self-understanding' or 'self-consciousness' of Jesus is generally viewed as one minefield it is preferable to steer clear of. Described as 'the last tabu' by one Johannine scholar,[1] the unavoidably speculative nature of the subject and the temptation towards anachronistic psychologizing renders academic investigation a precarious undertaking. A chapter subtitled 'the victim's self-cognizance' must therefore be prepared to mark out the boundaries of its inquiry with care, in order to allay suspicion and avoid confusion about what it attempts to achieve.

To further complicate the task, the concept of victimization is itself a multi-layered phenomenon and hence clarity is also needed concerning which aspect is being explored. This can be illustrated simply by reflection on the meaning of the subtitle of this book, which labels *Jesus as Victim in the Gospel of John.* Do I mean by this that what happens to him in the Gospel can be termed victimization—in other words that the *reader* is justified in bringing that label to the text as a hermeneutical aid? Or that the *text itself* uses victimization as a motif for the life of Jesus and by using its own labels defines him as a victim?[2] Or further, that *within the world of the text,* the character of Jesus understands himself to be victimized and/or to be a victim?[3] Immediately, three layers have been

---

1.   J.A.T. Robinson, 'The Last Tabu? The Self Consciousness of Jesus', in *Twelve More New Testament Studies* (London: SCM Press, 1984), pp. 155-70. Robinson notes that of all the 'no go' areas in New Testament scholarship, the most important point to remember is that 'of the self-consciousness of Jesus *we may say nothing*' (p. 155, emphasis added).

2.   For example by using titles such as 'lamb of God' and by association with victims familiar to the evangelist such as the suffering servant and the paschal lamb.

3.   It is important to grasp the difference in meaning between believing that you are being victimized and perceiving yourself to be a victim. The latter frame of mind is possible *whether or not* you are experiencing adverse circumstances and in fact in

identified and there are undoubtedly further levels on which the concept can be approached and defined. As is indicated by the title of this
chapter, the concern here is with that last layer: the awareness that the
Johannine Jesus displays of his experience of victimization and the understanding that he has of himself as a victim. It should be obvious that
we are in no way concerned with the self-consciousness of the historical
Jesus.[4] Nor is there is a suggestion that it is possible to trace back any

common speech, it is not unusual for someone to be accused of having a 'victim
mentality', which colours their perspective on life. Conversely, a person who suffers
actual victimization may never identify himself or herself as a victim.

4.   Bultmann voices a commonly held view when he states: 'we can, strictly
speaking, know nothing of the personality of Jesus' (*Jesus and the Word* [trans. L.P.
Smith and E.H. Lantero; New York: Charles Scribner's sons, rev. edn, 1958], p. 8;
see pp. 5-12 for the whole discussion). Robinson, while acknowledging the difficulties, is prepared to take the plunge: 'The materials clearly fail for reconstructing
Jesus' self-consciousness in psychological terms, for analysing his psyche, its history
or its type. The Gospels are no more in the business of supplying answers to
psychological questions than they are to sociological or economic ones—though this
does not mean that it is illegitimate *for us* to ask them.' ('The Last Tabu?', p. 159,
emphasis original). Those who have made attempts to tackle this subject have
normally done so in an attempt to determine whether Jesus thought himself to be
'God' or Israel's Messiah. The question of Jesus' messianic self-consciousness was an
important tenet of the quest for the historical Jesus. More recently it can be found in
Marinus de Jonge's examination of the self-understanding of the historical Jesus
(*Jesus, the Servant–Messiah* [New Haven: Yale University Press, 1991]). Writing of
the crucifixion he claims, 'had Jesus not stood in a unique relationship with God and
had he not been *fully aware of everything this involved*, the crucifixion would have been
robbed of its dignity and depth of meaning' (p. 32, emphasis added). His position on
the historical Jesus' self-understanding has consequently become a prerequisite for
his theology of the cross. The pitfalls inherent in such a line of inquiry become evident. Wayne Meeks, in a critique of de Jonge's approach, makes two points that
implicitly illustrate the futility of attempts to document the self-consciousness of the
historical Jesus. He rightly questions why a person's historic identity and their self-
consciousness must be identical: 'All of what I significantly am can surely not be
limited to what I am "fully aware" of being' ('Asking Back to Jesus' Identity', in
M.C. de Boer [ed.], *From Jesus to John: Essays on Jesus and New Testament Christology
in Honour of Marinus de Jonge* [JSNTSup, 84; Sheffield: JSOT Press, 1993], pp. 38-50
[43]). He follows this with the declaration, 'even if we could know in some detail
what images Jesus used to make sense of his own identity and his mission and of the
possibility that he might die violently, *that knowledge would not make much difference
theologically*' ('Asking Back to Jesus' Identity', p. 44, emphasis added).

James Dunn attempts to justify the legitimacy of searching for insight into the self-
knowledge of Jesus: 'Can the historian hope to penetrate into the self-consciousness

understanding the Johannine Jesus may have had of himself as a victim
to an attitude of the historical Jesus.[5] The means of inquiry is literary-
critical and the focus of attention is the character of Jesus as he appears
in the text. The self-cognizance of Jesus in the Fourth Gospel is simply a
facet of his characterization. It is entirely possible to demonstrate from
the text that the *character* Jesus believes himself to be victimized by the

(or self-understanding) of a historical individual? The answer must be in the affirmative, otherwise history would be nothing more than a dreary catalogue of dates
and documentation' (*Christology in the Making: An Inquiry into the Origins of the
Doctrine of the Incarnation* [London: SCM Press, 1980], p. 25). See also his popular
treatment of the subject in *The Evidence for Jesus*. Dunn discusses whether Jesus
understood himself to be the Son of God on the basis of the evidence and reliability
of the Fourth Gospel (pp. 30-52).

For a theological rather than historically motivated perspective on the subject, see
Karl Rahner: 'The human soul of Jesus enjoyed the direct vision of God during his
life on earth...as a basic condition of the created spiritual nature of Jesus...perfectly
reconcilable with a genuine, human experience' ('Dogmatic Reflections on the
Knowledge and Self-Consciousness of Christ', in *Theological Investigations*. V. *Later
Writings* [trans. K.H. Kruger; 20 vols.; London: Darton, Longman & Todd, 1969],
pp. 193-215 [215]).

Another interesting approach is that of E.A. Johnson, who discusses Jesus' self-
knowledge using a bipolar model of human consciousness. She concludes that at the
transcendental pole of self-awareness he had the subjective intuition that he was the
Word made flesh, but at the categorical pole of self-understanding he had to grow
concretely into that knowledge in the course of his lifetime. This is a novel perspective, if somewhat unsubstantiated (*Consider Jesus: Waves of Renewal in Christology*
[New York: Crossroad, 1990], pp. 35-47).

5.   This is exactly what Oscar Cullmann does when he claims that the title 'Suffering Servant' is an important christological designation because it goes back to
Jesus himself and therefore 'opens to us most clearly the secret of his self-consciousness' (*The Christology of the New Testament* [trans. S.C. Guthrie and C.A.M. Hall;
London: SCM Press, 1959] p. 81). De Jonge claims that it is plausible that Jesus used
three main models to interpret his own death (the 'envoy of God', the 'suffering
righteous servant' and the one who dies 'for others'). He concludes: 'The three
models of interpretation of Jesus' death found in the earliest layers of traditional
material can all provide some insights into Jesus' own understanding of his life and
death. (*Servant-Messiah*, p. 54, see pp. 32-54 for whole discussion).

From a liberation theology approach, Leonardo Boff believes it is possible to distinguish between 'the awareness that Jesus had of himself and his mission and the
forms used to express this'. The latter—reflections made about Jesus after the resurrection—he classes as Christology. The former he calls Jesusology (*Jesus Christ,
Liberator*, p. 145).

Jewish community of which he is a part. It is also possible to demonstrate that he understands himself to be a victim and that this is a fundamental aspect of the perception he has of his identity, shaping his
attitude towards his death.

Characterization of Jesus

Chapter 1 of this book began by suggesting that one of the reasons the
Fourth Gospel was perceived to be disconcerting could be found in its
portrayal of Jesus. Chapter 4 went on to explore aspects of the social
function of the text and the role of violence. I now return to look
specifically at the character of Jesus. It is not necessary here to discuss
characterization in detail—as a tool within general literature, biblical literature or, even specifically John's Gospel—as all of these have been
covered elsewhere.[6] A few general comments will be sufficient for my
purpose.

Leland Ryken gives helpful advice on 'how we know what a character is like'. Any of the following six mechanisms, he suggests, will
enable a character to be known to the reader:

1. actions, including speech
2. personal traits and abilities (the interpretation given to actions)
3. thoughts and feelings, including motivations and goals
4. relationships and roles
5. responses to events or people
6. archetypal character types.[7]

---

6. For general works on characterization see Forster, who classifies characters as
'flat' or 'round' depending on their complexity (*Aspects of the Novel*, pp. 54-84). See
also Chatman, *Story and Discourse*, pp. 107-38; and R. Scholes and R. Kellogg, *The
Nature of Narrative* (Oxford: Oxford University Press, 1966), pp. 160-206.

Discussions of biblical characterization appear in R. Alter, *The Art of Biblical Nar-
rative* (London: George Allen & Unwin, 1981), pp. 114-30 and Ryken, *Words of
Delight*, pp. 71-6. Both focus on characterization within Hebrew Bible narratives.
See also the contributions in E.S. Malbon and A. Berlin (eds.), *Characterization in
Biblical Literature* (Semeia, 63; Atlanta: Scholars Press, 1993).

For Johannine characterization see Culpepper, *Anatomy of the Fourth Gospel*, pp.
101-48; du Rand, 'The Characterization of Jesus'; Duke, *Irony in the Fourth Gospel*,
pp. 95-100; Stibbe, *John as Storyteller*, pp. 24-25 and Stibbe's commentary on John,
which includes a section on characterization for each chapter of the Gospel.

7. Ryken, *Words of Delight*, p. 74. Ryken also views the subject from the author's
point of view, identifying four techniques open to writers attempting to portray

In order to establish that the character of Jesus perceives himself to be both victimized and a victim, it will therefore be necessary to demonstrate that what the text tells us of his thoughts and feelings, speech and actions—in other words his general behaviour—is in support of this. However, Ryken also warns that the process of getting to know a character is not simply a descriptive process, but involves 'a series of interpretive leaps and conclusions on the part of the reader'.[8] This is not a licence to 'hack a speculative path through the conditional thickets of the possible',[9] but a degree of subjective intuition about a character *is* permitted. It is this act of interpretation that enables Ryken to call Jacob a trickster and con man,[10] and Culpepper to discern that 'there remains a heart of darkness in the character of Jesus'.[11]

From Christology to Victimology

There remains one further task that it is necessary to undertake at the beginning of this chapter. An attempt must be made to explore what is meant by the term 'victim' in order to be able to suggest how one might behave. While it is recognized that this is a complex and somewhat subjective undertaking, if it is avoided there will be nothing against which to benchmark the behaviour of Jesus. In the first instance, a distinction must be made between a sociological and a sacrificial, cultic understanding of what a victim is. There is sufficient textual evidence to legitimate the claim that, in the Fourth Gospel, the characterization of Jesus includes his identification as a sacrificial victim in the cultic sense of the term. This will be discussed in Chapter 9, where the way in which allusions to the paschal lamb influence interpretation of the crucifixion will be explored. For the purposes of this chapter, a basic psychological understanding of victimization will suffice.

characters: 'One of three characters—the narrator, someone else in the story, or the person himself or herself—can describe and assess the character, or the character's own actions (whether external or mental) will embody one or more traits' (p. 73). Similar statements are made by Alter in 'Characterization and the Art of Reticence', *Art of Biblical Narrative*, pp. 116-17.

    8.   Ryken, *Words of Delight*, p. 75.
    9.   Geoff Dyer writing in his critique of Norman Sherrin's biography of Graham Greene, *The Guardian*, 30 August 1994, p. 13.
    10. See Ryken's analysis of the characterization of Jacob in *Words of Delight*, pp. 75-81.
    11. Culpepper, *Anatomy of the Fourth Gospel*, p. 112.

Victimology[12] offers a comprehensive classification system and associated vocabulary for the examination of the dynamics between perpetrators and victims.[13] There is a clear distinction made by the discipline between two groups of victims: those who play no active part in becoming a victim, and those who promote their victimage. The first group, termed 'situational aggression victims', are the target of attack or repeated aggression because of circumstance. Disorders developing in these victims as a result of their experiences can be acute or chronic.[14] The second group, 'promotional aggression victims', are subject to attack or prolonged aggression because of a conscious or unconscious invitation. While situational victims may develop disorders, this group have disorders to begin with. These can fall into three types: impulsive, compulsive and characterological.[15] What is important about this group

12. Victimology is an offshoot of criminology that began to develop in the 1940s and can be defined as 'the study of criminal–victim relationships' (S. Schafer, *The Victim and his Criminal: A Study in Functional Responsibility* [New York: Random House, 1968], p. 3). For a full history of its development and socio-political implications see R. Elias, *The Politics of Victimization*.

13. Definitions of vocabulary of relevance to this study are as follows:

victim (n.)	someone killed, harmed by, or suffering from some act of aggression
victimage (n.)	that which belongs to the state or condition of being a victim.
victimal (adj.)	pertaining to or concerned with victiming
victiming (v.)	making oneself a victim; promoting victimage
victimization (n.)	the state of being victimized
victimized (v.t.)	to be made a victim of

(I.L. Kutash, 'Victimology', in R.J. Corsini [ed.], *Encyclopaedia of Psychology* [4 vols.; New York: J. Wiley & Sons, 2nd edn, 1994], III, pp. 564-66 [565]). Material for the following paragraph on the types and characteristics of victims is from this article. It should be noted that this is just one of many suggested victim typologies, but that most typologies imply the victim's participation in crime to some extent. Elias provides an overview in *Politics of Victimization*, pp. 59-60.

14. Acute disorders are a transient situational disturbance with symptoms such as exhaustion, grief, hostility, remorse and disorientation. Chronic disorders develop over a long period of being the victim of aggression and include symptoms of chronic anxiety, guilt, irritability and extreme apathy (Kutash, 'Victimology', p. 565).

15. Impulsive disorders occur when an individual receives a blow to self-esteem (e.g. job loss) and immediately endangers him or herself, consciously or unconsciously, as a response. Compulsive disorders occur when a person's early experiences have produced infantile feelings of anxiety or guilt so that the individual

is that there exists a 'nefarious symbiosis'[16] between the victim and offender, with the victim stimulating the victimizer towards a response.

To return to the Gospel of John, how can these theories be of assistance in understanding the dynamic between Jesus and his oppressors, and Jesus' identity as a victim? Any attempt to relate modern psychological understanding to the characters of a biblical text is naturally subject to accusations of anachronism and inappropriateness. However, one has only to read Mark Stibbe's commentary on John 21 to see how illuminating it can be, and the desire here is for illumination rather than methodological purity.[17] When, in his section on the characterization of Jesus, Alan Culpepper concludes that 'it is not hard to understand why he provokes hostility', he provides a good starting point.[18] Jesus engages in victimal behaviour in the Fourth Gospel. He provokes, incites, frustrates and confronts the Jews on several occasions, exposing himself to severe risk of physical danger (Jn 7, 8, 10). At the Feast of Dedication he succeeds in distracting the Jews from stoning him in one breath (10.32), only to make a statement that is designed to antagonize them further in the next (10.38). What conclusion can the reader come to, but that he invites aggression, he courts violence? Perhaps this is why, as Robinson concedes, the Johannine Christ is found by many to be 'intolerable or repellent'.[19] The real implication of Jesus' behaviour is that *he is in some way an active participant in his own victimization*. There is a level at which his victiming—placing himself in hazardous situations,

---

repeatedly invites punishment. Characterological disorders occur when a person has come to associate gratification (sexual or emotional) with physical or psychological pain and consequently develops a lifestyle that seeks it out (Kutash, 'Victimology', p. 565).

16. 'Many criminal deeds are more indicative of a subject–object relation than of the perpetrator alone. There is a definite mutuality of some sort', claims H. von Hentig in his seminal work on victimology, *The Criminal and his Victim: Studies in the Sociobiology of Crime* (New Haven: Yale University Press, 1948). Von Hentig saw a 'reciprocal operation of affinities between doer and sufferer', which ranged from complete indifference to conscious impulsion. He identified four attitudes of victims—apathetic, lethargic; submitting, conniving; co-operative, contributory; and provocative, soliciting (pp. 419-20).

17. Stibbe, *John*, pp. 209-15. Stibbe explores the relationship between Peter and Jesus, showing most effectively how Peter is helped to come to terms with his three-fold denial of Jesus.

18. Culpepper, *Anatomy of the Fourth Gospel*, p. 112.

19. Robinson, 'The Last Tabu?', p. 160.

goading his enemies—is a *collusion* with his oppressors. This is a serious accusation to make, even if we are only speaking of the characterization of the Gospel's protagonist, and the contents of this chapter will provide the justification for it. But some initial word of explanation is called for. The major question that comes to mind is, *why*? If it is possible to interpret Jesus' behaviour in this way, what would be his motive for doing so? I suggest that the reason must lie in his understanding of his role and identity. There is an obvious degree of circularity in this argument—his believing that he is a victim gives rise to victiming behaviour. But the point is this: From the very beginning of the narrative, Jesus is cognizant that his fate will be a brutal and humiliating execution. He speaks about it constantly and the text tells us that this knowledge influences his behaviour. It can hardly be denied, therefore, that this awareness shapes his expectations of and dealings with those who will be responsible for his death. At its most basic level his awareness of his identity as a victim is something of a self-fulfilling prophecy[20]—again we encounter circularity but, as Ursula Le Guin commented, 'you have to form a circle to escape from a circle'.[21] There are, however, dangers inherent in circularity, as she illustrates with the following tale:

> In the Far West...they tell stories about hoop snakes. When a hoop snake wants to get somewhere—whether because the hoop snake is after something, or because something is after the hoop snake—it takes its tale (*sic*) (which may or may not have rattles on it) into its mouth, thus forming itself into a hoop, and rolls. Jehovah enjoined snakes to crawl on their bellies in the dust, but Jehovah was an Easterner. Rolling along, bowling along, is a lot quicker and more satisfying than crawling. But, for the hoop snake with rattles, there is a drawback. They are venomous snakes, and when they bite their own tail they die, in awful agony, of snakebite.[22]

Alas, her invitation to 'take the tale in your teeth, then, and bite until the blood runs, hoping it is not poison'[23] runs a fatal risk—self-destruction. The connection with the Johannine Jesus? Cognizance of his

---

20. In other words, Jesus sees suffering as his primary occupation—it is what he is there to do. He therefore *expects* to suffer and consequently ends up putting himself in situations where he *does* suffer. It could be further argued that this is a source of psychological oppression for the character in the Gospel.

21. U. Le Guin, 'It Was a Dark and Stormy Night, or, Why Are we Huddled about the Campfire?', *Critical Theory* 7.1 (Autumn 1980), pp. 191-99 (193).

22. Le Guin, 'It Was a Dark and Stormy Night', pp. 193-94.

23. Le Guin, 'It Was a Dark and Stormy Night', p. 199.

identity as a victim is his deadly rattle which, in this narrative, he *does* take in his teeth, rolling and bowling towards the cross. It is in this way that he participates in his own victimization, flirting with violence and courting betrayal.

Perhaps, at this stage in the chapter, these claims seem dubious, but exegesis will bear them out. The examination of the character and behaviour of Jesus will demonstrate and illuminate this perspective on his victimage. Continually aware of the hatred encircling him, deeply conscious of the agony that awaits, his metaphors and mannerisms reveal, inevitably, the pain of existence and of immolation.

Jesus' Awareness of his Death

If one of the primary characteristics of victims is a fixation concerning their fate, it can be expected that the Johannine Jesus will demonstrate a preoccupation with his death from early on in his ministry. The extent to which this is the case becomes evident if a comparison with the Synoptics is drawn. In the Synoptics it is noticeable that, for most of his public life, Jesus rarely mentions the subject of his death, even in parables. With the exception of a few isolated references, the material is reserved for the end of each Gospel. There is a hint to the reader that Jesus is aware he will be leaving his disciples during the dispute concerning fasting etiquette (Mk 2.18-22; Lk. 5.33-39; Mt. 9.14-17). Here Jesus says that his disciples need not fast while the bridegroom is with them, but will do so when he is 'taken away' ($\dot{\alpha}\pi\alpha\rho\theta\tilde{\eta}$). There is no clear indication, however, that death is meant. It is not obvious to the reader, nor to Jesus' audience, what the full meaning of this saying is. The Matthaean Jesus knows by ch. 12 (vv. 14-15) that the Pharisees aim to kill him, but an open declaration of Jesus' fate does not occur until the end of his ministry is approaching in all three Gospels.

Jesus' first Synoptic prophecy of his death and resurrection follows Peter's confession that he is 'the Christ' (Mt. 16.21; Mk 8.31 and Lk. 9.22). The prophecy is repeated, although in Mark and Luke the disciples do not understand what Jesus is saying (Mt. 17.22-23; Mk 9.31-32 and Lk. 9.44-45). Despite a third announcement, in which Jesus does not exactly mince his words, the Lukan disciples have still not grasped what is about to happen, and we cannot be sure about Mark's either (Mt. 20.17-19; Mk 10.33-34; Lk. 18.31-34). In addition to these three pronouncements, the disciples are told that 'the Son of Man will suffer' (Mt. 17.12; Mk 9.12), that he will 'give his life as a ransom for many' (Mk 10.45), and that he will 'suffer many things and be rejected' (Lk. 17.25). These are the *only* references to his death prior to the passion narrative. The subject can hardly be said to feature prominently in the Synoptic Jesus' teaching, which is primarily concerned with the coming of the kingdom of God and the conduct of would-be believers. Conversely, in John the subject of Jesus' death is never far below the surface of any discourse and fatalistic predictions occur throughout his ministry in various forms.[24]

A further difference between the Synoptic and Johannine death predictions is the way in which they are delivered. In the Synoptics they never take the form of an accusation or announcement to the crowd. They are not publicly stated since the information is reserved solely for the twelve, whom Jesus privately informs about his forthcoming death in order to prepare them. In John the disciples do not function as an élite band of supporters in whom Jesus confides his knowledge about his fate. They hear his predictions and accusations together with the rest of the Jews and are not privy to additional information until their last evening together. Death is no secret in John. Not only is the reader bombarded with more or less explicit reminders from the evangelist, but Jesus does not let other characters forget what is going to happen to him and who is responsible for it.

Death, violence and rejection are fundamental to Jesus' understanding of his identity and experience. He does not gradually become aware of his fate as popular opposition to his ministry burgeons and the authorities become increasingly hostile. He knows from the very beginning of the narrative that he is on earth to die: this is the purpose of his mission. It is the will of the Father, and hence the work to be accomplished. The table overleaf documents the frequency of his death predictions as well as other statements that he makes about opposition and violence, whether metaphorical or literal.

---

24. Du Rand claims 'the protagonist knows what the outcome of his mission will be', but then describes it in terms of returning to the Father. This has the effect of shifting the focus on death, which is the real content of the mission and the means of return to the Father ('The Characterization of Jesus', p. 28).

Verse	*Reference or Prediction*
1.51	Alludes to the crucifixion ('ascending and descending')
2.4	Alludes to the hour of death ('my hour has not yet come')
2.19	Alludes to the destruction of his body ('destroy this temple')
3.11-12	Perceives rejection ('you do not receive …you do not believe')
3.14	Alludes to the crucifixion ('so must the Son of Man be lifted up')
5.38-47	Perceives disbelief/rejection ('you do not believe…do not receive')
6.36	Perceives disbelief ('you do not believe')
6.51-58	Alludes to sacrificial death ('the bread I shall give for the life of the world is my flesh')
6.70	Alludes to betrayal/perceives evil ('one of you is a devil')
7.5-8	Perceives the world's and (by implication) his brothers' hatred ('the world cannot hate you, but it hates me')
7.19	Accuses the crowd of hostile intent ('you seek to kill me')
7.33	Alludes to the nearness of death ('I shall be with you a little longer')
8.21	Indirectly refers to death ('I go away and you will seek me')
8.28	Alludes to the crucifixion ('when you have lifted up the son of Man')
8.37, 40	Two accusations of hostile intent ('you seek to kill me')
10.10-18	Alludes to sacrificial death ('I lay down my life for the sheep')
10.32	Queries reason for attempted stoning ('for which… do you stone me?')
12.7	Directly refers to death ('let her keep it for the day of my burial')
12.23	Directly refers to the hour of death ('the hour has come')
12.32	Direct refers to the crucifixion ('when I am lifted up')
12.35	Alludes to the nearness of death ('light is with you a little longer')
13.21	Directly refers to the betrayal ('one of you will betray me')
14.28	Alludes to death ('I go away')
15.18-25	Directly refers to persecution and hatred ('it has hated me…')
16.5-28	Alludes to death through return to the Father ('I go to the Father…')
16.32	Predicts he will be deserted ('you will be scattered')
17.1-5	Alludes to death ('the hour has come… glorify thou me')

Table 6: Jesus' Awareness of Opposition and Death (prior to actual arrest)

The table indicates the all pervasive nature of the relevant material, with an intensification during the farewell discourse as 'the hour' becomes imminent. It is possible to determine specific phases in Jesus' cognizance of his death, just as it is in the development of the plot. This was briefly outlined in the section on the Gospel's structure in Chapter 3 and is recapped overleaf:

– From John 1 to 5 Jesus refers to his death in veiled terms, using key theological words and metaphors such as 'the hour' and 'being lifted up'. He makes no direct accusations to the Jews about their part in his death but alludes to it when he proclaims '*you* destroy this temple'. By the end of John 5 the animosity between the Jesus and the Jews has been clearly established and their intention to kill him is stated by the evangelist.

– Jesus' indirect and metaphorical references to his death reach a climax when he delivers the discourse on the bread of life in John 6. This contains disturbing and violent language indicating the meaning of his fate and is interpreted literally by the Jews. The discourse concludes with Jesus' acknowledgment of the presence of his betrayer, which indicates a movement towards 'the hour'.

– From John 7 to 9 Jesus speaks openly and frequently about his death. He no longer uses metaphors, but while at the Feast of Tabernacles repeatedly accuses the Jews of wanting to murder him. He asserts his innocence several times and questions their motive for his death, as if struggling with its meaning and inevitability.

– In John 10 Jesus uses an extended metaphor, that of the good shepherd, to speak about his death and its sacrificial nature. He creates a scene that, on the surface appears peacefully pastoral, but in reality contains violent imagery.

– After the attempt to arrest him at the Feast of Dedication, Jesus does not specifically mention his death again until the end of his public ministry in John 12. At the tomb of Lazarus, however, he is greatly distressed, and this is related to the nearness of his own death. The section ends with the plot and prophecy by the High Priest legitimizing his execution.

The ensuing sections—the announcement of the hour in John 12 and the material in the farewell discourses in John 13–17—will be discussed below in Chapters 7 and 8 respectively.

Jesus' Early Ministry (1.18–5.47)

During the first five chapters of the Gospel Jesus sets about the business of establishing himself as an itinerant preacher and healer. He gathers together a group of followers, performs three miracles, explains his role and mission to different representatives of society in several discourses and takes a stand against the religious status quo by an act of vandalism in the temple. By the time the reader learns of the Jews' determination to kill him in 5.16, much has been revealed about Jesus' attitude to the community, understanding of his identity and awareness of his death. The next few pages explore five aspects of Jesus' character that the reader discovers in this section of the Gospel:

1. *He Displays a Deep Consciousness of his own Death*
This is not a truism about Jesus in general since, as has already been shown, there is a difference between the Synoptics and John on this matter. The Johannine character knows from the very beginning of his ministry that he is going to die and frequently alludes to the fact. His understanding of his death is theologically defined in these chapters.[25] The principal vehicle by which this is conveyed is his use of specific vocabulary which, in the Fourth Gospel, is associated with death. As this vocabulary is used continually throughout the narrative by both Jesus and the narrator, it is appropriate to pause briefly to consider its role and significance.

Johannine Theological Signifiers. The terms ὥρα (hour), δόξα/δοξάζειν (glory) and ὑψοῦν (lift up) are employed throughout the Gospel, either together or separately, to refer to Jesus' death, alerting the reader to various aspects of its significance. A great deal has been written about the theological consequences of these terms and the purpose here is not to rehearse these arguments but to mention the effect of their inclusion on the reader's understanding of narrative time and the way in which they repeatedly focus attention on the death of Jesus. Alan Culpepper, drawing on the work of Gérard Genette, discusses in detail the occasion

---

25. It could be suggested that one of the reasons for this is that there is no direct threat to his life during this section and so he has no experience on which to draw in order to speak about it.

and role of analepses and prolepses within the Gospel.[26] John's use of the above-mentioned terms can generally be seen to fall into the category of allusive internal prolepses—references to an event which will happen prior to the end of the narrative.[27] The reader who has an awareness of the meaning of these words within the narrative is repeatedly projected forwards to the crucifixion by their use. It is a means by which the evangelist continually informs us that death is the hermeneutical key to Jesus' words and actions.

The word ὥρα is used to indicate the hour of Jesus' death in John.[28] It is used 26 times in the Gospel, although several of these are simply temporal indicators.[29] One of its main uses is to provide an explanation as to why events took the course that they did. For example, in both 7.30 and 8.20 it is employed to explain why Jesus manages to escape arrest by a hostile crowd: ὅτι οὔπω ἐληλύθει ἡ ὥρα αὐτοῦ—'because his hour had not yet come'. The reader who recognizes the meaning of the term will be reminded each time it is used that Jesus' life grows ever

26. See, Culpepper (*Anatomy of the Fourth Gospel*, pp. 54-70) and in particular the diagrammatic representation of narrative time (p. 70).

27. Depending on one's theological stance regarding the extent to which the words refer to the crucifixion, they could be termed 'explicit repeating prolepses'. However, as Culpepper points out, it is pointless to force a distinction between these and suggestive allusions—'both are used for plot development and dramatic intensity' and there is a 'perceptible development toward greater explicitness...as one moves through the gospel' (*Anatomy of the Fourth Gospel*, p. 62). For the reader too, as he or she becomes familiar with the evangelist's literary style and the import of frequently used terminology, the prolepses naturally become more explicit.

28. E. Haenchen, *John* (trans. R.W. Funk; Hermeneia Commentaries; 2 vols.; Philadelphia: Fortress Press, 1984), II, p. 8; Barrett, *Gospel According to John*, p. 191; Miranda, *Being and the Messiah* ('The Gospel makes it abundantly clear that Jesus' "hour" is the hour of his death' [p. 103]. Nicholson, focusing particularly on its use in Jn 13, contends that it does not signify the hour of Jesus' death, but 'the hour of his return to the Father, in which hour the death played a part' (*Death as Departure*, p. 147). However, this interpretation does not allow for the close relationship between the hour and the 'glorification' of Jesus, for which death is the interpretative key. J.T. Forestell elaborates: '13.1 speaks of the hour in which Jesus is to pass from the world to the Father. *This is the characteristic Johannine way of referring to the death of Jesus*. His death is a passage to the Father and the means whereby he reaches the presence of God' (*The Word of the Cross: Salvation as Revelation in the Fourth Gospel* [AnBib, 57; Rome: Biblical Institute Press, 1974], p. 72, emphasis added).

29. For example, 1.39, 5.35, 16.21.

shorter as the hour approaches. Its use in 7.30 and 8.20 therefore effectively signals to the reader that Jesus was not caught this time, but he will not escape indefinitely because his hour of death grows closer and is unavoidable.

δόξα and δοξάζειν occur frequently in John's Gospel and are significant for the interpretation of Jesus' death.[30] δόξα is used in the prologue to refer to the 'glory' of the incarnate Logos, manifested through grace and truth (1.14), but also shown through his miracles (2.11, 11.40).[31] As 1.14 indicates, it is also dependent on Jesus' relationship with the Father (...δόξαν ὡς μονογενοῦς παρὰ πατρός).[32] The verb δοξάζειν refers specifically in the Gospel to the death of Jesus.[33] The crucifixion is the supreme act of both immolation and 'exaltation'[34] for Jesus. The δόξα is therefore derived from and is inextricably linked to the destruction of Jesus. The term is used by John to alert the reader to the significance of Jesus' words or to explain the behaviour of other characters. For example, in 7.39 the Spirit has not yet been given

30. The noun occurs 19 times (compare Mt.: 8; Mk: 3 and Lk: 13), and the verb 23 times (compare Mt.: 4; Mk: 1 and Lk.: 9).

31. According to Culpepper's classification, we can view references to δόξα as mixed analepses and prolepses as they speak of an event which begin prior to the commencement of the narrative and will continue past its ending (*Anatomy of the Fourth Gospel*, p. 61).

32. 'The δόξα of the Father and the δόξα of the Son are bound to each other', claims Bultmann (*Gospel of John*, p. 429).

33. Barrett claims that it is used 'as a *description* of the death of Jesus' (*Gospel According to St John*, p. 166, emphasis added). Forestell sees it used 'in reference to the passion as the hour of Jesus' glorification' (*Word of the Cross*, p. 65). For Nicholson, the glorification of the Son of Man does *not* refer to the death of Jesus, but 'to something which the Father does to the Son, either coincident with or subsequent to, the return of Jesus above' (*Death as Departure*, p. 149). However, Thompson, arguing against Käsemann's interpretation, points out: 'Whatever the precise nuance of "glory" (*doxa*) in the Fourth Gospel, it is certainly revelatory glory... *But there is no revelation in John apart from Jesus' death!...* There is no glory apart from the cross' (*Humanity of Jesus*, p. 111, emphasis added). Furthermore, one of the most convincing arguments for the interpretation of 'glorify' as a reference to death must surely be the use of the term in 21.19. Here we learn that Peter too will glorify (δοξάσει) God, and that this will be achieved *by his death*.

34. The use of the word 'exaltation' does not signify divinity here. In accordance with a low Christology, the nature of this glory or exaltation is best conveyed by honour accorded Jesus by God, rather than divine splendour displayed by Jesus himself. See Davies, *Rhetoric and Reference*, p. 132.

because, explains John, Jesus was not yet glorified ('Iησοῦς οὐδέπω ἐδοξάσθη). The disciples do not understand the actions of Jesus in 12.12-15, riding into Jerusalem on an ass, until after he has been 'glorified' and they recall the scriptural prophecy of Zech. 9.9. Similarly, they cannot understand the scriptural reference in Jn 2.19-22 until after the resurrection. These passages reveal that full comprehension of Jesus' words and deeds is not possible apart from an awareness of his glorification, which can *only* be understood from the perspective of his death. δόξα and πάθος are therefore inseparable—the use of one always carries an implicit reference to the other in the Fourth Gospel. They encompass the extremes of Jesus' human experience, permeating his life and climaxing simultaneously at the moment when he is most honoured by God and most humiliated by humanity, on the cross.

The third word to consider, ὑψοῦν, occurs five times in the Gospel. Jesus uses it on three separate occasions to refer to himself, at 3.14, 8.28 and 12.32. He speaks of the Son of Man being 'lifted up', indicating in the final reference in John 12 what is implied by this phrase: 'and I, when I am lifted up from the earth, will draw all to myself'. In case the reader misses the spatial clue ('from the earth') and the soteriological one ('draw all to myself'), the evangelist spells it out: 'He said this to show by what death he was to die' (v. 33).

ὑψοῦν has a double meaning every time it occurs in John.[35] For the purposes of this study it is sufficient to note that it refers the reader directly to the crucifixion of Jesus, indicating the type of suffering that his death will inflict and it is linked broadly to his exaltation and the manifestation of his glory during this process.

Returning to Jesus' awareness of his death in John 1–5, this vocabulary is used on a number of occasions. His justification for his initial refusal to perform the water-into-wine miracle is that his 'hour has not yet come' (2.4).[36] He explains to Nicodemus that 'the Son of Man must

35. See G. Bertram, 'ὑψόω', *TDNT*, VIII, pp. 606-13 (610). Nicholson's study identifies five ways in which the term is interpreted by scholars, four of which link it to the crucifixion. His own view, and that of Bultmann and Dodd as well, is that 'ὑψόω refers primarily to the lifting up to heaven, but this includes, or is achieved by, the cross', in other words, it is speaking primarily about Jesus' return to the Father, in line with his interpretation of ὥρα and δόξα/δοξάζειν (*Death as Departure*, p. 141).

36. Note, however, the doubts expressed by Brown and Beasley-Murray that

be lifted up' (3.14). The 'hour' surfaces again in discussion with the Samaritan woman (4.21, 23) and after the healing at Bethesda (5.25, 28) with the theme of glory also appearing after Bethesda (5.41-44).

Jesus refers to his death by using additional significant terminology in John 1. In response to Nathanael's amazement and acclamation following his display of omniscience, Jesus declares 'You will see heaven opened, and the angels of God ascending (ἀναβαίνοντας) and descending (καταβαίνοντας) upon the Son of Man' (1.51). The terms ἀνα-βαίνειν and καταβαίνειν contain an implicit reference to the death of Jesus,[37] and the image has been interpreted as alluding not simply to the *fact* of his death but the *method* as well.[38] Added to this is his use of the term τὸν υἱὸν τοῦ ἀνθρώπου, which is also closely linked to his suffering and death.[39] That Jesus uses the theme of his death in 1.51 to introduce himself to a would-be follower is surely an indication that it is fundamental to both his self-understanding and the way in which he expects others to perceive him.

The temple incident, discussed in Chapter 5, provides further detail about Jesus' cognizance of his death. The sign he intends to show the Pharisees (as a mark of authority for his actions) is his own death (Jn 2.19). As mentioned previously, he implicitly identifies the religious officials as those responsible for his destruction and we also learn that he knows he will be resurrected after three days. The phrase 'destroy this temple' is the first violent language Jesus uses about himself. The words are metaphorical, but the metaphor is a powerful and catastrophic one. He likens his own death to the tearing down of the immense building

Jesus is referring to his death this early on in the narrative (Brown, *Gospel According to John*, I, p. 100; Beasley-Murray, *John*, p. 35). There is no reason why this should not be the case.

37. They function as 'technical terms' for Jesus' descent from heaven and his going back up by way of the cross (*TDNT*, I, p. 521).

38. J.M.D. Derrett claims that Jacob's ladder now represents the cross (*Law in the New Testament* [London: Darton, Longman & Todd, 1970], p. 416): This, it has to be admitted, is slightly fanciful, although the comment of Barrett could be seen to imply similar: 'The Son of Man is both in heaven and on earth...he descends to give life to the world...he ascends again to his glory...but this ascent and glorification are *by way of the Cross*' (*Gospel According to St John*, p. 187, emphasis added).

39. Carson, *Gospel According to John*, p. 165. Dodd also sees it clearly connected to the work of the Suffering Servant (*Interpretation*, p. 247). Its use in 3.14 can also be seen to link with the crucifixion.

that his listeners are standing in—one that has taken over four decades to construct—implying a forceful and crushing destruction.

That Jesus is aware of the violent and shameful method by which he will be executed is also indicated in his discourse with Nicodemus, where he uses the term ὑψοῦν coupled with an image of the lifting up of an object of salvation on a pole (3.14).[40] The other feature of his death that comes through strongly in this speech is its salvific function: whoever believes will have ζωὴν αἰώνιον—a theme greatly elaborated by the narrator and to which Jesus returns in 5.21-24.

The investigation of the first tenet of Jesus' character—he displays a deep consciousness of his own death—has been necessarily protracted, as it is of primary importance to our understanding of his victim consciousness. It is clear that it is a significant motivator for Jesus. He has referred to it in some form or another in every conversation he has had in John 1–5. He has used it as the justification for acting (in the temple) or not acting (at Cana). It represents the climax of the community's rejection of him and he is already aware of those who will be responsible for it.

2. *He Believes that he is Being Rejected and Misunderstood*

By the time readers first hear Jesus speak in Jn 1.38, they already know that he will be rejected by his community as the prologue has made this clear. This does not mean the assumption can be made that the character of Jesus is aware that the proclamation of his message will be met with antipathy. Given what we know about his death cognizance, however, it is not surprising that early on in the narrative there is evidence that Jesus perceives himself to be rejected and misunderstood. This can be found in Jesus' discussion with Nicodemus, where he states, 'You do not receive our testimony...and you do not believe' (3.11-12). In fact, at this point in the plot, the only actual indication of hostility on the part of the Jews has been their outrage concerning the temple incident—an outrage provoked purely by the outrageous behaviour of Jesus' himself. That Jesus uses the second person plural when addressing Nicodemus

40. In addition, Jesus compares the Son of Man to a serpent, which was a symbol of death in the Hebrew Bible. Its role was to bring death to humanity in Gen. 3 and see also Ps. 58.4; Isa. 59.5; Jer. 8.17 and Micah 7.17. The reference here is to Num. 21.9 the 'setting on a pole' of a bronze serpent by Moses, which functions to save the people from the fiery serpents sent by God. To escape death, the people must look upon the symbol of death.

indicates that the accusation of disbelief is not directed solely at him but includes the religious authorities, who Jesus evidently believes oppose him.[41] In fact, Jesus' perception is corroborated by the narrator at the end of the chapter, who echoes '...no one receives his testimony' (3.32).

Jesus elaborates on his understanding of the rejection of the Jews in John 5, where he propounds that his witness and authority originate from the Father who sent him (vv. 30-45). We hear that the rejection of Jesus stems from the Jews' rejection of the word of the Father and his emissary (vv. 37-8). Their resistance to him is complete: they do not have his word abiding in them, do not believe in him, refuse to come to him, do not have his love, do not receive him, do not seek his glory, do not believe Moses, and so on. Perceiving such intransigence, Jesus exclaims in despair 'how will you believe my words?' (5.47).

3. *He Is Suspicious of the Motives of Others*

Allied to Jesus' awareness of his rejection by the community and the misunderstanding of his ministry is his suspicion of the motives of others. Not only does the narrator tell us plainly that Jesus does not trust those around him (Jn 2.24-25), but his behaviour also indicates this. His attitude towards Nicodemus reveals a blatant scepticism about whether or not he is genuinely interested in the truth. As mentioned above, Nicodemus is included among those Jesus accuses of not believing or receiving his testimony, but it is not the narrator who tells us this, it is Jesus' behaviour. Nicodemus' opening gambit arouses suspicion—'the tone sounds greasy', comments Goulder.[42] Jesus' reaction to him is negative. His initial response in v. 3 functions to exclude Nicodemus: he cannot possibly move beyond a basic appreciation of Jesus' signs because

---

41. Some commentators perceive the anachronistic inclusion of the evangelist's message to the authorities of his own day in the use of the plurals. In other words, it is not what Jesus said to Nicodemus, but what the church (we) is saying to the synagogue (you). So Bruce, *Gospel of John*, pp. 86-87. Carson's explanation is interesting: 'Jesus is sardonically aping the plural that Nicodemus affected when he first approached Jesus... "*we* know you are a teacher'". Jesus' response can be seen as a sneer: '"*we* testify to what *we* have seen"—as if to say, "*We* know one or two things too, *we* do!'" (*Gospel According to John*, p. 199).

42. 'Nicodemus', p. 154. Goulder identifies eleven reasons that indicate a negative portrayal of Nicodemus by John (pp. 154-55).

he has not been born from above.[43] Furthermore, his reply to Nicodemus's request for clarification about being born again is little short of sarcastic: 'Are you a teacher of Israel, and yet you do not understand this?' (3.10).[44]

While it might be expected that Jesus would suspect the motives of Nicodemus, it is more difficult to see why he would behave similarly towards some of the other players. This facet of his character comes to the fore when, on two occasions in John 1–5, he is requested to enact a miracle. His response to both his mother and the father of a dying child is brusque. 'Woman, what have you to do with me? My hour has not yet come', he chides Mary, as if she is trying to manipulate him into a compromising position in which he will have to reveal who he is (2.4).[45] His castigation of the distressed official also appears particularly harsh: 'unless you see signs and wonders you will not believe' (4.48).

43. Goulder sees this as a 'rasping rebuke' ('Nicodemus', p. 155).

44. So Culpepper, *Anatomy of the Fourth Gospel*, p. 110. Carson sees a 'sharp retort' (*Gospel According to John*, p. 198).

45. Τί ἐμοὶ καὶ σοί, γύναι; οὔπω ἥκει ἡ ὥρα μου. Commentators are universally unimpressed by Jesus' response to his mother: 'These words do not sound like the response of a loving son. Indeed, it sounds like a rebuke', chides Stibbe (*John*, p. 44). Culpepper admits there is 'a certain coldness' about his words (*Anatomy of the Fourth Gospel*, p. 110). Kysar sees 'considerable sharpness' (*John*, p. 45). Juan Alfaro comments that the phrase 'what do you want with me' can be used to address someone who represents danger or a threat to the speaker and includes a connotation of rejection ('The Mariology of the Fourth Gospel: Mary and the Struggles for Liberation', *BTB* 10 [1980], pp. 3-16 [7]). Fear is also seen to be a factor in the interpretation given to the phrase by the residents of Solentiname: 'Jesus may have been afraid. It's very natural for somebody to be afraid of death… But anyway Mary here does not seem to be afraid or to pay any attention to prudence, but she urges him to perform a miracle' (Cardenal, *Gospel in Solentiname*, p. 151).

Brown, on the other hand, concentrates on the *logical* problem caused by Jesus' words. Jesus refuses his mother's request but she proceeds as if he had not, and he then carries out the miracle without indicating any change of mind. Brown accepts the theory that 2.4 is a Johannine addition to a pre-Johannine miracle story which is intended to show that Jesus is not at the disposition of his family during his ministry ('The "Mother of Jesus' in the Fourth Gospel", in M. de Jonge (ed.), *L'évangile de Jean: Sources, rédaction, théologie* [BETL, 44; Leuven: Leuven University Press/ Uitgeverij Peeters, 1977], pp. 307-10). It is important to note that it is not the use of the vocative γύναι which indicates harshness, as there are examples in the rest of the Gospel of this being used without negative connotation (see Barrett, *Gospel According to St John*, p. 191). It is instead the content of the whole sentence which indicates the tone in which the address γύναι is spoken.

Although the plural form of the verbs is used here (ἴδητε, πιστεύσητε), as with Nicodemus, indicating that the reprimand is not directed solely at the official, nevertheless it is hardly an exhibition of the 'grace upon grace' that the reader is expecting from the Word made flesh.[46] Jesus is evidently unmoved by this man who has begged[47] him for assistance. He considers the request purely in terms of the demand that it makes upon him, accusing the father, together with anyone else within earshot, of 'only being interested in me for my miracles'. Although Jesus finally grants both Mary[48] and the official[49] their wishes, his behaviour leaves

---

46. Readers familiar with the Synoptic Jesus will find his behaviour particularly unpalatable. Compared to Synoptic healings—parallels Mt. 8.5-13 and Lk 7.1-10; the raising of the widow's son (Lk. 7.11-17) and the healing of Jairus' daughter (Lk 8.40-56)—where, on each occasion, Jesus' compassion moves him to act, the Johannine Jesus exhibits a noticeable lack of empathy with the petitioner. Lindars offers an explanation of the difference between Jn 4 and its parallels on the basis of the Fourth Evangelist's different handling of the theme of faith. In the Synoptics, Jesus responds willingly to the centurion's request, but is hindered by the centurion himself, who reveals that he believes Jesus' word alone is sufficient to cure. In John, claims Lindars, Jesus refuses the officer 'on the grounds that he has not shown a deep enough quality of faith, and only after he has tested him in this way utters the word of healing' ('Traditions behind the Fourth Gospel', in M. de Jonge [ed.], *L'évangile de Jean*, pp. 107-24 [110]). See also J.M. Robinson for a similar treatment of this passage in source critical terms: 4.47b-49a seem to him to have been added by the evangelist because Jesus' intervening comment is rather 'gratuitous' and is unrelated to the father's request that his son be healed. The 'rebuff' seems to be ignored as Jesus does go on to heal the child ('The Johannine Trajectory', in J.M. Robinson and H. Koester (eds.), *Trajectories through Early Christianity* [Philadelphia: Fortress Press, 1971], pp. 232-68 [246]). The treatment by Lindars and Robinson of this passage, as well as Brown's of Jn 2.4 (see previous note) demonstrates my different approach to these disconcerting passages. No refuge can be sought in theories about the evangelist's redaction of a pre-Johannine source. Instead the explanation is found in the different ways in which Jesus is characterized in the Synoptics and John, with the latter revealing that Jesus can be cold and unfeeling during an encounter with a man in need.

47. ἐρωτάω, 'to beseech' (someone on someone's behalf), BAGD, p. 312.

48. Stibbe sees Mary simply forcing Jesus' hand, refusing to be swayed by his resistance: 'Her reaction is to turn to the servants of the banquet and say, "Do whatever he tells you". This now leaves Jesus with no choice but to do something! He is involved now whether he likes it or not' (*John*, p. 45).

49. Stibbe's explanation as to why Jesus subsequently heals the official's son is less convincing. He sees a development from 'condemnation to compassion' when Jesus learns that the son is actually a little boy. 'Though the narrator does not

the reader feeling slightly uncomfortable. In the second miracle in particular, the petitioner appears to be presented in a more favourable light than Jesus himself. Despite being accused of deficient 'signs faith', the official is vindicated by the evangelist's comment that he believed in the *word* (λόγος) of Jesus, and not just him but his whole household (4.50, 53). Jesus' suspicion of his motives has therefore been unjustified.

4. *He Has Strong Emotions that Can Provoke Him to Violence*
Culpepper sees the Johannine Jesus as 'demonstrably less emotional' than his Synoptic counterpart.[50] While it is obvious that the two characters are portrayed as having extremely different personalities, there is certainly evidence of emotional response in John's Jesus. The difference in the Fourth Gospel is that the feelings expressed by Jesus are not always particularly attractive and are more difficult to interpret. As we have just seen, his response to the official with the sick son is decidedly emotional—'unless you see signs...'—but it is hardly sympathetic. We could speculate about what feelings are being displayed by Jesus—frustration, anger, scorn—but we would be hard pressed to find much warmth in them. Du Rand sums it up when he notes that, with the exception of a few individuals, Jesus seems to keep his interpersonal distance: 'Jesus is sketched as discussing love but he does not seem to be very loving himself'[51]—in other words, he does not practice what he preaches.

The most obvious display of emotion by Jesus occurs in the temple incident, as was mentioned in Chapter 5. Jesus is not averse to direct action in order forcefully to make a point, although what that point *is* is not at all clear to those watching. The narrator encourages us to

---

intervene to offer an insider's view of Jesus' thought processes, it is probable that the word *paidion* is to be taken as a catalyst for Jesus' change of attitude. A son could be a male of any age. A little boy is something altogether different. The official is therefore quickly told, "Your son will live"' (*John*, pp. 72-73). While Stibbe admits that his interpretation is speculative, I would suggest that it is actually wrong. There is little evidence in the text to give it any weight at all. The indication is not that Jesus has a change of heart, but rather that the official is so persistent that Jesus sees he will *have* to act in order to rid himself of the man. His words to him are terse and functional, bearing no hint of compassion.

50. Culpepper, *Anatomy of the Fourth Gospel*, p. 111.
51. du Rand, 'The Characterization of Jesus', p. 29.

attribute Jesus' rampage through the court to *zeal*[52]—a particularly powerful motivator—noting that this was the understanding of the disciples (2.17).[53] The justification that Jesus uses for his actions is his death, a possible indication that the motivation for the outburst is fuelled by emotions concerning his death, such as rage or fear. It is easy to see a character who is out of control in this scene, but to suggest more than this would be overly speculative.

5. *He Is Prepared to Flout Religious and Other Cultural Conventions*
The final facet of Jesus' character that the reader learns about from John 1–5 is his refusal to allow societal norms and expectations to constrain his behaviour. As a consequence, other characters often find his actions unusual or offensive. His proclivity to transgress religious conventions needs little comment. Examples in this early section of the narrative include the healing on the sabbath and his challenge to the temple system. His explanations indicate that he simply does not think the normal rules of behaviour apply to him (5.17, backed up by the claims of vv. 19–28). His discussion with a woman from Samaria at Jacob's well is so radical that it raises the eyebrows of the disciples—the first time that an indication of their surprise (and perhaps judgment) at his unconventional behaviour is noted. It was considered undesirable that a Rabbi should speak to a woman and for Jesus to spend time talking alone with a Samaritan woman of questionable repute would no doubt have been even more undesirable.[54] Jerome Neyrey, noting that the *dramatis personae* in John can be seen as representative figures, suggests that the narrator has concentrated in this woman many of the characteristics of the marginal persons that we see Jesus' regularly interacting with in the

---

52. Culpepper comments that Jesus actually acts out of anger, but that it is interpreted as zeal (*Anatomy of the Fourth Gospel*, p. 110). Stibbe is nearer to zeal: outrage inspired by devotion (*John*, p. 50).

53. The indication of the evangelist is that they did not use this interpretation until after the crucifixion and resurrection (Kysar, *John*, p. 49). If this is the intention, we should understand that Jesus' act would have been quite senseless, even to his followers, during his lifetime.

54. Barrett quotes *Nid.* 4.1: 'the daughters of the Samaritans are menstruants from their cradle (i.e., perpetually unclean)', and *P. Ab.* 1.5: 'talk not much with womankind… He that talks much with womankind brings evil upon himself and neglects the study of the Law' (*Gospel According to St John*, p. 240). Carson points out: 'Jesus himself was not hostage to the sexism of his day' (*Gospel According to John*, p. 227).

Synoptics—'she is the amalgam of cultural deviance'.[55] She is a Gentile, unclean, a sinner and a woman; *quadruply oppressed*, as we would say today.[56] The message to the reader is that Jesus considers his testimony to be relevant to everyone, including social outcasts, and that he will not be inhibited by the sensibilities of others, even his closest companions, in his commitment to bring it to whomever he wishes.[57]

The exploration of the major facets of Jesus' character through John 1–5 has produced an interesting picture of John's protagonist. It has been established that he is already fully conscious of the primary facts about his death; including the method to be used, its salvific function, the responsible party and the end result. His words and actions reflect this consciousness, although at this stage it is manifested through allusive and symbolic means rather than overtly.

The Bread of Death (6.26-66)

The discourse following the feeding miracle marks an important stage in the development of Jesus' victim consciousness, revealing significant details about his understanding of his death. The discourse is a milestone in the narrative as it marks the end of any 'popular following' Jesus might have had. His message is so repugnant to his audience that it completely alienates them and by the end of the pericope there is a desertion by the majority of Jesus' troup of supporters. The section will be explored in terms of the development of Jesus' message and its offensiveness using the structure on the following page.

55. J.H. Neyrey, 'What's Wrong with this Picture? John 4, Cultural Stereotypes of Women and Public and Private Space', *BTB* 24 (1994), pp. 77-91 (86). A representative of a class 'neither morally approved nor socially acceptable', comments C.H. Dodd ('The Portrait of Jesus in John and in the Synoptics', in W.R. Farmer, C.F.D. Moule and R.R. Niebuhr [eds.], *Christian History and Interpretation: Studies Presented to John Knox* [Cambridge: Cambridge University Press, 1967], pp. 183-98 [196]).

56. Given that this is the case, it is interesting to speculate whether the evangelist has created one character who embodies as many deviant characteristics as possible to avoid having to write a number of other episodes showing Jesus accepting numerous individuals with different flaws. After all, if Jesus accepts this 'no hoper', it can be taken as read that everyone else is in with a chance.

57. See S.D. Moore for a fascinating exploration of how Jesus also can be seen to be needy in this passage, and his need is just as great as the woman's ('Are There Impurities in the Living Water that the Johannine Jesus Dispenses? Deconstruction, Feminism, and the Samaritan Woman', *BibInt* 1.2 [1993], pp. 207-27).

The interrogation–response form of the discourse is now generally accepted to show similarities to first-century Palestinian midrashim.[58] Jesus builds up his message slowly, drawing in the listeners as he develops the metaphor, pausing to dispel misunderstanding and literal interpretations. The climax he works towards is not the statement ('I am the bread of life', 6.35), which we hear early on in the discourse, but the implications of this claim, which he does not spell out until vv. 53-58. That this last section is the climax becomes clear if it is suggested that the *aim* of the discourse is to spell out fully what is repellent about Jesus' message, in order that those who are not able to receive it are repelled. This will become clear in the following exegesis.

58. See P. Borgen, *Bread from Heaven: An Exegetical Study of the Concept of Manna in the Gospel of John and the Writings of Philo* (NovTSup, 10; Leiden: E.J. Brill, 1965). Borgen shows the discourse on bread (6.31-58) is an exposition of the Hebrew Bible, characterized by midrashic features with parallels found in Philo and in Palestinian midrashim. This is accepted by most of the major commentaries. See, for example, Lindars, *Gospel of John*, pp. 250-53.

Figure 3: *Jesus as Victim: Thematic Development in John 6*

1. 6.26–34 *Jesus challenges his listeners*
   Statement: '*you seek perishable food*'
   Development of theme:
   > Unperishable food is available
   > It can be accessed via belief in 'the one sent'
   > It comes down from heaven and gives life
   Response: '*give us this unperishable food!*'

2. 6.35–42 *Jesus alienates his listeners*
   Statement: '*I am the source of unperishable food from heaven*'
   Development of theme:
   > Those eligible will receive this food and eternal life
   > The Father identifies those eligible
   > Belief in 'the one sent' is the eligibility criterion
   Response: '*how have you come from heaven?*'

3. 6.43–52 *Jesus angers his listeners*
   Statement: '*the unperishable food must be eaten to gain life*'
   Development of theme:
   > The Father leads the eligible to Jesus
   > Access to eternal life is through Jesus
   > Eating the unperishable food results in eternal life
   > The unperishable food is Jesus' flesh
   Response: '*how can you give us your flesh to eat?*'

4. 6.53–60 *Jesus repulses his listeners*
   Statement: '*my flesh and blood must be eaten to gain life*'
   Development of theme:
   > Eating flesh and blood is essential for eternal life
   > Eating flesh and blood promotes mutual 'indwelling'
   > The Father is the origin of the unperishable food
   Response: '*this is a hard saying; who can bear it?*'

5. 6.61–66 *Jesus repels his listeners*
   Statement: '*there is a harder message than this*'
   Development of theme:
   > The ascent of the Son is more offensive than his descent
   The offence is spiritual not physical
   > Access to life is via belief in the spiritual offence
   > Access to belief is via the Father
   Response: *silence—desertion*

1. *Jesus Challenges his Listeners (6.26-34)*

The section begins with the people who had witnessed the feeding miracle searching out Jesus, confused as to how he could have crossed the
Galilean sea without a boat. Their question appears innocent enough:
'how did you get here?' but Jesus immediately suspects their motives.[59]
He responds with an accusation: 'You seek me, not because you saw
signs, but because you ate your fill of the loaves' (v. 26). On the surface,
this claim bears little resemblance to what has actually happened. As
Barrett points out, the people had at least understood that a miracle had
been performed and Jesus had been recognized as an 'exceptional' person.[60] It is Jesus, therefore, who is not satisfied that the crowd have worthy intentions and believes, in the final analysis, their motives to be
materially oriented. The exchange that follows, in which Jesus repeatedly attempts to haul the audience up from the physical onto the spiritual plane, abounds in Johannine irony. The subjects of work, belief
and food are explored, with the people requesting further proof of Jesus'
authority—'How about a feeding miracle?', they suggest. With his cor-
rection to their understanding of the manna from heaven episode[61] Jesus
sets up the listeners. It is the Father who provides the 'true' bread—'that
which comes down from heaven, and gives life to the world' (v. 33).
When they respond as expected, keen for a supply of this life-long
magical substance, the stage is set for Jesus' claim.

2. *Jesus Alienates his Listeners (6.35-42)*

Thus far the discourse has taken the form of questions from the crowd
who seek answers from Jesus, trying to discern if he is a prophet from
God. Jesus' replies have stated the truth about himself and his identity,
but in veiled terms that are not fully understood by his listeners. It is in
v. 35 that he begins to make a series of bold assertions that provoke,
confuse and finally outrage them. For their part, the audience antagonize Jesus with their insistence on literal interpretations of his words.

---

59. That the crowd had genuine motives in seeking Jesus is suggested by
Dorothy Lee: 'The crowd's desire to seek Jesus in vv. 22-25 is a sign of understanding on their part, since "seeking" is used elsewhere in the Gospel of embryonic
discipleship' (*Symbolic Narratives*, p. 141).

60. Barrett, *Gospel According to John*, p. 286.

61. As Borgen shows, Jesus' action of correcting their erroneous interpretation
of Scripture follows Jewish exegetical method (*Bread from Heaven*, pp. 61-69).

Jesus becomes the subject of the discussion in 6.35, in place of the manna. The effect of describing himself as the bread of life is to introduce himself as the unperishable food that must be consumed by the disciples. Forceful language is used to state his promise: the believer shall never hunger and never thirst,[62] but his listeners learn that it is only available to those who believe. Jesus' accusation to the crowd is clear: 'you do not believe' (οὐ πιστεύετε)—*you are not eligible* (v. 36). This is a clear rebuttal to those he perceives as rejecting his message on the basis of unbelief, but it soon becomes evident that the matter of eligibility is far from straightforward. The role of the Father in drawing believers to Jesus is paramount, and Jesus is totally dependent on the Father for the gift that he has to offer and its acceptance by the people.[63] This raises the question of who is rejecting whom. Jesus rejects those he believes reject him, but the reason they reject him is because they have been rejected by the Father. The end result is to relieve Jesus of the responsibility of being a popular preacher courting a large following—Johannine discipleship is for the exclusive few, not for the masses. Jesus is tacitly *permitted* to provoke desertion and even hostile opposition by the majority, because his task is merely to raise up the few who have already been given him. Courting rejection is part of his role. No need, then, to prettify the true content of his message; and, as we will see, he does not hesitate to state its implications in the bleakest of terms, phrasing his 'invitation to life' in a way that will utterly revolt his listeners. At this point, however, the main complaint[64] of his audience relates to the claim of heavenly origin,[65] which they dispute among themselves, creating an atmosphere of disbelief and animosity. By the time v. 41 is reached, Jesus has completely alienated a group of people who were

---

62. Beasley-Murray suggests that the negatives οὐ μὴ and οὐ μὴ πώποτε are very strong (*John*, p. 92).

63. Davies comments: 'Everything Jesus achieves is understood as the Father's gift... In his ministry Jesus does the "works which the Father *has granted* me to accomplish..." Any success in the ministry is also reckoned as God's gift: "All that the Father *gives* me will come to me"' (*Rhetoric and Reference*, pp. 168-69, emphasis original).

64. The use of γογγυσμός relates the attitude of the Jews to that of their forefathers, who 'murmured' against Moses when they had nothing to eat (Exod. 16.2-12), thus establishing a further link with the bread/manna theme.

65. Again we encounter Johannine irony. See Duke, *Irony in the Fourth Gospel*, pp. 64-65.

originally supportive and had sought him out for misguided, but not malicious motives.

3. Jesus Angers his Listeners (6.43-52)

Jesus openly confronts those gossiping against him. His challenge repeats several of his previous claims: those to be 'raised up' will be identified by the Father alone; he is the bread of life; the bread bequests eternal life (vv. 44-50). He then elaborates further on the nature of the bread and the believer's relationship to it:

> I am the living bread which came down from heaven;
> if anyone eats of this bread, he will live for ever;
> and the bread which I shall give
> for the life of the world is my flesh. (v. 51)

The claim is striking in that although it begins in a similar fashion to previous ones—'I am the living bread which came down...', mentioning eating and eternal life—it finishes with the identification of the bread with Jesus' flesh.[66] This shifts the discussion back onto the physical level, where the discourse originally started. Beginning with the multiplication of loaves (a literal miracle), both Jesus and the people moved onto a spiritual plane. They did not occupy the *same* spiritual plane—Jesus talks about the truly spiritual, the bread of life, whereas the people are stuck halfway between the physical and spiritual, talking of another miracle, one which is imbued with ancient religious significance. Jesus now reverts to the startlingly physical: his flesh. And with the reference to flesh, the death of Jesus again surfaces in the narrative.

The Jews reel with horror at his words, having interpreted them literally: 'How can this man give us his flesh to eat?'; (v. 52). Their 'murmuring' becomes a fully animated squabble, with μάχομαι indicating the strength of emotion aroused.[67] The extremity of their reaction makes it clear that their disgust is at the thought of eating human flesh. Jesus, however, makes no attempt to pacify them by retracting his words or dispelling their confusion. Instead, he chooses to state again, forcefully and more explicitly, his original statement.

---

66. Maarten Menken comments, 'Jesus *gives* what he *is*: the bread of life' ('John 6.51c-58: Eucharist or Christology?', *Bib* 74 [1993], pp. 1-26 [15]).

67. A very strong term, as noted by the commentators. Lindars translates it as 'battled' (*Gospel of John*, p. 226); Barrett as 'disputed violently with one another' (*Gospel According to St John*, p. 298). BAGD gives 'fight, quarrel, dispute' (p. 496).

4. Jesus Repulses his Listeners (6.53-60)

The language Jesus uses to express the heart of his message is overwhelmed with vocabulary that connects eating and drinking with his body. In the space of the five verses that comprise his answer there are 21 references using the following terms:

Term	Translation	Frequency
σάρξ	flesh	4
αἷμα	blood	4
τρώγω	chew	4
πίνω	drink	3
ἐσθίω	eat	2
ἄρτος	bread	2
βρῶσις	food	1
πόσις	drink	1

The vocabulary employed contributes to the violence of the metaphor evoked. The verb τρώγω, which has a coarser meaning—to munch or chew—is used in place of ἐσθίω in vv. 54, 56 and 57.[68] The crude picture would therefore be that the believers are to gnaw on the flesh of Jesus.[69] The use of such vocabulary has been seen by some to be anti-Docetic polemic, which would prevent the 'spiritualizing' of the

---

68. BAGD, p. 829. There has been some discussion about the significance of the various Greek verbs for eating. C. Spicq, after a survey which shows the blurring of the distinctions between the verbs τρώγω, φαγεῖν and ἐσθίω concludes: 'Jamais, jusqu'à saint Jean, *trogein* n'a été utilisé dans un texte religieux. L'Evangeliste l'emploie pour insister sur le réalisme dans la mandication, tout en indiquant qu'il ne s'agit pas d'une impossible "anthropophagie"' ('Τρώγειν: Est-il synonyme de φαγεῖν et d'ἐσθίειν dans le Nouveau Testament?', *NTS* 26 [1979–80], pp. 414-19 [419]). However, see Menken for the argument that although τρώγειν has a stronger sense than φαγεῖν in itself, this is not relevant because for John the two verbs are interchangeable ('John 6.51c-58', p. 17).

69. Note the advice of Chrysostom who, unperturbed by the imagery of the text, advised those wanting to be united with Jesus that they should not only see, touch and eat him, but 'fix their teeth in His flesh' (*Hom. Joh.* 46.3). R.A. Edwards also favours a literal interpretation, based on the use of τρώγω. He suggests: 'it was a word that was commonly applied to animals, a crude word, which might perhaps, as it applied to people, be translated "get your teeth into". If it intensified the energy of eating when Jesus said that it was to be done to the "Son of Man", I think he was challenging the romantic dreaminess that belonged to the idea' (*The Gospel According to St John: Its Criticism and Interpretation* [London: Eyre & Spottiswoode, 1954], p. 61).

eucharist.[70] Likewise, the use of the word σάρξ instead of σῶμα, which is used in the Synoptic accounts of the last supper, is claimed by some to be anti-Docetic[71] (although it ties in with the Johannine theology of ὁ λόγος σὰρξ ἐγένετο 'the word became flesh', 1.14). In addition, the use of σάρξ rather than σῶμα alludes to the sacrificial realm, evoking the image of the flesh of slaughtered animals placed on the altar for burning. Similarly, the mention of blood calls to mind the sprinkling of the sides of the altar with the blood of the beast by the priests. The mutilation implicit in the concept of eating flesh evokes the practice of dismembering the animal's body before burning (Lev. 1).[72]

The pattern of eating flesh and drinking blood is set up four times by Jesus, emphasizing their interrelatedness, as follows:

eat the flesh (of the Son of Man)	. . .	drink his blood	v. 53
eat my flesh	. . .	drink my blood	v. 54
my flesh is food	. . .	my blood is drink	v. 55
eat my flesh	. . .	drink my blood	v. 56

The offensiveness of the image to Jesus' audience can hardly be over-emphasized. The idea of eating flesh would have been naturally repugnant to the Jews, particularly since it is coupled with the drinking of blood. The consumption of blood was held as an abomination and strictly forbidden by Hebrew law. Blood was regarded as the life of a creature and was used for atonement (Gen. 9.4; Lev. 17.10-14; Deut. 12.23-25).[73] The very phrase 'eat my flesh and drink my blood' parallels the Deuteronomic prohibition; 'the blood is the life, and you shall not

70. Brown, *Gospel According to John*, I, p. 283; A.J.B. Higgins, *The Lord's Supper in the New Testament* (London: SCM Press, 1952), p. 82; Hoskyns, *Fourth Gospel*, p. 297.

71. O.S. Brooks, 'The Johannine Eucharist: Another Interpretation', *JBL* 82 (1963), pp. 293-300 (294). J.D.G. Dunn believes that the whole of 51c-58 is anti-Docetic and that this is the reason for its inclusion: John is trying to stress the offensiveness of the incarnation ('John VI: A Eucharistic Discourse?', *NTS* 17 [1971], pp. 328-38).

72. Note also that the discourse is being delivered at the time of the Passover, v. 6.4.

73. Hence the claim of Rudolf Schnackenburg that the drinking blood is only added to complement that eating of flesh and not in order to make the idea more shocking is clearly untenable. This is precisely the effect that it would have had. (*The Gospel According to St John* [trans. C. Hastings, *et al.*; HTKNT; 3 vols.; repr.; London: Burns & Oates, 1988 (1982)], II, p. 61.)

eat the life with the flesh' (12.23). The phrase to 'eat someone's flesh' is used as a metaphor indicating hostile action (Ps. 27.2; Zech. 11.9) as well as being a literal term for physical mutilation (Gen. 40.19; Micah 3.1-3). Together, the words flesh and blood signify the whole person in Jewish idiom,[74] hence the combination of the two statements 'eat my flesh' and 'drink my blood' carry the implication that Jesus is to be fully consumed—there will be nothing left of him.[75]

That this passage refers in a fundamental way to the violence of the death awaiting Jesus would appear to be obvious. Nevertheless, it is a point that remains unremarked upon by numerous Johannine commentators, the reason being that links with the eucharistic have been the primary focus of attention.[76] Commentators literally cling to this figurative interpretation: '...if Jesus' words are to have a favourable meaning, they *must* refer to the Eucharist', exclaims Brown.[77] It is not difficult to understand why scholars have succumbed to this temptation; after all, taken literally Jesus' words are not pleasant, conjuring up a gory

74. See J. Behm, 'αἷμα', *TDNT*, I, pp. 172-76 (172). σάρξ καὶ αἷμα was an established Jewish term for a man (Sir.14.18; *3 Bar.* 15.4).

75. Menken comments that the use of the word σάρξ denotes man (*sic*) in his frailty and mortality and makes it applicable to the dying Jesus: 'his death is the moment when he proves to be σάρξ' ('John 6.51c-58', p. 9).

76. Attention paid to the eucharistic significance of the passage has had the effect of screening out any other possible interpretations. Commentators rarely pause long enough in their discussion of 'eat my flesh/drink my blood' to state more than flesh = bread, and blood = wine. So, for example, Schnackenburg asserts that 'there could be no doubt of the reference to the eucharistic meal' (*Gospel According to St John*, II, p. 61). Likewise, Barrett, Bultmann and Higgins see 'unmistakable' and Lightfoot 'almost direct' eucharistic allusions (Barrett, *Gospel According to St John*, p. 299; Bultmann, *Gospel of John*, p. 235; Higgins, *Lord's Supper*, p. 82; R.H. Lightfoot, *St John's Gospel: A Commentary* [ed. C.F. Evans; Oxford: Clarendon Press, 1956], p. 156). Notable exceptions are Dodd and Carson. Dodd claims that the expression πίνειν τὸ αἷμα 'can hardly fail to suggest shed blood, and therefore violent death' (*Interpretation*, p. 339). Carson explains that as the primary symbolic reference to 'blood' in the Bible is to violent death 'it would be hard for any reader in the decades immediately after the cross not to think of Jesus' supreme sacrifice' (*Gospel According to John*, p. 296). Menken suggests that although the evangelist uses eucharistic material, the major theme of the passage is christological. The terms flesh and blood refer to the crucified Jesus and are used to combat both Docetic and Jewish understandings of Jesus' death ('John 6.51c-58').

77. Although why they must have a *favourable* meaning is not justified (*Gospel According to John*, I, pp. 284-85, emphasis added).

image of cannibalism. Many would join the first disciples in admitting that this is a hard saying (ὁ σκληρὸς λόγος, v. 60). Nevertheless, it is not acceptable to interpret the passage primarily in terms of the eucharist. All of the characters in the narrative (including the disciples) understand Jesus to be speaking literally. They have no knowledge of the eucharist to provide a convenient figurative interpretation. Of even greater significance is the fact that the narrator gives no hermeneutical nudge to the reader, indicating that the passage should be read figuratively, nor is it indicated that the disciples ever understood it in that way. We might justifiably have expected a word from the evangelist about how to interpret this passage; after all, the reader is provided with such assistance elsewhere.[78] There is, however, an ominous silence at this point. Jesus' words are to remain a hard saying for the reader as well. Given these points, there is no legitimate excuse for skating over the literal in order to plunge straight into the figurative. The *primary* message that Jesus is delivering is concerned with his suffering and death. Eucharistic significance is *secondary*, submerged some way beneath the surface layer of the text.[79]

78. For example in Jn 2.22 and 6.64, 71. Perhaps something along the lines of: 'when therefore Jesus was raised from the dead, his disciples understood that he was speaking about the eucharist', would have been suitable?

79. Just how secondary the eucharistic significance is can be gleaned if a comparison is made between Jn 6 and the Synoptic accounts of the last supper (Mk 14.22-25; Mt. 26.26-29; Lk. 22.19-24). The significant differences between the context and content of Synoptic and Johannine material unsurprisingly reveal different emphases on interpretation. The Synoptic Jesus utters his sacramental words in the context of a Passover meal at the end of his ministry. He is surrounded by his closest disciples in the privacy of the upper room in a supportive, non-threatening environment. Conversely, the Johannine Jesus speaks in public, surrounded by a large crowd of uncomprehending and, for the most part, unsympathetic Jews. The words he speaks address different issues and fulfil different functions. In the Synoptics Jesus' words are an instruction to the disciples about an act of remembrance to be performed, while in John they proclaim to the crowd what must be done to obtain eternal life. The Synoptic accounts are brief (around four verses long) and devoid of unnecessary detail. The description of the institution of the ritual is as basic as it possibly could be, with no extraneous theological explanation regarding its significance. The words used differ slightly in each case, although they all follow the same form: Jesus blesses the bread, breaks it and gives it to the disciples and then takes the cup, gives thanks and hands it to them, each time with a sentence of explanation. Mark is the briefest; his words indicating the globally sacrificial nature of the blood (19.22, 24), but they do not explain the significance of the bread being

Assistance in interpreting this hard saying can be found in the method used by Stephen Moore to understand the discourse with the Samaritan woman.[80] Moore shows how the woman muddies the distinction between the material and the spiritual in the discussion about the living

Jesus' body, nor do they contain the vital Johannine behest to eat and drink. Similarly, Luke omits the commands 'eat' and 'drink', but includes an explanation regarding the bread (22.19). The cup is mentioned (v. 22) and both the body and blood have redemptive value for disciples, although a wider application is not indicated. Luke ends with an immediate reference to the betrayer, linking Jesus' death with the act of remembrance. The Matthaean account is close to Mark's, omitting sacrificial words with the bread, including them with the wine and ending with a reference to the kingdom. It adds the imperatives λάβετε φάγετε and πίετε, emphasizing the disciples' active participation, but they are not commanded to continue this practice in his memory. Matthew also elaborates on the reason for the sacrifice: Jesus' blood is poured out εἰς ἄφεσιν ἁμαρτιῶν (v. 28), showing why his death is necessary. At its most basic level, the Synoptic tradition contains the representation of the bread and wine as the body and blood of Jesus and the sacrificial nature of the blood as essential elements of the eucharist. This concept is inoffensively phrased in simple language, avoiding anthropophagic overtones by its evident symbolic intention. The contrast with John's text is not difficult to see. Not only is the subject matter far wider—eternal life and 'abiding in Jesus' elaborating its redemptive role—but the feeding language has alternative connotations. Emphasis is not placed on the symbolism of the bread and wine, but rather on flesh and blood, which must be eaten by believers. The Synoptic disciples are not told that they must eat flesh, but merely that the bread *represents* Jesus' body; the connection with violence is lost. The text does not state whether or not the Synoptic disciples understand his words, but it can be assumed that they did not accord them a literal meaning as there is no indication of shock or confusion among them. Those who claim that Jn 6 is decidedly anti-Docetic in its aim view the language as being an attempt to combat Docetism by 'heavily, if somewhat crudely, underscoring the reality of the incarnation in all its offensiveness'. (Dunn, 'John VI', p. 336). The meaning of the Johannine eucharist is therefore acceptance of the scandal that the saviour is truly flesh and blood; 'to eat Jesus' flesh and drink his blood is none other than to accept his true humanity' (Brooks, 'Johannine Eucharist', p. 297). However, the meaning of John's eucharist, particularly when compared to that of the Synoptics is deeper than this. It is the acceptance of the physical suffering of the man. It is not just that the word became flesh, but that the flesh was destroyed. It is a recognition of the violence involved in the sacrifice of the Son. If the message of the Synoptic eucharist is that Jesus' life is to be remembered as that which is given for the believers, John's message is that Jesus' human form will be devoured by a hostile world.

80. Moore, 'Are There Impurities in the Living Water?', pp. 223-25. Lee notes that there are striking parallels between the feeding miracle and the discourse with the Samaritan woman (*Symbolic Narratives*, p. 144).

water on offer from Jesus. The water from Jacob's well does not merely satisfy her physical need, but also has a spiritual significance. It is not simply literal nor is it purely figurative but, like the water which will flow from Jesus' side, it is a 'literal figure' which 'overflows both containers'.[81] Furthermore, he claims, the two separate levels of meaning that have enabled Johannine irony to function throughout the narrative—the perishable and unperishable bread; being born again and reentering the womb—are collapsed by the death scene. Jesus himself dissolves the partition between heaven and earth, spirit and matter, figure and letter, manifesting as he does 'the unknowable otherness of God in finite flesh'.[82] Approaching Jesus' words in 6.53-60, the use of the concept of a 'literal figure' confronts the reader immediately with the overwhelming savagery of the image. Jesus began in v. 51 by linking an interpretative image, his flesh, with what he has been saying about the unperishable bread. But once this has been done the bread fades into the background. 'My flesh must be eaten, my blood must be drunk', he asserts again and again and again. Life for the believer and the ability to abide with Jesus will require his death (v. 56), but how brutal that death will be. Jesus speaks of two types of bread, but there is only one method of ingestion. This, then, is the way in which the unperishable bread will perish: by being devoured. The theophagic undertones to Jesus' words, with connotations of *sparagmos* are difficult to ignore and in order to explore further the 'literal figure' that Jesus has drawn, it is helpful at this point to pause and consider these issues in more detail.

Jesus and Dionysus: Seeing the sparagmos *in John 6*
To gain an insight into the literal implications of what Jesus claims must be done to his body, we need look no further than Dionysian myth. Johannine scholars who have recognised varying degrees of similarity between the figures of Dionysus and Jesus include Dodd,[83]

81. Moore, 'Are There Impurities in the Living Water?', p. 224.
82. Moore, 'Are There Impurities in the Living Water?', p. 222.
83. Dodd sees clear similarities between the wedding at Cana and Dionysian legends in which wine is miraculously generated, pointing to the reference in Pausanias (*Historical Tradition*, p. 224). Pausanias notes that empty pots in sealed rooms were miraculously filled overnight, and that at the feast of Dionysus 'wine flows of its own accord from the sanctuary' (Pausanias 6.26.1-2).

Bultmann,[84] Hengel[85] and Stibbe.[86] Stibbe identifies eleven parallels between the protagonists of John's Gospel and the *Bacchae* of Euripides. While he stresses that it cannot be claimed that John consciously incorporated aspects of the *Bacchae* into his Gospel, it is likely that he unconsciously chose the *mythos* of tragedy, rendering echoes between Dionysus and Jesus inevitable.[87] Dodd makes a similar statement:

> The time was not yet when apologists could safely draw parallels between Christ and the figures of pagan mythology. But folk-tales often forget their origins, and circulate in disguise, and certainly folk-tale motives, not native to Christianity, or even Judaism, are to be found in the Gospels.[88]

The principal point of contact between Dionysian myth and the words of Jesus in John 6 is the image of the *sparagmos*—the tearing apart and eating of the flesh of the sacrificial victim. Dionysiac ritual involved the pursuit of the god, who would appear to his followers in his animal form (principally a bull, lion, fawn or serpent) at the *oreibasia*. Once caught, the animal would be torn to pieces, its raw flesh eaten and its blood drunk in order to signify an immediate partaking of 'life in its essence as embodied by the god'.[89] Obvious similarities can be discerned with Jesus' identification of the benefits to be had from eating his

84. Like Dodd, Bultmann sees Jn 2 as 'a typical motif of the Dionysus legend' (*Gospel of John*, pp. 118-19).

85. Hengel notes the comparisons made between Jesus and Dionysus by Celsus in Origen's *Contra Celsum* 2.34 (*Johannine Question*, pp. 70, 191 n. 86).

86. Stibbe explores the links between the two figures in his detailed analysis of Jn 18–19 as tragic genre (*John as Storyteller*, pp. 129-47).

87. Stibbe, *John as Storyteller*, p. 134-35, 137.

88. Dodd, *Historical Tradition*, p. 225. R.T. Fortna wishes to go further than this, claiming that Dionysiac legend is present in the source: 'Just like Dionysus, Jesus shows who he is, what he can accomplish, and in that way reveals a kind of divinity' (*The Fourth Gospel and its Predecessor* [Edinburgh: T. & T. Clark, 1989], p. 52). Note also the claim of the non-Johannine scholar, L.H. Martin: 'The Dionysiac wine ritual was incorporated into Christian imagery by the Gospel of John' (*The Hellenistic Religions: An Introduction* [Oxford: Oxford University Press, 1987], p. 95). For further discussion of the perceived dependence of Christian myth on Dionysiac legend see M. Detienne (*Dionysos Slain* [trans. M. Muellner and L. Muellner; Baltimore: The Johns Hopkins University Press, 1977], pp. 68-69).

89. Martin, *Hellenistic Religions*, pp. 94. Description of the ritual can be found in the work of H.J. Rose, who notes that human victims were also sacrificed (*A Handbook of Greek Mythology: Including its Extension to Rome* [London: Methuen, 6th edn, 1972], p. 154). Lest this all seems far removed from twentieth-century civilized

flesh—abiding in him and eternal life.[90] Description of the ritual can be found in *The Bacchae*, where it is the antagonist, Pentheus, rather than Dionysus, who is dismembered by the celebrants, principal among them being his mother Agaue.[91] Euripides provides a graphic rendition of the scene:

> Grasping his left arm below the elbow
> and setting her foot against the unhappy man's ribs,
> she tore his shoulder out, not by her normal strength,
> but the god gave a special ease to her hands.
> Ino was wrecking the other side of him,
> breaking his flesh, and Autonoe and the whole mob
> of bacchants laid hold of him; all gave voice at once—
> he moaning with what breath was left in him,
> they screaming in triumph. One was carrying a forearm,
> another a foot with a boot still on: his ribs
> were being laid bare by the tearing; and each of the women
> with hands all bloody, was playing with Pentheus' flesh.[92]

The scene is a horrifying one, conveying effectively the bloody brutality of Pentheus's fate. Bearing it in mind when interpreting the exhortation of Jesus 'to eat his flesh and drink his blood' prevents the reader from diluting the image he has evoked. Having been forced to flee from a threatening, if enthusiastic, crowd the previous day (v. 15), Jesus now articulates the meaning of his death using the language of *sparagmos*. The 'literal figure' begins to appear less contrived.

behaviour, one only has to read Donna Tartt's chillingly realistic account of the attempt of a group of Vermont students to recreate a Dionysiac ritual in her first novel *The Secret History*. The allusions to The *Bacchae* are unmissable. Compare Euripides' description of the fate of Pentheus with the following: 'Charles...has a memory of struggling with something, pulling as hard as he could, and all of a sudden becoming aware that what he was pulling at was a man's arm, with his foot braced in the armpit' (*The Secret History* [London: Penguin Books, 1992], p. 199, see also pp. 190-200, 422-23).

90. Interestingly, Northrop Frye specifically terms the *sparagmos* 'Eucharist symbolism' (*Anatomy of Criticism: Four Essays* [London: Penguin, rev. edn, 1990 (1957)], p. 192).

91. Legend has it that Dionysus himself suffered a similar fate, being torn to pieces by Thracian women (Martin, *Hellenistic Religions*, p. 93). See also Detienne, who provides the somewhat gruesome details of the boiling and roasting of his flesh (*Dionysos Slain*, pp. 68).

92. G.S. Kirk, *The Bacchae of Euripides: Translated with an Introduction and Commentary* (Cambridge: Cambridge University Press, 1979), pp. 118-9.

That it has played some part in the understanding of the death of Jesus is evidenced by the contents of *Christus Patiens*, a poem about the passion composed in the twelfth century CE. The poem is believed to incorporate a section of text from The *Bacchae* which is now lost:

> Come old man, the head of the thrice-wretched one
> let us fit on correctly, and reconstruct the whole
> body as harmoniously as we may.
> O dearest face, O youthful cheeks,
> behold, with this covering I hide your head;
> and the bloodstained and furrowed
> limbs...   *Christus Patiens* 1466[93]

Twelfth-century Christianity, it would seem, did not balk at the extreme violence associated with the death of Jesus, importing the language of Euripides to assist in conveying the horror of the crucifixion.[94] Twentieth-century scholarship, as the reaction of Raymond Brown above has indicated, has generally done just that: balked. It is clear that, laid bare, John's text is as raw as Euripides'. The language used by the character of Jesus permits us to view his 'death-consciousness' in terms as savage as the *sparagmos*. That Jesus has coupled the promise of eternal life with this figure of death, rendering it redemptive, does not detract from the brutality of the image evoked. The end result is that the ambiguities that cohabit in the figure of Dionysus—'victim and god of mysteries'[95]—become visible in the Johannine Jesus.

93. Quotation and explanation from Kirk, *The Bacchae*, p. 131.

94. For further examples of the concept of *sparagmos* in early church worship see O.B. Hardison, *Christian Rite and Christian Drama in the Middle Ages: Essays in the Origin and Early History of Modern Drama* (Baltimore: The Johns Hopkins University Press, 1965). Hardison discusses the early history of medieval drama. Referring in particular to the Lenten Agon (Good Friday), he comments: 'The reading of the Passion of John... is one of the high points in the Easter drama. In it Christ emerges as the supreme instance of the Divine Victim, the "lamb led to the slaughter" of the original Passover. The Agon of the preceding weeks leads with ritual inevitability to abuse, defilement, torture, and destruction, the Christian embodiment of the *sparagmos* of pagan religion' (p. 130). See also Jan Kott: 'In *Exsultet*, perhaps the most dramatic Latin church hymn of the seventh and eighth centuries, still sung during Matins, Christ the Lamb, *sparagmos* and *omophagia*, appear with striking clarity' (*Eating of the Gods*, p. 210).

95. Detienne, *Dionysos Slain*, Preface, p. x.

In the light of the above, the response of the disciples, 'this is a hard saying; who can listen to it' (6.60), appears something of an understatement.[96] The implication is that those who have no stomach for Jesus' words can be identified with those not 'drawn by the Father' (v. 44). That this time the complaint is placed in the mouths of the disciples (μαθητής)[97] rather than the Jews (v. 52), emphasizes its validity. The offence has shifted up another gear.

5. *Jesus Repels his Listeners (6.61-66)*

The final pericope sees Jesus responding to the 'murmuring' disciples.[98] He has no reassurance to offer but only the challenge of further offence with a harder saying: 'Do you take offense at this? Then what if you were to see the Son of Man ascending where he was before?'; (v. 61b-62). There is more than a hint of scorn here.[99] The second question is incomplete, but the sense is clear; 'You don't like that? Well, try *this* for size...?'[100] Far from toning down his teaching to make it more palatable, Jesus confronts them with the greater scandal of the crucifixion, and death surfaces once more. Jesus has no patience with those whose sensibilities are offended by his words. Again we see his suspicion regarding the motives of those around him—he knows that they do not truly believe him.[101] Jesus is not interested in those who do not form part of the elect. They *cannot* believe because they have not been drawn by the Father. If the aim of his shocking discourse was the deliberate

96. Σκληρός ἐστιν ὁ λόγος οὗτος· τίς δύναται αὐτοῦ ἀκούειν. The αὐτοῦ could refer to λόγος or to Jesus. Barrett supports the latter, since ἀκούειν with a genitive has a personal subject more often than not in John, rendering it 'Who can listen to him?' (*Gospel According to St John*, pp. 302-303).

97. Seen by Jeffrey Trumbower as evidence that μαθητής does not always have a positive connotation in John (*Born from Above*, p. 85).

98. Barrett sees supernatural knowledge as the means by which Jesus perceives their discomfort, but simple observation of the hostile atmosphere that had developed was probably sufficient (*Gospel According to St John*, p. 303).

99. Davies sees it as a taunt (*Rhetoric and Reference*, p. 191).

100. As Bultmann suggests, *Gospel of John*, p. 445. Menken suggests an alternative understanding to the anacoluthon, which removes the scornful element. He sees the suppressed words following 'then what if you see...?' as being '...will you then accept my words?' This almost sees despair in the words of a man who wonders what he must provide as proof to his followers ('John 6.51c-58', p. 25).

101. Goulder suggests that this is because he has 'the all-piercing eyes of the καρδιογνώστης God' ('Nicodemus', p. 163). Alternatively, it could be claimed that he was simply an good judge of character.

'downsizing' of his troupe of followers, weeding out those who are not part of the Father's elect, Jesus has succeeded. The response to his final words is desertion by many disciples who turn away (ἀπῆλθον) from him, leaving only the core.

6. *Epilogue (6.67-71)*

The desertion of so many 'disciples' prompts Jesus to seek reassurance himself. His question, 'do you also wish to go away?' (μὴ καὶ ὑμεῖς θέλετε ὑπάγειν, v. 67), reveals a touch of anxiety. Barrett describes it as a 'tentative', 'hesitating' suggestion,[102] and it seems reasonable to propound that the rejection of so many has shaken his confidence in the commitment of the few who remain. Peter's subsequent confession of faith in Jesus as 'the Holy One of God' elicits a response that offers no clearer indication of self-assurance. This is commonly held to be a climactic statement of faith.[103] However, at this point in the narrative, Jesus appears little concerned with acclamations of glory. He does not confirm or deny the status accorded him by Peter; in fact, it passes without comment. His concerns are rejection and, beyond that, death. The twelve chosen by Jesus remain with him, yet he identifies one of these as 'a devil' (v. 70). The narrator elucidates, naming Judas as the culprit, but the words employed by Jesus—'did I not choose you?'—hint at the underlying ambiguity in their relationship. Their interdependence is implicit: Judas will betray, but Jesus has chosen. The discourse, with its violent metaphor of physical immolation, concludes on this ominous note, having identified the agent selected to initiate it.

Accusations in the Temple (7.1–8.59)

By the end of John 6, Jesus has managed to alienate all but twelve of his disciples, speaking in graphic and horrifying terms about the violence he anticipates. The next two chapters see him abandoning the 'literal figure' to speak unambiguously and publicly about his death. John 7 and 8 have already been discussed in some detail in Chapter 5, focusing on the chaotic and physically threatening action they contain. The following section will look briefly at events from Jesus' perspective. The two discourses that it contains[104] are punctuated with phrases by Jesus that

---

102. Barrett, *Gospel According to St John*, p. 306.
103. Morris, *Gospel According to John*, p. 388; Lightfoot, *St John's Gospel*, p. 170.
104. The fifth (7.14-19) and sixth (8.12-59).

indicate the effect that the hostility of the community has on his self-understanding. The tenets of Jesus' character identified in John 1–5 will be revisited. The first three—death, rejection and suspicion—have become somewhat interlinked, but it is possible to assess whether there has been further development in these areas.

1. *He Displays a Deep Consciousness of his own Death*

The section begins by stating that Jesus would not travel in Judea because the Jews sought to kill him (7.1). The conclusion that can be drawn from this is that he is avoiding confrontation and is aware of the danger that he is in. The words οὐ γὰρ ἤθελεν can be translated 'he dared not',[105] giving the impression that there is a potential element of fear in his decision. This is further supported by Jesus' subsequent behaviour. His response to his brothers' suggestion that he travel to the dangerous region of Judea is a forceful 'No'. The reason that he gives is linked with his death (ὁ καιρός)[106] and the hatred of the world.

Throughout the course of the discourses in John 7–8, the subject of Jesus' death continually rises to the surface. No longer does he speak in metaphors or veiled terminology. The first discourse is punctuated with overt accusations made to his audience, indicating that the threat of death is uppermost in his mind. He commences with an unprovoked accusation to the crowd (7.19), which is repeated in 8.37, 40. Having escaped one attempted arrest, he remarks to the Jews: 'I shall be with you a little longer, and then I go to him who sent me' (7.33); again a reference to his death although the Jews are confused as to the meaning of his words. His departure is mentioned again in 8.21 where there is a dispute about where Jesus will go and whether his words imply suicide. Jesus recognizes that time is short and his fate is predetermined. He uses the theological signifier ὑψοῦν in 8.28 to indicate further the method which will be used for his disposel. That his death is at the forefront of his mind during these discourses cannot seriously be disputed. Moreover, violent death is implied by the allusion to the crucifixion and the implication that the Jews too are murderers, like their father (ἀνθρωποκτόνος, 8.44).

---

105. Brown, *Gospel According to John*, I, p. 306.

106. Barrett notes that this is not distinguishable from the more common ὥρα, containing a reference to death (*Gospel According to St John*, p. 312). See also Miranda, *Being and the Messiah*, p. 103.

2. *He Believes that he is Being Rejected and Misunderstood*

The beginning of John 7 reveals a development in Jesus' perception of the extent to which he is rejected. The reader already knows that he will be an outcast from his community (1.11, 3.32, 4.43) and has heard him say that he is disbelieved and will be betrayed (6.36, 71). But the declaration by Jesus that he perceives himself to be universally hated takes a step further, being the strongest statement of opposition yet— 'the whole world is against me' (οὐ δύναται ὁ κόσμος μισεῖν ὑμᾶς, ἐμὲ δὲ μισεῖ, 7.7). Suspicion and opposition are high on the agenda.

Misunderstanding plays a large part in both discourses. It is centred on the meaning of Jesus' accusations as well as his identity and origin. For the most part, Jesus and the crowd operate on different levels of meaning. The crowd do not understand that they are the threat he is referring to. They think they know who Jesus is (7.27, 41), but of course they cannot perceive his true identity. Their accusations that he is a Samaritan and has a demon are a further evidence of their inability to comprehend Jesus' words—they are so alien the crowd conclude there must be something wrong with the man who utters them. Jesus is clear that misunderstanding represents rejection on their part (8.24, 37b). The reason his words have no meaning to them is because they are not among those drawn by his Father, but have another father: 'why do you not understand what I say?...You are of your father the devil' (8.43-44).

3. *He Is Suspicious of the Motives of Others*

That Jesus is suspicious of the motives of the crowd is blatantly obvious from the beginning of the fifth discourse. In the middle of the feast Jesus begins to teach an audience who are relatively positive about his message (indicated by ἐθαύμαζον). It soon becomes evident, however, that his intention is not to win back the supporters he lost after the discourse on the feeding miracle. His accuses them in a sudden outburst: 'why do you seek to kill me?' (τί με ζητεῖτε ἀποκτεῖναι, 7.19). The crowd are amazed and treat him as if he were mad, accusing him of being possessed: '*Who* is trying to kill you?' From their perspective he is not in any danger—at least not yet. Jesus, however, not trusting himself to them, pursues the subject. He is convinced that the world hates him and this crowd belong to the world, despite their protestations of innocence. He challenges the people, believing they are angry (χολᾶτε, 7.23) and have made a judgment on him (κρίνετε, 7.24). Their opposition and the danger the crowd pose is clear in *his* mind, as shown by his words, even if it is not in theirs.

In the sixth discourse, Jesus displays a similar scepticism towards his listeners. In the first half of the pericope Jesus gains 'believers' (8.30-31). He spends the second half provoking them with further accusations that they want to kill him, disbelieving their faith in him and questioning the reason for their opposition. Despite the fact that Jesus appears, at this point in the narrative, to have generated interested bystanders who do not present an obvious threat to him, he still behaves as if they were hostile and twice accuses them of wanting to kill him (vv. 37, 39). Jesus' suspicion of the crowd manifests itself in a goading that is quite out-rageous, and most definitely dangerous.[107] He confronts them directly, calling them children of the devil, whose true father is not Abraham, but a murderer. By implication they are murderers too and he is their victim. That the devil is a murderer 'from the begining' (ἀπ᾽ ἀρχῆς, 8.44), alludes not simply to the Genesis accounts of Adam losing his immortality,[108] or Cain's slaughter of Abel,[109] but additionally to the Word made flesh, who was also ἐν ἀρχῇ (Jn 1.1).[110] Jesus understands the threat to be continual and, as Trumbower notes, throughout the dialogue with the Jews in John 7–8, Jesus speaks of the Jews' response to him 'as if everything were a foregone conclusion'.[111] The deceitful nature of the devil and his children is also stressed. It is because Jesus speaks the truth that the deceitful world, the antithesis of truth, cannot abide him. He despairs of their rejection, exclaiming with frustration:

---

107. Von Hentig's comment seems somewhat appropriate when analysing Jesus' behaviour in John 7–8: 'In a certain sense the animals which devour and those that are devoured complement each other. Although it looks one-sided as far as the final outcome goes, it is not a totally unilateral form of relationships. They work upon each other profoundly and continually, even before the moment of disaster' (*The Criminal and his Victim*, p. 385). This is a courtship of death that requires complicity on the part of the victim.

108. Barrett, *Gospel According to St John*, p. 349; Hoskyns, *Fourth Gospel*, p. 343.

109. Brown, *Gospel According to John*, I, p. 359.

110. Girard comments that here a 'triple correspondence' is set up between Satan, the original homicide, and the lie. To be a son of Satan is to inherit the lie; the lie that covers the homicide. This lie is a double homicide since its consequence is always a new homicide to cover up the old one. To be a son of Satan is the same thing as being the son of those who have killed their prophets since the foundation of the world (*Things Hidden since the Foundation of the World*, p. 161).

111. Trumbower, *Born from Above*, p. 87.

'which of you convicts me...*why* do you not believe me?', but the question is a rhetorical one. His mistrust of these 'believers' is based on his perception of their origin; the reason they do not hear the words of God is that they are not of God (8.47). They are fundamentally and irreconcilably opposed to him. When the discourse erupts into physical violence, Jesus is not surprised as this is in accordance with their nature. The reader should note, however, that it was Jesus who put the idea of murder in their heads to start with (7.19; 8.37, 40).

4. *He Has Strong Emotions*
We do not see evidence of Jesus' emotions provoking him to physical violence in this section, but there is an indication that his emotions are strong. The continual questioning of the Jews regarding their rejection of him betrays his frustration with them. He accuses them of being angry with him, yet he is angry with them too. The dispute on Jesus' origin and identity in the sixth discourse elicits the exclamation 'why on earth am I still speaking to you at all?'[112] (v. 25), a phrase that Robinson claims exhibits 'scarcely-suppressed exasperation', revealing emotional strain.[113]

5. *He Is Prepared to Flout Religious Conventions*
Jesus' challenge to religious conventions in this section is primarily to the truths the Jews held to be important—the traditions of Moses (Jn 7.22-23) and Abrahamic ancestry (Jn 8.33-42). In addition, he justifies his sabbath healing (Jn 7.23). Bearing in mind the language and imagery that has been used in John 6, by this stage of Jesus' ministry there is little additional left for him to challenge.

The prominence of rejection and death as overt themes in John 7–8 is evident. Jesus continues to display a deep consciousness of them, resulting in suspicion of those who come to listen to him at the feast. Far from being calm and collected, Jesus behaves in a manner that

112. Bultmann's translation (*Gospel of John*, p. 353). The verse is frequently trans-lated as the more obscure: 'even what I have told you from the beginning' (Brown, *Gospel According to John*, I, p. 347). However, the alternative is quite possible and was supported by the Greek Fathers (Chrysostom and Cyril). Sanders and Mastin also refer to it as 'an expression of hopelessness' (*Gospel According to St John*, p. 224). Westcott simply sees a 'sad exclamation' (*Gospel According to St John*, p. 142).

113. J.A.T. Robinson, *The Priority of John* (ed. J.F. Coakley; London: SCM Press, 1985), pp. 355-56.

resulting in suspicion of those who come to listen to him at the feast. Far from being calm and collected, Jesus behaves in a manner that indicates he is threatened, and this is verbalized several times. He is provocative and offensive, his behaviour on occasion appearing victimal.

The Mauling of the Shepherd (10.1-18)

The final public discourse of the Gospel, the parable of the good shepherd (10.1-18), marks a watershed in Jesus' understanding of his own death. John 9 has concerned itself with the religious authorities' official rejection and 'casting out'[114] of Jesus and his followers, but death now resurfaces and further detail about how Jesus perceives it is provided. The evangelist informs us that Jesus uses a παροιμία[115] to speak to his listeners, commonly rendered a 'figure of speech'. As with John 6, this can be seen as a *literal figure* that uses a metaphorical framework to convey a direct message about Jesus' death.[116] BAGD defines παροιμία in Johannine usage as a 'dark saying', which, as will be shown, is particularly appropriate.[117]

The section can be divided into three parts:

1. 10.1-6   The comparison between the shepherd who knows his sheep and the thief from whom they flee.
2. 10.7-10   The comparison between the 'door' that brings life and those that came before it who steal and kill.
3. 10.11-18 The comparison between the good shepherd who faces the wolf and the hireling who flees.

It is the third section that is really of importance to this study; how-

---

114. For the significance of ἀποσυνάγωγος, see Martyn, *History and Theology in the Fourth Gospel*.

115. The παροιμία is frequently seen to be the Johannine version of the Synoptic parables. For details see R. Kysar, 'Johannine Metaphor—Meaning and Function: A Literary Case Study of John 10.1-8', *Semeia* 53 (1991), pp. 81-111. See also J. Painter, 'Tradition, History and Interpretation in John 10', in J. Beutler and R. Fortna (eds.), *The Shepherd Discourse of John 10 and its Context: Studies by Members of the Johannine Writings Seminar* (Cambridge: Cambridge University Press, 1991), pp. 53-74 (55).

116. Kysar sees the contents of this figure as 'no mere similes or teaching vehicles. They are rather 'true metaphors' with poetic power to initiate a new kind of experience' ('Johannine Metaphor', p. 99).

117. BAGD, p. 629.

discussed.[118] Additionally, it should be stressed that the focus here is on Jesus' understanding of his role and fate and not on pinpointing with great precision the identity of each symbolic player in the picture he creates.[119]

1. *The Shepherd and the Thief (10.1-6)*

In vv. 1-6 Jesus introduces the thief/robber, the shepherd, the gate-keeper and the sheep. It becomes evident that the shepherd represents Jesus, and the sheep are believers who 'hear his voice' (v. 3). The emphasis of this παροιμία is on the relationship between the shepherd and his sheep and the inability of the intruder to usurp the shepherd's role. The stranger is not able to lead the sheep; in fact, they flee from him because they do not recognize his voice. This indicates that the threat to the sheep in these verses is of being misled by the false words of impostors. The sheep are in danger here, but the danger is not strictly death; rather deception. The shepherd is not in danger; his role is to know and be known by his sheep and subsequently to lead them the correct way.

2. *The Door and the Thief (10.7-10)*

The Jews[120] cannot comprehend the meaning of Jesus' words, so in vv. 7-10 he elaborates, using a slightly different figure. This time he is the door of the sheep (ἡ θύρα τῶν προβάτων, v.7). Instead of being the shepherd, who legitimately enters by the door, he becomes the entrance itself. The thieves and robbers feature again as enemies of the sheep in this part of the discourse and the threat remains that of deception—hence the assertion that the sheep did not heed (οὐκ ἤκουσαν) them. Jesus repeats his claim to be the door in v. 9 and gives it soteriological significance: entering 'through him' leads to salvation and 'pasture', the means of sustenance for the sheep. Verse 10 marks a

---

118. Numerous attempts have been made by commentators to rearrange the contents of this chapter to facilitate interpretation and to identify what the original sayings were and how they have been joined together. These questions will not be tackled, but see the commentaries of Bultmann and Bernard for discussion. Dodd's quote on John 10 is now infamous: 'the wreckage of two parables fused into one' (*Historical Tradition*, p. 383).

119. For an attempt to do this see G.S. Sloyan, *John* (Interpretation; Atlanta: John Knox Press, 1988), pp. 130-32.

120. Presumably, although they are not specifically mentioned until v. 19.

turning point in the discourse. Previously the thieves and robbers have threatened to mislead and steal the sheep, but now, with the introduction of the subject of salvation, the issue of death is also raised. Jesus claims, 'the thief comes only to steal and kill and destroy'. The discourse takes an ominous turn as the sheep are at risk of slaughter (v. 10). Jesus' role is diametrically opposed to that of the thief: he promises abundant life, while the thief threatens violent death. However, the provision of life by Jesus will necessitate his own slaughter and the third section of the discourse shifts in emphasis from the risk to the sheep, to the risk to the shepherd.

3. *The Shepherd and the Hireling (10.11-18)*

Verses 11-18 contain two sections on the good shepherd and his relation to the sheep. Both concern aspects of Jesus' death. The first is reminiscent of the bread of life discourse in John 6 and the second reveals a development in Jesus' understanding of what awaits him. Jesus' identification of himself as 'the good shepherd' (ὁ ποιμὴν ὁ καλός), begins both sections and is then qualified by the function he performs. In vv. 11-13 the subject is sacrificial death. Jesus explains that the test of a true shepherd is in 'laying down his life' (τὴν ψυχὴν αὐτοῦ τίθησιν ὑπὲρ τῶν προβάτων). This phrase is highly significant in the rest of the passage, occurring five times. In v. 11 the concept of immolation is introduced, which is then expanded in vv. 17-18. Jesus brings two new characters onto the scene in v. 12; ὁ μισθωτός (the hireling), who serves to highlight the actions of the good shepherd and τὸν λύκον (the wolf), who is the agent of death. He describes the actions of the hireling in detail, making it evident what the consequences are for the good shepherd. The hireling sees the wolf, abandons the sheep and flees. The wolf snatches them and scatters them in a chaotic scene of brutal carnage. As their guardian, Jesus cares for and will not desert the sheep, to the point of suffering mutilation on their behalf. The English rendition 'lay down his life' is rather euphemistic, concealing the real horror of the picture Jesus has graphically painted. It is the shepherd who is snatched (ἁρπάζω)[121] by the wolf in place of the sheep and the image he creates is that of a man literally being torn to pieces by a savage beast.

---

121. A violent term, used of wild animals dragging away their prey. An example given in BAGD is in Gen. 37.33 where, on seeing Joseph's coat, Jacob fears that he has been torn apart by a wild beast. BAGD also notes that the adjective ἅρπαξ means '*rapacious, ravenous* of wolves' (p. 109, emphasis original).

That Jesus uses such forcefully violent metaphors to speak of himself as a human victim affords the reader an insight into his perception of his death. The *sparagmos* imagery of John 6 is evoked, where again his flesh and blood are devoured. The figure of the good shepherd is commonly perceived to be a comforting pastoral one. Barnabas Lindars, for example, claims that it 'makes an immediate appeal to the imagination', providing 'one of the most *endearing* aspects of the Johannine portrait of Jesus'.[122] However, to consider the picture from the point of view of the victim gives rise to a different interpretation. The bloody destiny of a man standing between a wolf and a flock of sheep hardly makes for an endearing scene. That Jesus' words depict an episode which is, in the final analysis, extremely brutal and gory is a fact unrecognized by all of the major commentaries.[123] While the concept of the good shepherd has an initially protective, bucolic connotation, the death that Jesus envisages the shepherd suffering conveys the violence that he anticipates.[124] The meaning he gives to 'laying down his life' (τὴν ψυχήν μου τίθημι) is the mutilation of his own body.

Verses 14-18 further reveal Jesus' attitude towards his death, expressed theologically rather than metaphorically. He begins by restating his identity as ὁ ποιμὴν ὁ καλός, proceeding to describe the closeness of the relationship between himself, his sheep and the Father. It is this that causes him to sacrifice himself. His care for the sheep costs him his life and his obedience to the Father also demands it, as this is the charge (τὴν ἐντολήν) he has received. Jesus' words about his death in this pericope are significantly different from his previous utterances. They are no longer questioning or accusatory, but indicate an acceptance of what must befall him. The key phrases in this section reveal that his recognition of the voluntary nature of his sacrifice, and the power this gives him are the significant factors. The expression used by Jesus, τίθημι τὴν

122. Lindars, *Gospel of John*, p. 352, emphasis added.

123. Those consulted being Bultmann, Barrett, Brown, Lindars, Beasley-Murray, Schnackenburg, Sanders, Hoskyns, Bernard, Sloyan, Stibbe and Westcott.

124. Robert Kysar sees the images in John 10 as 'shocking', but only in the sense that 'the series of images shares the shock of true metaphorical language'. In other words, form rather than content is the vehicle of shock—'the poetic metaphor startles the imagination by the comparison it offers and thereby opens up a new and unanticipated possibility of truth' ('Johannine Metaphor', p. 98).

ψυχήν, is a rare one in Greek and probably represents the Hebrew מסר
נפשו, meaning 'to hand over one's life'.[125] This encapsulates both the
active and passive nature of Jesus' death. It is active in the sense that he
voluntarily lays it down, but passive in the sense that he has no choice
but to lay it down, and in doing so he becomes the victim of the violence of others.

Verses 17-18 are structured in a way that highlights Jesus' autonomy,
within the framework of his obedience to the Father:

> *the love of the Father*
> > *the laying down and taking up*
> > > *the voluntary nature of Jesus' action*
> > *the laying down and taking up*
> *the charge from the Father*

The significant feature of v. 18 is that twice he states that he has control
over his circumstances: 'No one takes it from me, but I lay it down *of
my own accord*. I have *power* (ἐξουσίαν) to lay it down, and I have *power*
(ἐξουσίαν) to take it again'. His assertions of power are tempered by
the inevitability of his destiny. They do not mean that he can avoid
death, nor that he can control his circumstances. He has no power to
alter his fate and escape the suffering that awaits him. He *will* die—this
has already been determined. Theologically, it is the reason that the
Word became flesh. Practically, the Jews are already determined to kill
him. There is no possible alternative ending to the Gospel. Hence, the
ἐξουσίαν that Jesus is referring to is not an ability to change his circumstances—the die is already cast. The only 'power' that he possesses is the
ability to become powerless, and this is expressed in the voluntary nature of his sacrifice. He does this by consciously 'laying down' his life,
rather than having it taken from him. That he uses authoritative terms
to stress his passivity reveals the tension between the voluntary and
involuntary nature of his role as the Lamb of God. He uses forceful
phrases to qualify his renouncement of power. The allegory of the
shepherd and his sheep, threatened by the wolf, contextualizes and aids
in the interpretation of his words. When faced with danger, the hireling
is able to flee, but the shepherd has no choice but to remain with the
sheep, because his very nature is as the *good* shepherd. He has a relationship with the sheep and it is his duty to protect them—if he did not

---

125. Hoskyns, *Fourth Gospel*, p. 376; Schnackenburg, *Gospel According to St John*,
II, p. 296 n. 83. Both refer to Str-B, II, p. 537.

he would not be the good shepherd. He has no option but to accept the situation—to choose vulnerability in the face of a vicious enemy, to become a victim.

Facing the Tomb (11.1-54)

Following the exposition of his death in John 10, Jesus does not speak of it again in detail until the very end of his public ministry. However, there is a significant event in this next section that merits discussion as it reveals a great deal about his feelings as he approaches the end.

John 11 narrates the raising of Lazarus from the dead—the final public 'sign' that marks the climax of all Jesus' miracles performed before his death.[126] For my purposes, the passage can be divided up as follows.[127]

1. 11.1-4   request for the miracle
2. 11.5-14   contextualizing the miracle: physical context
3. 11.17-27 contextualizing the miracle: theological context
4. 11.28-38 contextualizing the miracle: emotional context
5. 11.39-44 execution of the miracle
6. 11.45-53 ramifications of the miracle

It is the emotional context that is of interest here, although a few points should be noted about the first three stages. Jesus appears to be in control of the situation in vv. 1-16, having a clear idea of what he will do. He waits until Lazarus is dead, explaining his actions to his disciples, first metaphorically and then, when they fail to grasp his meaning, literally. An indication is given that the miracle to be performed is closely linked to Jesus' death by the hint in v. 4: the illness is not unto death (πρὸς θάνατον), at least not for Lazarus, but it is for the glory of God: ἵνα δοξασθῇ ὁ υἱὸς τοῦ θεοῦ δι' αὐτῆς. The glorification of the Son refers forward to the crucifixion, hence Jesus himself acknowledges the role

126. Some would see John 21 as a miracle carried out after the resurrection. Stibbe notes that it is the seventh miraculous sign and since seven is a number connoting perfection in Judaism it can be seen as the climactic one ('A Tomb with a View: John 11.1-44 in Narrative-Critical Perspective', *NTS* 40 [1994], pp. 38-54 [39]).

127. For alternative suggestions on structure see Lee, who believes that in both literary and theological terms the narrative should include the anointing and the plot to kill Lazarus and hence ends at 12.11 (*Symbolic Narratives*, pp. 191).

this miracle will have in causing his death. The reader is reminded of the physical danger that travelling to Bethany will pose for Jesus (vv. 8, 16), with Thomas evidently believing that death was imminent for all of them. After delaying two days, Jesus travels to Bethany and is met by Martha.[128] Their subsequent discussion results in her climactic expression of faith: 'I believe that you are the Christ, the Son of God, he who is coming into the world' (v. 27).[129] It is not until he encounters Mary and the other mourners that Jesus' composure wavers and he displays strong emotions.

Mary unintentionally leads the Jews that Martha has been attempting to protect Jesus from, straight to where he is. He is immediately exposed and becomes vulnerable. However, the responses of the Jews and of Jesus are not what the reader might expect. Jesus is confronted with a grieving party. Both Mary and the Jews are weeping (κλαίω) and Mary reproaches Jesus for failing to act in time to save Lazarus (v. 32). The atmosphere alters from one in which there is a calm grief, through which it has been possible to elicit a response of faith, to one of chaotic and uncontrollable grief. Extreme emotions and actions are demonstrated, with Mary throwing herself at Jesus' feet. Jesus' response also shows great strength of feeling:

Jesus...was deeply moved in Spirit and troubled (ἐνεβριμήσατο τῷ πνεύματι καὶ ἐτάραξεν ἑαυτὸν, v. 33)
Jesus wept (ἐδάκρυσεν ὁ Ἰησοῦς, v. 35)
Jesus...deeply moved again (πάλιν ἐμβριμώμενος ἐν ἑαυτῷ, v. 38)

128. That Martha meets him alone has been seen to emphasize the risks of appearing in public for Jesus: 'His danger was fresh in her mind; the rage of His enemies... might break out again more violently when they heard of his arrival' (J. Calvin, *The Gospel According to St John* [ed. D.W. and T.F. Torrance; trans. T.H.L. Parker; 2 vols.; Calvin's Commentaries; Edinburgh: Oliver & Boyd, 1959, 1961], II, p. 7). Wilhelm Wuellner notes that the opening setting of the pericope is 'fraught with tragedy because it forces Jesus and his partners out of hiding back into the public and hostile arena' ('Putting Life Back into the Lazarus Story and its Reading: The Narrative Rhetoric of John 11 as the Narration of Faith', *Semeia* 53 [1991], pp. 113-32 [116]).

129. σὺ εἶ ὁ χριστὸς ὁ υἱὸς τοῦ θεοῦ ὁ εἰς τὸν κόσμον ἐρχόμενος. A.Y. Collins claims that Martha's confession of Jesus as the Christ is 'at least as prominent and climactic as Peter's confession in chapter 6' ('New Testament Perspectives: The Gospel of John', *JSOT* 22 (1982), pp. 47-53 [53]).

Without doubt, the verb ἐμβριμάομαι is one of anger and indignation.[130] It occurs in Dan. 11.30, Lam. 2.6, Mk 1.43 and Mt. 9.30 with the sense of 'shaking with anger'. The term ταράσσω similarly has negative import. In John it always contains an element of fear,[131] and could be interpreted 'he was in turmoil'.[132] The reason why the grief of Mary and the Jews would provoke the fury of Jesus has been a source of speculation for commentators. Some suggest that it is because he is angered by the faithlessness of the Jews,[133] or because he found himself 'face to face with the realm of Satan'.[134] That he is simply expressing grief in sympathy with the mourners[135] is insufficient to explain his anger. The combination of the two terms used indicates a powerful expression of wrath, with Carson noting: 'it is lexically inexcusable to reduce this emotional upset to the effects of empathy, grief, pain or the like'.[136] Barrett's explanation is the most plausible: Jesus perceives that

130. BAGD, p. 254. Carson notes that in extra-biblical Greek, it can refer to the snorting of horses. In humans it suggests 'anger, outrage or emotional indignation' (*Gospel According to John*, p. 415).

131. Barrett states it means a 'fearful perturbation' (*Gospel According to St John*, p. 399). BAGD gives the following meaning: 'mental, spiritual agitation…be troubled, frightened, terrified' (p. 805). The use of ταράσσω in the Synoptics also indicates fear. See Mt. 2.3 (Herod); Lk. 1.12 (Zacharias); Mt. 14.26, Mk 6.50 (disciples at Jesus walking on water) and Lk. 24.38 (disciples at the appearance of Jesus).

132. Miranda, *Being and the Messiah*, p. 106. Even Stibbe, who claims that this emphasis of humanity in the narrator's description of Jesus is surprising, but should not obscure the divine attributes which are still present, concedes that ταράσσω denotes a 'deep emotional disturbance' ('A Tomb with a View', p. 45).

133. Bultmann, *Gospel of John*, p. 407; Hoskyns, *Fourth Gospel*, p. 404.

134. Brown, *Gospel According to John*, I, p. 435.

135. So, Lindars, *Gospel of John*, p. 399; and J.N. Sanders, *A Commentary on the Gospel According to St John* [ed. B.A. Mastin; London: A. & C. Black, 1968], p. 272. Delbert Burkett's interesting source-critical analysis of John 11 in fact places the words 'Jesus wept' immediately after 'When he saw her crying and the Jews who had come with her crying…' (v. 33b), making a causal link between the two in his 'account B'. His subsequent comment on the insertion of 'account A' material (vv. 33c-34) notes that Jesus' weeping has now been separated from its cause, leaving it 'strangely isolated' ('Two Accounts of Lazarus' Resurrection in John 11', *NovT* 36 [1994], pp. 209-32 [223, 227]).

136. Carson, *Gospel According to John*, p. 415. See also Schnackenburg who claims 'any attempt to reinterpret [ἐμβριμάομαι] in terms of internal emotional upset caused by grief, pain or sympathy is illegitimate' (*Gospel According to St John*, II, p. 335). Cullen Story, after examining the history of scholarship on this pericope, posits his own interesting theory on the cause for Jesus' anger. It reflects Jesus' regret

the sorrow of the mourners is almost forcing him to perform a sign, and furthermore, that 'this miracle will be impossible to hide (cf. vv. 28-30)...and will be the immediate occasion for his death'.[137] Jesus faces a crisis point. He has no option but to act. He *must* raise Lazarus in order that God's glory be revealed, but the request to act is in reality the request to lay down his own life. Wuellner sees this as an oxymoron— the conjunction of death and glory.[138] Like the shepherd in John 10, he must make the sacrifice required of him; there is no escape from the purpose for which he has come. Indeed, this victimal act is the stamp of his identity. He is filled with anger and fear and the pressure on him is unbearable as this miraculous act will seal his fate. Faced with the ulti- mate challenge of his mission—to lay down his life to raise up Lazarus, to sacrifice himself for his sheep—he is not a calm, exalted figure, but is utterly traumatized. It is here that the Johannine Jesus is overwhelmed by pathos, outraged in spirit and troubled. He bursts into tears[139] and is deeply distressed on facing the tomb. Again, the meaning of ἐδάκρυσεν ὁ Ἰησοῦς (v. 35) is not an expression of sympathy for the mourners,[140] or caused by the thought of Lazarus in the tomb,[141] but rather he cries for *himself*. His tears are an expression of grief over his *own* death, which

over his delay in arriving at Bethany and allowing Lazarus to die, thus causing such grief to the family. He therefore sees an element of 'self-recrimination or self-cen- sure' in Jesus' emotions ('The Mental Attitude of Jesus at Bethany: John 11.33, 38', *NTS* 37 [1991], pp. 51-66 [64]).

137. Barrett, *Gospel According to St John*, p. 399. Also see Rensberger on the link between the raising of Lazarus with the decision to execute Jesus (*Overcoming the World*, p. 75). Lee also sees the reason for Jesus' distress as linked to the passion, noting that one other place in the Gospel when ταράσσω is used is in 12.27, where Jesus recognizes the advent of the hour. She proceeds to interpret his experience in terms of the pain of childbirth: 'Jesus' distress relates symbolically to his impending passion and resurrection. His role is a maternal one in giving life to the believers through pain and suffering' (*Symbolic Narratives*, p.p. 211-12).

138. Wuellner, 'Putting Life Back into the Lazarus Story', p. 117.

139. Barrett notes the aorist of δακρύειν has this meaning (*Gospel According to St John*, p. 400; also Sanders and Mastin, *Gospel According to St John*, p. 272). See Hengel for a description of Jesus' 'very human emotions' (*Johannine Question*, p. 70).

140. So, Barrett, *Gospel According to St John*, p. 400.

141. So, Brown, *Gospel According to John*, I, p. 426. Also O' Grady: 'the human Jesus feels pain and sorrow at the death of a loved one' ('The Human Jesus in the Fourth Gospel', p. 63).

is now inevitable.[142] The Jews mistake his tears for ones of sorrow for
the dead Lazarus: 'See how he loved him!' But Jesus has no sorrow for
Lazarus, who he knows will live again. Instead, he weeps as he lays
down his own life. The difference between the grief of Jesus and that of
the Jews is emphasized in the different verbs used to describe their
action—κλαίω for the wailing mourners and δακρύειν for himself.
They are not united in grief for a friend,[143] but Jesus is alone, afraid and
in turmoil, confronted with his own destruction.

Jesus 'shakes with anger' once more on reaching the grave (v. 38).
The moment has now arrived, and what he sees assaults him. The tomb
containing the body is a grim encounter with the reality that will befall
him. He performs the miracle that is his duty without hesitation and
with a short prayer of thanks to the Father for the benefit of those lis-
tening. The miracle is executed with the minimum of description on
the part of the narrator. Lazarus vacates his tomb and is unbound. Nothing is added about the subsequent emotions of the onlookers, the resurrected man or his sisters. Jesus has carried out the act that will seal his
fate as a victim soon to be bound himself and lead to his death. It is in
the next chapter that his body will be anointed for burial at the same
house in Bethany, and by Lazarus's sister, Mary.

The Ramifications of the Miracle
This section has been concerned with Jesus' understanding of his death,
his cognizance of his identity as a victim. However, as has already been

142. A psychoanalytic reading of the text would see Jesus experiencing 'existence
pain' in this scene as he is unable to deny the inevitability of his own death. Irvin
Yalom comments on the human tendency towards death denial: 'We know *about*
death, intellectually we know the facts, but we—that is, the unconscious portion of
the mind that protects us from overwhelming anxiety—have split off, or dissociated,
the terror associated with death. This dissociative process is unconscious, invisible to
us, but we can be convinced of its existence in those rare episodes when the
machinery of denial fails and death anxiety breaks through in full force. That may
happen only rarely, sometimes only once or twice in a lifetime. Occasionally it
happens during waking life, sometimes after a personal brush with death, or when a
loved one has died (*Love's Executioner and other Tales of Psychotherapy* [London:
Penguin Books, 1989], pp. 5-6). This would be one way of understanding Jesus'
severe anxiety at the tomb of Lazarus.

143. Contrast Wuellner, who sees a focus on shared grief and anger between
Jesus and the other characters ('Putting Life Back into the Lazarus Story', p. 119).
The anger and grief of Martha and Mary are caused by the death of Lazarus. The
anger and grief of Jesus are caused by his own death.

noted, the raising of Lazarus is the precursor to the official decision to execute Jesus and a brief word will be added on the last section of this chapter (11.45-57).

The raising of Lazarus does not prompt a faith response from all of the onlookers. There are spies among them who report Jesus' latest act to the Pharisees. Gathering together the council, the religious authorities determine the necessary action to be taken. Boff notes that:

> Religious fanaticism, the will to power, and the desire to maintain guaranteed privileges were...the main reasons that brought Jesus' enemies—divided among themselves but united against him—to liquidate the annoying prophet of Nazareth.[144]

The authorities complain that Jesus will be the cause of the destruction of 'the [Holy] place and the nation' (τὸν τόπον καὶ τὸ ἔθνος, v. 48). The response of Caiaphas shows that he agrees this is a threat, but he provides a solution: 'You know nothing at all; you do not understand that it is expedient for you that one man should die for the people and that the whole nation should not perish' (vv. 49b-50).

Beutler notes that the suggestion of Caiaphas sounds like an example of *Realpolitik*—better to sacrifice one than risk the many.[145] As noted by most commentators, and stated by the evangelist in the following verse, irony peaks. Caiaphas's use of language is telling. Jesus will die for (ὑπέρ) the nation and hence is clearly identified in sacrificial terms as a scapegoat.[146] His sacrifice is seen as 'socially therapeutic'. Girard's words on the suffering of Job are pertinent: 'it is not so much a question of curing certain individuals as of watching over the well-being of the entire community'.[147] The full force of the hatred and opposition of the Jewish community is made clear by the condemnation of its most powerful members. Jesus is an individual without value, an expendable victim.

---

144. Boff, describing what the authorities decide to do in Jn 5.18 and 11.49-50. (*Jesus Christ, Liberator*, p. 104).

145. J. Beutler, 'Two Ways of Gathering: The Plot to Kill Jesus in John 11.47-53', *NTS* 40 (1994), pp. 399-406 (401). Davies comments that it 'is both a cynical, political remark in the story and a true elucidation of the significance of Jesus' death, an ironical meaning which is so important in the narrative that it is made explicit' (*Rhetoric and Reference*, p. 37).

146. Carson, *Gospel According to John*, p. 422; Beutler, 'Two Ways of Gathering', pp. 404-6.

147. Girard, *Job, the Victim of his People*, p. 79.

Concluding Comment: The Victim's Self-Cognizance

This chapter has examined evidence for the Johannine Jesus' awareness of himself as a victim. Five sections of the Gospel have been discussed and have revealed different aspects of this character's self-cognizance through his words and behaviour. From the early indication that his ministry should be understood in terms of his death, through the unravelling of its meaning and the violence associated with it, the reader becomes acquainted with a man who is, and understands himself to be, a victim. His response to the harassment and rejection of the community is not sovereign and unemotive. On the contrary, the Johannine Jesus reveals sentiment, but this sentiment is of a different nature from that of his Synoptic counterpart. During the course of this chapter we have seen him react to other characters with sarcasm, anger, antagonism and antipathy. Even those whose requests seemed genuine experienced a somewhat glacial response when they sought his help. It has not been the intention to characterize Jesus in purely negative terms, but merely to highlight these aspects of his attitude, which are clearly present in the text and contribute to our understanding of his victim persona.[148] The hatred that engulfs him influences much of what he says and does. His sarcasm and coolness derive from his suspicion of others. His anger springs from distress about his own death. His habit of goading his opponents is a means of participating in his own victimization, colluding with those who will deliver him up. That Robinson sees in him the marks of 'emotional strain and psychic disturbance'[149] now seems less an example of illegitimate psychologizing than of thoughtful exegesis.

148. Certainly the picture that has been painted is far removed from that seen by D. Harrington, who claims that the evangelist's portrait of Jesus 'makes his hero an attractive character'. 'At the end of each episode', claims Harrington, 'Jesus emerges as noble and wise' (*John's Thought and Theology: An Introduction* [Good News Studies, 33; Wilmington, DE: Michael Glazier, 1990], p. 8). This seems difficult to substantiate on a close reading of the text.

149. Robinson, 'The Last Tabu?', p. 160; or *The Priority of John*, p. 355.

7

Relationship with Death I:
Facing the Hour

The way in which John 11.55–12.50 functions as a link passage between the two parts of the Gospel—looking back on Jesus' ministry and forwards to his death—has already been outlined during the section on structure in Chapter 3. The purpose of this chapter is to explore some of the insights that the passage affords us for the interpretation of Jesus as a victim.

The unit will be discussed as follows:

1. 11.55–12.11   The Anointing
2. 12.12-19   Entry into Jerusalem
3. 12.20-36   Announcement of 'the Hour'
4. 12.37-50   The Message and its Rejection

The first two sections outline the two final scenes in Jesus' public ministry, with the last one functioning as a comment by the evangelist on the effectiveness of that ministry. Jesus ties them together with the middle section, which announces the imminence of 'the hour' and calls for the glorification of the Father.

The Anointing (11.55–12.11)

Immediately preceding the Passover, Jesus returns to Bethany to the house of Lazarus, Martha and Mary. The evangelist reminds us who Lazarus is ('the man Jesus raised from the dead'), 12.1, not because the reader will have already forgotten, but as a means of focusing on what the subject matter of this pericope is to be. This house is a place that is linked with death for Jesus and, having confronted it once at the grave of Lazarus, he returns this time to make ready for his own impending death. It was noted in Chapter 6 that the raising of Lazarus was an occasion of intense emotional trauma for Jesus (ἐνεβριμήσατο τῷ πνεύματι καὶ ἐτάραξεν ἑαυτόν, 11.33 and vv. 35, 38). It was claimed that this was because Jesus knew this final sign would precipitate his execution, and indeed it is followed immediately by the plot of the Pharisees to kill him (11.45-53). It is fitting, therefore, that he now returns to this location. Just as the preparation applied to Lazarus's dead body was undone here, as the bandages that embalmed him were unbound, so Jesus, faced with the imminence of 'the hour', presents his own body to be prepared for death.[1]

The role of Martha and Mary in this pericope will not be explored in detail here, as it has been examined elsewhere.[2] It is sufficient to draw attention to the following points: Mary performs an act of extreme sacrifice with deep prophetic significance for Jesus. John, like the other evangelists who narrate similar events,[3] emphasizes the costliness of her gift, both directly by noting that it was costly (πολυτίμου, 12.3), and through Judas' exclamation of horror at her wastefulness, thinly disguised as concern for the poor (v. 5).[4] However, her act is not simply financially costly but also costs her her dignity as it is an act of humble servitude that she carries out as a disciple of Jesus.[5] The anointing of the feet was generally the task of a slave, being seen as a humiliating activity. However, Brown notes that 'occasionally disciples would render this

---

1. A further link between the raising of Lazarus and the anointing can be seen in 11.2. John identifies Mary as 'the one who annointed Jesus with ointment and wiped his feet with her hair' *before* the event has actually happened. This is new information for the first-time reader, who at this point does not actually know whether the anointing of Jesus will happen before or after his death. The verse functions not simply as another indication that death is near, but that this family, beloved of Jesus, is closely connected with his death.

2. See S.M. Schneiders, 'Women in the Fourth Gospel and the Role of Women in the Contemporary Church', *BTB* 12 (1982), pp. 35-45; T.K. Seim, 'Roles of Women in the Gospel of John', in L. Hartman and B. Olsson (eds.), *Aspects on the Johannine Literature: Papers Presented at a Conference of Scandinavian New Testament Exegetes at Uppsala, June 16–19, 1986* (ConBNT, 18; Uppsala: Almqvist & Wiksell International, 1987), pp. 56-73; and Schüssler Fiorenza, *In Memory of Her*, pp. 329-31.

3. Mk 14.3-9; Mt. 26.6-13; Lk. 7.36-50 (although the Lukan version has a completely different context and cannot strictly be seen as a parallel).

4. Judas merely 'deplored that the money had eluded him' (Bultmann, *Gospel of John*, p. 415).

5. Mary is 'explicitly characterized as a beloved disciple whom the teacher has specifically called' (Schüssler Fiorenza, *In Memory of her*, p. 330). So too Stibbe, *John*, p. 132.

service to their teacher or rabbi'.[6] She also looses her hair to wipe his feet, an action that could be interpreted as wanton behaviour.[7] Mary's conduct can be seen as a foreshadowing of Jesus' own act of debasement before his disciples in 13.1-11. In fact, Mary sets an example of humility that Jesus subsequently mimics. The two statements can clearly be seen as parallels:

> She anointed the feet of Jesus
> and wiped his feet with her hair (12.3)

> He began to wash the disciples' feet
> and to wipe them with the towel with which he was girded (13.5)

The obvious differences are that Mary specifically anoints[8] the feet of Jesus, whereas Jesus simply washes those of his disciples. In addition, they use different items to dry the feet—for Mary it is part of her own body, heightening her humiliation.

Culpepper comments that Mary represents the response of 'devotion and uncalculating, extravagant love' to Jesus and that 'she does not even understand the significance of her anointing of Jesus'.[9] There is, however, absolutely no evidence in the text that she does not understand her act as one of anointing for burial, as opposed to simply an expression of love for Jesus.[10] It is Judas[11] who does not understand the act of Mary and is indignant at the unnecessary squander of this silly woman. Mary is contrasted with Judas in this pericope[12]—her actions are born out of generosity and truth, while his emanate from greed and dishonesty. Her

6. Brown, *Gospel According to John*, II, p. 564; also Lindars, *Gospel of John*, p. 446. These references are drawn from the commentary on John 13, where it is Jesus who carries out the footwashing.

7. Haenchen notes that only a prostitute would have 'run around' with her hair loose (*John*, II, p. 84).

8. The meaning of ἀλείφω is literally 'to anoint' (BAGD, p. 35). Barrett appears to play down the significance of Mary's act by claiming that it means 'merely "to smear with oil", as after the bath' (*Gospel According to St John*, p. 412).

9. Culpepper, *Anatomy of the Fourth Gospel*, p. 141-42.

10. The fact that the verb used to describe Mary's act indicates that she was *anointing* his feet could be seen to indicate that she had some conception of the import of her behaviour.

11. And in the Synoptics the other male members of the party—the disciples in Mt. 26.8, the Pharisees in Luke and Mk 14.4.

12. The evangelist intends to portray 'the true disciple Mary of Bethany as counterpart to the unfaithful disciple Judas Iscariot' (Schüssler Fiorenza, *In Memory of Her*, p. 330). So too Stibbe, *John*, p. 132.

response can also be compared to the inadequate response of Peter in 13.8-9. Peter does not understand and cannot accept Jesus' actions, arguing vehemently with him. We will see in the next chapter that he is unable to behave as Jesus bids him until he is literally faced with the possibility of expulsion from the group of disciples (13.9). In contrast, Mary is a disciple who behaves appropriately before Jesus, knows how to respond to his needs and is commended for it.

The reprimand of Judas elicits an immediate and fierce response from Jesus in defence of Mary: 'leave her' (ἄφες αὐτήν, v. 7). He proceeds to interpret her deed in relation to his impending death,[13] but also identifies himself as one who is *more* needy than the marginalized group identified by Judas:

> Let her keep it for the day of my burial.
> The poor you always have with you,
> but you do not always have me. (vv. 7-8)

In stating that the disciples will always have the poor to attend to, but will not always have him, Jesus identifies himself with this group as one of the oppressed, but he goes further by implicitly comparing their adversity with his. The indigent are among the many needy victims of society, *but Jesus too is a victim*. He has an immense and acute need which is recognized and tended to by Mary through her sacrificial care for him.

Entry into Jerusalem (12.12–19)

The day after Jesus has been anointed for burial, he begins his last journey into Jerusalem where he will be put to death. Stibbe notes that this is 'the urban setting which spells hostility, danger and unbelief'[14] and indeed a first-time reader would surely be surprised by the uncharacteristically enthusiastic behaviour of a crowd whose normal reaction to Jesus is of a more threatening nature.[15] In contrast to the Synoptic accounts, where many details of the acquisition and preparation of the

---

13. What precisely is meant by 'let her keep it for the day of my burial' is uncertain and Barrett explores the many possibilities (*Gospel According to John*, p. 414). Suffice to say that it functions as a somewhat morbid statement by Jesus indicating that death is uppermost in his mind.

14. Stibbe, *John*, p. 133.

15. As has been anxiously commented upon by the disciples as recently as Jn 11.5.

donkey at Jesus' request are recorded (Mt. 21.1-7), John notes that Jesus found and sat on an ass in response to the cries of the crowd. Sanders suggests that Jesus is embarrassed at the situation and that his reaction was 'a prompt repudiation of the crowd's acclamations'.[16] He claims that Jesus' embarrassment was due to the fact that he did not want to be mistaken for a military messiah and so he undermined the triumphal entry by sitting peacefully on the ass. No doubt another reason why Jesus acts as if he is uncomfortable as the recipient of the adulation of the Jews is because of an inability to trust the inclinations of a group who have transformed themselves at short notice into a lynch mob on more than one occasion. Indeed, the evangelist alerts us to their fickle nature with his warning that their desire to see him is linked to the raising of Lazarus (v. 18)—the crowd have an inadequate 'signs faith'. The experienced reader already knows that the cries of 'Hosanna' will soon become 'crucify'.

The pericope ends with a comment by the Pharisees, which, far from being a statement of despair over the extent of popular support that Jesus commands,[17] is in reality simply an excuse to justify the action they had already determined to take: 'the decision that Jesus must die is confirmed in their minds: they had been right! If they do not act as they had decided, the danger will never be banished.'[18]

Announcement of the Hour (12.20–36)

Jesus' final encounter with the crowd before he goes into hiding (12.36b) follows the entry into Jerusalem prior to the Passover. If the raising of Lazarus was the climax of Jesus' public acts, then this scene contains his climactic public words. He speaks openly to the crowd about the purpose of his death and his struggle with it. The request of some Greeks to see Jesus indicates that the universal intention of his mission is being fulfilled; however, it causes him some distress, prompting a long monologue regarding the imminence and benefits of his death. His speech is full of the significant Johannine terms which were discussed in Chapter 6—ὥρα, δόξα/δοξάζειν and ὑψοῦν—which illu-

---

16. Sanders and Mastin, *Gospel According to St John*, p. 287-88.

17. In contrast to the Synoptic plot to kill Jesus where Jesus' popularity causes a real problem for the authorities—'not during the feast, lest there be a riot among the people', Mt. 26.5.

18. Bultmann, *Gospel of John*, p. 419.

minate the meaning of his death. The evangelist is anxious to impress upon the mind of the reader the nearness of Jesus' death. In the passage comprising 12.20-36, he employs his full arsenal of theological signifiers, as well as all the violent and negative terminology he can muster to put his point across, as can be seen below:

Term	Translation	Frequency
δοξάζω	glorify	4
ὥρα	hour	3
ἀποθνῄσκω	die	3
ὑψόω	lift up	2
σκοτία	darkness	2
θάνατος	death	1
μισέω	hate	1
κρίσις	judgment	1

The vocabulary used cannot fail to create an atmosphere of danger and impending death.

Jesus' speech falls into three sections:

1. announcement of the hour and explanation of its benefits (12.23-26);
2. inevitability of the hour and confirmation from the Father (12.27-33);
3. imminence of the hour and explanation to the crowd (12.34-36).

The announcement of the hour is followed by the description of three benefits of the hour: (1) death is the precursor to fruitfulness, and Jesus' death will mark the birth of the church; (2) death to life in this world will grant eternal life for the believer, and (3) death is the place to which the disciples must be prepared to follow Jesus, but the disciples will receive the presence of Jesus and the honour of the Father. The words of advice for would-be followers indicate the sacrificial aspect of following the one who was himself a sacrifice.

Contemplating the implications of the hour sends Jesus into great distress. 'How is my soul troubled' (τετάρακται, v. 27), he says, reflecting his experience at the tomb of Lazarus. 'The prospect of death, now seen to be imminent, fills the human soul of Jesus with terror.'[19] He phrases his predicament in the form of a question; 'And what shall I say? "Father save me from this hour?"'. Deeply disturbed, he searches for a means of

19. Sanders, *Gospel According to St John*, p. 294. Hengel also recognizes the 'profound emotion' expressed by Jesus here (*Johannine Question*, p. 70).

escape from the horror ahead.[20] The only way out would be to petition the Father, but in the same breath he recognizes the futility of this action. There would be no point in asking the Father to save him, because the hour is the very moment for which Jesus has been sent in the first place. Resigned to this fact, he calls on his Father to fulfil his purpose, with the words 'Father, glorify (δόξασόν) your name', inviting the hour to begin. As Jn 12.27-28 is commonly viewed as the Johannine equivalent of the Synoptic Gethsemane,[21] it is appropriate to pause and consider the implications of such an association at this point.

The Gethsemane Experience in the Synoptics and John
There are two main issues to be considered when comparing the Synoptic Gethsemane with the experience of the Johannine Jesus:

1. The attempt of the protagonist to avoid death.
2. The distress suffered by the protagonist on considering his death.

The Synoptic Gethsemane recounts the desire of Jesus to avoid the fate that will befall him if at all possible (Mt. 26.36-46; Mk 14.32-42; Lk. 22.39-46). In Mark and Matthew, Jesus petitions the Father on three distinct occasions and in Luke there is one long petition. What is clear is that the Synoptic request to the Father to 'let this cup pass from me'[22] is a genuine one. Jesus truly wants to be released from his forthcoming ordeal and must believe that such release is in some way possible, praying earnestly for it three times.[23] Leonardo Boff claims the Synoptic Jesus perceived the possibility of death but was not absolutely certain of it, and retained the hope that God would save him from death, even when on the cross.[24] In the Fourth Gospel, Jesus does not ask to be spared his ordeal; he does not 'throw himself on the mercy of God'.[25] Stibbe claims this is because John's Jesus needs no helpers—not even

---

20. 'The quandary of Jesus is an index to the inner tension which he suffers' (Lindars, *Gospel of John*, p. 431).

21. Brown, *Gospel According to John*, II, p. 475; Lindars, *Gospel of John*, p. 430; Sanders, *Gospel According to St John*, p. 294; Barrett, *Gospel According to St John*, p. 424; Haenchen, *John*, II, p. 97; Sandmel, *Anti-Semitism in the New Testament?*, p. 113.

22. Mk 14.35-36, where he also asks for the hour to pass; Mt. 26.39; Lk. 22.42.

23. In Mt. and Mk. In Lk. it is only once, or twice if vv. 43-44 are accepted.

24. So, Boff, *Jesus Christ, Liberator*, p. 116.

25. M.W.G. Stibbe, '"Return to Sender": A Structuralist Approach to John's Gospel', *BibInt* 1 (1993), pp. 189-206 (195).

God.[26] He is characterized as the quintessential, superhuman, solitary hero in the Gospel.[27] However, it is not heroic intentions that prevent Jesus from asking for an escape. As has been indicated above, his words show he knows it is *never within the realms of possibility*. There can be no 'delusion of reprieve'[28] for the Johannine Jesus. He has already accepted the inevitability of his death, having faced this crisis prior to raising Lazarus, but this does *not* prevent him from experiencing great fear at the thought of it.

Moving on to the second point, comparison of Jn 12.27 with the Gethsemane event invariably results in comments about the minimal level of distress displayed by the Johannine Jesus. So Haenchen observes: 'The anguish of Jesus, depicted by Mark, is for John only like a small cloud that appears momentarily to darken the sun.'[29] Furthermore, Stibbe claims that Jesus exhibits his sovereignty in this passage, showing a 'mastery of his emotions'.[30] The anguish which is conveyed by the verb ταράσσω becomes 'feelings of unease',[31] which are transcended when Jesus focuses on the importance of his calling. Stibbe adds: 'instead of wilting before the prospect of his death he *rejoices* in its conse-quences'.[32] While Jesus certainly outlines what the consequences of his death will be (12.24-26), there appears to be no evidence in the text of any rejoicing on his part. Indeed it is *after* he has spoken of these benefits that he is overwhelmed with fear. It is therefore difficult to accept that they function as a source of comfort to him.[33] A closer look at the text indicates that this is a hermeneutical error.

---

26. Stibbe's analysis of Jesus' 'helper' follows Greimas's actantial model.

27. Stibbe, 'Return to Sender', p. 195.

28. A term used to describe when a condemned man, immediately before his execution, gets the illusion that he may be reprieved at the very last minute. See V.E. Frankl, *Man's Search for Meaning: An Introduction to Logotherapy* (trans. I. Lasch; London: Hodder & Stoughton, 1964), p. 8.

29. Haenchen, *John*, II, p. 97. See Bultmann for another watered down, but slightly more bizarre interpretation: 'It is not the struggle of his soul that should become visible, but the decision that he actually made' (*Gospel of John*, pp. 427-29).

30. Stibbe, *John*, p. 153.

31. Stibbe, *John*, p. 153.

32. Stibbe, *John*, p. 153, emphasis added.

33. The fact that the occasion does not end on an altogether positive note could also be indicated by Jesus' departing and hiding when he has finished speaking (v. 36b). It would be speculative to claim that this was a response to his distress, but

Perhaps the primary error in interpreting this passage has arisen from the assumption that John has collapsed the distress of Gethsemane into two verses. In reality it has been *extended* rather than abridged, appearing in three chapters and spanning the public and private ministry of Jesus. Gethsemane appears traumatic. Matthew and Mark have Jesus greatly distressed and troubled[34] with a soul sorrowful (περίλυπός) unto death, falling to the ground to pray. Luke has Jesus in agony and sweating blood.[35] But John's Gospel also provides plenty of evidence for a trau-matized Jesus. On three separate occasions—at the tomb of Lazarus, during his last public speech and at the point of the betrayal—the evangelist indicates that Jesus is deeply troubled. The terms used are strong ones. I have already mentioned ἐμβριμάομαι, ταράσσω and δακρύω which occur in John 11. In Jn 12.27 and 13.21 Jesus is specifi-cally mentioned again as being deeply distressed (ταράσσω). The Syn-optics, on the other hand, do not indicate that Jesus suffered anguish when considering his death outside of Gethsemane. There is no men-tion of emotion when the betrayal is mentioned; indeed it is the dis-ciples who are sorrowful, not Jesus (Mk 14.19). The only occasion where we see Jesus weeping in the Synoptics is in Lk. 19.41, but it is not in connection with his death but the fate of Jerusalem.[36] The con-clusion that we can draw is that the Johannine Jesus is not demonstrably less traumatized about his death—if anything the reverse is the case.

Returning to John's text, Jesus' petition to the Father to 'glorify his name' elicits a direct response. Again, this indicates the retrospective and prospective nature of Jesus' 'glorification' through suffering: 'I have glo-rified it, and I will glorify it again' (καὶ ἐδόξασα καὶ πάλιν δοξάσω, 12.28). The affirmative response from heaven leads Jesus to declare that the moment of judgment has arrived and to hint again at his method of execution. The humiliation of the cross beckons, and he ends his contact with the crowd with a last invitation to believe in the light, even as the darkness approaches.

there is no hint in the text that it is due to any threat from the crowd (compared with 8.59, for example).

34. Mt. 26.37, Mk 14.33; λυπεῖσθαι καὶ ἀδημονεῖν.

35. ἐγένετο ὁ ἰδρὼς αὐτοῦ ὡσεὶ θρόμβοι αἵματος, 22.44, although there are difficulties with this verse. I.H. Marshall notes that many manuscripts omit vv. 43-44 and that the textual evidence for omission is strong (*The Gospel of Luke: A Commentary on the Greek Text* [NIGTC; Exeter: Paternoster Press, 1978], p. 831).

36. Note also that the verb is κλαίω, not δακρύω.

The Message and its Rejection (12.37-50)

The evangelist rounds off Jesus' public ministry with a word to the reader, aided by two quotes from the Hebrew Bible, about why he was rejected. He hints that the cause was an inadequate 'signs faith', in fulfilment of Isaiah's words:

> Lord, who has believed our report,
> and to whom has the arm of the Lord been revealed (v. 38b)?

and:

> He has blinded their eyes and hardened their heart,
> lest they should see with their eyes and perceive with their heart,
> and turn for me to heal them (v. 40).

The subject of unbelief alludes to the prologue and the statement that Jesus came to his own, but was not received by them. The reality of these words has been fully explored during the course of the narrative, the evangelist claiming that it was all foretold long ago by the prophets. Rejection is predestined, as is execution. Jesus' experience of victimization is thus sanctioned by the evangelist.

The argument follows hesitant lines:

> They *could not* believe.
> But many did.
> But they did not confess it
> because they loved men more than God.
> Therefore they were not *real* believers.

Rejection is the overriding reaction to Jesus—that some attained some level of belief is almost added as an afterthought. They cannot be seen as *bona fide* followers as they loved the way of the world more than the δόξα of God (v. 43). They were not prepared to take on the role of victim themselves, risking expulsion from the community in the way that Jesus had done.

John closes the chapter and this section of Jesus' ministry with a long list of claims that summarize his message. They make clear to the reader Jesus' relation to the Father, the origin of his authority and the believer's relation to him. Readers are now fully aware of what Jesus has been sent to do, what he has *not* been sent to do, and who it is that has sent him. They are also aware that the next stage will be the hour of death.

8

Relationship with the Disciples I:
Departure

Jesus' relationship with his disciples is played out most explicitly through his words and actions during the last evening that he spends with them. Through it we learn of his attitude towards them and the relationship he expects them to have with each other and the outside world. He elaborates on a number of important themes as he attempts to prepare his followers for the trauma of his death. Departure and return, the sending of the Spirit and the preparation of the Father's house are but a few of the subjects discussed. This chapter will explore John 13–17[1] in two sections: the footwashing and associated material (13.1-29); followed by the major discourses and prayer of Jesus (14–17).

The Footwashing and Betrayal(s)

The footwashing and the betrayal by Judas are interlinked and should be interpreted together. This is because the theme of betrayal runs throughout the whole of the footwashing incident: mention of it precedes (v. 2), interrupts (vv. 10-11), concludes (v. 18) and follows it (vv. 21-30). This has the function of heightening the bathetic nature of the whole scene. Both the reader and the protagonist know that the act of perfidy is imminent, yet Jesus' behaviour at this moment is utterly unexpected. He chooses to communicate with his disciples through an intensely intimate action, which renders him consciously and deliberately humiliated.

---

1.   The compositional problems associated with these chapters are noted but will not be discussed. For discussion, see F.F. Segovia, *The Farewell of the Word: The Johannine Call to Abide* (Minneapolis: Fortress Press, 1991), pp. 21-47; or J.W. Pryor (*John, Evangelist of the Covenant People: The Narrative and Themes of the Fourth Gospel* [Downers Grove, IL: InterVarsity Press, 1992], pp. 102-106).

Exactly *what* is being communicated has been the subject of widespread scholarly debate.[2] This section will focus purely on what can be learned about Jesus' victim-consciousness from the event.

The footwashing is commonly seen as a loving and gracious gesture by Jesus towards his disciples,[3] but its deliberately subservient nature and the strong theme of betrayal provide clues for an alternative interpretation of his motives. As will be seen, Jesus performs an act of self-abasement that prefigures the degradation of his execution.[4] It is enacted before not one, but two betrayers, and it is the interaction between these three major characters that provides much of the dramatic tension in the pericope.

For our purposes, John 13 can be divided up as follows:

2.   For discussion of the various interpretations of footwashing see the work of J.C. Thomas (*Footwashing in John 13 and the Johannine Community* [JSNTSup, 61; Sheffield: JSOT Press, 1991]). Prominent theories have been: an example of humility (Lagrange, Bernard); a symbol of baptism (BAGD, MacGregor); an act of cleansing/forgiveness (Dunn, Beasley-Murray); a separate sacrament (Koch); a soteriological sign (Hoskyns, Bultmann); polemic against baptism or purification (Kreyenbühl, Fridrichsen) (see pp. 11-18 of *Footwashing* for details). For another recent treatment of the passage see Ruth Edwards, who explores the possible interrelationship between the exemplary, sacramental and christological interpretations. Her viewpoint is that footwashing is '*a sacrament of identification with Jesus in his humble service and death*' ('The Christological Basis of the Johannine Footwashing', in J.B. Green and M. Turner [eds.], *Jesus of Nazareth. Lord and Christ: Essays on the Historical Jesus and New Testament Christology* [Carlisle: Paternoster Press, 1994], pp. 367-83 [378, emphasis original]).

3.   Thomas notes that where there are ancient examples of individuals who, without being obliged to, wash the feet of others, love is most frequently the motive (*Footwashing*, p. 187). Carson sees it as 'simultaneously a display of love, a symbol of saving cleansing, and a model of Christian conduct' (*Gospel According to John*, p. 463). The text itself, of course, situates the behaviour of Jesus within the context of love for the disciples: 'he loved them to the end' (13.1).

4.   Numerous scholars see the footwashing prefiguring the crucifixion. See, for example, Mlakuzhyil, who views it as 'the symbol of the supreme, loving and life-giving sacrifice of Christ on the cross (*Christocentric Literary Structure*, p. 325).

1. 13.1-4   General Context
                —the hour of death has come
                —introduction of the first betrayer

2. 13.5-11   Execution of the Footwashing
                —introduction of the second betrayer
                —conflict between Jesus and the second betrayer
                —reference back to the first betrayer

3. 13.12-20 Discussion of the Footwashing
                —commission of disciples
                —reference to betrayer(s)

4. 13.21-30 Execution of First Betrayal
                —query of second betrayer
                —commissioning of first betrayer
                —departure of first betrayer

5. 13.31-38 Prediction of the Second Betrayal
                —predicted death (glorification) of Jesus
                —prediction of departure of Jesus
                —prediction of second betrayal

1. General Context (Verses 1–4)

The chapter begins with a lengthy introduction that sets the scene temporally and theologically. The narrator describes Jesus as knowing (εἰδὼς) two things: first, that his 'hour' has come to depart out of the world (v. 1), and secondly that the Father to whom he is going has 'given all things into his hands' (v. 3). Between these two, the narrator places another fact that Jesus knows: 'the devil had already put it into the heart of Judas Iscariot, Simon's son, to betray him'. The reader is given little opportunity to envisage a cosy scene of supportive fellowship between Jesus and his followers during this private supper. He who was a murderer from the beginning has been at work, and his emissary, the betrayer, is in their midst. This ominous statement, coupled with Jesus' obvious awareness of the nearness of death, creates a confused suspense when the sentence finally ends with his undressing and donning a towel.

2. Execution of the Footwashing (Verses 5–11)

Jesus' behaviour towards the disciples is embarrassing and shocking, as will be witnessed by the reaction of one of the recipients.[5] In order for modern readers to be shocked by Jesus' behaviour it is necessary to refer briefly to the cultural context of his act. Chris Thomas outlines examples of footwashing in the Jewish and Graeco-Roman environment. He concludes that footwashing was clearly associated with servitude and could even be used as a synonym for slavery: 'to wash another's feet symbolized the subjugation of one person to another'.[6] In performing this task Jesus does a job that was so menial it was reserved for Gentile servants, women and children. It was not something that a Jewish male servant should have been required to do.[7] Jesus behaves not merely as a slave, but as the lowest kind of slave. He joins the ranks of 'non-people'—those who are the true victims of a patriarchally structured society. He lays down the status of a free, Jewish male and takes up that of a slave, a Gentile, a woman, a child, to perform a task that places him on the underside of life. While the Synoptic Christ concerns himself with the plight of the downtrodden through his contact with tax-collectors, prostitutes and outcasts, the Johannine Christ's contact is immediate and personal. His role is not to minister to society's victims but to *become* one. His becoming a victim is not realized merely through a superficial empathy with the oppressed, but is an integral part of his identity. The deliberate nature of his self-abasement within this context makes his behaviour appear victimal.[8] The disciples would have been scandalized. Although they might have expected to wash *his* feet, they could never have conceived that he would wash *theirs*.[9] What makes it all the more unexpected is the fact that this is the very occasion on which Jesus could have been expected to exert, rather than relinquish, his authority. Throughout his ministry his claims have been disputed

5. So, Carson, *Gospel According to John*, p. 462.

6. Thomas, *Footwashing*, p. 56.

7. Claims Barrett, referring to *Mekhilta* Exod. 21.2 (*Gospel According to St John*, p. 440).

8. Sandra Schneiders disagrees that this is an act of self-humiliation, but rather one of service between friends. This disregards the nature of the act and the way that it would have been interpreted by its recipients ('The Foot Washing [John 13.1-20]: An Experiment in Hermeneutics', *CBQ* 43 [1981], pp. 76-92 [88]).

9. Thomas sees Jesus' action as unique since it is that the *only* example of a superior voluntarily washing the feet of inferiors to be found in antiquity (*Footwashing*, p. 59).

and his authority to proclaim them denied by his hearers. In the context of the last supper he is surrounded by those who *do* believe him, where his authority is accepted as teacher and lord, yet he chooses to act as one with none at all. Instead of behaving like a rabbi, he debases himself as a slave,[10] indicating the true nature of his identity.

The text describes his preparation for the act: 'he rose from supper, laid aside his garments (τίθησιν τὰ ἱμάτια) and girded himself with a towel' (v. 4). The use of τίθημι provides an intertextual link with the action of the shepherd in 10.17-18 and hints at the significance of this derobement.[11] That the plural form ἱμάτια is used also indicates that he took off more than just his outer robe.[12] As Lindars puts it: 'he strips for action'.[13] With the 'laying down' of his clothing he assumes the poverty and vulnerability of a near-naked slave. In addition to this Jesus girds himself with a towel—the recognizable act of a slave preparing for service (Lk. 17.8).[14] In the eyes of the disciples, the transformation is complete; from κύριος to δοῦλος.

The text does not indicate how many pairs of feet Jesus has washed, nor how willingly they received him, before he is forced to pause by the objection of Peter. Peter's reaction is vigorously negative. He sees no act of laudable humility; rather one of shameful humiliation. He has no admiration for a Master who stoops to serve him and is horrified at this display of self-abasement.[15] Jesus is vitiated by his own disciples

---

10. Barrett states that the degrading nature of the task should not be exaggerated, adding that 'wives washed the feet of their husbands, and children of their parents'. This is surely the point (*Gospel According to St John*, p. 440).

11. J.D.G. Dunn sees τίθημι as providing a link between the footwashing and Jesus' death ('The Washing of the Disciples' Feet in John 13.1-20', *ZNW* 61 [1970], pp. 247-52 [248]). See also R.A. Culpepper, 'The Johannine *Hypodeigma*: A Reading of John 13', *Semeia* 53 (1991), pp. 133-52 (137).

12. Jn 19.23 indicates that he wore enough items for four soldiers to divide between them.

13. Lindars, *Gospel of John*, p. 450.

14. Beasley-Murray also notes that in the Midrash on Gen. 21.14, when Abraham sent Hagar away he gave her a bill of divorce, took her shawl and girded it around her loins 'that people should know that she was a slave' (*John*, p. 233; following Str-B, II, p. 557). For the doubly symbolic action of 'girding' and its possible connections with death see Ruth Edwards, who points to the girding of Peter in Jn 21.18-19 as symbolic of his martyrdom ('Christological Basis of the Johannine Footwashing', p. 373).

15. Culpepper, among others, sees Peter's response to Jesus indicating 'wonder

through washing their feet and it is to this that Peter objects. Initially his
protest is tentative and questioning: 'Lord, do you wash my feet?' (v. 6).
By addressing him as 'Lord', Peter attempts to right the relationship that
Jesus has just capsized by behaving as his subordinate. Jesus understands
Peter's discomfort and tries to reassure him that all will become clear in
good time. Peter, however, cannot accept Jesus' action. It is too radical,
too frightening for him to permit and he fights to retain the rabbi–
disciple archetype with which he is familiar. Allowing Jesus to wash his
feet would irrevocably violate this, as Jesus would lose his respectability
and status within the group by performing such a servile task.[16] Peter
refuses to submit his teacher to disgrace in this manner and his protest is
strongly phrased: 'You shall never wash my feet' (οὐ μὴ νίψῃς μου τοὺς
πόδας εἰς τὸν αἰῶνα, v. 8).[17] By speaking to Jesus in this way, Peter
treats him as if he *were* a slave. In his attempt to prevent the humiliation
of Jesus, he actually participates in it by desperately trying to exert his
own power over him, commanding: 'You will never...', as if to say: 'I
forbid you...'.[18] Ironically, through the very act of forbidding, Peter takes
on the role of master and participates in the oppression of 'Jesus as slave'.
As his relationship to the world is that of a victim, so too his relation to
even his own can take this form.

Jesus does not respond with a similar assertion of power. He does not
order Peter to submit to being washed. He simply states a fact that presents Peter with a clear choice: 'If I do not wash you, you have no part

and amazement', but given the context and the nature of the task, shock and dismay
are more likely. ('The Johannine *Hypodeigma*', p. 138).

16. Schneiders, in her discussion of this passage, also argues that Peter is reacting
to Jesus' dismantling of familiar power structures, although she relates this to a
different understanding of Peter's motives for power and Jesus' motives for service:
'Peter realizes that Jesus, by transcending the inequality between himself and his
disciples and inaugurating between them the relationship of friendship, is subverting
in principle all structures of domination, and therefore the basis for Peter's own
exercise of power and authority' ('The Footwashing', p. 87).

17. F. Blass and A. Debrunner note that οὐ μὴ with the future indicative is the
most definite form of negation regarding the future (*A Greek Grammar of the New
Testament and other Early Christian Literature* (ed. R.W. Funk; Cambridge: Cambridge
University Press, 1961), p. 184.

18. Bultmann comments: 'the natural man simply does not want this kind of
service'. The reason, he concludes, is that it is part of the basic way that men think
to refuse to see the act of salvation in what is lowly, or God in the form of a slave.
This is, of course, at the heart of Peter's discomfort (*Gospel of John*, p. 468).

in me' (v. 8). This is not a threat, but it *is* an ultimatum.[19] Being washed by Jesus is so important that having a 'part'[20] with him is conditional on acceptance of this act. The most obvious meaning of the term indicates a share in eternal life,[21] but Thomas sees the meaning as extending to sharing the destiny or identity of someone.[22] Jesus' message is clear: to have a part with him, Peter must accept this manifestation of his identity—the full meaning of the Word made flesh. This manifestation is not one of power and glory through Messiahship, but of abasement and disgrace through victimization. If Peter cannot accept this act, how will he ever cope with the shame that it prefigures—that of the cross? The dilemma facing Peter is simple enough: in, or out? Nevertheless, he avoids tackling it head on, choosing rather to complicate the issue. His exclamation: 'Lord, not my feet only but also my hands and my head' (v. 9) could be seen as an enthusiastic request for the fullest possible inclusion with Jesus,[23] but in fact it implicitly contains a further denial to allow Jesus to behave as a slave. The significance of Peter's request for his hands and head to be washed is discussed by Thomas, who draws the following conclusion:

> Clearly Peter has misconstrued the entire episode. At first, he misun-
> derstands Jesus as performing an act of hospitality. Then, when he is con-
> vinced of the necessity of the washing, he seeks to suggest the particular
> kinds of washings most appropriate. In typical Johannine fashion, his mis-
> understanding awaits the discourse by Jesus for clarification.[24]

19. Although Fernando Segovia sees it as 'a severe threat' this seems to be an incorrect reading. Jesus is not threatening to expel Peter, but merely stating what is and is not possible if Peter wishes to remain with him ('John 13.1-20: The Foot-washing in the Johannine Tradition', *ZNW* 73 [1982], pp. 31-51 [43]).

20. Or 'share' in the sense of having a place with someone. BAGD, p. 506.

21. So, Brown, *Gospel According to John*, II, pp. 565-66. Brown notes that μέρος is used in the LXX to translate the Hebrew חלק, the word that describes the God-given heritage to Israel.

22. For example, he refers to usage in Mt. 24.51 and *Mart. Pol.* 14.2 (*Footwashing*, pp. 93-94).

23. So, Carson: 'unrestrained exuberance' (*Gospel According to John*, p. 464). Likewise Brown: 'if the footwashing brings heritage with Jesus, then the more wash-ing, the better' (*Gospel According to John*, II, p. 566). Lindars too thinks Peter views the washing quantitatively. More washing will gain a better place with Jesus (*Gospel of John*, p. 451). Culpepper sees Peter's request for more washing as pious ('The Johannine *Hypodeigma*', p. 140).

24. Thomas, *Footwashing*, p. 97.

This interpretation overlooks the most important and interesting element of the interaction between Jesus and Peter: the fact that it is an
occasion of severe conflict. The reason for this may be that the interpretation is founded on a view of Peter that sees him as having a
positive role in the Fourth Gospel.[25] The conflict can therefore be minimized and reinterpreted as a misunderstanding on the part of the
ebullient disciple, which Jesus is able to correct. If, however, Peter's
character is viewed less favourably, then the conflict can be used to explain his reaction to Jesus' ultimatum in a rather different way.[26] Whatever Peter understands to be the reason for the footwashing—hospitality
or otherwise—it is evident that he is strenuously opposed to it by the
language he uses and the fact that he refuses it twice. The first reassurance of Jesus is not effective and it is difficult to see how his second
statement, the ultimatum, could render the necessary task any more
palatable to Peter.[27] However, if Peter can persuade Jesus to wash his

25. A commonly held view propounded by, among others, Oscar Cullmann, in
Peter: Disciple, Apostle, Martyr (trans. F.V. Filson; London: SCM Press, 2nd edn,
1962). The competition between Peter and the beloved disciple merely emphasizes
their separate roles (pp. 28-31). See also R.E. Brown, K.P. Donfried and
J. Reumann (eds.), *Peter in the New Testament: A Collaborative Assessment by Protestant
and Roman Catholic Scholars* (London: Geoffrey Chapman, rev. edn, 1974). Brown *et
al* see no evidence of rivalry between Peter and the beloved disciple—'to speak of
rivalry is probably an exaggeration, if it implies polemic or animosity, since that
would not be true to the Johannine portrait of Simon Peter' (pp. 138-39). Paul
Minear's assessment of Peter is common: 'well-meaning, but dull and slow, if not
stupid' ('The Beloved Disciple in the Gospel of John: Some Clues and Conjectures',
NovT 19 [1977], pp. 105-23 [117]).

26. For a convincing examination of the representation of Peter in John's Gospel
that concludes that he is very definitely depreciated, while the Beloved Disciple is
elevated, see A.H. Maynard ('The Role of Peter in the Fourth Gospel', *NTS* 30
[1984], pp. 531-48). See also A.J. Droge, 'The Status of Peter in the Fourth Gospel:
A Note on John 18.10-11, *JBL* 109 (1990), pp. 307-11. Droge muses that Simon
Peter has been named a 'rock' not for his solid leadership, but because of his
persistent obtuseness, and sees him as 'a man who has come dangerously close to
being placed beyond the Johannine pale' (p. 311). J.L. Staley suggests that although
Peter is initially introduced as a positive model of discipleship through verses such as
1.42 and 6.67-69, he is later revealed as the character who is unable to understand
what Jesus is about to undergo in 13.6-9, 36-38 and 18.10-11. He goes on to
explain how readers come to disassociate themselves from Peter for this reason
('Subversive Narrator/Victimized Reader: A Reader Response Assessment of a
Text-Critical Problem, John 18.12-24', *JSNT* 51 [1993], pp. 79-98 [92-94]).

27. However, note the opposite view, from Brown: 'Peter had protested to Jesus

hands and head as well, this would undermine the servile nature of the original task and have quite a different meaning. Rather than indicating misguided enthusiasm, Peter's request for additional washing can be seen as an attempt to manipulate Jesus back into the role of master. To wash the hands[28] and head[29] would distance the task from that of a slave's basic duty. In particular, having his head washed by Jesus would be behaviour that Peter would feel far more comfortable with since, rather than kneeling at his feet in an evidently subordinate position, Jesus would be standing over him, performing a deed that resembled an anointing. And so, Peter asks not just for his feet (as that can *only* be demeaning), but his hands and head too (as that would transform it into a 'commissioning', and impart authority to the anointer). The request therefore must be seen as a continued refusal by Peter to permit Jesus to carry out his task.

Jesus rejects Peter's request. His refusal is both logical and theological, but interestingly it is not addressed directly to Peter. *He* who has bathed[30] (not 'you') is clean and needs no further washing, apart from his feet,[31] which is why Jesus is carrying out this task. Jesus pronounces; 'and you are clean', but is forced to qualify this pronouncement—'but

but had quickly accepted the footwashing when Jesus pointed out its salvific purpose' (*Gospel According to John*, II, p. 568).

28. The washing of hands is linked to ritual purity. Thomas notes that because of their continual contact with a number of items, the hands are regarded as always being unclean unless they have just been washed. The implication is that they can render the whole person unclean (*Footwashing*, p. 96). See Jacob Neusner for detail on the Mishnaic reasoning for handwashing: 'what is unclean in the first remove makes hands unclean' (where the first remove means original contact with a primary source of uncleanness) (*Judaism: The Evidence of the Mishnah* [Chicago: University of Chicago Press, 1981], pp. 105-106).

29. The head can be used as the equivalent of the person and his or her whole existence. It therefore becomes the part of the body on which, for example, anointings (Mk 14.3) and judgments (Acts 18.6) are made. See K. Munzer, 'Head', *NIDNTT*, II, pp. 156-63 (158). These were evidently not actions carried out by slaves, but by those in authority.

30. Generally seen as a reference to baptism. See Dodd, *Interpretation*, p. 401; Haenchen, *John*, II, p. 108. Schnackenburg, however, asserts that it is impossible to conclude with any certainty that baptism is alluded to here (*Gospel According to St John*, III, pp. 21-22).

31. For arguments on the inclusion of εἰ μὴ τοὺς πόδας, which is omitted by Codex Sinaiticus, the Vulgate, some Old Latin texts, Tertullian and Origen, see Thomas (*Footwashing*, pp. 9-25).

not all of you' (v. 10). Neither bathing nor washing guarantee that cleansing has actually taken place. Jesus is commonly seen to be referring to Judas with these words,[32] although there is no reason why there could not also be a hint of Peter's own betrayal.[33] Peter has already been set up as the disciple who rejects the service of Jesus. He barely scrapes through the final selection process for discipleship.[34] The narrator confirms in v. 11 that Jesus is cognizant of who will betray him and that we are to equate uncleanness with betrayal. Again, Judas is the obvious culprit, but before the end of the passage, the reader will learn that Jesus knows of another betrayer. The narrator's comment ensures that the theme of betrayal remains uppermost as a hermeneutical tool with which to interpret the footwashing.

The reader cannot doubt that along with the feet of the 'clean', Jesus knew he was washing those of the treacherous. This is a deliberate act of servitude—self-abasement before the man whose heart the devil has already corrupted. We can only speculate about the reason that Jesus does this. Why, for example, does the footwashing occur *before*, rather than *after* Judas leaves the room? Carson suggests that the reason for the inclusion of Judas can be found in the 'unfathomable love and forbearance of the Master'.[35] Love as the potential motive for the footwashing was briefly mentioned above, but the text states that Jesus loved *his own* (v. 1) and Judas is clearly excluded from this select group. Love for Judas cannot credibly be claimed as a motive. If, however, part of the purpose of the footwashing is that it functions as a preparation ritual, then the

32. For example, Thomas, *Footwashing*, p. 106; Barrett, *Gospel According to St John*, p. 442; Segovia, 'John 13.1-20', pp. 46-47. Culpepper extends it to 'those who would deny the salvific significance of Jesus death and go out into the world' ('The Johannine *Hypodeigma*', p. 140).

33. Trumbower argues that without verse 13.11, the reader would automatically assume that Jesus' statement 'you are not all clean' included Peter as well as Judas because Peter had just exclaimed 'you shall never wash me into eternity'. He does not follow the argument to its logical conclusion, namely that a reference to the betrayal (or denial) of Peter is intended (*Born from Above*, p. 132).

34. Dodd sees the entire episode as being the final 'sifting' of the disciples—'the faithful remnant is finally selected out of the unbelieving world' (*Interpretation*, p. 402). Maynard comments; 'Judas fails the test and is 'sifted out', and Peter almost fails!' ('Role of Peter in the Fourth Gospel', p. 535).

35. Carson, *Gospel According to John*, p. 466.

necessity of washing Judas' feet becomes obvious.[36] Judas has a task to perform and Jesus must prepare him for its execution. The deed can be seen as representing the nadir of his victimage at this point in the narrative. In voluntarily undertaking this deed he implicitly colludes with his betrayer, preparing Judas for his own perfidious work. The act itself is degrading: to render oneself vulnerable and shamed before beloved companions is one thing, to do the same to the man whose goal is treachery is quite another. But the meaning of the act has a significance beyond humiliation. It can be seen as a further indication of victimal behaviour as Jesus plays his part in ensuring Judas is ready for his task. The devil has already put it into Judas's heart to betray him, Jesus prepares him by washing his feet. There is one final task to be carried out by both of them.

3. *Discussion of the Footwashing (Verses 12-20)*

Verse 12 marks the end of this 'sign' as Jesus takes up (ἔλαβεν) his clothes and reclines again. The RSV translates the phrase καὶ ἀνέπεσεν πάλιν as 'he resumed his place'. This is indeed what he does, both literally and figuratively as he reclaims his status as 'teacher' and 'Lord' (v. 13). His speech falls into two parts, as was indicated by the structure at the beginning of the chapter. The meaning of his statement is encapsulated by the words: 'for I have given you an example, that you should also do as I have done to you' (v. 15). It is a call to victimage for the disciples, even as he has made himself their victim. He speaks to them about their duty as slaves as they too must wash each other's feet. This cannot be seen simply as an admonition to humble service,[37] but a warning that the disciples must be ready to become worthless in society's reckoning and experience similar degradation.[38] Jesus' statement

---

36. Thomas documents the close connection between footwashing and preparation for a specific task, experience or relationship. He notes that the phrase 'with unwashed feet' came to mean 'without adequate preparation' in the Graeco-Roman world. He therefore sees this emphasis on preparation as significant for John 13–17, which is devoted to Jesus' preparation of his disciples for his departure (*Footwashing*, p. 59).

37. Says Segovia, 'John 13.1-20', p. 45.

38. See also Thomas's arguments that ὑπόδειγμα should be interpreted as more than a call to service but is in fact a mandate from Jesus to carry out the practice of footwashing (*Footwashing*, p. 110). Culpepper, on the other hand, notes the use of the term in the LXX to refer to an exemplary death which served as a model for others to follow ('The Johannine *Hypodeigma*', p. 143).

that a servant is not greater than his master ironically appears to prop up the disciples' concept of ordered patriarchal relations. It is, nevertheless, this very rule that Jesus has just broken. This 'master' has made himself less than his 'servants' by washing their feet and so has undermined this hierarchical structure. This highlights the deeply radical implications of 'the Lord' becoming a victim. The message to those easily offended is that if the one who bears the title 'the holy one of God' must stoop to such disgrace, then they can expect no less. However, this too has the result of levelling master and slave, as the difference in status is lost through their common experience of servitude.

Jesus' instructions are not directed towards all present at supper. There is one who is excluded from this commission by the fact that he has *not* been chosen by Jesus. The betrayer's work is not to submit to humiliation, but to inflict it—not for him the role of victim. It is to the subject of the betrayal that Jesus turns in the second part of his speech, relating the event to the fulfilment of the Scriptures. His reference is to a slightly altered version of Ps. 41.9: 'He who ate my bread has lifted his heel against me' (ὁ τρώγων μου τὸν ἄρτον ἐπῆρεν ἐπ' ἐμὲ τὴν πτέρναν αὐτοῦ, v. 18).[39] In its context in John's Gospel the verse is loaded with significance. The use of τρώγω provides a linguistic link with the

39. Hanson notes that the evangelist's quotation of this text is quite unlike the LXX, which reads: ὁ ἐσθίων ἄρτους μου ἐμεγάλυνεν ἐπ' ἐμὲ πτερνισμόν—'he who ate my loaves has magnified against me the supplanting' (40.10) (*Prophetic Gospel*, pp. 173-74). It is generally held that the Hebrew text, rather than the LXX, was the source of John's quotation. So Barrett, who sees John rewriting freely (*Gospel According to St John*, p. 444). In his analysis of this text, M.J.J. Menken suggests that the evangelist has made his own translation from Hebrew, with the variations between the two being explained by the influence of 2 Sam. 18.28 (a passage analogous to Ps. 41.10). He argues that John could not have used the LXX version because it made use of πτερνισμός, which introduced the nuance of 'beguiling'. The idea of Judas beguiling Jesus did not accord with his position on Jesus' omniscience ('The Translation of Psalm 41.10 in John 13.18' *JSNT* 40 [1990], pp. 61-79). J.R. Michaels sees this text, as well as its companion fulfilment citation, Jn 15.25, as functioning on two levels. In the first instance they refer directly to Jesus' betrayal and passion, but in addition they can be seen to prophesy about the experience of the disciples after Jesus' departure. Through these verses, Michaels argues, the twin themes present in Mt. 10.21-22 and Mk 13.12-13—betrayal from within and hatred from without—have been incorporated into John's work ('Betrayal and the Betrayer: The Uses of Scripture in John 13.18-19', in C.A. Evans and W.R. Stegner [eds.], *The Gospels and the Scriptures of Israel* [JSNTSup, 104; Sheffield: Sheffield Academic Press, 1994], pp. 459-74).

discourse on the feeding of the five thousand in John 6, the former evidently providing a hermeneutical clue to the usage in 13.8.[40] The phrasing is similar:

ὁ τρώγων μου τὴν σάρκα   6.54, 56
ὁ τρώγων μου τὸν ἄρτον   13.18

The violent connotations of the 'munching', 'chewing' vocabulary, combined with the eating of bread/flesh have already been mentioned in the context of *sparagmatic* consumption. The language of physical destruction reappears here in conjunction with the betrayal. Judas is one who has figuratively devoured the flesh of Jesus, but not for the purposes of gaining a share in the life of the 'god'. On a more obvious level, of course, the poignancy of his words again emphasize Jesus' vulnerability. This is the treason of a companion with whom he has shared table fellowship. This will be highlighted when the Scripture is literally fulfilled in v. 26 when Jesus hands over the sop to Judas.

The second half of the verse continues the theme of physical abuse. The term ἐπῆρεν ἐπ᾽ ἐμὲ τὴν πτέρναν αὐτοῦ is undeniably abusive in intention. Lindars proposes the meaning 'has kicked me from behind'[41] and Hoskyns likens it to 'the sudden kick of a horse'.[42] Whatever the precise original meaning,[43] it is evident that the metaphor used is a malignant one and in this context it is particularly appropriate: the feet that Jesus has washed respond with violence and a metaphorical kick. This accentuates the contempt[44] of the betrayer and his rejection of Jesus' deed.

---

40. The significance of the use of τρώγω instead of the LXX's ἐσθίω has been discussed in the section on Jn 6. Michaels has difficulty seeing what the point of this parallel is, concluding that in all likelihood it is simply a matter of Johannine style, preferring τρώγειν to ἐσθίειν as the present tense of the verb 'to eat' ('Betrayal and the Betrayer', p. 467). However, I would argue that the fact that there *is* a clear parallel automatically implies that the evangelist saw a point.

41. Lindars, *Gospel of John*, p. 454. This suggests a similar sort of treachery to being shot in the back.

42. Hoskyns, *Fourth Gospel*, p. 441.

43. Bruce suggests the Hebrew, which is literally 'has made his heel great against me' can be rendered 'has given me a great fall', or 'has taken cruel advantage of me' (*Gospel of John*, p. 287).

44. For argument that the term contains an element of contempt see E.F.F. Bishop—'a revelation of contempt, treachery, even animosity' ('"He that Eateth Bread with me Hath Lifted Up his Heel Against me": Jn 13.18 [Ps. 41.9]', *ExpTim* 70 [1958–59], pp. 331-33 [332]).

4. Execution of the First Betrayal (Verses 21-30)

Verse 21 moves the narrative onto the next stage. Given the continual references to the betrayal throughout the chapter, the reader can hardly be unprepared for the coming scene. Jesus, who has appeared calm during the footwashing and ensuing discussion, now seems overcome by emotion.[45] The moment for the traitor to act has arrived and the text states ἐταράχθη τῷ πνεύματι ('he was troubled in spirit', v. 21). The use of ταράσσω has already been discussed in the section on the raising of Lazarus and was seen there to have connotations of fear and anxiety. Its use here recalls the mental suffering of Jesus at the tomb; something as momentous as the raising of a dead man is about to happen. It could be argued that it is Jesus' distress that compels him to utter his next words—after all he has up until now only alluded to the betrayer and clearly the disciples are none the wiser about what is to happen.[46] The baldness of his allegation ensures that there is no doubt about its meaning: 'Truly, truly, I say to you, one of you will betray (παραδώσει) me'. Now it is the disciples' turn for anxiety: *who* will betray Jesus?[47] Peter's worry prompts him to action, and he asks this question through the mediation of the beloved disciple, who is physically[48] and (presumably)

45. Carson comments, 'his anguish was visible, and caught the attention of his disciples' (*Gospel According to John*, p. 472). J.N. Suggit, commenting on the betrayal, sees John showing that 'the treachery harms Judas more than Jesus, for Jesus always knows what is to happen and is always in control' ('John 13.1-30: The Mystery of the Incarnation and of the Eucharist', *Neot* 19 [1985], pp. 64-70 [69]). It is difficult, however, to minimize the emotional distress displayed by Jesus in v. 21. In addition, knowing who his betrayer is does not imply that he is in control of the situation.

46. Perhaps the two statements in vv. 10 and 18 can be seen as hints to Judas to make his move. When Judas fails to act, the mental torment caused by waiting is such that Jesus forces his hand. Mlakuzhyil sees it as 'another attempt of Jesus to touch the heart of the betrayer' (*Christocentric Literary Structure*, p. 326).

47. Culpepper seems to suggest that the disciples do not understand Jesus' words—they are met with a lack of comprehension. However it surely is not what Jesus is saying, but whom he is speaking of, that causes their uncertainty ('The Johannine *Hypodeigma*', p. 145).

48. For the various theories on the seating arrangements of the disciples at the supper, the location of the place of honour (on the left or the right), and who occupies it, see the following scholars: Brown, *Gospel According to John*, II, p. 574; Barrett, *Gospel According to St John*, p. 446; Sanders, *Gospel According to St John*, pp. 312-13; and K. Quast, *Peter and the Beloved Disciple: Figures for a Community in Crisis* (JSNTSup, 32; Sheffield: JSOT Press, 1989), pp. 59-60. In all likelihood it is the beloved disciple and Judas who are sitting closest to Jesus.

emotionally closest to Jesus.[49] Peter's interest in the identity of the betrayer is more than just curiosity, it has a personal dimension to it.[50]
Trumbower suggests that Peter's anxiousness could be 'the author's
subtle indication of Peter's fear that *he* might be the betrayer'.[51]
Although the reader knows that Judas is the one to whom Jesus is referring, the characters do not and hence this interpretation is perfectly
feasible, particularly bearing in mind Jesus' words to Peter earlier on in
the scene (v. 10).

Jesus does not respond to the question with a name, but informs the
beloved disciple how he will unmask the culprit. Whether the other
disciples are cognizant of the meaning of Jesus' sign is not clear, but we
can make the assumption that at least three at the table are waiting to see
to whom Jesus hands the morsel.[52] The choice of a deed rather than a
word, and the nature of the deed itself is highly significant. It is all the
more notable in its differences from the Synoptic account.[53] While

49. On the role of the beloved disciple at this point in the narrative, see Carson
(*Gospel According to John*, pp. 473-74) and Stibbe (*John*, p. 149). Minear sees the
position of the beloved disciple vis-à-vis Jesus paralleling that of God and the Logos
in 1.18: 'In both places the phrase suggests intimacy of vision and knowledge that
qualifies a person to mediate divine grace and truth ('The Beloved Disciple in the
Gospel of John', p. 117). D.J. Hawkin sees him as having not just intimacy with
Jesus, but also superior knowledge of him. He is the 'special confidant' of Jesus
('The Function of the Beloved Disciple Motif in the Johannine Redaction', *LTP*
33.2 [1977], pp. 135-50 [143]). For general works on the identity of the Beloved
Disciple, see the relevant section and associated bibliography in Quast (*Peter and the
Beloved Disciple*, pp. 16-17).

50. Quast claims that in this passage it is almost impossible to differentiate
between Peter the individual and Peter the stylized representative of the disciples
(*Peter and the Beloved Disciple*, p. 63). Bultmann is also among those who see Peter
acting on behalf of the disciples (*Gospel of John*, p. 481). However, the above
discussion of Peter's objections to the footwashing show that he is portrayed very
definitely as an individual.

51. Trumbower, *Born from Above*, p. 132, emphasis added. Contra Schuyler
Brown, who comments: 'It does not occur to Peter to ask, "Is it I?"' ('The Beloved
Disciple: A Jungian View', in R.T. Fortna and B.R. Gaventa (eds.), *The Conversation
Continues: Studies in Paul and John: In Honor of J. Louis Martyn* (Nashville: Abingdon
Press, 1990), pp. 366-77 [374]).

52. The beloved disciple, Judas and Peter, assuming that the beloved disciple
answered Peter's question by relaying Jesus' words. This assumption is open to
dispute. Frans Neirynck, for example, claims that the beloved disciples does not tell
Peter ('John 21', *NTS* 36 [1990], pp: 321-36 [330, 333]).

53. Mt. 26.23; Mk 14.20. Luke does not include the incident.

Mark has Judas dipping bread into the dish with Jesus, in John Jesus dips the bread himself and hands it to Judas.[54] What, then, is being communicated by this act? The meaning clearly does not lie simply in the identification of the betrayer to other disciples as they now fade from the picture. The meaning lies in what is being communicated to the betrayer. Suggestions from commentators have included an appeal to Judas to reconsider,[55] or a gesture of supreme love and understanding.[56] For our purposes, the significance lies in the *active* nature of handing the sop to Judas and the consequences of this action.[57] This 'handing' (δίδωμι) is a cue to the one who will 'hand him over' (παραδίδωμι) to his death. But it is what happens after the morsel is given that is so striking: 'then after the morsel, Satan entered into him' (καὶ μετὰ τὸ ψωμίον τότε εἰσῆλθεν εἰς ἐκεῖνον ὁ Σατανᾶς, v. 27). The action of Jesus prepares the way for the action of Satan. Few modern scholars seem prepared to posit that the possession of Judas by Satan is caused by anything other than the hardening of Judas' resolve against Jesus at this crisis point.[58] Nevertheless, the text could be interpreted as indicating that Jesus' act has a causal element. The devil has already primed Judas (v. 2), but as yet he has been passive and has eaten, drunk and had his feet washed along with the other disciples. Jesus announces the betrayal and to indicate who will execute it he dips and gives a morsel to Judas. We know that Judas takes the morsel (the text states this in v. 30). The arguments of those who see Judas refusing a gift of Jesus which is

54. Quast debates briefly which one is likely to be the original eyewitness material and concludes: 'whatever the direction of change between John and the Synoptics, the direct action of Jesus in John is noteworthy. Jesus is obviously communicating something by his actions and words' (*Peter and the Beloved Disciple*, p. 65).

55. Sanders feels that as Judas has not been unmasked publicly, he could still change his mind (*Gospel According to St John*, p. 314). J.H. Bernard sees it as 'the last appeal to his better nature' (*A Critical and Exegetical Commentary on the Gospel According to St John* [ed. A.H. McNeile; ICC; 2 vols.; repr.; Edinburgh: T. & T. Clark, 1942 (1928)], II, p. 474). T.L. Brodie sees it as an effort by Jesus to 'recall Judas from his developing entanglement with Satan' (*The Gospel According to John: A Literary and Theological Commentary* [Oxford: Oxford University Press, 1993], p. 453-44).

56. Carson, *Gospel According to John*, p. 474.

57. Schnackenburg sees it as 'a clear expression of Jesus' initiative , taken to remove the traitor' (*Gospel According to St John*, III, p. 30).

58. So Carson, *Gospel According to John*, p. 475. Brodie resists seeing Judas as a puppet in the plan of salvation, claiming that the morsel did not destroy his freedom nor push him into the grip of Satan (*Gospel According to John*, p. 453).

symbolized by the morsel (i.e. love, a last chance etc.), therefore do not
quite follow through logically as Judas does *not* refuse it. He takes it and
then Satan enters into him. Barrett claims, 'μετά states a temporal but
not a causal relation; receiving the morsel did not make Judas Satan's
tool'.[59] But can we really rule out all elements of causality here?
Although Haenchen's statement that it is 'the magical morsel with
which Satan entered',[60] or Wrede's reference to the 'Satanic sacrament'[61]
may seem a little crass, the text shows Jesus participating in, facilitating,
even initiating the chain of events leading to the departure of Judas.[62]
This is emphasized by his subsequent command: 'what you are going to
do, do quickly'. [63] As Culpepper notes, 'it is not Satan that prompts
Judas to leave and carry out his betrayal'.[64]

The reference to a 'Satanic sacrament' is one that merits consideration. Some debate has existed over whether the morsel can be seen to
be eucharistic. Moloney discusses this point in detail, concluding that
the use of τρώγω in v. 18,[65] coupled with the inclusion of the words
λαμβάνει καί in v. 26b of many ancient manuscripts provides sufficient
evidence for a eucharistic interpretation.[66] This renders the text 'So
when he had dipped the morsel, *he took it* and gave it to Judas, the Son
of Simon Iscariot', mirroring the Synoptic format for the institution of
the eucharist. The eucharistic interpretation has posed problems for
many interpreters, since immediately following the morsel from Jesus,

---

59. Barrett, *Gospel According to St John*, p. 448.

60. *John*, II, p. 111. Haenchen thinks this is the work of a 'foolish redactor' who
has crassly attempted to emphasize Jesus' transcendence in this passage (p. 112).

61. Wrede notes 'it is a kind of satanic sacrament, which Judas takes to himself'.
Quoted in Bultmann, *Gospel of John*, p. 482 n. 8.

62. Edwin Freed sees 13.27 conflicting with 13.2 and comments that it is 'one of
those enigmatic contradictions inherent in the method of Jn which cannot be
explained' (*Old Testament Quotations in the Gospel of John* [NovTSup, 11; Leiden: E.J.
Brill, 1965], p. 92). There is reason, however, to see a contradiction.

63. Carson notes that τάχιον may be a comparative; 'do *more quickly* (than you
were planning)' (*Gospel According to John*, p. 475). If this is the case it could be seen
as a further indication of distress on Jesus' part, almost a plea to Judas to make his
move.

64. Culpepper, 'The Johannine *Hypodeigma*', p. 145.

65. Since this refers the reader back to Jn 6, which he sees as overwhelmingly
eucharistic.

66. F.J. Moloney, 'A Sacramental Reading of John 13.1-38', *CBQ* 53 (1991),
pp. 237-56.

the devil enters Judas.[67] Moloney sees it as an indication of the remarkable self-giving love of Jesus.[68] However, my interpretation of the events of John 6, and the *sparagmatic* hermeneutic of the body and blood makes sense of any 'eucharistic' connotations that the morsel may have. The eating of Jesus' body and drinking of his blood signify his physical destruction. Jesus gives the morsel to Judas because it is Judas who is to initiate the process. The taking and giving of something that represents his body[69] to the man responsible for his betrayal stresses his active involvement. Jesus enables the first step to be taken towards his own destruction. Perhaps the most significant question here is: who is colluding with whom? The devil places the seed in the heart of Judas. Jesus prepares the betrayer with two deliberate and intimate deeds— washing his feet and choosing, dipping and handing him a piece of food. The actions of Jesus function as a kind of foreplay for the entry of Satan into Judas. Once again we are faced with an interpretation that shows Jesus playing a victimal role.

At the beginning of this section it was suggested that the distress of Jesus indicated that something momentous was about to happen. The evangelist ends the scene with a phrase that confirms this by its dramatic content: 'and it was night' (ἦν δὲ νύξ, v. 30b). Darkness, symbolic of evil in the Gospel, is directly opposed to the light that Jesus represents (1.5; 9.4-5; 12.35). That night has now come indicates that the moment for the power of darkness has arrived and the hatred of the world has closed in on Jesus.

---

67. Augustine has a detailed comment about the problem of Satan entering Judas subsequent to Jesus handing him the sop. He resolves this by saying that what is important is 'not the character of the thing that is given, but of him to whom it is given' (*Hom. Ioh.* 42; *LNPNF*, VII, pp. 312-14).

68. Moloney sees Jesus shining forth in his unconditional love for ignorant disciples who betray and deny him: 'No narrative could portray such incredible love better than a story telling that Jesus of Nazareth, on the night before he died, gave the eucharistic morsel to Judas. It is not as if Judas is yet another example of a failing disciple. He is the evil disciple, the betrayer... Yet the morsel is given to Judas' ('Sacramental Reading', p. 251).

69. This relies on the morsel being bread, which, along with Moloney, I am assuming. For the argument that it is meat, see M.-J. Lagrange: 'Le pain étant à la disposition de chacun, on offre plutôt un morceau de viande' (*Evangile selon Saint Jean* [Paris: J. Gabalda, 7th edn, 1948], p. 362).

5. *Prediction of the Second Betrayal (vv. 31-38)*

Immediately after the departure of Judas, Jesus announces that the Son of Man is glorified. The vocabulary of glorification is used five times in vv. 32-33, indicating the nearness of death. In addition, Jesus comments: 'yet a little while I am with you', indicating once more that the time of departure/death is close. As he gave them an example to follow in 13.15, he now gives them a commandment, and this is a commandment to love to the extent that he has loved them. In other words, εἰς τέλος. If humility and humiliation are expected of them through footwashing, then the willingness to die is expected through the love they must show. Culpepper comments;

> Jesus' death is the model for the community. The footwashing and the new commandment are related as two facets of the same instruction for the community: Do (footwashing/love/die) for one another as I am doing for you.[70]

Once more Simon Peter questions Jesus, revealing a lack of understanding of his words. He is still not able to accept Jesus' way of doing things. Jesus tells him he will follow afterward, but he wants to follow now (vv. 36-37). It almost seems to be the rashness of his promise that prompts Jesus' prediction of his own betrayal, which sounds not unlike a rebuke: 'Truly, truly, I say to you, the cock will not crow, till you have denied me three times'. Schnackenburg notes that Jesus' use of words makes his statement emphatic (ἀμὴν ἀμὴν...οὐ μή..., and comments that his words sound 'extremely oppressive'.[71] Peter's promise rings hollow to Jesus and he immediately disavows him of his delusions of human glory through martyrdom.[72] Peter's protestations are truly pathetic and reveal his *continued* misunderstanding of Jesus' words and actions.[73] Perhaps, though, there is another reason why Jesus responds to him in the way he does. Peter is unpredictable and although Jesus

---

70. Culpepper, 'The Johannine *Hypodeigma*', p. 146.

71. Schnackenburg, *Gospel According to St John*, III, p. 57.

72. J.M. Reese notes that Peter presumptuously promises to lay down his life for Jesus using the same word as Jesus, who lays down his life for the flock ('Literary Structure of Jn 13.31–14.31; 16.5-6, 16-33', *CBQ* 34 [1972], pp. 321-31).

73. Maynard believes that further evidence of anti-Petrinism can be seen in the fact that Peter is alone in his stated willingness to die for Jesus in John, while in the Synoptics, other disciples join in. He suggests that the evangelist wants it to appear that only Peter misunderstands Jesus at this point and therefore his inadequacy is heightened ('The Role of Peter', p. 537).

knows he is weak, there may be a risk that he will do something rash to upset the chain of events that will lead to the cross. The subtle dynamics between Jesus and Judas have resulted in the latter leaving to carry out his task. Jesus does not want Peter jeopardizing this in any way, just as in a few hours time he will not want him jeopardizing the arrest. Consequently he immediately discourages any ideas of heroic action on Peter's part by identifying and exposing his true cowardice.

In concluding this section, it is worth noting that, although both intimate and climactic events have taken place in chapter 13, and we have learned quite a bit about Jesus' relationship with his disciples—he loves them, he is willing to debase himself before them, he expects the same of them—the focus has been on his interaction with individuals, rather than the group as a whole. Now that the business is done, the focus shifts to the wider group and to Jesus' role as their leader.

The Charismatic Leader?

If the footwashing was Jesus' means of communicating with his disciples through a sign, his attempt to communicate through discourse is seen in chs. 14–16. The remainder of the supper is primarily a monologue on the part of Jesus in which he comforts, educates, chides and warns those who are closest to him. These discourses contain material about a number of different themes and can be structured as follows:

1. 14.1-31   Jesus' departure and the coming of the Spirit
2. 15.1–16.4a Jesus' warning about the conditions and dangers
               of discipleship
3. 16.4b-33   Jesus' departure and role of the Spirit
4. 17.1-26   Jesus' prayer for the believers

The first three sections are of greatest relevance and the purpose and outcome of Jesus' words will be discussed in some detail below. Prior to this, it is necessary to consider the context in which the speech is taking place and the dynamics of the interaction between Jesus and the others present.

1. Context of the Discourses

As previously mentioned, the situation we are confronted with in these chapters is not that of a cosy supper, slightly tinged with sadness, as a leader calmly explains to his supporters what to expect when he has

leader calmly explains to his supporters what to expect when he has
gone. The scene is, in fact, a very tense one. Both Jesus and the disciples
display anxiety in their words and behaviour. The preceding events have
no doubt contributed to this uneasy atmosphere. From the disciples'
point of view, Jesus has just carried out an unexpected and shocking act
by washing their feet; had a serious argument with Peter; accused one of
them of being his betrayer;[74] told them he is leaving them and finished
off with further bitter words to Peter, scorning his fealty. From Jesus'
point of view, he has attempted to carry out an act of service to his
disciples which has humiliated him, and all the more so because it was
misinterpreted and resulted in conflict. He has had to bear the presence
of the one who is about to betray him, enduring great distress as he
identifies the culprit and sends him out to complete his task. Following
Judas' departure, Jesus has had to tell those closest to him that he will be
taken from them, but has been interrupted by Peter who, with his shal-
low promises, has revealed an utter lack of comprehension about the situation. Indeed, we can surmise that the atmosphere is extremely tense.

2. Jesus' Objectives
To understand the dynamics of the interaction between Jesus and the
disciples we must first explore what it is Jesus is trying to achieve, followed by some assessment of how successful he is. Jesus' words indicate
that he has the following objectives in mind:

- — to comfort and reassure his disciples
- — to explain where he is going and why
- — to instruct them about how they should behave
- — to warn them about future dangers

Underlying all of these objectives, however, is a fear. Jesus is afraid that
when he leaves them, they will all 'fall away' (σκανδαλίζειν,[75] 16.1),
and he must try to prevent this. He is faced with a major challenge in
communication and needs to persuade them to remain firm. Given the
tension between them, coupled with his own anxiety, this will not be
easy, but he must try to get across these few messages effectively as this
is now his last opportunity to do so.

---

74. They obviously do not all understand that this has been resolved by the
departure of Judas—see 13.29.

75. Barrett notes that this term has 'considerable force', meaning 'to cause to
give up the Christian faith' (*Gospel According to St John*, p. 484)

Comfort and Reassurance. There are many indications in John 14–16 that Jesus is deeply concerned about the current anxiety and future distress of his followers. He attempts to console them and relieve their fears, by encouraging them to trust him and to trust God. The section begins in this vein, with the words: 'Let not your hearts be troubled (ταρασ-σέσθω), believe in God, believe also in me' (14.1). That Jesus uses the same word to describe their anxiety as was used to describe his own in 13.21 (ταράσσω) is an indication of the strength of the emotions involved.[76] Much of his teaching seems to spring from this desire to comfort them and his means of reassurance is to explain where and why he is going and how he will return. He uses comforting images of home-making (14.2-3, 23). He sees they are orphans, but promises to come to them (14.18). He again encourages them not to be anxious and fearful (ταράσσω, δειλιάω 14.27), and promises that he is leaving his peace with them[77] and that joy will follow (15.11). He recognizes their overwhelming sorrow (16.6), but says that it is of necessity. In the end, he has to recognize that their mental state is such that he can tell them no more (...'You cannot bear them now', 16.12).

Explanation about Jesus' Departure. As mentioned above, one of the ways in which Jesus tries to comfort his disciples is by explaining the reason for and effects of his departure. This is an abiding theme throughout John 14–16. He is departing to go to the Father (14.2, 28; 16.28), but will return to them (14.3, 28). The subject of his departure is, according to Painter, a crisis which is depicted in 'emotional, psychological terms' —'how can the disciples overcome the trauma caused by the departure of Jesus?'[78] The discourse focuses, as Bruce Woll comments, on 'the harsh fact of separation between teacher and disciple. Jesus' followers are told that they will not be able to follow him!'[79] Jesus assures them,

---

76. Schnackenburg also notes that the use of the word καρδία refers to the emotional attitude in Semitic anthropology (*Gospel According to St John*, III, p. 58).

77. I. John Hesselink sees Jesus promising the disciples 'an assurance, a tranquility, an inner strength which they will enjoy from the resurrection onwards' ('John 14.23-29', *Int* 43 [1989], pp. 174-77 [175]). He therefore sees the peace of Jesus as having an eschatological dimension to it. This is one way of explaining why Jesus' promise of peace does not seem to take immediate effect.

78. Painter, 'The Farewell Discourses', p. 532.

79. B.D. Woll, 'The Departure of "the Way": The First Farewell Discourse in the Gospel of John', *JBL* 99 (1980), pp. 225-39 (229).

however, that there will be benefits for the disciples as a result of his departure—preparation of a place with him and the Father (14.2-3) and the sending of the Paraclete (16.7-11), who will act as their guide (16.13).

Instruction on Behaviour. Jesus must use this time to communicate to his disciples how he expects them to behave when he has gone. He has already given them the example of the footwashing, but this must be bolstered with firm instruction. The disciples are required to keep the 'words' or commandments of Jesus (14.12, 15, 21, 24; 15.10), to 'bear fruit' (15.2), to 'abide in Jesus' (15.4, 9). These are evidently interlinked, but Jesus explains the bottom line in 15.12: 'This is my commandment that you love one another as I have loved you'.[80] To fulfil this command, disciples must be prepared to make the ultimate sacrifice, the one that Jesus himself is about to make; to give up their own lives. Minear sees this as a kind of 'suicide pact between the Good Shepherd and his undershepherds'[81]—if he is to give up his life for his friends, so too must they.

Warning about Future Dangers. Jesus' fear that the disciples will fall away once he has gone prompts him to give them two sets of warnings. One set details what will happen to them if they remain steadfast, keeping Jesus' command; the other tells of what will happen if they do not. The latter is contained in 15.1-11: Jesus indicates that the disciples have no choice but to abide in him. If they do not they will bear no fruit and be cast off the vine. They will wither and be thrown into the fire to burn (v. 6).[82] The consequences of failing to remain true to Jesus are deadly and these words sound as much like a threat as a warning.[83]

80. This is the pre-eminent command of Jesus, according to Segovia, underscored by both the use of the definite article and the emphatic use of the possessive pronoun (*Farewell of the Word*, p. 155).

81. Minear, *John: The Martyr's Gospel*, p. 45.

82. Segovia notes the admonitory function of 15.1-11: 'the call to abide is accompanied by a severe, sustained portrayal of the consequences for the disciples of a failure to heed the call…those who do not bear fruit…will not only be removed from the vine but also undergo death and destruction' (*Farewell of the Word*, pp. 163-64).

83. Segovia sees the choice facing the disciples formulated in the 'sharpest terms possible'—'either fulfil your proper role as disciples, or lose not only your discipleship but ultimately your life as well' (*Farewell of the Word*, p. 164).

The consequences of abiding in Jesus, however, may also be deadly, as is indicated in 15.18-16.4a. The disciples must expect hatred, persecution, expulsion from the synagogue and even death.[84] Victimization is an inescapable part of discipleship for those who abide in the victim. These words of Jesus confirm what we already know about his understanding of his relationship with the world. The severity of the world's hatred as he experiences it is emphasized by the overwhelming use of negative vocabulary. In this short section we have the following occurrences:

Term	Translation	Frequency
μισέω	hate	7
διώκω	persecute	2
ἀποσυνάγωγος	expel (from synagogue)	1
ἀποκτείνω	kill	1

Jesus perceives relentless abhorrence towards him. He has suffered it from the beginning of his ministry and knows that when he has gone, the same hatred will pursue his followers. The world abhors Jesus to such an extent that, he claims, it will rejoice (χαρήσεται) at his torturous and bloody death (16.20).

In vv. 22-24 Jesus speaks of the wilful nature of the world's rejection and sin. If the κόσμος was ignorant it would be innocent, but it is *not* ignorant and Jesus' mission has testified to its evil works (7.7). He has stated his identity, performed 'signs' and taught them, yet the response of those who have heard and seen him has been malevolent, and this is painful for Jesus. 'For all their judicial objectivity, the words are unmistakably suffused with emotion', comments Dodd.[85] Rejection of his revelation renders them culpable. Jesus, however, is not culpable. He

---

84. This section is commonly seen as being an attempt by the evangelist to warn the community about impending violent persecution to encourage them to remain firm. Moloney comments that this section is 'deeply rooted in the concrete experience of the Johannine community'. 'For the evangelist and his community', he goes on, 'it was important to see and understand that the experience of hatred and violence...was part of the experience of Jesus and is also part of the experience of his disciples' ('The Structure and Message of Jn 15.1–16.3', *AusBR* 35 [1987], pp. 35-49 [43, 41]). See also Lindars, 'Persecution of Christians' and the discussion in Chapter 4.

85. Dodd, 'Portrait of Jesus in John', p. 191.

perceives himself as the object of their unwarranted victimization, claiming 'They hated me without a cause' (15.25).[86] To claim that he was hated without reason does not render the world's opposition unintelligible to the reader. We have seen the escalation in enmity between Jesus and his persecutors over the last few chapters, some of which appears to have been provoked by Jesus himself. For the Fourth Gospel, however, there has never really been any story to be told other than that of the incompatibility between the λόγος and the κόσμος and the dynamics of violence at the point at which they meet.

3. *The Disciples' Reactions*

Having discussed Jesus' objectives and the messages he has attempted to communicate to his team, it is appropriate to look at how successful he seems to have been from their perspective. Their reaction to his words is the best indicator of how well he has achieved his objectives of comforting, explaining, instructing and warning. Although, for the most part, these chapters comprise a monologue by Jesus, the disciples interact with him on several occasions and these will be explored to reveal the nature of the communication taking place.

Jesus Comforts? The fact that Jesus needs to repeat his words of comfort on a number of occasions during his speech would seem to indicate that they are failing to take effect. Employing a variety of different images and metaphors, he tries to impress on the disciples the fact that joy will follow their sorrow. Promises of greater works, a counsellor, his own return—all these are used to boost *esprit de corps*. He ends his speech with what sounds like a last ditch attempt to motivate them and win their trust in him and his promises: 'In the world you have tribulation; but be of good cheer, I have overcome the world' (16.33).[87] To under-

---

86. This could derive from either Ps. 34.19 or Ps. 69.4, although the latter seems probable as this is a text used elsewhere in the Gospel. Verse 9 appears in Jn. 2.17 and v. 21 in Jn. 19.29, quite apart from the general relevance of its theme of suffering, which marks it out as a messianic psalm. See Barrett, *Gospel According to St John*, p. 482 and Dodd, *Historical Tradition*, p. 38.

87. This verse is generally interpreted in an overwhelmingly triumphalist manner. For example, Beasley-Murray understands 'I have conquered the world' as 'the word of the Victor who, by his enduring θλῖψις in obedience and unwavering love, conquered the evil in the world, as he overcame the 'prince' of this world' (*John*, p. 288). D.G. Miller is not unusual in his portrayal of a very militaristic Jesus: 'I have faced your enemy and vanquished him... I have fought your battle... I have routed

stand why Jesus is not particularly effective in raising the morale of his team, we need to look at the messages he is projecting. Woven into his words of comfort are accusations that reveal Jesus' ambivalence about what he is trying to achieve. He has mixed feelings about their feelings. He wants to comfort them, of course, because he does love them, but he is also angry that he has to console them at all, because this reveals the paucity of their love for him—'If you loved me you would have rejoiced, because I go to the Father' (14.28). I showed in Chapter 6 how Jesus was suspicious of the motives of those around him. Here too we see this trait. Jesus suspects the reason for their sorrow is not concern for him at all, but for themselves. They selfishly do not wish to lose their leader. It is hardly surprising, then, that he is unable to comfort them— his heart is not really in it.

Jesus Educates? Given that Jesus wants his followers to understand the need for his departure, it might be expected that he would welcome their questions about it. This appears not to be the case. Jesus reacts in a hostile manner to most of their queries.[88] This has the effect of intimidating the disciples, who then dare not ask him any more questions (16.5), and resort to speculating among themselves about what he means (16.17-18).[89]

Considering the response that Peter received when he questioned Jesus about following him in 13.36-37, it must have required some degree of courage for Thomas to do likewise. He too is a disciple who has expressed a willingness for martyrdom (11.16). Thinking only on an earthly level, he again indicates his desire to be a follower, but misunderstands the destination. Jesus' reply attempts to educate—'*I am the way*'—but his next words are a reproach: 'If you had known me, you would have known my Father also' (14.7).[90] The clear implication is

the foe' ('Tribulation but...', *Int* 18 [1964], pp. 165-70 [169]). It is natural to interpret the phrase in this manner if one's overall picture is of Jesus as the exalted victor. As a victim, however, Jesus 'overcomes' the world in a different way: not by defeating the κόσμος but by embracing its θλῖψις.

88. Contra Reese, who sees a pattern of revelation–question–clarification in each interaction between Jesus and his disciples, but does not evaluate any of these negatively ('Literary Structure').

89. Du Rand claims that the disciples find him 'enigmatic' and 'mysterious', but the sense of the text is rather that they are afraid to ask him ('Characterization of Jesus', p. 30).

90. Carson claims that Jesus is 'sensitive to Thomas' misunderstanding', but there

that the disciples do *not* know Jesus in the way they are expected to. Eager to understand, Philip puts in a request to see the Father.[91] This, however, provokes an outburst from Jesus which is directed against Philip personally: 'do you not know me, Philip...how can you say...do you not believe...?' (vv. 9-10). Jesus is both angry and incredulous that Philip could ask this of him.[92] If Philip cannot believe Jesus himself, he should look to his works for the evidence that he desires.[93] Judas ventures a question about how Jesus will be manifested, which is better received. Nevertheless, there is a warning contained in the response concerning those who do not love him and do not keep his words.

The disciples have great difficulty understanding Jesus' message, but his style is not to educate them through mutual discussion; rather he lectures them, admonishing them if they reveal their ignorance. He tries to rescue the situation in 16.6 and 19 by answering what he thinks are their questions, but they do not respond to this. Finally, in 16.28, he makes his message clear and they make an expression of faith in him, but he now reveals that he does not trust their words. Instead of seeing in them an indication that the disciples have come to *some* understanding about his departure, he scorns them with a retort: 'Do you now believe? The hour is coming, indeed it has come, when you will be scattered, every man to his home, and will leave me alone' (16.31-32).[94]

is no evidence of this in the text (*The Farewell Discourse and Final Prayer of Jesus: An Exposition of John 14–17* [Grand Rapids: Baker Book House, 1980], p. 27). Woll sees in Thomas's question an indication that he thinks a successor to Jesus will be required. Jesus is emphatic in his denial of this—'I *remain* the way' (The Departure of "the Way"', p. 230).

91. Gordon Fee sees Jesus' answers as too tantalizing for Philip: 'He has had enough of the mystery, the obfuscation...no more guessing at what Jesus means and what he is all about. Let us just have one good look, that will satisfy us' ('John 14.8-17', *Int* 43 [1989], pp. 170-74 [170]).

92. Calvin shares Jesus' frustration: 'It seems quite absurd that the apostles should continually argue with the Lord. For why did He speak at all except to teach them what Philip was asking about? (*Gospel According to John*, II, p. 78).

93. This is clearly an insult, since Jesus is scathing about those who need such props for belief. See Jn 2.48.

94. Carson sees Jesus answering them 'with gentle irony', which hardly fits the mood of the scene according to this interpretation (*The Farewell Discourse*, p. 167).

Jesus Instructs? Whether or not Jesus has managed to instruct his disciples effectively in what is required of them will, in reality, only be borne out by their subsequent behaviour. We can expect, however, that Jesus will not be overly optimistic about their ability to follow his instructions. After all, it seems the crux of his directive is love, and he has already accused them of not loving him (14.28); what hope is there that they will manage to love each other? Do they know what is expected of them? Their actions provide no evidence that they do. Jesus' final words in John 16 reveal that he knows he has failed to make the necessary impact on the listeners. Instead of remaining (μένω) they will leave him alone (μόνος). Moreover, Peter is imminently about to fail a test of 'laying down his life for his friend' through his denial, and, along with his companions, to desert discipleship in favour of fishing once Jesus is dead (21.2).

Jesus Warns? It could be argued that the one thing Jesus does manage to do effectively in this section is to warn the disciples about the dangers ahead. He spends some considerable time on this subject, and by the end of John 16 they are surely aware that tribulation awaits. It should be remembered, however, that the reason behind the warnings is Jesus' fear that the disciples will fall away under pressure. Admonition about the consequences of failing to abide and forewarning about the likely threat from the world were intended to inspire the disciples to remain true to their leader. The success of the warnings can, again, only be measured by the effect that they have on the disciples' behaviour. As already noted, they are almost immediately disregarded as they scatter 'every man to his home' (v. 32).

In conclusion, I suggest that Jesus has not managed to achieve his objectives particularly successfully. He loves his disciples and has attempted to inspire a love in them that results in loyalty unto death, but recognizes himself that he has failed to do this. As an exercise in team building, the results have been disappointing.[95] In preparing his team for the challenge ahead, this leader has failed to communicate the plan, motivate the individuals and win overall commitment.[96] In the light of this, there is only one option left for Jesus.

95. Although amazingly, Reese sees the section ending on a 'note of assurance' ('Literary Structure', p. 330). This does not seem to be borne out by the text.
96. Discussing Jesus' leadership style, Bruce Malina notes that charismatic leaders

4. *Jesus' Last Option*

The one course of action left open to Jesus is to pray to the Father. His attempt to strengthen the disciples' faith and prevent desertion may not have worked, but he can at least petition the Father for assistance in this matter.[97] The prayer is his final option and should not be viewed as a 'solemn', 'high-priestly prayer', which 'replaces the prayer-struggle of the Synoptic Jesus'.[98] It is the deeply emotional plea and a desperate man's last wishes. He prays for those given him by the Father, those who received the word (17.6, 9). He recognizes that while he was in the world, he was able to guide and protect them (v. 12). Now he is leaving the world and they must remain. He therefore asks the Father in vv. 13-19 for assistance in achieving the objectives already identified. As far as consolation is concerned, he asks that they are given joy (v. 13). Speaking of his return to the Father, he acknowledges that neither he nor they are of this world (v. 16). Recognizing the hatred that will surround them, he prays that they may be kept from the evil one

require strong personal authority and inspire impassioned loyalty from their followers. He sees Jesus having none of these; he has no power over people, only demons and occasionally nature, and of his disciples, 'one betrays him, one denies him, the others flee from him in time of need' ('Jesus as Charismatic Leader?', *BTB* 14 [1984], pp. 55-62 [58]). Furthermore, Malina sees charismatic leaders exuding confidence in their abilities and thriving on power, neither of which are characteristics of Jesus. Instead, he sees him as 'the great reputational, legitimate leader', who 'affirms the traditional values and structures of his society by repudiating personal power' (p. 61).

If Jesus' leadership style during his farewell speech was analysed according to more modern management theory, it is interesting to speculate which category he would fall into. According to Likert's styles of management leadership, for example, he would perhaps fit the description of exploitative–authoritative leaders, who are, 'highly autocratic, place little trust in subordinates and use fear and punishment as motivators, with only occasional rewards. They retain all powers of decision-making and only engage in downward communication' (R. Dixon, *Management Theory and Practice* [Oxford: Butterworth–Heinemann, 1991], pp. 65-66).

97. I am not suggesting that Jesus *only* prays to the Father because he feels his speech has not had the desired effect. Any one of a number of reasons could be suggested for the inclusion of the prayer. My interpretation, however, sees his recognition of failure (16.31) setting the context for the petition to the Father.

98. Windisch, 'John's Narrative Style', p. 53. Edward Malatesta also seems to minimize the emotional distress of the passage in his discussion of the structure of this 'sublime prayer' ('The Literary Structure of John 17', *Bib* 52 (1971), pp. 190-214 [190]).

(v. 15). He asks too that they be consecrated in the truth, stating that he consecrates himself for their sake (vv. 17, 19). His sacrifice is made so that they can behave in a similarly sacrificial manner, in fulfilment of his command.[99]

Jesus' prayer is borne out of a knowledge that the end has now come for him—'the hour has come' (ἐλήλυθεν ἡ ὥρα, 17.1)—and he is about to be deserted by the followers with whom he has shared everything. He concludes with a final word to the Father on behalf of other believers, but the pericope ends with no response from those who have heard his petition.

Concluding Comment: Jesus' Farewell to his Disciples

Jesus' last meal with his followers has added further dimensions to the understanding of him as a victim. In Chapters 5 and 6 we saw how he was victimized by all sections of the community—from the crowd to the authorities—and explored how he reacted to this. Now we have seen that he exhibits victimal behaviour in private and in the company of those closest to him. This has been a crucial factor in the footwashing and betrayal. Moreover, Jesus sees his disciples, and expects them to see themselves, as victims. His ability to encourage them to be faithful to this calling has been limited, perhaps because of a preoccupation with his own fate. His prayer to the Father has, however, revealed his desire for them and for those after them—for a unity through love which is not possible before the hour of death has been embraced.

---

99. Beasley-Murray sees ἁγιάζειν as having a sacrificial context, in accordance with the meaning of 'consecrate' in the Hebrew Bible (*John*, p. 301).

Relationship with Death II:
Embracing the Hour

It has been shown throughout the preceding chapters that Jesus' experience during his ministry is one of victimization and persecution. In examining the events surrounding his death, we might anticipate that these aspects of his experience would be heightened. After all, it is to be expected that a man who is arrested, put on trial and executed should be pictured as suffering violently at the hands of others. It should not be a surprise if there is a narrative of his being beaten and abused and it would be natural for him to be referred to as a victim. However, such has not been a principal emphasis of Johannine scholarship in its treatment of the passion. The focus has been rather on the triumphant nature of the passion, with Jesus hailed as a victor rather than a victim, as is clearly expressed by these words of Raymond Brown:

> Jesus goes through the passion not as a victim, but as a sovereign and superhuman Being who at any moment could bring the process to a halt.[1]

The passion of the Johannine Jesus is portrayed primarily in terms of his glorification, and it is this perspective that pervades all aspects of the interpretation of the final chapters of John. This appears to be particularly the case when John is compared to the Synoptics, whose accounts are viewed as more violent and harrowing for Jesus. Collins asserts that

1.   Brown, *Gospel According to John*, II, p. 787. Ashton comments: 'In the case of the Fourth Gospel "passion" is a misnomer; Jesus controls and orchestrates the whole performance' (*Understanding the Fourth Gospel*, p. 489). Similarly, R.H. Fuller sees Jesus having a large degree of autonomy, as he 'initiates the passion and calls the shots' ('The Passion, Death and Resurrection of Jesus According to St John', *ChS* 25 [1986], pp. 51-63 [57]). For Stibbe, Jesus' 'sovereign control' over the events of chs. 18 and 19 simply reflect the 'superhuman and solitary heroism' of his character ('Return to Sender', p. 195).

'were it only the Gospel of John that had been handed down to us, it is unlikely that we would speak of the "passion of Jesus" at all'.[2] He makes this claim because he considers a passion narrative to be 'an account of suffering and of passivity, that is, suffering that occurs at the hands of others'[3] and that this is *not* what he thinks is depicted in John. An alternative view, which I would argue, is that if the only narrative of Jesus' death available to us was John's, we would indeed view it as a passion (by Collins' definition or otherwise). This is because the chain of events, which describe Jesus' betrayal by a false follower, denial by a friend, torture by his own people, trial at the hands of a weak ruler, condemnation, abuse, degradation and crucifixion, cannot easily be viewed any other way. In addition, the violence inherent in John's narrative would not be minimized by comparison with the events depicted in the Synoptics. As this is a common step in elevating the Johannine Christ from victim to victor during his passion, it will be helpful to begin the section with a discussion on this subject.

Comparison of the Synoptic and Johannine Passions

It would not be an unfair generalization to say that scholars have held that John's account is less violent and less shocking than that of the Synoptics, portraying Jesus controlling his last hours and dying in a more triumphant fashion.[4] There are two tenets of the traditional scholarly Johannine treatment of the passion which have to some extent become preconceptions, colouring the way the account is commonly viewed. These will be discussed before exegesis of the text is carried out. The first is that John does not portray Jesus suffering the same level of violence and degradation as in the Synoptics. Sobrino claims that John 'prettifies' Jesus' death to soften its scandalous impact.[5] There are seen to be fewer accounts of Jesus' physical ordeal, minimizing the torture he

---

2. R.F. Collins, *These Things Have Been Written: Studies on the Fourth Gospel* (Leuven: Peeters, 1990), p. 89.

3. Collins, *These Things Have Been Written*, p. 87.

4. For example, 'Jesus' reaction to his own impending death shifts [in John] from that depicted in the Synoptic Gospels. Whereas there it seems to be a fearful ordeal to be endured, now it becomes a deliberate positive act' (L.R. Bailey, *Biblical Perspectives on Death* [Overtures to Biblical Theology; Philadelphia: Fortress Press, 1981], p. 95).

5. Sobrino, *Christology at the Crossroads*, p. 185.

suffers.[6] The second is that Jesus is majestically in control of the proceedings. From the time of the arrest, through the trial and up until the
moment of his death, he displays a serene detachment from the chaos
about him, as he calmly completes his Father's work. This view is widespread among writers probably primarily because it accords so readily
with the theology of the 'hour of glory', lending itself to an interpretation tinged with triumphalism.[7] The theory is that as Jesus approaches
death, so the hour of glory becomes ever more prominent. Jesus is in
control of this process and of events that lead up to the hour.[8] He is
omniscient and composed as he completes this work, taking the time to
ensure that he fulfils Scripture and ministers to the needs of others, even
in the midst of the terrible agony of crucifixion. So Collins can conclude that 'as John tells the story of the passion, he does not tell us about
the one who suffers at the hands of others; rather, he tells the story of
one who takes the initiative and remains in full control until the consummation of his revelation'.[9]

John's narration of the passion is certainly different from that of the
Synoptics, both in terms of the sequence of events and the style used to
convey them. However, neither of the two preconceptions mentioned
above can be supported. The first point is relatively straightforward: to
counter the claim that the Johannine Jesus has a passion experience less
brutal than his Synoptic counterpart one need only to place the texts
side by side. A comparison of the Synoptic and Johannine accounts
(Figure 4) shows the course of events ordered by the evangelists and

---

6.   'It is not correct to characterize the Jesus of John's Gospel as suffering ...
John...does no more than hint that Jesus' death involves him in the suffering which
the Synoptics strongly suggest' (Moody Smith, 'Presentation of Jesus in the Fourth
Gospel', p. 368).

7.   'It is the hour for Jesus to be glorified, and so Jesus remains in control of
events until they are triumphantly completed' (Lindars, *Gospel of John*, p. 535).

8.   Jesus is 'majestically, completely in charge of the situation right up to the
very end' (Sobrino, *Christology at the Crossroads*, p. 185). Similar sentiments from
Sloyan, *John*, p. 200; Stibbe, *John*, p. 181 and Evans, 'The Passion of John', p. 57.
Forestell is slightly less ambitious in his claims: 'In a general way the evangelist
avoids portraying Jesus in a humiliating light at the supreme moment of his career'
(*Word of the Cross*, pp. 82-83). Marianne Thompson, while claiming that Jesus'
'sovereignty and victory over his opponents loom large', concludes that the passion
narrative does not minimize the humanity of Jesus (*The Humanity of Jesus*, pp. 105,
110).

9.   Collins, *These Things Have Been Written*, p. 89.

Event	Synoptics (Mk 14.43–15.40; Mt. 26.47–27.56; Lk. 22.47–23.49)	John (18.1–19.37)
Arrest	Jesus approached by a crowd with weapons Jesus is betrayed with a kiss *Jesus is seized by crowd* Slave's ear cut off (healed in Luke) Jesus rebukes arresters for coming to him in darkness	Jesus is approached by a band with weapons Jesus confesses his identity Crowd 'fall back' Jesus pleads for release of his disciples Slave's ear cut off *Jesus is seized and bound*
Jewish Trial	Jesus is led to high priest's (Caiaphas) house False witnesses speak against Jesus Jesus is interrogated Jesus is condemned to death *Jesus is mocked and abused* Jesus is denied by Peter	Jesus is sent to Annas (Caiaphas has already condemned Jesus to death) Peter denies Jesus Jesus is interrogated *Jesus is struck by soldier* Jesus is sent to Caiaphas Peter denies Jesus again
Roman Trial	Jesus is delivered to Pilate (Judas hangs himself—Matthew) Jesus is interrogated Barabbas is released in Jesus' place Crowd call for Jesus to be crucified Pilate washes his hands (Matthew) *Jesus is scourged* (Mark, Matthew) *Jesus is mocked and abused*	Jesus is delivered to Pilate Jesus is accused by priests of being an evildoer Jesus is interrogated Barabbas is released in Jesus' place *Jesus is scourged* *Jesus is mocked and abused* Priests call for Jesus to be crucified Jesus is interrogated again Jesus is presented to the crowd Crowd calls for him to be crucified again
Crucifixion	Jesus is led out for crucifixion Simon of Cyrene carries Jesus' cross (Wailing and lamenting of women - Luke) Jesus refuses wine and myrrh (Mark, Matthew) *Jesus is crucified* Soldiers cast lots for his clothes Jesus is mocked by crowd, priests and robbers (Jesus forgives soldiers/one robber repents—Luke) Jesus cries out Jesus is given sponge of vinegar *Jesus dies* Temple curtain torn in two (Tombs of the righteous open—Matthew)	Jesus is led out for crucifixion *Jesus bears his own cross* *Jesus is crucified* Soldiers cast lots for his clothes Jesus entrusts his mother to the beloved disciple Jesus is given sponge of vinegar Jesus says his last words *Jesus dies* *Jesus' side is pierced*

indicates in italics the occasions of physical violence suffered by Jesus. As can be seen, the Johannine version does not reduce the occasions of torture, although Markan style elaborates on the details of the abuse and mocking more than John does. If anything, it is the Lukan version that makes the least of the violence inflicted on Jesus and this suggestion will be explored further in the section on the crucifixion.

The second point needs more careful consideration. It is clearly one of the great ironies of John's Gospel that during his passion, the Jesus who is being mocked as the King of the Jews is actually being presented to the reader as the true king whose kingdom is not of this world. Nevertheless, scholarship seems to have relied on somewhat earthly concepts of kingship to interpret the text, imposing its own understanding of what a king should be. The regal terms so often applied to Jesus during these passages—sovereignty, majesty, enthronement, triumphant—must be considered in the context of what type of king Jesus is actually presented as being. To recognize the irony of the interplay between the earthly and heavenly king or the earthly and heavenly authority (19.11), but then proceed to apply royal terminology of the earthly type (with all its old notions of earthly power) to the heavenly king is to miss the point of what the evangelist is saying. The old terminology turns Jesus the King into Jesus the Monarch, the Emperor, the Supreme Ruler. This cannot be the right picture for John; especially as Jesus himself rejects the earthly context and indicates that it should not be applied to him—he has no servants fighting to prevent his arrest because he is not that kind of king (18.36). He is the kind of king that deconstructs our notion of kingship.

How then are we to understand the kingship of Jesus at this stage in the drama? Surely it must be an understanding that is consistent with the picture we have already seen. I have traced the character of Jesus the victim through the narrative thus far and, although his behaviour may alter, his character will endure to the end. The text has shown him to be a man of deep emotions, including fear and anger, who is not always in control. When we arrive at the passion, we do not expect the evangelist to just flip him over and reveal that he is a potentate after all. A consistent interpretation will view Jesus as king in the same way he was viewed as master in 13.1-20, or as healer in 4.46-54, or as teacher in 3.1-15. This heavenly king is truly a king from below. He is a king who has friends rather than servants (15.15). He is not an overlord who inflicts his rule on his subjects; instead he is the first to enact his own commandment and to do so *in extremis*—his subjects do not die for him, he dies for them. Rather than obsequiousness, he asks for a genuinely servile approach to be practised among his people and again, he is the first to show them what this means. He does not demand mere loyalty, but the practice of a love that is prepared to lay down its life and not solely for the king, but also for fellow subjects. Signs of status, dignity and honour as we know them are absent; the dignity of this king is displayed in his debasement before his friends and enemies as he washes their feet. His kingship is not about exerting authority but bearing witness to the truth. His 'sovereignty' must also be understood in this context as he is a king who eschews the exercise of power as we know it. Pilate's power may be derivative, but Jesus' power is also limited. He is a king with power to do one thing alone: to lay down his life (10.18). He does not speak on his own authority (12.49) and he does what another commands (14.31). Even stranger, that 'other' is his father. If there is one thing an earthly king does not have, it is a father—'The King is dead. Long live the King'. These points will be further explored during the following discussion on the arrest, trials and crucifixion, but suffice to say here that Jesus' identity as a victim cannot preclude his identity as a king. The former must be used to reinterpret the latter.

The Arrest of Jesus (18.1-12)

From the point of Jesus' arrest his oppression and subjection to physical threat evidently intensify as he becomes a political prisoner. Although his ability to move about the country has been restricted for some time (7.1; 11.8), he now loses his liberty entirely. The 'elusive Christ'[10] has finally been ensnared and is at the mercy of hostile Jewish and Roman authorities. The occasion of his arrest has the potential to be far more violent that it actually turns out to be. Jesus is 'seized and bound' (v. 12), but the only real casualty is Malchus, the high priest's slave, who has his ear amputated in a burst of enthusiasm by Peter.

An examination of the contents of the text reveals an operation of such scale and drama that the scene is almost farcical. Jesus has gone with his disciples across the Kidron valley to a familiar meeting place in a garden. We can assume that the sum total of his party consists of twelve men—Jesus and the remaining eleven disciples. In the garden they are confronted by the betrayer's party, consisting of a Roman

10. As Stibbe sees him ('Elusive Christ', pp. 19-38).

cohort (τὴν σπεῖραν), numbering six hundred armed soldiers[11] carrying torches,[12] a number of officers from the chief priests and Pharisees, and Judas himself. The Synoptics do not paint such an official and imposing picture of Jesus' apprehenders.[13] They talk of a crowd[14] which has among it a contingent of religious authorities, but does not yet involve the Romans. It could be argued that the reason for mobilizing a sizeable army to arrest one man was to counteract any trouble there may have been from supporters of Jesus, although it can hardly be said that the support of the people is something that Jesus can rely on in John. Despite their cries of 'Hosanna' as he enters Jerusalem (12.12-13) and the worries of the Pharisees that the world has gone after him (12.19), we know that they are fickle in nature, as is evidenced by 7.30 and 8.59. The Johannine Jesus in no way commands the popular support of his Synoptic counterpart, whose arrest is delayed for fear of the people rioting (Mt. 26.5 and parallels).

The effect that the inclusion of the Roman cohort in the narrative has is to emphasize the immense force ranged against Jesus in the Johannine account. On a practical level, it could be that, due to the failure of the authorities to capture Jesus in the past, notably at the Feast of Tabernacles (7.25-52), they are not prepared to risk his escaping their clutches again and so they take the precautionary measure of marshalling all available men. Symbolically, what Jesus is faced with here is the hatred

11. So claims Lindars, (*Gospel of John*, p. 539). BAGD concurs: 'the tenth part of a legion, normally 600 men' (p. 761). Sloyan disagrees, however, exclaiming 'surely not the literal six hundred men …but a small fraction' (*John*, p. 201); and Fuller sees the size of the cohort as being 'grossly exaggerated' ('Passion, Death and Resurrection', p. 55). The text allows us to assume that it is the full cohort and it becomes less incredible if the authorities had in mind the possibility of civil unrest following the arrest. Ernst Haenchen goes further, suggesting the whole Roman–Jewish company would have amounted to around 800, armed and with lanterns to prevent any of Jesus' party escaping in the darkness (*John*, II, p. 164).

12. A note unique to John and possibly a reference to τις περιπατῇ ἐν τῇ νυκτί, προσκόπτει, ὅτι τὸ φῶς οὐκ ἔστιν ἐν αὐτῷ (Jn 11.10).

13. For a thorough study of the differences between the Johannine and Synoptic accounts see M. Sabbe, 'The Arrest of Jesus in Jn 18.1-11 and its Relation to the Synoptic Gospels', in M. de Jonge (ed.), *L'Evangile de Jean: Sources, Rédaction, Théologie* (BETL, 44; Leuven: Leuven University Press/Uitgeverij Peeters, 1977), pp. 203-34. Sabbe's article is a refutation of the claim by Anton Dauer that Jn 18.1–19, 30 is a combination of the redactional work of the evangelist with a written pre-Johannine source.

14. Mk 14.43 and Lk. 22.47 use ὄχλος; Mt. 26.47 uses ὄχλος πολύς.

and opposition of the entire world.[15] He is confronted with the might of the Roman army (representing the Gentile world), and the power of the chief priests and Pharisees (representing his community), all of whom have overtly hostile intentions. Bearing this in mind, the evangelist's comment in 18.4 that Jesus 'knew all that was to befall him' seems hardly surprising. There is no need for supernatural knowledge here—it would have been patently obvious to all present what was about to befall Jesus.[16] The time for escape is now ended, as practical preparations for the hour of death are set in motion with the arrest. Faced with this absurdly one-sided situation, it is Jesus who takes the initiative, as the leader of his own party, by approaching and addressing the masses with the question 'whom do you seek?' (v. 4). They too have a leader; a representative of the world that rejects Jesus, but it is obviously not Judas whom Jesus addresses, or who makes the reply 'Jesus of Nazareth' (v. 5). Nor is it Judas who identifies Jesus to the rest of his entourage; but rather, Jesus identifies himself. The role of the betrayer is minimized to gathering a sufficiently impressive band and leading it to the garden. There is no need for words or a kiss between the two men.

The reason for the dramatic response of the assemblage to Jesus' admission ἐγώ εἰμι ('I am he') has been the source of much speculation. Some hold that falling to the ground is the typical response to a theophany, which is what has occurred here,[17] whether or not the use of the divine name is implied.[18] An alternative suggestion if use of the divine name is accepted is that the crowd are not so much floored by the theophany as horrified at the blasphemy.[19] Others believe that it is

---

15. Barrett claims that the inclusion of the Romans was due to John's intention to show that 'the whole κόσμος was ranged against Jesus' (*Gospel According to St John*, p. 516).

16. Some scholars hold that there is supernatural knowledge on Jesus' part (Barrett, *Gospel According to St John*, p. 519; Haenchen, *John*, II, p. 165; and Sabbe, 'The Arrest of Jesus', p. 217). The reader already knows that Jesus has a strong awareness of his impending death.

17. Brown, *Gospel According to John*, II, p. 818; Lindars, *Gospel of John*, p. 541, Barrett, *Gospel According to St John*, p. 520. All refer to other examples of biblical theophanies, for example, Dan. 10.9; Acts 9.4, 22.7, 26.14.

18. So Haenchen, 'the revelatory formula of the divine man' (*John*, II, p. 165).

19. Compare the ritualistic melodrama with which the high priest responds to Jesus' blasphemy in the Synoptics: 'by tearing his garments' (Mk 14.63 and parallels).

simply the 'intimidating effect'[20] of the 'divine majesty'[21] of the person
of Jesus. An interesting, if implausible, suggestion is that of Stibbe, who
muses that the captors respond in this way primarily because they are
astounded that they have finally succeeded in ensnaring their victim:
'They fall back in amazement not so much because Jesus is divine as
because they have at last apprehended the elusive Christ'.[22] The irony of
the scene is rich. Six hundred professional soldiers are sent to arrest one
man, who fells them all with two words. Also ironic is the fact that this
is the one point when Jesus exhibits any kind of power over his adversaries, and it is the very moment at which he loses his liberty. A
tremendous sense of anticipation is created by the writer at the end of v.
6: Jesus is surrounded by a hostile multitude, but suddenly they are all
incapacitated. *What will happen next?* If we did not already know the
ending we might wonder if he was going to seize his chance and flee,
just as he did in 7.30, 8.59 and 10.39. This time, however, he simply
stands there and impatiently repeats his question and its answer. His
second statement is cleverly phrased in a way that will enable his disciples to escape detention, even if he cannot: 'I told you that I am he; so,
if you seek me, let these men go' (v. 8). Thus the desertion of his followers is legitimized in John on theological grounds.

Missing from the Johannine account of Jesus' arrest is his accusation
that the authorities had no need to apprehend him under the cover of
darkness as they could have approached him in the temple at any time
(Mt. 26.55 and parallels). This would have been patently inappropriate
in John, since they frequently *had* attempted to arrest him at other times,
but without success. Nor does he lament the fact that they have come
after him with swords and clubs, like a robber (Mk 14.48 and parallels).
The Johannine Jesus already knows that the authorities afford him
no respect and in all likelihood expects this sort of rough treatment.
Matthew's pious platitude, 'for all who take the sword will perish by the
sword' (26.52) is also missing. The Jesus of the Fourth Gospel is no paci-
fist and scorns Peter's impetuous bravery not for the reason stated above,
or even because he could, if he wanted, marshal his own angelic army,
but because it is *another sabotage attempt on the fulfilment of his work.* Just as
Jesus rebuked Peter during the footwashing scene for attempting to
pressure him into behaving in a manner Peter found more comfortable

20. Sloyan, *John*, p. 201.
21. Sanders, *Gospel According to St John*, p. 385.
22. Stibbe, *John*, p. 184.

(13.6-10), so he does not trust Peter's motives here either. Once again Peter finds an ignominious master unpalatable. He cannot seriously have intended to take on the Roman forces single-handedly. The implication is that he would rather have Jesus a hero, dying in a blaze of glory, than surrendering in a cowardly fashion, shamefully shackled and destined for the most dishonourable death. Jesus' attitude is clear from the reason that he gives for rejecting Peter's actions: 'Shall I not drink the cup which the Father has given me?' (v. 11). There is no response from Peter, who presumably now flees with the other disciples. For them, Jesus' fate has been sealed and all is lost. However, for Jesus there was never an alternative to the Father's cup. He behaves with dignity and resignation during this scene, rather than with potency,[23] as finally the κόσμος closes in and he is seized and bound.

The Jewish 'Trial' and Peter's Denial (18.13-27)[24]

The Jewish trial and the denial of Jesus by Peter are interwoven, with the contrasting behaviour of the two individuals being used by the evangelist to illuminate the themes of bearing witness and concealment. In comparison to the Synoptic account of the Jewish trial, John's portrayal appears purely perfunctory in nature. This is even more evident when this scene is compared to the subsequent interrogation before Pilate in the Fourth Gospel, which is highly elaborate. The events of 18.13-27 do not advance the plot in any significant manner, serving merely to re-emphasize Jesus' innocence in the face of the accusations of the Jews. The reason for this cursory treatment of the Jewish trial in John is simply that, by this time, there is little more to be added about the reason why Jesus is rejected by the Jews and the fate that awaits him at their hands.[25] The reader has known why they wish to kill him since

23. Stibbe sees the scene ending with Jesus exhibiting 'Socratic composure...in control of events' (*John*, p. 181). There is, however, a difference between being in control of *oneself* and being in control of one's *environment*. It is the former, rather than the latter that is the case here.

24. The word trial appears in inverted commas because, unlike the Synoptic accounts, it would appear that John's account does not relate a proper trial before the Sanhedrin, but an informal interrogation (Brown, *Gospel According to John*, II, p. 826; Rensberger, *Overcoming the World*, p. 91).

25. Andrew Lincoln notes that there is no account of a Jewish trial before the Sanhedrin because 'throughout his public ministry Jesus can be viewed as on trial before Israel and its leaders' ('Trials, Plots and the Narrative of the Fourth Gospel',

Jn 5.18. Caiaphas has already pronounced judgment in 11.50 and the reader is reminded of this in 18.14.

The events are simply structured, with the interrogation and model testimony of Jesus bordered by the double failure of Peter to remain faithful when challenged. Peter and 'another disciple'[26] follow Jesus to the residence of Annas, where he is to be interrogated by the high priest. Peter is unable to enter the court until the other disciple, who has connections with Annas, negotiates with the doorkeeper on his behalf (v.16). While it is reasonable to assume that Peter's intentions in following Jesus were derived from a concern as to what would happen to him, once inside the courtyard he becomes little more than another betrayer. His response to the doorkeeper's question, 'Are not you also one of this man's disciples?' is the curt declaration οὐκ εἰμί ('I am not'). His words are significant as they do not simply serve to refute his identification with Jesus' party, but echo the very words that Jesus uses to identify himself, ἐγώ εἰμί.[27] In addition to Peter's promise of fidelity in 13.37, which prompted Jesus' prediction of denial, the reader is also reminded of his 'great affirmation' of 6.69, 'You are the holy one of God', to which this pericope contrasts as Peter's 'great repudiation'. There is no elaboration by Peter after his initial statement, or further challenge by the servants and officers at this point.[28] He simply attempts to blend in with the crowd in order to warm himself by their fire.

Meanwhile, the questioning of Jesus by the 'Grand Inquisitor'[29] has begun. There is no need for false witnesses to establish a charge against Jesus, or even to ascertain whether he thinks he is the Christ, as is necessary in the Synoptics.[30] The questions are described vaguely as being

---

JSNT 56 [1994], pp. 3-30 [6]). Similarly, Barrett notes that John has already given 'with great fullness' his account of the controversy between Jesus and the Jews in John 7–10 (*Gospel According to St John*, p. 523).

26. Whether this is the beloved disciple is not significant for this study, but see the summary of opinion and support for this hypothesis in Quast (*Peter and the Beloved Disciple*, p. 77).

27. Brown, *Gospel According to John*, II, p. 824; Quast, *Peter and the Beloved Disciple*, p. 83; Stibbe, *John*, p. 181.

28. In contrast to the Synoptic versions; Mk 14.66-71; Mt. 26.69-75; Lk. 22.56-60.

29. As the high priest is referred to by Ernst Haenchen, who paints an interesting picture of the scene, drawing on Dostoyevsky's *The Brothers Karamazov* for inspiration (*John*, II, pp. 168-69).

30. Mk 14.56-59; Mt. 26.59-61; Lk. 22.67-71.

'about his disciples and his teaching' (v.19), quite possibly an attempt to gather more intelligence about the identity of Jesus' followers and their subversive activities.[31] However, Jesus' answer does not give information about either of these things, nor does he take the opportunity to further rehearse his claims:

> I have spoken openly to the world;
> I have always taught in synagogues and in the temple,
> where all Jews come together;
> I have said nothing secretly.
> Why do you ask me? Ask those who have heard me,
> what I said to them, they know what I said. (vv. 20-21)

This statement is not so much an 'innocuous response... a declaration of openness and innocence'[32] as an impudent refusal to co-operate with the authorities and possibly to incriminate others by name. Not only does Jesus emphasize the accessible way in which his teaching has been disseminated, but he cleverly challenges Annas to call the many witnesses who have heard him speak on his behalf in order that a proper trial can be held. This is no doubt the reason he earns himself a blow (ῥάπισμα) from one of the guards (v. 22).[33] Undeterred by the physical violence,[34] Jesus questions the legitimacy of this action with a request that the Jews bear witness to what he has done to deserve the beating. In contrast to the witness of Jesus, which has been openly spoken, there is no such witness forthcoming from the high priest or officials. John does not intimate whether this is because they have no justification for the abuse, because they *need* no justification for it, or simply because it is deemed to be pointless to carry on interrogating this contumacious prisoner. The trial is over and Annas dispatches Jesus, still bound, to Caiaphas' house where he is to be kept until dawn.

---

31. As suggested by Sanders, *Gospel According to St John*, p. 392.

32. Sloyan, *John*, p. 203.

33. Brown notes that the behaviour of Jesus was probably startling, pointing to the normal attitude of a prisoner before a judge as seen in Josephus (*Gospel According to John*, II, p. 826). Josephus states 'for no matter who it was that came before this Sanhedrin for trial, he has shown himself humble and has assumed the manner of one who is fearful and seeks mercy' (*Ant.* 14.172).

34. The word used by Jesus, δέρω, 'to beat', suggests that he has sustained a more severe form of abuse than simply a slap round the face. The meaning is literally 'to flay' or 'to skin' (BAGD, p. 175).

Back in the courtyard, Simon Peter is still warming himself by the fire (18.25). Further questioning by those present, including a potential relative of Malchus, elicits two more definitive denials by Peter that he is a disciple and was with Jesus in Gethsemane (vv. 25, 27). The crowing of the cock closes the scene, although John's readers are expected to remember the prediction of Jesus in 13.38 since there is no mention that Peter does, nor, indeed, that he shows any remorse for his actions.

The contrast between Peter and Jesus in this scene is played out through the language and behaviour attributed to each character. Jesus is candid and defiant, but also clever—he has hidden nothing, bearing witness without betraying his disciples. He is brave in the face of physical threat from the guards, while still being bound as a prisoner. Peter, on the other hand, has not been particularly clever. Having been suspected of being Jesus' follower once, he remains close to the fire, presumably for the sake of physical comfort, but of course he can easily be seen here and is consequently challenged twice more.[35] He is dishonest, breaking his vow of fidelity to Jesus and concealing his discipleship. The bravado of Gethsemane has dissipated. It is ironic that, as Jesus challenges Annas to bring in one who has heard his message to testify for him, so his chief disciple is outside denying all association with him.[36] The Jewish trial plays out the rejection of Jesus by his own (1.11), but this time even one of those who did receive him stands with ὁ κόσμος against him.

The Roman Interrogation (18.28–19.16)

The trial of Jesus by Pilate has received a high level of attention from scholars because of the unique arrangement of the events in the Fourth Gospel when compared to the Synoptics. The section is divided into seven scenes which occur alternately inside and outside of the praetorium, as detailed in Figure 5. This will function as a useful framework for examining what is a large and complex piece of Johannine material.[37]

---

35. Staley sees negative connotations in Peter's choosing to stand with the temple police and chief priest's slaves, associating himself with them ('Subversive Narrative/Victimized Reader', p. 93).

36. Peter's denials happen in a period of time simultaneous with Jesus' interrogation (Quast, *Peter and the Beloved Disciple*, p. 85).

37. Based on the structure first suggested by Raymond Brown (*Gospel According to John*, II, pp. 858-59).

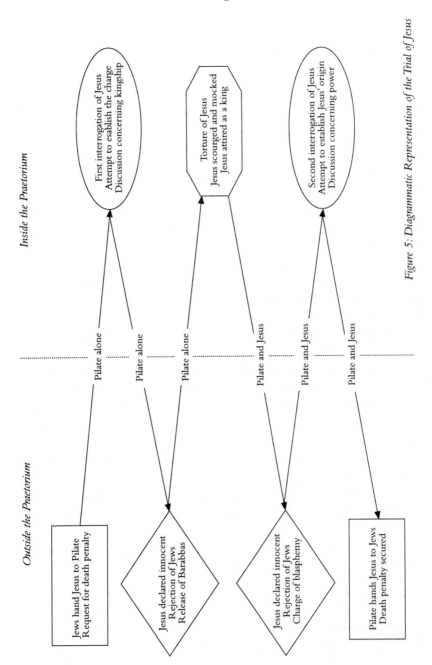

Figure 5: Diagrammatic Representation of the Trial of Jesus

The issues that will be investigated from the perspective of this study will be those of power and political oppression. Quite apart from being marginalized within his own community, Jesus is a member of a race that is subject to the domination of the Romans and political wrangling plays no small part in the execution of judgement on his case. For this reason, some time will be spent exploring the relationship between Pilate and the Jews and the role that he plays.

Scene 1: In which Jesus is Handed over to Pilate for Judgment (18.28-32)
The Jews bring Jesus to Pilate for judgment under Roman law. However, when Pilate questions them about the accusation against Jesus, they simply sneer, 'If this man were not an evildoer, we would not have handed him over' (v. 30). This does not succeed in arousing Pilate's interest in the case and the Jews are forced to reveal their true intentions—they have not brought Jesus to Pilate for the purpose of having him tried, but to have him condemned. They have, after all, judged Jesus themselves and already established the cause of his guilt.[38] All they need now is the rubber stamp on his death sentence. The tension is caused by the fact that the power to execute the sentence rests with their Roman oppressors, not within the Jewish community, and this is therefore a painful reminder of their subjugation.[39] Pilate is not someone to whom the Jews feel they need to justify their actions (and hence the sneer); he is an obstacle to be manipulated into delivering their designs for Jesus. It is, of course, ironic that as the victim of the Jews, Jesus is prevented from being executed as a result of their *own* oppression by the Romans. Once their purpose has been made clear, the Jews have no problem in securing Pilate's interest—'he is at once willing to proceed with the hearing when he learns that a crucifixion is in the offing'.[40]

38. For breaking the Sabbath and 'making himself equal to God' (5.18), although this is not the pronouncement of a formal Sanhedrin. Schnackenburg notes that 'The petulant answer of the Jews is less to illustrate the tension between the representatives of the Jewish authorities and the Roman procurator, than to show up their inability to bring a water-tight charge against Jesus.' There can be no doubt by this stage that Jesus is guilty on several charges of breaking Jewish law (*Gospel According to St John*, III, p. 245).

39. There is a dispute over whether or not the Jews were able to inflict capital punishment during this period. In favour are Lindars, *John*, p. 557; E. Lohse, *History of the Suffering and Death of Jesus Christ* (Philadelphia: Fortress Press, 1967), p. 74; and Sanders, *Gospel According to St John*, p. 395.

40. Rensberger, *Overcoming the World*, p. 92. Rensberger's portrayal of Pilate as a

Scene 2: In which Pilate Interrogates Jesus for the First Time (18.33-38a)
Establishing that Jesus is to be charged with a capital offence, Pilate
proceeds to interrogate him. The Jews have not accused him of political
rebellion or of claiming to be the King of the Jews,[41] but Pilate is
interested in insurgency and so begins with this question. The ensuing
dialogue is intensely frustrating for Pilate as Jesus obfuscates a question
that merely requires a monosyllabic answer.[42] He has little patience with
Jesus. He scorns him for his rejection by his own people, remarking 'Am
I a Jew? Your own nation and the Chief priests have handed you over
to me' (v. 35), and ending the interview abruptly, spitting out the words
'what is truth?' (v. 38a).[43] Jesus' answers seem to have been calculated to
allay the concerns of Pilate that he may be a political threat,[44] and on the
face of it they indicate that he does not possess worldly power and
hence cannot defend himself. He too recognizes his rejection by the

strong character, undeniably hostile to the Jews and unconcerned with the fate of
Jesus, using him to ridicule their nationalistic hopes, is far more convincing than
those that see him as sympathetic to Jesus. The latter is generally the stance of the
older commentaries such as Barrett, *Gospel According to St John*, p. 531; and Brown,
Gospel According to John, II, p. 863. Sanders comments: 'Pilate has a certain sympathy
with Jesus. He sees that they are both victims of a plot, and wants to free both Jesus
and himself' (*Gospel According to St John*, p. 397). See also Sloyan, *John*, p. 206; and
Culpepper: 'Pilate represents the futility of attempted compromise' (*Anatomy of the
Fourth Gospel*, p. 143). Arguments for Pilate as a sympathetic figure are refuted by
David Flusser: 'Pilate... is the same cruel, cynical hater of Israel we know from the
Jewish sources' ('What Was the Original Meaning of *Ecce Homo*?', *Immanuel* 19
[1994–95], pp. 30-40 [40]).

41. Compare with the Synoptics, where this is the charge brought to Pilate in
Lk. 23.2. Mark and Matthew also record it as Pilate's first question (Mk 15.2; Mt.
27.11). The reader of John already knows that the Jews' charge against Jesus is
religious not political, but Pilate does not discover this until 19.7, when the Jews
claim ὅτι υἱὸν θεοῦ ἑαυτὸν ἐποίησεν. Ironically, political glory is something that
Jesus has expressly avoided (6.15); however, the entire trial scene is packed full of
such ironies. For a full description of them see Duke, *Irony in the Fourth Gospel*, pp.
126-37 and Stibbe, *John*, pp. 189-92.

42. As is emphasized by his second attempt to get a straight answer in v. 37.
Culpepper notes that in general in the Fourth Gospel Jesus seems to be 'congenitally
incapable' of giving a straight answer (*Anatomy of the Fourth Gospel*, p. 112).

43. Pilate's question is not one of a serious seeker: 'if it were, he would stay for
an answer' (Rensberger, *Overcoming the World*, p. 93).

44. He 'proceeds at once with such a definition of his kingship as removes it
from the sphere of sedition and rebellion' (Barrett, *Gospel According to St John*,
p. 536).

Jews and distances himself from his community—it is against the Jews,
not the Romans, that his servants would fight were he an earthly king.
However, the meaning of Jesus' words encompasses a dimension that
Pilate cannot hope to comprehend. 'His kingship is, *in origin*, not ἐκ τοῦ
κόσμου and hence it is ἐκ τῶν ἄνω ('from above', 8.23)'.[45] Although it
is frequently asserted that Jesus is implying that he has authority over the
earthly province as well,[46] this is not really the point that he is making
here. He does not have secular power—it would not be commensurate
with his mission,[47] which is to bear witness to the truth. Ironically,
again, it is bearing witness that has brought the violence and hatred of
the world upon him.

*Scene 3: In which Jesus Is Declared Innocent and Barabbas Released (18.36b-
40)*
Pilate's verdict is that Jesus is harmless.[48] He taunts the Jews by offering
to release their pathetic 'king', flaunting his own power as procurator
over them. The opposition to his offer is violent; they scream out 'Not
this man but Barabbas'[49]—a forceful and effective further rejection of
Jesus. Barabbas is described as λῃστής (v. 40), a term used for bandits
and guerrillas;[50] thus the Jews call for the earthly revolutionary, who is
struggling for secular power and involved in fighting their oppressors.[51]

45. Nicholson, *Death as Departure*, p. 84.
46. '...this realm does not have its roots in this world. Thereby, however, it sets
before the world a sovereignty that fundamentally surpasses every other' (Heinrich
Schlier, quoted in Rensberger, *Overcoming the World*, p. 97). So also Brown, *Gospel
According to John*, II, p. 869.
47. However, it is not correct to claim that it is 'not a political movement and
therefore makes no use of political means' (Haenchen, *John*, II, p. 179).
48. '...this is not a political matter and Jesus' claim to kingship is not a threat to
Caesar' (Forestell, *Word of the Cross*, p. 84).
49. Ἐκραύγασαν is a strong word, 'suitable for a mob' (Barrett, *Gospel According
to St John*, p. 539). So also BAGD, p. 447.
50. Brown (*Gospel According to John*, II, p. 857) and Lindars (*Gospel of John*,
p. 563) refer to usage by Josephus. Josephus mentions the attempt of Felix, the
procurator of Judea, to clamp down on the activities of the brigand chief Eleazar and
other bandits (λῃστής) in *War* 2.253.
51. Pilate's tactic of taunting the Jews with their impotence can only be seen to
have backfired at this point as he is forced to release a man who is a *real* threat to
political stability. As Stibbe points out, this is surely the last thing that he wanted!
(*John*, p. 188). Flusser claims that this would have increased Pilate's animosity towards Jesus: 'Shortly before the time set for the execution, Pilate turned to the

Scene 4: In which Jesus is Mocked and Beaten (19.1-3)

The torture of Jesus follows the crowd's demand for his death. Jesus is flogged and subjected to a ritualistic humiliation. Claims that Pilate aimed to mollify the Jews with this action, in order that he could then release him, are not justified.[52] The Jews want Jesus dead, not just disabled. Pilate has himself and his men a little sport, with the overall aim of deriding the crowd, making Jesus a ridiculous example of Jewish nationalism.[53] The mocking is an episode particularly rich in Johannine irony. The crown of thorns and purple robe are symbols used in the mock coronation of the pathetic caricature who represents to the Romans the best the Jews have to offer—their king. For the evangelist, of course, he is in reality the *true* king. The jeering and feigned obeisance of the soldiers is punctuated by further physical abuse before Jesus is dragged back out to face the mob.

crowd of Jewish demonstrators and proposed the granting of amnesty to Jesus, the Galilean prophet, whom he considered the least dangerous to his rule. But the high priests had already persuaded the crowd to demand the release of Barabbas, a popular hero; Pilate, who depended on the support of the local leadership, was forced to give in and pardon Barabbas. From then on, his natural cruelty was directed towards Jesus.' ('What Was the original meaning of *Ecce Homo*?', p. 32).

52. Stibbe: 'a sort of mass catharsis' (*John*, p. 188). So too Culpepper, *Anatomy of the Fourth Gospel*, p. 142; Haenchen, *John*, II, p. 181 and Hoskyns, *Fourth Gospel*, p. 523.

53. Flusser contends that it is probable that Pilate himself participated in the mocking of Jesus. A similar incident occurred in Alexandria in 117 during which a Roman prefect took part in such an event. 'It is not impossible, then, that Pilate, blinded by his hatred of the Jews and drawn by his predilection for pointless ceremonies, participated in this mock-acclamation of the King of the Jews, thereby performing an act which was both provocative and politically unwise' ('What Was the original meaning of *Ecce Homo*?', p. 39). As regards the flogging, the Greek suggests that Pilate does this himself: τότε οὖν ἔλαβεν ὁ Πιλᾶτος τὸν Ἰησοῦν καὶ ἐμαστίγωσεν. This would serve to emphasize the callous nature of the procurator and his disinterest in the well-being of Jesus. Brown, however, claims that the subsequent verse implies that the flogging is carried out by the soldiers (*Gospel According to John*, II, p. 874). Schnackenburg, perceiving Pilate to be a weaker figure, claims that he 'allows himself to be carried away so far as to have Jesus scourged'. This is not borne out by the text—Pilate is evidently enjoying himself (*Gospel According to St John*, III, p. 253). Also, Rensberger, *Overcoming the World*, p. 94.

Scene 5: In which Jesus is Declared Innocent, but his Death is Demanded (19.4-8)

Pilate exits the praetorium to present this mock-king to the Jews, declaring his innocence as he does, and emphasizing his frailty and humanity with the proclamation: 'Behold the man' (v. 5).[54] Jesus wears the symbols of power and authority, but they are meaningless. To Pilate he is merely another man whom he is able to thrash, deride, crucify or release as he chooses. All attention is focused on the pitifully ridiculous figure that emerges—hardly recognizable as a man at all, disfigured by abuse with his 'blood-smeared and swollen features',[55] the sight of whom incenses the priests even further. The new monarch is hailed by his subjects with the cry σταύρωσον σταύρωσον, but Pilate continues to taunt them with their impotence: 'Take him *yourselves* and crucify him' (v. 6)—something clearly impossible. The Jews try a different tack, making a play for a conviction on the basis of religious transgression, which is, after all, the real issue. They have called Pilate's bluff, as he was the one who advised them to judge Jesus by their own law in the first place (18.31). Now they make an appeal to this law, claiming that according to its precepts he should die since 'he made himself the Son of God'.[56] This has an immediate effect on Pilate, who suddenly becomes alarmed[57] at the accusation levied against Jesus and realizes that he must now take him a little more seriously.

Scene 6: In which Pilate Interrogates Jesus for a Second Time (19.9-11)

Pilate hurries Jesus back into the praetorium for a further round of questioning, concerned to establish who he really is. His question πόθεν

54. Pilate's statement simply means 'Look at him! This is the King you want crucified!' (Morris, *Gospel According to John*, p. 793). Schnackenburg sees it as a means of drawing attention to Jesus in his appearance as a mock-king (*Gospel According to St John*, III, p. 256).

55. Haenchen, *John*, II, p. 181.

56. Many claim that Pilate now becomes *even more* afraid. See Haenchen, *John*, II, p. 182; Brown, *Gospel According to John*, II, p. 877 and Culpepper, *Anatomy of the Fourth Gospel*, p. 143. However, this cannot be the case as his words and actions have exhibited no fear up to this point and it is possible to translate the Greek 'he became afraid instead', or 'he was very much afraid' (Barrett, *Gospel According to St John*, p. 542).

57. The cause of Pilate's anxiety could be either pagan superstition (Lindars, *Gospel of John*, p. 568), or a concern that he may be reported to Rome for failing to respect local religious practices (Brown, *Gospel According to John*, II, p. 878).

εἰ σύ; ('where are you from?') is phrased using the significant vocabulary of the fourth evangelist, for the origin of Jesus is the question that is addressed by the entire Gospel.[58] As the Jews have tried to ascertain where Jesus has come from (and hence the source of his authority), so now Pilate wishes to know. His question is greeted by an enigmatic silence from Jesus that is open to various different interpretations.[59] Is it due to 'the impossibility of giving Pilate an answer he will understand';[60] because 'the divine is not a mundane object with specific attributes, with respect to which one can make inquiries';[61] or because 'only faith can receive an answer to this question'?[62] Perhaps he is exercising a dignified right to silence, or maybe he has been so brutalized by Pilate's men that he is no longer able to function properly. Whatever the reason, it only serves to agitate Pilate further as he now attempts to bully Jesus into answering. His assertion of power after Jesus' fate in v. 10 is delivered as a threat—'if you know what's good for you, you'll co-operate with me', he threatens. But Jesus is not intimidated and provides a response that convinces Pilate it would be a good idea to have this man released. Lindars comments: 'Jesus pricks the bubble of Pilate's conceit by reminding him of the derivative nature of all earthly power'.[63] The reader knows that the power given to Pilate, ἄνωθεν, is derived from the Father, which is also from whence Jesus came,[64] but what Pilate makes of this statement is open to question. It is entirely possible that he interprets Jesus' words in a purely political sense, reflecting on the potentially precarious nature of his own power base. From his point of view, the power given to him 'from above' is that of the Roman State, and he could well be confused into thinking that the death of Jesus would have serious ramifications for him if the news reached Caesar.[65]

58. From John 1, ἐν ἀρχῇ ἦν ὁ λόγος...καὶ ὁ λόγος σὰρξ ἐγένετο, through 3.13; 5.30; 7.27; 9.29; 14.5 and throughout the last supper.
59. As Sloyan points out; 'it does not happen often in John'! (*John*, p. 209).
60. Sanders, *Gospel According to St John*, p. 401.
61. Haenchen, *John*, II, p. 182.
62. Forestell, *Word of the Cross*, p. 85.
63. Lindars, *Gospel of John*, p. 568.
64. Barrett, *Gospel According to St John*, p. 543.
65. This would be supported by Brown's comment that local religious practices were to be respected by the procurator. See n. 56 above.

Scene 7: In which Jesus is Handed back to the Jews for Crucifixion (19.12-18)
Pilate exits the praetorium a final time in order to negotiate with the
Jews. Here his fears are confirmed: the motive behind this crucifixion *is*
political and now the Jews are holding him to ransom—'If you release
this man you are not Caesar's friend' (v. 12). Faced with the prospect of
a mob of rowdy Jews accusing him of treason, Pilate does not dither.[66]
Jesus is hauled back out of the praetorium, and over to the βῆμα ready
for judgement.[67] Pilate just cannot resist one more sarcastic taunt;
'Behold your King', he says of the pitiable figure before them. This
merely serves to heighten their contempt and hatred and they reject
Jesus for the third and final time, betraying not only him but also their
nation and their god with the cry 'we have no king but Caesar' (v. 15).
Pilate has finally triumphed.[68] The outcome could really not have been
better from his point of view and he dispatches Jesus immediately for
execution.

Epilogue: The Titulus (19.19-22)
Pilate carries out one final task in the Gospel. He writes the *titulus* that is
fixed to the cross, proclaiming the wretched figure whose humiliating
death is publicly displayed to be Ο ΒΑΣΙΛΕΥΣ ΤΩΝ ΙΟΥΔΑΙΩΝ. Paul
Duke calls this his 'last revenge on the Jews' and his 'last twisted homage
to Jesus'.[69] Certainly it is an immense affront to the religious authorities

---

66. Flusser notes that 'this particular line of argument was the most likely to
move Pilate, whose loyalty and obsequiousness towards Caesar were salient features
of his personality' ('What Was the original meaning of *Ecce Homo?*', p. 36).

67. The text is ambiguous as to whether it is Jesus or Pilate who sits on the
judgment seat—a further case of Johannine irony—is Pilate judging Jesus or vice
versa? See Bultmann, *Gospel of John*, p. 664 and Schnackenburg, *Gospel According to
St John*, III, pp. 263-64 for arguments for the former. I. de la Potterie argues for the
latter based on the transitive use of καθίζειν. This accords with his theological
agenda as he concludes that the real judging that takes place is between Jesus and the
Jews: '... les vrais antagonistes en présence ne sont pas Jésus et Pilate mais Jésus et les
Juifs. Jésus est représenté ici comme le juge des Juifs' ('Jésus, Roi et Juge d'après Jn
19.13', *Bib* 41 (1960), pp. 217-47 [247]).

68. Haenchen claims that at this point Pilate 'throws in the towel' (*John*, II,
p. 183). This simply cannot be supported since he has just succeeded in eliciting 'an
abnegation of their highest national hopes' (Rensberger, *Overcoming the World*,
p. 95).

69. Duke, *Irony in the Fourth Gospel*, p. 136.

who have expended a great deal of energy asserting that Jesus is *not* their king.[70] It is also another slap at Jesus, who has attempted to distance himself from this title[71] and a further emphasis of the subjugation of the Jews—to the Romans, this 'king' from Nazareth[72] ridicules the nationalistic aspirations of the Jews.

The trial of Jesus has been discussed in this chapter primarily from the aspect of the oppression of the Jewish community and the victimization of one of their members. Jesus plays a passive rather than an active role in this drama, all the while maintaining his dignity and composure. He is buffeted about between Pilate and the Jews while both sides try to ensure they get what they want from the event—crucifixion for the Jews and maximum political gain plus a little entertainment for Pilate.

The Crucifixion

It is the Johannine account of the death of Jesus, more than any other part of the Fourth Gospel, which is viewed by current scholarship as presenting him as a victor rather than a victim. There is no place in John's theology of the cross, it is claimed, for a suffering and humiliated Jesus. The crucifixion is the occasion of enthronement of Christ and is his hour of glory and triumph. It would not be difficult to reproduce manifold quotations from the history of Johannine scholarship which have read the crucifixion story in this light, but pride of place on this issue should really go to Ernst Käsemann, whose view on John's passion narrative is that it is a 'mere postscript' to the Gospel.[73] For Käsemann, Jesus is 'the one who passes through death without turmoil and with jubilation'.[74]

---

70. 'To suggest that a powerless, condemned, and dying outcast was the king of their nation was a studied insult. To state only that the crazy fellow had claimed to be king would be harmless' (Barrett, *Gospel According to St John*, p. 549). Also Flusser, 'the inscription on the cross was an attack against the Jewish belief in a Messianic King who would come to free Israel of the Roman yoke' ('What Was the original meaning of *Ecce Homo?*', p. 32).

71. 'My kingship is not of this world...I might not be handed over to the Jews', 18.36.

72. The sign recalls Jesus' 'humble, if not despised, background in Nazareth' (D.A. Hubbard, 'John 19.17-30', *Int* 43 [1989], pp. 397-401 [398]).

73. Käsemann, *The Testament of Jesus*, p. 7.

74. Käsemann, *The Testament of Jesus*, p. 20. Gerstenberger, commenting that in

It is not simply the characterization of Jesus that is seen to have been customized by the evangelist. In the process of reinterpreting the tradition, John has cleaned up the whole scene, deleting some of the more gruesome aspects that appear in the Synoptic tale.[75] So C.F. Evans can claim that 'what in Mark is mystery and realism, and in Luke is pathos and humanity, in John is majesty and irony'.[76] Indeed, John has been so successful that, for Barnabas Lindars, he has managed to transform an event horrifying in its brutality and degradation into one that emits 'a pervading calm, like an Italian primitive painting'.[77]

As it would seem that the weight of traditional scholarship sees in John's rendition of the passion an account where 'elements of affliction

John the passion is 'no longer an enigma' since it is the hour of Jesus' exaltation, claims further that 'there emerges the impression that the suffering does not seriously affect him, but rather he is exalted above it'. This is due to the fact that the cross is '*only* the place of his return to the Father' (E.S. Gerstenberger and W. Schrage, *Suffering* [trans. J.E. Steely; Nashville: Abingdon Press, 1980], p. 171, emphasis added). Note also the following: John 'does not wish to depict the agony of Jesus... but wants to portray the one on the cross who is still king' (Haenchen, *John*, II, p. 192). 'In the Fourth Gospel...the humiliation of the Cross has practically disappeared; it is no longer a σκάνδαλον, but a shining stairway by which the Son of God ascends to his Father' (V. Taylor, *The Atonement in New Testament Teaching* [repr.; London: Epworth Press, 3rd edn, 1963 (1958)], p. 148). 'Christ's execution was his enthronement, the cross became his throne, and the passion was the Revealer's triumphant return to heaven' (H.R. Weber, *The Cross: Tradition and Interpretation* [trans. E. Jessett; London: SPCK, 1979], p. 132). 'The crucifixion of Christ is presented as an enthronement' (Forestell, *Word of the Cross*, p. 86). Barrett and Lindars are less effusive: 'Jesus remains a majestic figure' (Lindars, *Gospel of John*, p. 573). 'John brings out the theme of the royalty of Jesus' (Barrett, *Gospel According to St John*, p. 547).

75. Lindars notes that all the details which 'add horror' to the scene in the Synoptics are omitted. By this he means the mocking of bystanders, the darkness at noon, and the cry of dereliction (*Gospel of John*, p. 573). Others simply explain the absence of these items by reference to source-critical theories. Dodd doubts that John had access to these traditions (*Historical Tradition*, pp. 121-24). Indeed, Brown claims: 'All these Johannine omissions can scarcely be explained as deliberate excisions, for such details as the mockery by the priests, the darkness over the land and the rending of the temple curtain would have served as admirable vehicles for Johannine theology' (*Gospel According to John*, II, p. 914). Schnackenburg, however, claims that John has simply left out 'distracting' elements in order to concentrate on what is important to him (*The Gospel According to St John*, III, p. 268).

76. Evans, 'The Passion of John', p. 62.

77. Lindars, *Gospel of John*, p. 573.

and agony are alien and in which there remain only the victorious over-coming and consummation',[78] it might seem a precarious undertaking to attempt to make claims about the victimization of Jesus on the cross. The task will be approached from two angles. First, working from the text itself, the material marshalled by scholarship to propound the traditional view will be explored. Secondly, elements within the narrative that allow us to explore the crucifixion from the perspective of Jesus as a victim will be discussed. During this process I also hope to demonstrate that of all the Gospels it is Luke, and not John, who paints the least traumatic picture of Jesus.

Part 1 : Jesus as Victor
It would true to say that for some scholars, the view of Jesus as triumphant on the cross appears to originate principally from the high Christology that has been discerned in the Gospel in general.[79] Others, however, identify particular features of the Johannine passion narrative that they see minimizing the physical suffering of Jesus and enhancing his potency. The most significant of these issues is the effect of the 'hour of glory' on the suffering of Jesus, and this will be discussed first and in some detail. Following that, other reasons which have been put forward by scholars will be discussed.

Jesus Can Be Seen as the Victor who Eludes Suffering Because...

1. *...the Crucifixion is his 'Hour of Glory'.* One of the primary reasons why Jesus' death is regarded as being an occasion of exaltation, rather than a humiliation, is because the crucifixion is his 'hour of glory'. In the writings of many scholars, glory is juxtaposed with suffering and the two appear to become mutually exclusive. So Smalley can claim that 'his "hour" is an hour of glory, not agony',[80] and likewise Moody Smith that 'Jesus' death is his glorification *not* his humiliation'.[81] Bultmann

---

78. Haenchen, *John*, II, pp. 193-94.

79. The obvious example here is Käsemann, but see also Moody Smith and Haenchen.

80. Smalley, *John, Evangelist and Interpreter*, p. 224. Loisy makes a similar statement: 'La mort [du] Christ n'est pas une scène de douleur; c'est le commencement du grand triomphe' (*Le Quatrième Evangile*, p. 883).

81. Moody Smith, 'Presentation of Jesus in the Fourth Gospel', p. 370, emphasis

elaborates: as his moment of glorification, the passion is 'the crown' of Jesus' work; '*fundamentally* therefore he does not appear in the Passion story as the sufferer'.[82] Nicholson relates the portrayal of the crucifixion to the understanding the evangelist wants his community to have of the event: 'not an ignominious death but a return to glory'.[83] The significance of the terms δόξα and ὥρα has already been discussed in Chapter 6, where it was claimed that their use in the Fourth Gospel refers to the death of Jesus and, moreover, that the glorification of Jesus cannot be understood without reference to the crucifixion. One cannot occur without the other, which is why Käsemann's assertion that the Johannine passion is a postscript must be rejected and Fortna's suggestion that the Fourth Gospel is 'one continuous passion narrative'[84] accepted. This perspective uses the death of Jesus to interpret the concept of glorification, rather than *vice versa*. In reality, John sees the two as interdependent, but approaching the subject from this angle yields an interpretation that tempers more traditional views, which have obscured the reality of the agonizing death suffered by the Johannine Jesus by the focus on glory. The agony of Jesus on the cross is not cancelled out by the glory, quite the reverse; his suffering is an *integral part* of the glorification process, without which it would not take place.

The human experience of this barbaric death is the will of the Father for Jesus. This in itself is a distressing thought for Jesus, as is evidenced by his struggle with it in 12.27-28. But the physical suffering of Jesus on the cross must also be interpreted with reference to what he says about it during his ministry and his attitude towards it. I have already shown in Chapter 6 that Jesus perceives his death as being violent, bloody and physically tortuous. The language he uses in John 6 and John 10 to speak about death is full of violence and indicates his fear of the experience. The text makes it clear that, throughout his ministry, Jesus regards his death as a terrifying ordeal that draws ever nearer. The crucifixion itself cannot be viewed in isolation from the rest of his life, as it is in fact the very reason why the Logos became incarnate. Suffering and

added. This a very common statement which frequently surfaces in articles on various aspects of the Fourth Gospel as a fact which seems to be taken for granted. For example, see Droge, 'Status of Peter in the Fourth Gospel', p. 310.

82. Bultmann, *Gospel of John*, p. 633, emphasis added.
83. Nicholson, *Death as Departure*, p. 163.
84. Fortna, 'Christology in the Fourth Gospel', pp. 502-504.

glorification are not, therefore, mutually exclusive, but are two sides of the same coin.

That glory and suffering/death are not to be divorced is further evidenced by the comment made by the evangelist regarding Peter's death in 21.19: 'This he said to show by what death he was to glorify (δοξάσει) God'. It has been demonstrated in the discussion on the use of δοξάζειν (Chapter 6) that the juxtaposition of these terms with reference to Peter is a strong argument for their interdependence in the mind of the evangelist. The verse can be used further to shed light on the glorification through death of Jesus. Unlike Jesus, Peter will not be 'lifted up' and will not 'draw all to himself'. Lifting up would be particularly inappropriate terminology for one who was crucified upside down and Peter's role is to nurture those that Jesus has drawn to himself ('feed my sheep'). However, his death will glorify God. That John sees the death of one who is undeniably human (and not even a particularly successful disciple in John) as resulting in the glorification of God *must* have a bearing on the evangelist's understanding of the glorification of Jesus. Peter's death, undeniably, was the brutal, tortuous and humiliating death of a human being who was oppressed and finally executed. Peter, undoubtedly, suffered agony on his own cross, yet it was still a vehicle for the glorification of God. If this point is accepted, it cannot be legitimately claimed that John's use of the terminology when referring to the death of Jesus automatically implies the absence of suffering on his part.

Those who claim that humiliation and suffering are not central to the passion of John fail to see that they are central to the *entire life* of Jesus in the Fourth Gospel. Death beckons Jesus from Jn 1.29 onwards, and permeates the narrative throughout. All the players know this—Jesus knows, the Jews know and the reader knows—we know about the fear and we know about the agony. There is really no need for a drum roll when it finally arrives. Rather than viewing the Johannine passion as one that 'celebrate[s] the victor who followed the unswerving cause of God to his last breath',[85] we see the narrative celebrating the *victim* who remained faithful to the will of the Father through immolation.

2. *...He Endures its Physical Demands Single-handedly.* This reason focuses on 19.17, in which it is stated that Jesus carried his own cross: 'So they took Jesus, and he went out, *bearing his own cross*, to the place called the

85. E. Haenchen, 'History and Interpretation in the Johannine Passion Narrative', *Int* 24 (1970), pp. 198-219 (219).

place of the skull, which is called in Hebrew Golgotha'. That the Johannine narrative has Jesus carrying his own cross, rather than having Simon
of Cyrene carry it for him, is hailed by some to be another pointer to
his sovereignty—'John wished once more to emphasize the all-suffi-
ciency of Jesus; he needed no help in effecting the redemption of the
world'.[86] Others see the absence of Simon as polemical,[87] political[88] or
source-critical.[89] Brown suggests that the evangelist may have in mind a
parallel between Jesus and Isaac, who carries the wood for his own
sacrifice, and this concept will be further explored later in the second
part of this chapter.[90] Alternatively, if the omission can be accorded any
significance at all, it could simply serve to emphasize that Jesus must face
death alone. He bears his own cross not because he has no *need* of
assistance, but because there is no one who *can* assist him—no one else is
able to share in his ordeal.[91] The *via dolorosa* is simply the last stage in a
long journey towards death that, for the Johannine Jesus, has been
principally and necessarily a solitary one.

3. *...He is Able to Attend to the Needs of Others.* Having described the
crucifixion and the division of Jesus' clothes,[92] John narrates a scene
unique to the Fourth Gospel. Four of Jesus' followers are watching him

---

86. Barrett, *Gospel According to St John*, p. 548. Echoed by Stibbe: 'he has no
need of helpers because he is an all-sufficient king' (*John*, p. 197). Harrington sees it
as evidence that Jesus is 'master of his own destiny' (*John's Thought and Theology*,
p. 105).

87. It was omitted to counter the Gnostic heresy, which asserted that it was
Simon who was crucified in place of Jesus, who exchanged his form with him. See
Irenaeus, *Adv. Haer.* 1.24.4; *ANCL*, V, p. 91.

88. '...he may simply be emphasizing that Jesus died the death of an ordinary
criminal' (Sanders, *Gospel According to St John*, p. 405).

89. 'The contradiction is probably to be explained on the assumption that a
different tradition lies behind Jn's account, for the statement is quite unstressed'
(Bultmann, *Gospel of John*, p. 668, n. 3). Dodd claims that it echoes Lk. 14.27;
'whoever does not bear his own cross and come after me cannot be my disciple'
(*Historical Tradition*, pp. 124-25). Thisis supported by Lindars (*Gospel of John*, p. 574).

90. Brown, *Gospel According to John*, II, p. 917.

91. This would be supported by Hanson's claim that John wanted to represent
Jesus as bearing the burden of human sin and therefore thought it more appropriate
that he carried his own cross (*Prophetic Gospel*, p. 208).

92. An indication that Jesus suffers the humiliation of being crucified naked
(Weber, *The Cross*, p. 133). Hubbard comments; 'their removal speaks of dispos-
session, vulnerability, shame' ('John 19.17-30', p. 399).

die and he speaks to them, declaring that his mother should now adopt the beloved disciple as her son and that he should care for her (19.25-27). Again, this is seen as evidence of the exalted and victorious Lord—'Jesus thinks not of his own pain but of the needs of his mother. *This is the selfless heroism of a divine figure.*'[93] Du Rand, on the other hand, sees Jesus' action in selfish, rather than selfless, terms: 'His concern for his mother in the final moments of his life should be interpreted as that of the Son of God in full control of every situation, and *not* that he was acting from compassionate motives'.[94] Nicholson does see compassion as a motive for Jesus, but seems to indicate that this in some way cancels out his torment: '*Instead* of suffering humiliation and pain on the cross, the Johannine Jesus takes care of his mother'.[95] Exegetes have suggested a welter of theological motifs for this passage,[96] but what we are interested in here is whether the fact that Jesus shows concern for the fate of his mother while he is on the cross renders his performance more triumphant. The person whom Jesus beholds from the cross is another victim—a woman[97] who is experiencing grief and humiliation herself at the unjust and barbaric execution of her son. That he is able to react sympathetically, attempting to minimize her misery by identifying a source of support and comfort for her in the beloved disciple, is an indication of *humanity*, rather than divinity. Jesus' own experience of human suffering compels him to respond to that of another in a manner that is compassionate, rather than condescending.

93. Stibbe, *John*, p. 197, emphasis added.

94. du Rand, 'The Characterization of Jesus', p. 29, emphasis added. Fuller also sees Jesus maintaining enough control to think of practicalities, noting that 'Jesus sovereignly disposes his affairs before he dies' ('Passion, Death and Resurrection', p. 58).

95. Nicholson, *Death as Departure*, p. 165, emphasis added. This statement is particularly hard to comprehend since surely the sight of his anguished mother beneath the cross would *add* to the pain and humiliation suffered by Jesus, rather than detract from it.

96. For example, Bultmann sees Mary as representing Jewish Christianity that has overcome the offence of the cross, and the beloved disciple representing Gentile Christianity (*Gospel of John*, p. 673). Brown sees the tableau evoking the themes of 'Lady Zion's giving birth to a new people in the new messianic age, and of Eve and her offspring' (*Gospel According to John*, II, p. 926).

97. That Jesus perceives her as an individual in her own right, rather than solely in relation to himself as his mother, is evidenced by his use of the word γύναι. That his request to his mother and the beloved disciple is expressed so briefly could also be seen to indicate that he was physically weakening.

It is interesting at this point to compare the Johannine Jesus with his Lukan counterpart. Luke presents us with a picture of a most considerate man. So attentive is he towards the needs of those around him that he appears quite unconcerned about his own death. Pausing on his way to Golgotha, Jesus delivers a lengthy prophetic speech to the daughters of Jerusalem (Lk. 23.28-31). As he is being crucified, he petitions the Father for the forgiveness of those responsible (23.34), and once on the cross he is able to listen and respond to the debate on retribution between the other two prisoners, promising salvation to one of them (23.39-43). If any of the Gospels can be seen to portray Jesus as triumphant on the cross, it is surely Luke, rather than John.

4. *... He Is not Ridiculed while He Is on the Cross.* Scholars contend that the fact that the Fourth Gospel does not surround the cross with hostile onlookers who hurl insults at him, as is the case in the Synoptics, has a bearing on the atmosphere of the scene: 'The royal character of the crucified Jesus is further emphasized by the absence of any mockery during his crucifixion'.[98] Haenchen adds that John's passion 'exhibits nothing of the hatred and bitter irony of the world related by Mark, nothing of the enmity of the environment tormenting the crucified... Jesus is no longer ostracized and ridiculed by the world.'[99] We cannot, however, assume the absence of mockery at the cross. There is undoubtedly a crowd present watching the crucifixion, as is indicated by v. 20. Writing about the *titulus*, John notes that many of the Jews read it because the place of Jesus' crucifixion was near to the city. It was not read solely by Jews, for John is at pains to state that it was also written in Greek and Latin.[100] The *titulus* is a symbol of the contempt of the world, emphasizing Jesus' failure to the onlookers. The reader is well aware of the contempt with which the Jews, particularly the authorities, view Jesus. The Roman trial has been the principal vehicle for displaying the vehement public derision and humiliation of Jesus and there is little need here for further explicit comment—the mockery is implicit.

98. Weber, *The Cross*, p. 131.

99. Haenchen, *John*, II, pp. 193, 200.

100. The authorities attempt to use this as a further opportunity to discredit Jesus, indicating that he is a fraud: μὴ γράφε, ὁ βασιλεὺς τῶν Ἰουδαίων, ἀλλ᾽ ὅτι ἐκεῖνος εἶπεν, βασιλεύς εἰμι τῶν Ἰουδαίων (v. 21). Pilate, however, will not cooperate.

5. ... *He Does not Utter a 'Cry of Dereliction'*.

> The tragic dimensions of Jesus's death, his own anguish and suffering in
> the face of it, are largely absent from John. He dies as man is scarcely
> known to die. If in Mark Jesus utters a cry of dereliction and in Luke a
> pious prayer, in John he marks the end of his own earthly ministry and
> work with an imperious pronouncement, 'It is finished'.[101]

Whether it is an imperious pronouncement, 'cry of victory',[102] 'majestic
word'[103] or 'affirmation of fulfilment',[104] the last words of the Johannine
Jesus are almost universally interpreted in a positive light. The use of the
word τετέλεσται is seen to indicate that Jesus has triumphantly finished
his work on earth. It also rules out any implication of distress on the part
of Jesus due to desertion by the Father.[105]

τετέλεσται cannot seriously be interpreted as a triumphant cry. In the
first instance it is not a cry at all—the evangelist clearly states that Jesus
said his last word (εἶπεν).[106] The Synoptic accounts, on the other hand,
inform the reader that Jesus' last utterances were made with a loud voice
(φωνῇ μεγάλῃ).[107] In addition, the interpretation of τετέλεσται is open
to question. Its translation is generally accepted as 'it is finished',[108]

101. Smith, 'Presentation of Jesus in the Fourth Gospel', p. 371.

102. Sanders, *Gospel According to St John*, p. 410. Also Smalley, *John: Evangelist and
Interpreter*, p. 224 and L. Newbigin, *The Light Has Come: An Exposition of the Fourth
Gospel* (Edinburgh: Handsel Press, 1982), p. 256.

103. Lohse, *Suffering and Death of Jesus Christ*, p. 98.

104. Barrett, *Gospel According to St John*, p. 547. Similarly Lagrange, 'Jésus a
exprimé dans un cri la satisfaction du Fils qui a accompli l'oeuvre que lui avait
confiée son Père' (*Sain Jean*, p. 497).

105. John 'does not allow himself even to suggest that Jesus was deserted by
God' (Barrett, *Gospel According to St John*, p. 547).

106. Lindars, however, supplies it for him, commenting that 'John does not
mention the loud cry, but *tetelestai* is presumably his idea of what the cry was'
(*Gospel of John*, p. 582). Brown also sees it as a cry (*Gospel According to John*, II,
p. 930). Others simply add an exclamation mark when translating the statement to
make the point (Bultmann, *Gospel of John*, p. 675).

107. Mk 15.34, 37; Mt. 27.46, 49; Lk. 23.46. It is generally assumed that, in
contrast with John, the last cry of Jesus in Mark and Matthew is a negative one,
following as it does his cry of abandonment. It should be noted that this is purely an
assumption on the part of commentators, for example Lohse (*Suffering and Death of
Jesus Christ*, p. 98).

108. BAGD, p. 810. Although some translate it 'accomplished', which renders a
more triumphalist meaning. See, for example, Bultmann, *Gospel of John*, p. 675 and
Sanders, *Gospel According to St John*, p. 410.

although the nuance of the phrase can be understood in different ways. R.A. Edwards, for example, claims that the words heard by John[109] were actually 'it's all over'.[110] This would certainly be a negative interpretation, as the word would appear to indicate defeat rather than victory. It would take a good deal of manipulation of the evangelist's theology to imagine him placing a word of defeat on the lips of the dying Jesus, particularly since it cannot be denied that John considers this to be the moment at which God's name is 'glorified'. However, we should guard against interpreting it as an outright statement of triumph on the basis of comparison with the Synoptic accounts.[111] Brown and Thompson both warn against using a theology other than Johannine to interpret the Fourth Gospel's passion narrative (primarily on the grounds of the different sources used by John and the Synoptics). Thompson notes: 'it would be rash to state that John substitutes a pronouncement of triumph for a cry of dereliction, or to interpret John's words in the light of the Synoptic record'.[112] John's emphasis is on the obedience of Jesus to the Father's will to the very end, signifying that what has been finished is the work that Jesus was sent to carry out.[113] Is this a victory?[114] It can only be seen as 'victorious' in the same sense that his brutal and ignominious death is seen as 'glorious'. This must surely mean a re-examination of our concept of victory along less triumphalist

109. He held that the Gospel was the eyewitness account of John, the son of Zebedee.

110. 'We can have no manner of doubt that what he heard, then when he saw the head at last fall forward, was the dreadful close of what had been the passionate confidence and unlimited hope of youth, the shattering assertion that he had been mistaken. The Messiah episode, with all its exciting inspiration, was over' (Edwards, *Gospel According to St John*, p. 158). Edwards suggests that, meditating on the phrase, the evangelist *later* believed the real sense of the words were the majestic 'it is finished'. The point here is not that Edwards believes this is an eyewitness account of what was really said on the cross, but that the interpretation of τετέλεσται can be seen to have such negative import.

111. Compared with Luke's great shout and pious commendation: πάτερ, εἰς χεῖράς σου παρατίθεμαι τὸ πνεῦμά μου (23.46), John is surely less triumphant.

112. Thompson, *Humanity of Jesus*, p. 109.

113. Thompson again, 'Rather than suggesting the death of one untouched by human suffering, his words point to the death of one obedient to God's command for him' (*Humanity of Jesus*, p. 109).

114. Brown too ponders on this question: 'If "It is finished" is a victory cry, the victory it heralds is that of obediently fulfilling the Father's will' (*Gospel According to John*, II, p. 931).

lines. Jesus links the terms together himself during his last prayer before betrayal. He glorifies God on earth by finishing the work which he was given to do (17.4). The work of Jesus has been his life of rejection, suffering and oppression and now his victimization reaches its zenith with his crucifixion—'Jesus dies not only because he had done the Father's will but also because *for him to die is itself the Father's will*'.[115]

6. ... *He Gives up his Own Spirit*. The death of Jesus is seen to be his final sovereign act, showing that he maintains control right up to the last breath,[116] before appearing to choose the moment to die.[117] He is described as follows: καὶ κλίνας τὴν κεφαλὴν παρέδωκεν τὸ πνεῦμα ('and he bowed his head and gave up his spirit', 19.30). The meaning of these actions is said to indicate the voluntary nature of his death;[118] however, neither the bowing of the head nor the handing over of the spirit can be interpreted so simplistically. In his article on κλίνω Bauer informs us that:

> since the bowing of the head came before the giving up of his spirit, and since especially in the Fourth Gospel the Passion is a voluntary act of Jesus to the very last, the bowing must not be regarded as a sign of weakness; the Crucified One acted of his own accord.[119]

Haenchen too does not see any weakness on the part of Jesus in this action, claiming that: 'he bows his head as in sleep'.[120] However, Bultmann finds this untenable, commenting:

> ...it is true that in Jn the Crucified does not really appear as one who suffers but as one who acts, yet it would be too ingenious to find in κλίνας τ. κεφ. the independence of the action: e.g. Jesus reclined the head not because of weakness but in order to sleep.[121]

115. Hubbard, 'John 19.17-30', p. 401.
116. Lindars, *Gospel of John*, p. 582.
117. Stibbe, *John*, p. 197.
118. Sanders, *Gospel According to St John*, p. 410; Lindars, *Gospel of John*, p. 582.
119. BAGD, p. 436.
120. Haenchen, *John*, II, p. 194.
121. Bultmann, *Gospel of John*, p. 675. See also M. Hengel, who sees both Jesus' thirst and the sinking of his head as expressions of his creatureliness ('The Old Testament in the Fourth Gospel', in C.A. Evans and W.R. Stegner [eds.], *The Gospels and the Scriptures of Israel* [JSNTSup, 104; Sheffield: Sheffield Academic Press, 1994], pp. 380-95 [393]).

It is not obligatory, of course, to view Jesus' action as one of *defeat* or not befitting a king just because it is, undoubtedly, a sign of weakness in an exhausted man who is about to die.

The giving up of the spirit is more problematic. The verb used is not a common one and John is unique in using it in this context. The Synoptics all use different terms,[122] although they seem to use a similar metaphor for death—the 'handing over of Jesus' spirit'. Several commentators flirt with the idea that the phrase means 'hand over the Spirit' (in other words the Holy Spirit) but then reject this on the basis that John describes the giving of the Holy Spirit in 20.22.[123] In the end these scholars settle for a meaning along the lines of the Lukan version, 'into thy hands I commend my spirit'.[124] Nicholson sees a link with John 10, where Jesus states that he will lay down (τίθημι) his life of his own accord. He claims 'this is graphically born out by the fact that he gives up (παρέδωκεν) his spirit (19.30) before the soldiers can club him to death'.[125] However, if John really had this in mind surely he would have used τίθημι, or even perhaps alluded to it by using παρατίθημι. The fact is that he uses παραδίδωμι, andwhat commentators fail to mention is the context in which this verb is used in John. It occurs fifteen times in the Gospel; nine of which refer to the betrayal, or to Judas, 'the betrayer'. The rest refer to the 'handing over' of Jesus to Pilate by the Jews.[126] Of the latter group, Duke claims that the meaning is not simply to 'hand over' but to 'betray', since this is actually the meaning of the verb in this Gospel.[127] That this overwhelmingly negative term is used to

---

122. Mk 15.37, ἐξέπνευσεν; Mt. 27.50, ἀφῆκεν τὸ πνεῦμα; Lk. 23.46, παρατίθεμαι τὸ πνεῦμά μου.

123. Barrett, *Gospel According to St John*, p. 554; Sanders, *Gospel According to St John*, p. 410; Lindars, *Gospel of John*, p. 582. Hoskyns believes that it does refer to the handing over the Spirit to the believers, towards whom he has inclined his head, but concedes that it is 'very strange language' (*Fourth Gospel*, p. 532).

124. Lindars, *Gospel of John*, p. 582.

125. Nicholson, *Death as Departure*, p. 165.

126. 6.64, 71; 12.4; 13.2, 11, 21; 18.2, 5, 30, 35, 36; 19.11, 16; 21.20 and, of course, 19.30.

127. Duke, *Irony in the Fourth Gospel*, p. 128. W.K. Grossouw agrees that John uses this verb only for Jesus being delivered up to death, and in particular for the betrayal by Judas. He goes on: 'the only exception to this "technical" use of παραδίδοναι occurs in xix 30... Perhaps one should here see an intentional contrast with all other places where the word is used. Jesus voluntarily gives up his "spirit" to God—the only true παράδοσις' ('A Note on John XIII 1-3', *NovT* 8 [1966],

describe Jesus' last action cannot fail to influence our interpretation of the verse. Hanson sees a possible echo of Isa. 53.12c, the LXX of which reads: ἀνθ' ὧν παρεδόθη εἰς θάνατον ἡ ψυχὴ αὐτοῦ, 'because his soul was given up to death'. The Masoretic Text can be translated 'because he poured out his life to (the) death' (תחת אשר הערה למות נפשו).[128] If there was an allusion to this text it would certainly imply a negative meaning—surrendering his spirit to death rather than to the Father, as in Luke. The concept of Jesus *betraying* his spirit is a very difficult one, and a betrayal could be seen to imply that Jesus had failed either in his work or in death. It begins to make some sense, however, if it is interpreted with reference to his victimal role. This betrayal is his final collusion with darkness. It is the last act of a man who has both longed for and dreaded his fate and has played a conscious role in ensuring it comes to pass. Delivering up his spirit is not a gesture of sovereignty; it is the ultimate victimal act. He has courted betrayal from the begining—betrayal by his people, priests and disciples. Now he betrays his own life, handing himself over to death. The courtship is over, this is the consummation.[129]

What general conclusions can be drawn from the exploration of the way in which the characterization of Jesus during his passion has been handled by the commentators? First, many aspects marshalled in support of the triumphant crucified Jesus in reality do not contribute much to argument. Without doubt, the crucifixion is depicted as the enthronement of Jesus, but what an ignominious enthronement, and what an inglorious king. This, though, is the true irony—that this disgraced victim *is* John's king, that humiliation is how his dominion is manifested. Supremacist interpretations do not sit comfortably with the text. The glory of the Father is, and indeed must be, displayed through the scene

---

pp. 124-31 [127]). This suggestion is a weak one. There is no reason to suppose that Jn 19.30 is an exception to the 'technical' usage that the evangelist has built up throughout the rest of the Gospel.

128. Hanson, *Prophetic Gospel*, p. 218.

129. Just who or what Jesus hands his spirit over to is a matter for debate. It is significant to note that the text does *not* say he handed it over to the Father. Many of the commentators assume this to be the case—it is implicit if the phrase is interpreted 'into thy hands I place my spirit', as mentioned above, and Schnackenburg makes it explicit (*Gospel According to St John*, III, pp. 284-85). As the text does not mention the Father, other interpretations are possible, and I would argue that this is Jesus' final surrender to his fate. In this sense he hands himself over to death.

that the evangelist creates, but it is a sombre affair. As Hengel comments; 'for ancient hearers and readers no 'God walking over the earth' dies like this—disgraced and naked, and hanging on the cross.'[130] Victory has been wrought through the victimization of the Father's son. There is suffering, there is compassion, grief and dignity, but surprisingly for the fourth evangelist, there is little by way of dramatic flourishes. There are no supernatural signs, no last minute repentances and no dramatic loud cries. John's only tools have been a few texts from the Septuagint and a basic description of events. The death of Jesus has been a constant theme running through his narrative. There has been no need to accentuate the shame and savagery of a scene with which his readers would have been all too familiar.

Part 2: Jesus as Victim

I have examined ways in which commentators see Jesus presented as victorious, triumphant and sovereign on the cross. The next section will examine an alternative perspective on the death of the Johannine Jesus. I have tried to indicate already that he is not an imperious figure who avoids suffering while on the cross. To the contrary, he is a figure of great pathos. However, to see him in this light, what is needed is a means of approaching the story afresh, so that the aspects that portray Jesus as a victim are brought into sharper relief. The method employed will be to use Old Testament material within the text as an interpretative tool for the rest of the narrative.

It was mentioned at the end of the last section that one of the main tools used by the evangelist in shaping his narrative was the Old Testament. Hanson notes that John's passion contains 'a constellation of references to scripture, explicit and implicit'.[131] The fulfilment of Scripture is mentioned directly on three occasions during the passion narrative

130. Hengel, *Johannine Question*, p. 71.

131. Hanson, *Prophetic Gospel*, p. 203. In another work on the subject, Hanson discusses attempts by scholars to categorize John's treatment of Scripture as midrash, targum and haggada; as well as the use of typology, allegory and the importance of salvation history. He concludes that John's use is not 'atomistic'—he does not simply cite Scripture out of context, but intends to show that the whole person and career of Jesus was the fulfilment of Scripture ('John's Use of Scripture', in C.A. Evans and W.R. Stegner [eds.], *The Gospels and the Scriptures of Israel* [JSNTSup, 104; Sheffield: Sheffield Academic Press, 1994], pp. 358-79). For further discussion on the Fourth Gospel's use of the Old Testament see Freed, *Old Testament Quotations*; and Hengel, 'The Old Testament in the Fourth Gospel', pp. 380-95. Hengel notes the lack of

and scholars have seen allusions to several more texts through the vocabulary used. It should be stressed that it is not being claimed here that the evangelist was necessarily deliberately alluding to all of these texts (although this appears to be what Hanson claims), but just that the vocabulary used has encouraged scholars to see 'intertextual echoes'[132] between John and the particular text. It will become immediately evident that the references are to figures who are victims in the Hebrew Bible. In fact, they can be seen as victim 'prototypes'—those whose stories are automatically associated with violence and suffering. Exploring the characteristics of their victimization and the links between their experiences and Jesus' will assist in interpreting John's passion narrative. In this way they can be seen to function as *leitmotifs* for the story. As Dodd points out, these references must not be regarded as 'mere literary embroidery', as they give the narrative its specific religious and theological character.[133]

The texts generally considered to be relevant are detailed in the table below. Where it is claimed by a scholar that a text is alluded to, and the evangelist does not specifically state that he is using scripture, the reference is mentioned. In addition, where a text is claimed to have different references in the Old Testament, both are mentioned.

Reference in John	Reference in the Old Testament	Usage	Character Identified
19.14	Exod. 12.46/Num. 9.12	Alluded[134]	Paschal Lamb
19.17	Gen. 22.1-19	Alluded[135]	Isaac
	Isa. 53.11c	Alluded[136]	Suffering Servant

scholarly attention that this subject has received in the past and argues that John's use and ordering of citations is part of a 'well-considered, unified plan' (p. 395).

132. A term used by Stibbe when referring to similarities between John and passages from the Old Testament. This is a far more satisfactory way of discussing links between narratives than attempting to claim that there are direct parallels or deliberate allusions (*John*, p. 58). Likewise, Dodd refers to passages 'sometimes recalled to the reader by verbal echoes' (*Historical Tradition*, p. 31).

133. Dodd, *Historical Tradition*, p. 31.

134. Hengel, *The Johannine Question*, p. 189; Stibbe, *John*, p. 192; Barrett, *Gospel According to St John*, p. 51.

135. Brown, *Gospel According to John*, II, p. 917; Barrett, *Gospel According to St John*, p. 548; Westcott, *Gospel According to St John*, p. 273.

136. Hanson, *Prophetic Gospel*, p. 208.

Reference in John	Reference in the Old Testament	Usage	Character Identified
19.24	Ps. 22.18[137]	Direct	Psalmist
	Zech. 3.1-5	Direct	Joshua
19.28	Ps. 69.21[138]	Direct	Psalmist
19.29	Exod. 12.22	Alluded[139]	Paschal Lamb
19.30	Job 19.26-7	Alluded[140]	Job
	Isa. 53.12c	Alluded[141]	Suffering Servant
	Ps. 31.11a[142]	Alluded[143]	Psalmist
19.36	Exod. 12.46/Num. 9.12	Direct	Paschal Lamb
	Ps. 34.20[144]	Direct	Psalmist
19.37	Zech. 12.10	Direct	Shepherd–King

Table 7: Use of the Old Testament in the Johannine Passion

Three of these representative figures will be discussed in the second part of this chapter as a means of exploring the theme of the Johannine Jesus' death as a victim: Isaac, the Suffering Servant and the Paschal Lamb.

The Sacrifice of Isaac. That there are intertextual echoes between the story of Abraham and the offering of Isaac, and that of the Father and Jesus in the Fourth Gospel is no new concept. Both Jn 3.16 and 19.17 have been linked with Genesis 22. In the first instance, the mention of Jesus as God's only begotten son reminds the reader of Isaac.[145] The second reference, 19.17, mentions Jesus carrying his own cross.[146] The features that Jesus and Isaac have in common are as follows:

137. Ps. 22.19 in the LXX.
138. Ps. 69.22 in the LXX.
139. Stibbe, *John*, p. 196; Barrett, *Gospel According to St John*, p. 553.
140. Hanson, *Prophetic Gospel*, p. 216.
141. Bernard, *Gospel According to St John*, II, p. 641; Hanson, *Prophetic Gospel*, p. 218.
142. Ps. 30.11a in the LXX.
143. Hanson, *Prophetic Gospel*, p. 215
144. Ps. 33.21 in the LXX. See Hanson for a full discussion on the relevance of this passage to Jn 19.36 (*Prophetic Gospel*, p. 219).
145. Barrett, *Gospel According to St John*, p. 216; Stibbe, *John*, p. 58. P.R. Davies and B.D. Chilton also see a 'conceivable' allusion to Gen. 22 in Jn 3.16 ('The Aqedah: A Revised Tradition History' *CBQ* 40 [1978], pp. 514-46 [531]).
146. This interpretation was frequent among the Church Fathers. For example, see Chrysostom, *In Joh. Hom.* 85.1.

Isaac was depicted as an adult who voluntarily accepted death, a combination of the Gen. 22 story with the theme of the Suffering Servant. An additional link was

a. *They Are both the Only Son of their Fathers*. This is emphasized in the Hebrew Bible, Isaac being referred to three times by God as Abraham's only son (22.2, 12, 16, בִּנְךָ אֶת יְחִידְךָ). The LXX uses different language, calling Isaac Abraham's 'beloved son whom you have loved' (τὸν υἱόν σου τὸν ἀγαπητόν, ὃν ἠγάπησας, v. 2), but the meaning conveyed is similar. In John, Jesus is both the only begotten[147] and the beloved son[148] of the Father. This emphasizes the tragic aspect in each story and the value of the sacrificial victim—Abraham does not have another son to generate his descendants; Isaac is his only hope as well as his much longed for child. One cannot but help remembering another 'only begotten' child of the Hebrew Bible who is also sacrificed at the hands of her father: Jephthah's daughter, who, with great dignity, submits to the fate of becoming a whole burnt offering as a consequence of a foolish vow of her father (Jdg. 11.29-40).[149] Unlike Isaac, for this child there is no reprieve—'no solace comes from God..., no ram in the thicket'.[150]

b. *Their Sacrifice Will Bring Benefits to Others*. The willingness of Abraham to sacrifice Isaac brings blessings not only for himself but for his descendants and the nations of the earth (Gen. 22.18). The sacrifice of Jesus secures the salvation of the world (Jn 3.17). However, both benefits can only be mediated through faith—the faith of Abraham that Yahweh will somehow manage to be true to his promise of Gen. 17.5-8

established with the Passover lamb and the sacrifice of Isaac as it was dated 15th Nisan (*Gospel According to John*, II, p. 917). Barrett also concedes that John may have some Isaac typology in mind, however, Hanson thinks this is unlikely, contending that there is 'no trace' elsewhere in the Gospel for Aqedah theology (*Prophetic Gospel*, p. 207). It should, however, be noted that it is allusion to Gen. 22 and *not* to the Aqedah that is being discussed. See Davies and Chilton for a description of Aqedah doctrine and justification for not identifying allusions to Gen. 22 with the Aqedah ('The Aqedah: A Revised Tradition History', p. 514).

147. μονογενής, 1.14, 18; 3.16, 18.

148. Jesus tells us this on several occasions. See 3.35; 5.20; 10.17; 15.9-10.

149. For the whole story, see P. Trible, *Texts of Terror: Literary-Feminist Readings of Biblical Narratives* (Overtures to Biblical Theology; Philadelphia: Fortress Press, 1984), pp. 93-116; and J.C. Exum, *Tragedy and Biblical Narrative: Arrows of the Almighty* (Cambridge: Cambridge University Press, 1992).

150. Exum, *Tragedy and Biblical Narrative*, p. 58.

and the faith of the believer in the name of the only Son of God (Jn
3.18).

c. *They both Carry the Materials for their Death.* Abraham makes Isaac carry
the wood out of which the sacrificial altar will be made (Gen. 22.6).
Jesus too must carry the crossbar of his crucifix, as discussed above (Jn
19.17). This is a somewhat macabre touch in the Genesis story as Isaac is
unaware that he is the one destined to be placed on top of the pile to be
slaughtered. Jesus is, of course, fully cognizant of the purpose of the
wood that he carries.

d. *Both Victims are Bound.* Isaac is bound by his father in preparation for
his slaughter (Gen. 22.9). Likewise, it is mentioned several times during
the arrest and trial that Jesus is bound (for example Jn 18.12) and
presumably he was also bound to the crossbar of his crucifix. The denial
of liberty is an essential prerequisite to the murder of the victim.

e. *Both are Innocent Victims.* That Isaac is perceived as an innocent victim
is indicated by the two references to him as a young lad (τὸ παιδάριον,
Gen. 22.5, 12). He is also, of course, oblivious as to what is about to
happen to him, as is evidenced by his truly pathetic question to Abraham: '...but where is the victim?' (v. 7). Jesus is also specifically stated as
being innocent twice by Pilate during his trial ('I find no crime in him',
Jn 18.38, 19.4).

f. *Both are Betrayed.* The betrayal of Jesus is a familiar and unquestionable
fact in the Gospel—his cognizance of the perfidy of Judas is noted from
as early as Jn 6.71. But what about Isaac? The response Isaac gets from
Abraham to his question about the whereabouts of the victim is: 'God
will provide'. There are several ways in which this could be interpreted.
Perhaps Abraham truly believes that God *will* provide a lamb. However
tempting this interpretation might seem, there is not much evidence for
it in the text. This tale tells us nothing about Abraham's faith, only his
fear. Perhaps, then, Abraham wishes to protect Isaac from the awful
truth? Almost certainly he would want to do that; after all, he loves Isaac
(22.2). But what if he did tell Isaac the truth and Isaac, understandably,
was not so committed to the plan? Abraham is alone with his son by this
stage (22.5) and if the boy tried to escape, how would he, a very old
man, ever catch him? Abraham cannot take this risk; after all, he has

been charged with the responsibility of slaying Isaac by Yahweh, whom he fears deeply. He therefore holds back the truth from Isaac in order that the plan will not be jeopardized and his own life potentially at risk. He deceives him to ensure that he will be able to betray him, to hand him over, to Yahweh.

All of the above similarities between the filial experiences of Isaac and Jesus are obvious enough; however, the factor that is most significant and will assist in illuminating Jesus' identity as a victim has not yet been mentioned. This is the fact that *they both have fathers who are prepared to sacrifice them.* We do not see Abraham so much as flinch when he receives the command from God to sacrifice Isaac—he rises early the next morning and sets off to carry out the task. We do not discover until afterwards that his impetus has been fear of God (φοβῇ τὸν θεὸν σύ, 22.12). God's motive for the sacrifice of Jesus, on the other hand, is love for the world (οὕτως γὰρ ἠγάπησεν ὁ θεὸς τὸν κόσμον, 3.16). What both of these fathers have in common is an overriding priority that supersedes paternal affection. That they love their sons is not in doubt, but their commitment to another rules out the possibility of mercy for the victim. We hastily accept fear (which is often translated into devout fear, piety, etc., but *never* cowardice) as a mitigating circumstance for Abraham's attempt at infanticide in order to soothe feelings of deep discomfort about the whole scenario in Genesis 22. When it comes to the relationship between the Johannine Father and Son, it is difficult to view the death of the Son from anything other than a theological perspective, within the context of the salvation of the κόσμος. The basic fact is that Jesus is subjected to a brutal and bloody death by the will of his father: 'God himself led the victim to the slaughter place, and with a fixed smile, watched the execution'.[151] We have quickly strayed into taboo territory here. We have to admit that the complexities of the interdependence of the Father and the Son in John's Gospel are practically unfathomable and certainly outside of the remit of this study. Jesus is the son who, in the same breath, is at one with the Father (14.10, 10.30) and subordinate to him (14.28); at the command of the Father (14.31), doing nothing on his own authority (8.28) and yet has all things in his hand (3.35). Though the Father loves the Son, (3.35), he *so* loves the world that Jesus must be sacrificed to save it (3.16). Sacrifice, however, is more akin to violence and hatred than love and is not so

151. Kott, *Eating of the Gods*, pp. 219-20.

distantly related to murder.[152] 'Violence is not to be denied, but it can be diverted to another object, something it can sink its teeth into',[153] and this is what happens to the sacrificial victim. There is no denying that somehow the love of the Father for Jesus is bound up with the sacrifice of Jesus (be it voluntary, propitiatory, expiatory or whatever); with his experience of a barbaric, humiliating death: 'For this reason the Father loves me, because I lay down my life, that I may take it again' (10.17).[154]

The sacrificial perspective of the victimization of Jesus will be further explored in the section on the Paschal Lamb. Brown concludes that 'Isaac symbolism is ... one factor in leading us to think that John looked upon Jesus as a sacrificial victim who died at the same hour that the paschal lambs were being slaughtered in the Temple'.[155] What is being claimed here is that Jesus not merely a victim in the general sense of the term, but a sacrificial victim who is sacrificed for the world at the will of his Father.

The Suffering Servant. The suffering servant theme of Deutero-Isaiah occurs more frequently outside of the passion narrative than within it in the Fourth Gospel. It is used explicitly in Jn 12.37-40 and implicitly elsewhere.[156] Stibbe sees Deutero-Isaiah as a 'rich resource' for the author of the Gospel,[157] and indeed it is an important source of material for the understanding of Jesus as a victim.[158] It assists in the

152. R. Girard, *Violence and the Sacred* (trans. P. Gregory; Baltimore: The John Hopkins University Press, 1977), p. 1.

153. Girard, *Violence and the Sacred*, p. 4.

154. There is an irony in the fact that it is the 'father of the world', the devil, who is accused of being a 'murderer from the beginning' (8.44).

155. Brown, *Gospel According to John*, II, p. 918. Kott sees the sacrifices of Isaac and the Passover lamb as prefigurations of Jesus' own sacrifice (*Eating of the Gods*, p. 210).

156. So, 1.29, 36.

157. Stibbe, *John*, p. 136. 'The reader is meant to see the death of Jesus as the sacrifice of the Servant of Yahweh' (p. 137).

158. Other scholars who have recognized the importance of Isaiah on the Fourth Gospel include F.W. Young, who discusses the allusions and quotations in detail ('A Study of the Relation of Isaiah to the Fourth Gospel', *ZNW* 46 [1955], pp. 215-33) and Morris (*Gospel According to John*, p. 145). C.A. Evans sees John 12.1-43 as a midrash on Isa. 52.7-53.12 ('Obduracy and the Lord's Servant: Some Observations on the use of the Old Testament in the Fourth Gospel', in C.A. Evans and W.F.

interpretation of the 'lifting up' sayings (3.14, 8.28, 12.32)[159] and the 'glorification' of Jesus[160] and is linked to the understanding of Jesus as the lamb of God.[161] Whether or not the fourth evangelist actually saw Jesus as the Suffering Servant is not really the issue for discussion here, although there are plenty who argue that this was the case.[162] Speaking from the perspective of liberation theology, Segundo claims that:

> It is not going too far to say that the tradition of the suffering servant [within the early New Testament church] was *the* messianic tradition par excellence for interpreting the destiny of Jesus of Nazareth. We can see this in the Pauline school... and in the Johannine school (1.29, 32-34; 3.11; 8.12, 32, 45).[163]

This undoubtedly overstates the case, but it is not difficult to see why an emphasis on understanding of Jesus as a figure such as the servant of

Stinespring [eds.], *Early Jewish and Christian Exegesis: Studies in Memory of William Hugh Brownlee* [Atlanta: Scholars Press, 1987], pp. 221-36).

The identification of Jesus (Synoptic and Johannine) with the Suffering Servant was most fashionable in the 1950s and 1960s, being propounded by scholars such as Cullmann (*Christology of the New Testament*, pp. 51-82); and J. Jeremias ('παῖς θεοῦ', *TDNT*, V, pp. 654-717, especially pp. 705-17). It was Morna Hooker's comprehensive study, *Jesus and the Servant: The Influence of the Servant Concept of Deutero-Isaiah in the New Testament* (London: SPCK, 1959), that shattered many of the assumptions that had been held concerning the influence of the Servant Songs on New Testament Christology and it is now an area in which scholars tread with more care. Marinus de Jonge notes that 'we shall have to conclude that the influence of Isa. 52.13–53.12 on the earliest Christian kerygma can hardly be demonstrated' (*Servant-Messiah*, p. 50). Ruth Edwards, however, feels that the backlash against 'the older piety', which equated Jesus with the Servant, has gone too far. She comments, 'while the precise degree of dependence on individual texts may be disputed, a general influence of the Isaianic passages (esp. 52.13–53.12) seems inescapable' ('Christological Basis of the Johannine Footwashing', p. 382).

159. Beasley-Murray, *John*, p. lxxxiv; Stibbe, *John*, p. 137.

160. Evans, 'Obduracy and the Lord's Servant', p. 232.

161. Cullmann, *Christology of the New Testament*, pp. 71-2.

162. See Schnackenburg, *Gospel According to St John*, I, pp. 297-300; Smalley, *John, Evangelist and Interpreter*, p. 225; Hanson, *Prophetic Gospel*, p. 218.

163. Segundo, *Jesus of Nazareth Yesterday and Today*, p. 51. Likewise, Sobrino claims that the title 'servant of Yahweh' soon fell into disuse as a name for Jesus as the meaning of his death began to be reinterpreted and toned down by the later evangelists. The title, which was 'the most direct pointer to Jesus' cross' and 'the most basic explanation of Jesus' person' was replaced by others which stressed his existence as one already exalted in heaven (*Christology at the Crossroads*, p. 186).

Yahweh would be attractive to liberation theologians. Again, it is merely the 'intertextual echoes' between Isaiah and John that permit us to engage the hermeneutical assistance of the suffering servant when looking at the crucified Christ.

The עבד יהוה is a figure of great pathos in the Hebrew Bible. To view the Johannine Jesus from the perspective of the servant of Yahweh will necessitate leaving behind images of a man who is sovereign, serene and somehow eludes the agonies of his oppression. The servant is a pitifully tragic figure, whose fate is outlined in Isa. 52.12–53.13.[164] The following section will discuss the common experiences of Jesus and the servant.

a. *They Experience Intense Physical and Mental Pain.* At the risk of stating the obvious, it is worth noting that both Jesus and the servant *suffer.* The justification for this is that there are those who would perhaps dispute that this was something they had in common. The servant's suffering is extreme—so extreme that it has been the cause of his infamy, becoming part of his popular name. The Johannine Jesus, on the other hand, is *not* famous for his experience of extreme suffering, as has been noted throughout this study. The servant's experience of physical and psychological pain runs throughout the whole chapter: he is so disfigured he barely appears human; he was 'acquainted' with pain and suffering; he was pierced, crushed and wounded; he was oppressed and afflicted, crushed and made to suffer. These things are described in the LXX version of Isa. 53.3:

> But his form was ignoble, and inferior to that of the children of men; he was a man in suffering, and acquainted with the bearing of sickness, for his face is turned from us: he was dishonoured and not esteemed.

Jesus has endured the physical threats of the Jews throughout his ministry, escaping impromptu attempts to murder him several times (as can be seen from Tables 1–5 in Chapter 2). Following detention he is subjected to the torture of scourging and an agonizing execution—a fate which doubtless left him disfigured beyond human semblance.

b. *They are Spurned by Society.* The servant is an outcast from his own community. People who saw him were appalled at his appearance. They

---

164. No attempt will be made here to discuss the contents of the other three servant songs, as the fourth is the most appropriate in terms of subject material.

spurned him and despised him to the extent that he withdrew from society (again, Isa. 53.3). We have already mentioned above that Jesus is alienated from and rejected by his people. The fact that he is 'from above' and therefore not 'of this world' cannot be used to minimize his actual experience of rejection from his own community. This manifests itself practically in expulsion from the synagogue (Jn 9.22) but can also be seen in attempts by the Jews to associate him with other outcast groups, accusing him of being a Samaritan and demon-possessed (8.48).

c. *They are Innocent Victims.* I touched on the innocence of Jesus when discussing Isaac. Isaac's innocence is implied by his vulnerability as a young boy, whereas the innocence of the servant provides a more effective parallel with that of Jesus. The servant is portrayed as having endured violence and slander, despite the fact that he had not committed violence nor spoken dishonestly (Isa. 53.9b). His vindication comes in 53.11b: 'As a righteous one my servant shall justify many'.[165] Both victims experience wrongful arrest and unjust conviction on account of their innocence. The servant has no one to defend him on his detention—'who shall declare his generation?'; (53.8).[166] Likewise, Jesus has no defenders when Pilate raises the possibility of his release on the grounds of his innocence. He is confronted instead with the roar of 'crucify, crucify' from the crowd (Jn 19.6).

d. *Their Suffering is 'Unto Death'.* Whether the servant actually dies as a result of the violence inflicted on him is a point of disagreement among scholars. It has generally been held that he does,[167] but see R.N. Whybray for arguments to the contrary.[168] Verse 53.12b is seen to indicate

165. The Hebrew may be: 'he is proved innocent before the multitudes' (D.J.A. Clines, *I, He, We, and They: A Literary Approach to Isaiah 53* [JSOTSup, 1; Sheffield: JSOT Press, 1976], p. 13).

166. The Hebrew may be rendered 'no one raised a protest at his fate' (Clines, *I, He, We, and They*, p. 13).

167. So C. Westermann, *Isaiah 40–66: A Commentary* (trans. D.M.G. Stalker; London: SCM Press, 1969), pp. 257-69; J.L. McKenzie, *Second Isaiah* (AB; New York: Doubleday, 1983), p. 135; J.D.W. Watts, *Isaiah 34-66* (WBC, 25, Waco, TX: Word Books, 1987), p. 230; G.A.F. Knight, *Deutero-Isaiah: A Theological Commentary on Isaiah 40-55* (New York: Abingdon Press, 1965), p. 222.

168. R.N. Whybray, *Thanksgiving for a Liberated Prophet: An Interpretation of Isaiah 53* (JSOTSup, 4; Sheffield: JSOT Press, 1978), p. 92. H.M. Orlinsky also argues that the servant did not die. He interprets Isa. 53.10 to mean the servant would live

that the servant perished—'because his soul was delivered to death' (ἀνθ' ὧν παρεδόθη εἰς θάνατον ἡ ψυχὴ αὐτοῦ)—which provides us with the verbal link with Jn 19.30. Both victims give up their soul 'unto death'. For our purposes it is not really of great significance whether the servant dies. The point is that his affliction is so severe that death is not far away, in fact the expectation is that he will die as he is assigned a grave (Isa. 53.9). For Jesus, of course, victimization is fatal.

e. *Their Suffering Brings Benefits to Others.* As discussed above, the sacrifice of Jesus secures salvation (Jn 3.17) and the process by which this is secured is through a vicarious, atoning death. He is the good shepherd who lays down his life for the sheep (10.11). The servant of Yahweh also endures pain on behalf of the errant sheep ('and the Lord gave him up for our sins', Isa. 53.6).[169] The extent to which this can be claimed to be vicarious is another cause of dispute. All of the Isaian commentaries cited above[170] claim that the servant's suffering *is* vicarious. Westermann even goes as far as to claim that the translation of 53.12b can be rendered 'because he poured out his blood to death', suggesting a sacrifice of expiation corresponding to the sacrificial term for a guilt offering (אשם).[171] Whybray disagrees, claiming that the concept of vicarious suffering was alien to Jewish thought and has been introduced retrospectively to the interpretation of this passage from the Christian theology of the atonement.[172] What is important for our purposes is that it heightens the injustice borne by the servant. Not only is he innocent, but his torments are caused by the guilt of others and, in some way, his suffering is for them ('and he bore the sins of many', 53.12c).

a long life (*Studies on the Second Part of the Book of Isaiah: The So-Called 'Servant of the Lord' and 'Suffering Servant' in Second Isaiah* [VTSup, 14; Leiden: E.J. Brill, 1967], p. 61). Clines notes that the references to the Servant's death are all ambiguous and sees it as one of the enigmas in Isa. 53 (*I, He, We, and They*, p. 29).

169. Hanson sees this aspect of the servant's role accounting for the omission of Simon of Cyrene in the Johannine passion. The evangelist has 'deliberately represented Jesus as carrying his own cross because in Isa. 53.11 it was prophesied that the Servant of the Lord, whom John identified with Jesus, should bear the sins of many' ('John's Use of Scripture', p. 369).

170. In other words, Westermann, McKenzie, Watts and Knight.

171. Westermann, *Isaiah 40–66*, p. 268.

172. Whybray, *Thanksgiving for a Liberated Prophet*, p. 75. This is the position also held by Hooker (*Jesus and the Servant*, p. 158).

f. *Their Suffering Is Legitimated by God.* Both Jesus and the servant are victims of the will of God. Their agony is caused because God requires it. McKenzie comments that the servant has been afflicted beyond the ordinary affliction of the poor and lowly—'he has been touched by the wrath of God'.[173] We know that this is true in the case of Jesus; his death is the will of the Father as he was 'given' for this very purpose in order that the believers might be saved (Jn 3.16). As mentioned above with the sacrifice of Isaac, the relationship between the Father and the son must be interpreted in the light of the barbaric execution of the son.

There are further textual links between the servant and Jesus, but it is not necessary to belabour them at this point. Similar vocabulary is used, for example, of their exaltation (δοξάζειν) and lifting up (ὑψοῦν) (Isa. 52.13),[174] and the picture of the servant as a lamb (Isa. 53.7) evokes the lamb of God imagery used in John (Jn 1.36). What is interesting is that scholars who feel comfortable identifying the Johannine Jesus with the Servant do not take the step of viewing Jesus as a victim in the way that the servant evidently was.[175] The whole point about the Servant is that he suffers and experiences pain, rejection and mutilation. It is not acceptable to make comparisons and links between the two figures without recognizing this suffering and dealing with the hermeneutical implications.

The Paschal Lamb. The concept of Jesus representing the paschal lamb in the Fourth Gospel is derived primarily from two places in the text—the beginning of Jesus' public ministry and the end of his life. The first references occur in Jn 1.29 and again in 1.36, where John the Baptist hails him as the lamb of God who takes away the sin of the world.[176] The

173. McKenzie, *Second Isaiah*, p. 133. The Masoretic Text of 53.10a reads; 'yet it was the Lord's will to crush him and cause him to suffer' (דכאו החלי). The LXX has a different emphasis, seeing it as a cleansing or purging by God (καὶ κύριος βούλεται καθαρίσαι αὐτὸν τῆς πληγῆς).

174. See Evans, 'Obduracy and the Lord's Servant', pp. 232-33; Hengel, 'The Old Testament in the Fourth Gospel', p. 393.

175. An example of a failure to do this can be seen in Stibbe's commentary. While recognizing the influence of Deutero-Isaiah and stating that 'the reader is meant to see the death of Jesus as the sacrifice of the Servant of Yahweh, the one led like a lamb to the slaughter', he maintains that 'divine sovereignty' is the major feature of his characterization during the passion (*John*, pp. 137, 197).

176. Although see P.J. du Plessis for arguments against interpreting these verses as allusions to the Passover Lamb: 'the title is a Messianic one and a *terminus gloriae*.

second set of references occur during the passion and were introduced in Table 7. They make up what Hengel refers to as the 'emphatic Passover sacrifice typology of the day of Jesus' death'.[177] In 19.14 the evangelist provides a time marker at the point which Jesus is sentenced, which synchronizes his death with the slaughter of the Passover lambs.[178] In 19.29 the reference to ὑσσώπῳ has been seen to allude to the use of a sprig of hyssop dipped in the blood of the Passover lamb and sprinkled on the door posts of the Israelites (Exod. 12.22).[179] In Jn 19.36 the evangelist mentions the fulfilment of Scripture following the *crurifragium*: 'Not a bone of him shall be broken' (ὀστοῦν οὐ συντριβήσεται αὐτοῦ). This could be derived from Exod. 12.46, the rule that the bones of the Passover lamb should not be broken (καὶ ὀστοῦν οὐ

Like the other titles it expresses, from a different angle, the Divine Sonship of Jesus' ('The Lamb of God in the Fourth Gospel', in J.H. Petzger and P.J. Hartin [eds.], *A South African Perspective on the New Testament: Essays by South African New Testament Scholars Presented to Bruce Manning Metzger during his Visit to South Africa in 1985* [Leiden: E.J. Brill, 1986], pp. 136-48 [147]). Cullmann sees Jesus as the Lamb of God being both the Suffering Servant *and* the Paschal lamb (*Christology of the New Testament*, p. 70). So too Hooker, *Jesus and the Servant*, p. 104.

177. Hengel, *Johannine Question*, p. 189, n. 68.

178. The chronology of the crucifixion and the Passover is an area of some dispute, particularly since it is so obviously at odds with the Synoptics. Carson attempts to harmonize the Johannine and Synoptic accounts by claiming that παρασκευὴ τοῦ πάσχα means 'Friday of the Passover week' rather than the actual day before the Passover. This would meant that both John and the Synoptics had the last supper on Thursday—in other words it was a Passover meal (*Gospel According to John*, pp. 603-604). For the view that Jesus was crucified at the moment when the Passover lambs were being slaughtered, see Hengel, *Johannine Question*, p. 66; F.M. Young, *Sacrifice and the Death of Christ* (London: SPCK, 1975); C.K. Barrett, 'The Lamb of God', *NTS* 1 (1954), pp. 210-218 (specifically, p. 211); V.C. Pfitzner, 'The Coronation of the King: The Passion in the Gospel of John', *CurTM* 4 (1977), pp. 10-21; Smalley, *John, Evangelist and Interpreter*, p. 224 and Hanson, *Prophetic Gospel*, p. 219. Stibbe comments: 'Here narrative chronology and narrative Christology are inseparable' (*John*, p. 192).

179. Dispute over this point has been primarily due to the fact that the hyssop is a small wall-growing plant and would not be strong enough to support a wet sponge. See Haenchen, *John*, II, 194. The suggestion is that the word ὑσσώπῳ has erroneously replaced ὑσσῷ, a particular type of Roman javelin. See Beasley-Murray, *John*, p. 318. In defence of the Paschal reading, Strack-Billerbeck suggest that although a branch of hyssop could not support a wet sponge, a stalk could (Str-B, II, p. 581). See also Carson, 'the branches of hyssop at the end of a stalk could form a little "nest" to cradle the sponge' (*Gospel According to John*, p. 621).

συντρίψετε ἀπ' αὐτοῦ in the LXX), or a similar statement in Num. 9.12.[180] The piercing of Jesus' side itself, with the flow of blood and water, is seen by J.A. Grassi to be a reference to the Passover blood and a further indication that the evangelist sees Jesus' death in paschal terms.[181]

Viewed together, the direct references in John's Gospel to the lamb of God, coupled with the 'intertextual echoes' of the timing of his death, the hyssop and the *crurifragium* show that there is a clear line of paschal thinking in John that can be used to interpret our picture of Jesus as a victim. This raises the thorny problem of the theological meaning of the slaughter of the lamb and the way in which Jesus can be seen to be a sacrifice. Is he 'the Passover Lamb dying for the sin of the world',[182] or is this concept, with its connotations of vicarious expiation, simply too crude? Barrett claims that although describing Jesus as the lamb of God draws 'special attention' to his sacrificial death, drawing out the analogy between Jesus and the paschal sacrifice in the crucifixion scene, the evangelist does *not* explain the death of Jesus in sacrificial terms.[183] Others hold that salvation in the Fourth Gospel is mediated not by an atoning expiation from sin, but through 'revealing the truth that self-sacrificial love lies at the heart of God's dealings with man'[184]—in

---

180. This position is supported by, among others, Hoskyns, *Fourth Gospel*, p. 533 and Bernard, *Gospel According to St John*, II, p. 651. The alternative view is that the evangelist has the Psalter in mind. Although some scholars accept that both Ps. 34 and the paschal reading are relevant, Dodd claims that there is *no* link to the paschal victim, the psalm being used as it suggests the promise of Christ's resurrection (*Historical Tradition*, p. 131).

181. Because of Exod. 12.13—'the blood shall be a sign for you'. J.A. Grassi comments; 'this blood is extremely important for [the evangelist] because Jewish law required the actual *flow* of blood for a valid sacrifice' ('Eating Jesus' Flesh and Drinking his Blood: The Centrality and Meaning of John 6.51-58', *BTB* 17 [1987], pp. 24-30 [28, emphasis original]).

182. Pfitzner, 'Coronation of the King', p. 21.

183. Barrett, *Gospel According to St John*, p. 81. So too Taylor, who claims that although there is no doubt that sacrificial ideas are present in the Gospel, as seen in the allusions in 1.29, 6.54-6, 12.24, 17.19 and 19.36, the emergence of a definite sacrificial theory in John is restrained by the evangelist's preoccupation with Christ's glorification. He is therefore not presented as the One Great Sacrifice (*Atonement in New Testament Teaching*, pp. 148-49).

184. Smalley, *John, Evangelist and Interpreter*, p. 226.

other words it has an exemplarist function.[185] Carson argues that this view is exegetically doubtful, illogical, and reductionist.[186]

It does seem that the references to the lamb of God and the Passover in John are difficult to make sense of without *some* concept of the atoning sacrifice of Jesus.[187] Hengel is adamant: 'From John 1.29 to 17.19 there is a whole series of statements in the Gospel which refer clearly to the vicarious atoning death of Jesus.'[188] That the original paschal lamb was not considered a sin offering by the Jews is an issue that is tackled by Brown, who claims that by the time of Jesus, a sacrificial aspect had begun to become associated with the Passover.[189] Frances Young also comments that sin offerings dominated the temple

---

185. So Forestell—the death of Jesus is the culmination of his revelatory work (*Word of the Cross*, pp. 101-102). See also J. Painter, *John, Witness and Theologian* (London: Darton, Longman & Todd, 1975), p. 63.

186. As indicated by the following argument: 'exegetically doubtful, because there are too many passages in John whose most obvious meaning includes the notion of sins dealt with by means of Jesus' sacrificial death; illogical, because, as James Denney pointed out...it is as meaningless to detect profound, revelatory love in a cross of Christ that achieved nothing as it would be to detect profound love in a man who tries to prove his devotion to his fellow human beings by jumping off Brighton pier and drowning, with no purpose in view and no result achieved; and reductionist, because we are being forced into an "either/or" argument when the Fourth Gospel itself demands a "both/and"' (Carson, *Gospel According to John*, p. 153).

187. Du Plessis' complaint that the paschal lamb cannot be associated with the lamb who takes away the sin of the world because 'a lamb, in terms of imagery, does not sacrifice itself. He is the victim', misses the point completely. 'Taking away the sin of the world' and being a victim are not mutually exclusive, in fact, quite the reverse. They are both the objective and the *modus operandi*. In other words, Jesus is able to take away the world's sin *through* being a victim. This certainly means that there is an element of passivity about Jesus' saving work. Rather than seeing it as some glorious heroic action, there is more of an inclination to understand it as the inflicting of extreme suffering and violence on Jesus, to the point of immolation. The reason for du Plessis' assertion becomes obvious from his ensuing sentence: 'As for the Gospel of John, the passion narrative reveals just the opposite: Jesus is firmly in command from beginning to end. Even the so-called Paschal allusions in John offer no more than glimpses of lowliness, suffering and sacrifice... Käsemann's description of the passion...resembling "a triumphal procession" is not far wide of the mark.' ('The Lamb of God in the Fourth Gospel', p. 144).

188. Hengel, *The Johannine Question*, p. 66.

189. Brown, *Gospel According to John*, I, p. 62.

rituals in the time of Christ.[190] The prophetic interpretation of the exile as a punishment for a sinful nation emphasized the need for constant expiation and so sin offerings came into prominence, also affecting the meaning of the 'holocausts'.[191] Cullmann simply states that 'for the Jews the purpose of sacrificing the paschal lamb is to achieve atonement for the sins of the people'.[192]

Having discussed briefly the background to the understanding of the concept of the Passover lamb in John, it is appropriate to make some suggestions about the relevance that this has for our understanding of the victimization of Jesus. We have discussed already in Chapter 6 the way in which Jesus expresses the relationship between his body, his death and sacrifice. It is at the time of Passover that Jesus tells the crowds that his flesh will be given for the life of the world (6.51b). Moreover, when he speaks of laying down his life for the sheep, Jesus makes use of the violent physical imagery of being mauled by a wolf (10.11-12). The crucifixion is the occasion of that sacrifice, wherein Jesus is not simply victimized in the general sense of the word, but becomes more specifically a sacrificial victim, with all the violence that entails. J.H.M. Beattie, in an anthropological study of sacrifice, claims that 'almost always sacrifice is seen as being, mostly, about *power*, or *powers*'.[193] A characteristic of victims is the denial of their liberty, with the subsequent domination by the power or another individual or community group (a factor that is emphasized by being bound before slaughtered). Sacrificial victims are not sovereign and in control—quite the reverse. They are power*less* and are exploited and violated at the will

190. Young, *Sacrifice and the Death of Christ*.

191. Young, *Sacrifice and the Death of Christ*, p. 27.

192. Cullmann, *Christology of the New Testament*, p. 71.

193. J.H.M. Beattie, 'On Understanding Sacrifice', in M.F.C. Bourdillon and M. Fortes (eds.), *Sacrifice* (London: Academic Press, 1980), pp. 29-44 (37). Beattie identifies a fourfold classification of aspects of sacrifice based on the type of and relation to power: (1) Sacrifice to obtain/maintain closer contact with God. (2) Sacrifice to achieve separation from such spirits. (3) Sacrifice to acquire for the sacrificer an increase of non-personalized power. (4) Sacrifice to achieve separation from/removal of such diffuse power.

It is not feasible to explore in detail here the various theories of sacrifice and the ways in which they have been applied to the biblical literature. However, see J.G. Williams for a concise overview, from Hubert and Mauss through the structuralists to Girard (*The Bible, Violence, and the Sacred: Liberation from the Myth of Sanctioned Violence* [New York: HarperCollins, 1991], pp. 14-20).

of others, their bodies becoming the locus of the community's expression of violence. One of the foremost exponents on this relationship between the sacrificial victim and the community is René Girard and it is appropriate at this point to outline briefly his theories and consider their implications for this study.

The Girardian Scapegoat

The theories of Girard, detailed for the most part in his seminal works *Violence and the Sacred* and *The Scapegoat*[194], set out a framework for understanding the origin of violence in human communities and the mechanism for dealing with it. Essentially the key concepts are as follows.[195]

– Human desire is mimetic rather than autonomous. The mimesis of a model who is not separated from the subject temporally, spatially or socially (as is in the case of a distant hero), is ultimately destructive. This is because the imitation of another's desires turns them into a rival and an obstacle and the focus of more than one desire on the same object creates conflict. Chilton comments; 'the desire to have what the other has, a basic, human passion, is the root of violence: it is both ineluctable and incompatible with the existence of human culture'.[196]

– Mimetic rivalry erodes differences between individuals who, in the process of emulation, become more alike. This causes the collapse of the social hierarchy, with a loss of identity for individuals, and acts as a catalyst for crisis when the community comes under pressure or attack.

– 'If left unappeased, violence will accumulate until it overflows its confines and floods the surrounding area',[197] states Girard. The violent crisis is therefore resolved by means of a sacrifice—the sacrifice of a surrogate victim on behalf of the community and on whom hostility can be

194. R. Girard, *Violence and the Sacred* (trans. P. Gregory; Baltimore: The Johns Hopkins University Press); *idem*, *The Scapegoat* (trans. Y. Freccero; Baltimore: The Johns Hopkins University Press, 1986).

195. As well as the two texts mentioned above, I have drawn on the succint and comprehensible analysis by Richard Golsan for my summary of Girard's theories (*René Girard and Myth: An Introduction* [New York: Garland Publishing, 1993]). Additional analysis of Girard's approach to the Bible is to be found in James Williams's *The Bible, Violence, and the Sacred*.

196. B.D. Chilton, *The Temple of Jesus: His Sacrificial Program Within a Cultural History of Sacrifice* (Pennsylvania: Pennsylvania State University Press, 1992), p. 16.

197. Girard, *Violence and the Sacred*, p. 10.

focused through a mimetic transfer. 'The role of sacrifice is to stem this rising tide of indiscriminate substitutions and redirect violence into "proper channels"'.[198] The scapegoat is innocent, but is chosen by the crowd because of its marginal or exceptional status and is defamed and persecuted before being murdered.

– The death of the scapegoat results in the return of harmony and order to society. Subsequently, a further development occurs in the community's relationship with the victim, who now becomes sanctified as its saviour, having resolved the crisis through its death.

The above summarizes Girard's general theory, which he applied initially to classic novels, Shakespeare and Greek Tragedies as well as ancient myths and rituals.[199] When it comes to the Bible, however, Girard places it in a different category to other texts. To him, the Bible, as Golson comments, 'is not a text to be dissected with modern critical tools but is itself the scalpel'.[200] This is because the Bible subverts the human structures of violence, unmasking scapegoating as a truly arbitrary mechanism and revealing that God does not desire it. The key biblical revelation is that God, and those on God's 'side', take the perspective of the persecuted victim rather than the persecuting community. This is most fully evidenced in the gospels, which 'disclose both the secret of the mythic camouflage of violence and the way of liberation through a love that refuses violence'[201] via the story of Jesus, the innocent victim. Having summarized, albeit sketchily, the broad composition of Girard's thought, some general comments about connections with John's Gospel can be made. This will be done by addressing some of the key tenets of his theory under the following headings:

1. The Identification of an Appropriate Scapegoat

The key characteristic of those who qualify as scapegoats is that they are marked out from society. In a community that has become undifferentiated, they stand out as being different in some way—physically, psychologically, emotionally or though their elevated status. They display

---

198. Girard, *Violence and the Sacred*, p. 10.

199. The novels examined include, for example, *Don Quixote*, Stendahl's *Scarlet and Black* and the works of Dostoyevsky. He also writes extensively on Oedipus and Dionysus as well as African, Scandinavian and Aztec myths.

200. Golson, *René Girard and Myth*, p. 85.

201. Williams, *The Bible, Violence and the Sacred*, p. 12.

'victimary signs' that polarize the hostility of the community. Girard elucidates:

> We notice at first glance beings who are either outside or on the fringes of society: prisoners of war, slaves, pharmakos. In many primitive societies children who have not yet undergone the rites of initiation have no proper place in the community; their rights and duties are almost non-existent. *What we are dealing with, therefore, are exterior or marginal individuals, incapable of establishing or sharing the social bonds that link the rest of the inhabitants.* Their status as foreigners or enemies, their servile condition, or simply their age prevents these future victims from fully integrating themselves into the community.[202]

We instinctively know this is the truth about the victims in our world today. They are those who are on the fringes of our various definitions of society; the dispossessed, who can be subjected to oppression for reasons of poverty or gender or race, because they are people who *do not matter*—they are easily expendable. And the reason they do not matter is because they have no power. Girard claims, moreover, that it is not simply the marginalized status of individuals which makes them suitable sacrifices. There is another crucial factor:

> Between these victims and the community a crucial social link is missing, so that they can be exposed to violence without fear of reprisal. Their death does not automatically entail an act of vengeance. The considerable importance this freedom from reprisal has for the sacrificial process makes us understand that *sacrifice is primarily an act of violence without risk of vengeance.*[203]

Again, this emphasizes the absence of any value accorded the victim's life by the community. And because they do not matter and do not belong there is no one to stand up for them, and hence no danger of reprisal. There is no one whose life is worth less.

Much of this is clearly applicable to the presentation of Jesus in the Fourth Gospel. Jesus is congenitally incapable of being integrated into the community. He is the ultimate foreigner—he is not even from this world, but is *from above*. His identity and claims marginalize him, precluding acceptance from the very beginning of the Gospel, and this is evidenced by his expulsion from the heart of the community, the

---

202. Girard, *Violence and the Sacred*, p. 12, emphasis added.
203. Girard, *Violence and the Sacred*, p. 13, emphasis added.

synagogue.[204] Jesus articulates this experience of alienation and rejection in the farewell discourses, speaking of the hatred of the world and his separation from it. The issue of reprisal at the death of this victim is another occasion for deep irony. Neither the Jewish leaders nor the crowd display any qualms about engineering and demanding the death of Jesus. The crowd who clamour for Jesus' crucifixion manipulate the situation so that it is the Roman procurator, another foreigner, who will suffer political reprisals if Jesus is not executed (19.12).

2. The Execution of the Scapegoating Mechanism
Following identification, the scapegoat will be subject to persecution by the community. In particular, the victim may be falsely accused of violent crimes or religious transgressions. These which serve to ensure the scapegoat assumes a persona adequately evil to be responsible for the social crisis. For this reason, the crimes are all fundamental ones: 'They attack the very foundation of cultural order, the family and the hierarchical differences without which there would be no social order'.[205] This is precisely the situation in John's Gospel. The principal accusation levelled against the Johannine Jesus is that of religious profanation. The specific charge of the Jews to Pilate is that Jesus has made himself 'the son of God' (19.7). However, he has already been accused of blasphemy and Sabbath breaking. The many other examples of insults which dehumanize Jesus (being a Samaritan, demon possessed, illegitimate, from Nazareth, an evildoer), have already been documented in the tables in Chapter 2. These have the desired effect during the course of the narrative since by John 11, Jesus can be accused of jeopardizing the religious and political stability of the entire community—'If we let him go on thus... the Romans will come and destroy both our holy place and our nation' (11.48).

Material evidencing the development of a sacrificial crisis in the Fourth Gospel can also be found in the text. The increasing amount and degree of public animosity toward the Johannine Jesus as the narrative proceeds could, using Girard's framework, be attributed to mimetic desire and explain the absence of a popular following, as seen in the

---

204. Jn 9.22. This applies not only to Jesus but his followers, who are also excluded from community life. This is obviously the experience of the Johannine community and fuels their 'sectarian' attitude—it is precisely their aim *not* to be integrated into society.

205. Girard, *The Scapegoat*, p. 15.

Synoptics. Instead of an increasing swell of support for Jesus, there is a swell of opposition as mimetic contagion takes hold. The culmination of this is, again, the plot of the Pharisees to kill him in Jn 11. As High Priest, Caiaphas must surely function as a powerful model for the Jewish community and his declaration that Jesus is the acceptable victim who can alleviate the crisis becomes the desire to be imitated. Thus when the crowd have the opportunity to choose their victim in Jn 18.39-40, Barabbas (whose crimes are not nearly as heinous as those of Jesus by this stage) clearly will not do. In choosing Jesus as the victim the crowd imitate Caiaphas their mediator rather than Pilate, even though Pilate has just declared Jesus' innocence.

Having looked briefly at some indicators of the scapegoating process in John, we move on to look at the specific claims of Girard about biblical texts mentioned above. Firstly the gospel's subversion of the mimetic process by revealing the arbitrary choice of the victim, and secondly that the 'God of the Gospels' is the God of non-violence who does not intend there to be victims.

3. *The Gospel as the Unmasker of Mimetic Violence*
The key component of the revelatory force of the Gospel is seen to be the exposure of the arbitrariness the scapegoating mechanism:

> ...acts of foundational, sacrificial violence, are viewed from the standpoint of the victim rather than the persecutor... Seen through their eyes, the punishment—the persecutor's violence—is shown to be completely arbitrary. The persecutors themselves... are exposed as a vengeful mob in the throes of a mimetic crisis and in search of a scapegoat. The innocence of the victim is confirmed.[206]

Without doubt, the innocence of Jesus is asserted in the Fourth Gospel. He is hated without cause (15.25) and Pilate twice declares him 'without crime'. However, there is very little that is arbitrary about the selection of Jesus as a victim. While James Williams may claim that in John Jesus' fate must *necessarily* be that of expulsion because 'human darkness and deceit cannot tolerate the presence of One who does not distinguish people and values according to structures of violence and sacrifice',[207] there is a further element to be taken into consideration. I have already discussed in detail in Chapter 6 the collusive nature of Jesus' victimage.

---

206. Golsan, *René Girard and Myth*, pp. 85-86.
207. Williams, *The Bible, Violence and the Sacred*, p. 205.

Jesus is not a passive player in this drama and to indicate that the reason for his expulsion is simply that his ontological nature is intolerable to the world does not recognize his own contribution to the outcome. Not only does Jesus effectively fan the flames of the sacrificial crisis but he positions himself as the sacrificial victim. It may be that the statement of Jesus' innocence in the narrative functions to expose the illegitimacy of the sacrifice as a means of solving the mimetic crisis, but this does not alter the fact that, through his victim consciousness, he is facilitating the process. Undeniably, we see the violence of the persecuting community in all its ugliness, but we have also beheld the nefarious symbiosis between the community and the promotional aggressive behaviour of Jesus. After all, death is the necessary outcome because it is the purpose for which he has come (12.27). Is he playing them at their own game?

4. *The God who Does not Intend Violence*
In the light of the above what conclusions can be drawn about the Girardian declaration that God does not support the violent structures inherent in human society, opposing the mimetic process and taking the side of the victim. Is he 'a non violent deity [who] can only signal his existence to mankind by having himself driven out by violence—by demonstrating that he is not able to establish himself in the Kingdom of Violence',[208] as Hamerton Kelly indicates? Again, although it could be said that the Father in the Fourth Gospel takes the side of the victim, can it really be claimed that he does not intend the violence that befalls the Son? In the previous section relating to Abraham and Isaac, the Father's commitment to the world was discussed as being his the over-riding priority. The Father too plays an active part in this. He 'has glorified and will glorify' his name, and we know what that means in John's Gospel. Is he a non-violent deity, or is he a deity who permits violence to be done in order that the structures of violence can be dismantled, the end justifying the means? Jesus, then, becomes a suitable sacrificial victim, the focus for the aggression of his own community. His body is the receptacle for their barbarism, which is played out through his physical violation culminating in an immolating death.

The three figures that have been discussed above have provided useful insights to an understanding of Jesus as a victim. They are interlinked

208. R. Hamerton Kelly, *Sacred Violence: The Hermeneutics of the Cross in the Theology of Paul*, p. 80.

through their experiences of oppression and physical abuse and all share, in some sense, the fate of a sacrificial victim. They are not the only figures that could have been employed from a collection of literature where, as Girard comments, 'victims, always and everywhere, are prominent'.[209] From Abel, through the Levite's concubine, to Tamar, Job and the prophets, stories of senseless violence and murder abound within the confines of the canon.[210] The Psalms too are fertile ground for descriptions of physical and emotional distress caused by the savagery of others, and these are used by the evangelists as appropriate laments for the dying Christ.

Concluding Comment: Victor or Victim?

I have attempted throughout the course of this chapter to explore and develop a perspective on the passion of the Johannine Jesus that counteracts the traditional view. The degradation he suffers is no less than that endured by the Synoptic Jesus, but the common conception of him as detached and serene, eluding pain by virtue of his divine status, has obscured this fact. Jesus' experience of victimization, and his behavioural response to it, should be viewed within context of the experience of other victims. Others suffered and yet retained their composure— Jephthah's daughter, for example, accepted her pointless fate with courage and did not beg her father to remove her cup of suffering. John Parr comments that liberation theologians generally see Jesus standing in the line of Old Testament prophets, dying for the same reasons that prophets in every age die. 'The values he lived for were more important to him even than his own life. In this sense his death was unremarkable.'[211] We do not have to look far to find examples of modern-day prophets and liberators who have displayed great courage and dignity in the face of injustice, persecution and brutal death. The attitude of Steve Biko is a case in point:

209. Girard, *Job the Victim of his People*, p. 8.

210. See Trible, *Texts of Terror*, for literary-feminist examination of four female victims.

211. J. Parr, 'Jesus and the Liberation of the Poor: Biblical Interpretation in the Writings of Some Latin American Theologians of Liberation' (Unpublished thesis, University of Sheffield, 1989), p. 114.

You are either alive and proud or you are dead, and when you are dead,
you can't care anyway. And your method of death can itself be a politi-
cizing thing… if you can overcome the personal fear for death, which is a
highly irrational thing, you know, then you're on the way.[212]

When it comes to Jesus' trial, he is defiant not because he has power
over the proceedings, but because he does not recognize the authority
of the court (19.11). Similarly, as Nelson Mandela stated: 'I challenge
the right of this court to try me… because I fear that I will not be given
a fair and proper trial'.[213] Discussing how Jesus is derided and tortured
during his interrogation, Leonardo Boff comments that this is a scene
'quite frequent in police circles throughout the world'.[214] Likewise,
William Wipfler notes that the treatment Jesus receives is 'a classical
example of the brutalization of a political prisoner'.[215] Jesus' coping
tactics are also not unusual: his attempt to retain his dignity through
silence or a few well-chosen words is surely the aim of many who experience such atrocities. Is he really in control of the chain of events
throughout the passion narrative, or is he just in control of himself? And
if it is the latter, is this not a wholly *human* response to a situation of
personal adversity? Is it not the behaviour required of a leader whose
community is suffering persecution, in order to inspire the respect and
devotion of those who are to emulate him? Jesus' 'hour of glory' is not
his 'glorious hour', with all the brassy, triumphalist overtones conveyed
by that term. Instead it is the hour of liberation through *pathos*. Salvation
is mediated through the internment, torture and immolation of the
victim of God.

---

212. Steve Biko, interview published in *New Republic* magazine, January 1978
and quoted in D. Woods, *Biko* (London: Penguin Books, rev. edn, 1987). Likewise
the comments of Nelson Mandela at his own trial in Rivonia, 1964: 'Our struggle
is… a struggle of the African people, inspired by our own suffering and our own
experience. It is a struggle for the right to live. During my lifetime I have dedicated
myself to this struggle… I have cherished the ideal of a democratic and free society
in which all persons live together in harmony and with equal opportunities. It is an
ideal which I hope to live for and to achieve. *But if needs be, it is an ideal for which I
am prepared to die.*' (Woods, *Biko*, p. 32, emphasis added).

213. Mandela, quoted in Woods, *Biko*, p. 22.

214. Boff, *Jesus Christ, Liberator*, p. 107.

215. W.L. Wipfler, 'Identifying Jesus the Victim in the Victims of Repression',
Tugon 11.2 (1991), pp. 259-68 (264).

10

Relationship with the Disciples II:
Reunion

The exegesis of John from the perspective of Jesus as a victim is almost completed. The life and death of Jesus have been explored, showing how his experiences and behaviour can be interpreted in the light of his physical and emotional suffering. But the story does not end with the entombment of Jesus and, consequently, it would be wrong to finish the exegesis at this point. John's narrative tells of Jesus' resurrection and of several acts that he subsequently carries out before the Gospel draws to a close in 21.25.[1] The following chapter will discuss this final section, John 20–21, exploring what happens to the theme of victimage after the death and resurrection of the victim.

The primary focus of this chapter will be the personal encounters between Jesus and his followers. The structure employed will treat John 20–21 as a coherent and sequential unit,[2] being the section of narrative which describes the behaviour of Jesus following his death.

1.   I am not concerned here with the debate over the position of Jn 21 with regard to the rest of the Gospel, be it an appendix or an epilogue. As Frans Neirynck has aptly put it: 'The observations pro and contra have been made many times and the evidence evaluated as convincing or unconvincing' ('John 21', p. 336). See Stibbe, however, for a discussion of the literary arguments for John 20 being the original conclusion to the Gospel (*John*, pp. 198-99).

2.   I recognize that there are difficulties inherent in this. Ashton claims that to attempt to make sense of just 20.1-23 as continuous narrative is 'to enter an Alice-in-Wonderland world where one event succeeds another with the crazy logic of a dream' (*Understanding the Fourth Gospel*, p. 503).

Structure of John 20-21: Jesus beyond Death

1. (20.1-10   Discovery of the empty tomb)
2. 20.11-18   Jesus encounters Mary
3. 20.19-23   Jesus encounters the disciples
4. 20.24-29   Jesus encounters Thomas
5. (20.30-31   Summary of Gospel's Purpose)
6. 21.1-23   Jesus encounters Peter
7. (21.24-25   Conclusion to Gospel)

The most obvious question that springs to mind about the resurrected Jesus is: 'Is he still a victim?' If we conclude that he is, then what implications does that have for the meaning of his death? But if he is not, then what has he become and how is this transformation evidenced in the text? In the final analysis, does John's Jesus actually become a victor? This question can be explored by looking at his interaction with the characters Jesus encounters in his resurrected state, all of whom are followers of his. It was noted in Chapter 8 that Jesus' attitude towards his followers immediately before his death was a combination of concern and frustration—deep desire that they would endure, and fear that they would not. He attempted to prepare them for his death and for their own persecution, but lacked the ability to inspire them to the extent required to bring comfort and ensure short-term perseverance. He stood with them as a victim among victims.

Jesus Encounters Mary

Mary is the first to discover the empty tomb and to encounter the risen Jesus.[3] Matera notes that her reaction to the empty tomb is both rational and comprehensible: she thinks grave bandits have stolen the body[4] and she reports this to the disciples.[5] Although Peter and the beloved disciple

---

3.   The significance of this, both for John's Gospel and for church tradition generally, is discussed by Schneiders ('Women in the Fourth Gospel', p. 43). See also P. Perkins, '"I Have Seen the Lord" (John 20.18): Women Witnesses to the Resurrection', *Int* 46 (1992), pp. 31-41.

4.   W.E. Reiser notes that the separate position of the napkin and the other grave clothes was seen by the church fathers to be an apologetic against the claim that the body had been stolen. No bandit would have bothered to place them in such a manner ('The Case of the Tidy Tomb: The Place of the Napkins of John 11.44 and 20.7', *HeyJ* 14.1 [1973], pp. 47-57).

5.   F.J. Matera, 'John 20.1-18', *Int* 43 (1989), pp. 402-406 (402).

examine the tomb, which invokes belief in the resurrection in the latter,[6] they then leave Mary and return home. 'She alone remains to continue the search while they hide for fear of the Jews', comments Schneiders.[7] The text describes the behaviour of someone in a state of profound grief (20.11). She has lost Jesus twice—once in death and now through the removal of his body[8]—and her stooping to look into the tomb suggests an inability to accept this loss.[9] She knows he has gone; the disciples have verified this, but perhaps if she checks again... It is not Jesus she sees in the tomb, however, but two angels who ask her why she is crying. Her response to them indicates she does not yet have the belief of the beloved disciple but is still intent on finding the body of a dead man. She consequently turns around to look elsewhere, seemingly uninterested in the presence of the angels, when she does not find Jesus in the tomb (v. 14). Perhaps this is a further indication of her distress: the occupants of the tomb are clearly identified as angels (ἀγγέλους),[10] yet she does not ask them where Jesus is, nor does she query their presence in the tomb. There is no indication of fear, or in fact any

---

6.   See Stibbe's commentary for an interesting theory on why this is, based on the argument that the beloved disciple is Lazarus (*John*, p. 204). Chrysostom, among others, assumes that Peter too believes (*In Joh. Hom.* 86.1). This is not borne out by the text.

7.   Schneiders, 'Women in the Fourth Gospel', p. 39. She adds that her behaviour displays 'the blind folly, tough-minded devotion, desperate despair, and rapturous joy of the ardent lover' (p. 38).

8.   Brown suggests this was not the normal lamentation of a friend over the deceased. She wept because she thought Jesus' body had been stolen (*Gospel According to John*, II, p. 988).

9.   Mary's personal experience has been one of extreme trauma over the past few days. She has witnessed the brutal death of a deeply loved friend, the leader of her community, and is only beginning to experience this loss. Now she is has the further shock of the empty tomb. Her behaviour is indicative of a person in the first stage of grief, which may last from hours to weeks. This is characterized by feelings of numbness and paralysis, periods of confusion and mental lucidity and varying degrees of disbelief and denial. See S.R. Shuchter and S. Zisook, 'The Course of Normal Grief', in M.S. Stroebe, W. Stroebe and R.O. Hansson (eds.), *Handbook of Bereavement: Theory, Research and Intervention* (Cambridge: Cambridge University Press, 1993), pp. 23-43 (24).

10. As opposed to men (ἄνδρες), Lk. 24.4; or a young man (νεανίσκον), Mk 16.5.

emotional reaction, on seeing the angels,[11] but she simply answers their question and turns away. Her behaviour seems strange and suggests the disorientation or even panic, commensurate with a person in a state of shock. Turning away from the tomb brings her face to face with the body she has been seeking, yet she fails to recognize him.[12] Jesus' words to her are brief but indicate tender concern: 'woman, why are you crying? Whom do you seek?'; (20.15). The scene that John paints is not one that dramatically manifests a powerful, glorious resurrection, such as we see in Matthew, who provides an earthquake, a formidable angel and a risen Lord whose greeting, 'Hail!', results in the prostration of the hearers (Mt. 28.9). The Johannine Jesus' first concern seems to be not to proclaim that he has risen, but rather to minister to the need of this grieving woman. His inquiry as to the cause of her grief elicits an answer from Mary which would be barely comprehensible to a gardener

---

11. Compare Lk. 24.5, where the women are frightened and prostrate themselves; Mk 16.5 where they are amazed; and Mt. 28.4-5 where the guards are afraid and it could be assumed that the women were too, in view of the angel's words, Μὴ φοβεῖσθε ὑμεῖς.

12. If Jesus is recognizable, then Mary's failure to do so indicates further the depth of her grief. She is in a desperate state at the loss of his body. The last thing she expects to see is this body standing upright and talking to her and this is why she does not initially recognize him. Schnackenburg comments: 'pain and ardour make her blind' (*Gospel According to St John*, III, p. 317). In the light of this, Bultmann's accusation of 'foolishness' on her part seems inappropriate (*Gospel of John*, p. 686). Theories abound as to why Mary does not recognize Jesus. A full discussion of possible reasons is provided by Brown (*Gospel According to John*, II, pp. 1008-10). The appearances to Mary and to the disciples in 21.4-7 seem to suggest that Jesus is not easily recognizable. In the latter case, the disciples who have already seen him post-resurrection twice do not initially recognize his appearance or his voice on the beach in 21.4. Perhaps, however, the boat is too far out from the shore for them to see or hear him properly. In the appearances of 20.19-23 and 20.26-29, however, there seems to be no difficulty identifying Jesus. A possible explanation as to why Mary does not recognize him could be found in the suggestion of Mary Rose D'Angelo that the 'state' of Jesus is different when he meets Mary as to when he meets the disciples, because his transformation is in some way incomplete. D'Angelo follows Origen in this matter; however, they part company in the conclusions that they draw from it. Origen sees it denigrating the appearance to Mary as it follows that there is an incompleteness in her message (see his *Commentary on John* 13.30); whereas D'Angelo concludes that 'the uniqueness of the appearance may award Mary a special status' ('A Critical Note: John 20.17 and the Apocalypse of Moses 31', *JTS* 41 [1990], pp. 529-36 [535]).

who had just approached the tomb,[13] and which further indicates her distress and her determination to find the body of the one she is mourning. Jesus cuts through her grief and confusion with one word: her name. Mary immediately responds, correctly identifying him as ραβ-βουνι (v. 16). We can assume that she expresses her joy and relief in a physical manner by the content of Jesus' subsequent words to her: 'do not hold me' (μή μου ἅπτου).[14] There is no reason to see his words as a rebuke.[15] They function as a practical command which is given for a

13. It assumes that the gardener understands that the body has gone missing and knows the identity of the body. For theories on the relevance of the gardener see N. Wyatt, '"Supposing him to be the Gardener" (John 20.15): A Study of the Paradise Motif in John', *ZNW* 81 (1990), pp. 21-38. Wyatt sees significance in the location of the tomb in a garden as well as Jesus being mistaken for a gardener, claiming that they allude to the Garden of Eden. In support of this he notes that the royal connection of the garden and the man who inhabits it was widespread among Jews who expected the messiah and that this allusion would not have been wasted on the evangelist's contemporaries (p. 38).

14. Barrett notes that 'the present imperative with μή in a prohibition signifies the breaking off of an action already in progress, or sometimes the attempt to perform an action'. It is implied, therefore, that Mary had already seized Jesus or was about to do so (*Gospel According to St John*, p. 565). This interpretation is disputed by D'Angelo, who compares the passage with a similarly strange one in the Apocalypse of Moses. She argues the translation should be 'Do not touch me' and the warning 'enters the realms of purity and danger because the appearance takes place in some sort of intermediary stage' ('A Critical Note', p. 532).

15. So the ancient commentators; Chrysostom and Augustine both see the words as a rebuke to Mary's inappropriate response to his altered state. 'She should give more reverent heed to Him', chides Chrysostom (*In Ioh. Hom.* 86.2). Augustine sees her as still believing in Jesus carnally, not recognizing that he is now 'equal with the Father' (*In Ioh. Hom.* 121.3). Calvin also felt that Mary (along with the Synoptic female witnesses) was overly concerned with Jesus' physical state: 'He saw that they were too much occupied with embracing his feet... they fixed their attention on his bodily presence' (*Gospel According to St John*, II, p. 198).

Modern commentators who interpret Jesus' words as having a negative connotation include Ashton, *Understanding the Fourth Gospel*, p. 502. See also Brown for a list of some of the more 'banal' and 'fanciful' theories about why Jesus does not want Mary to touch him (*Gospel According to John*, II, pp. 992-93). Brown himself seems to imply a negative interpretation with the following comment: 'Admixed in Magdalene's recognition and the love it reflects is an all too human element or, as John would phrase it, an element of this world below' ('The Resurrection in John 20: A Series of Diverse Reactions', *Worship* 64.3 [1990], pp. 194-206 [200]).

theological reason.[16] Mary, who at the beginning of the scene appeared greatly upset, somewhat confused and in shock, is now given an important commission by Jesus.[17] His presence, his word and his task have a therapeutic effect on her, enabling her to carry out the commission faithfully.

Once the encounter is over, we are not told what happens to Jesus, but the effect that the meeting has had on Mary is evident: she is a changed woman, who has 'passed from confusion and grief to recognition as she announces "I have seen the Lord"'.[18] Schneiders sees the message that Mary is given to relay as being the Johannine version of the kerygma, which she announces using the technical credential statement of revelation, and which is received without any indication of disbelief by the other disciples.[19] Commenting on the role of women witnesses in the resurrection narratives, Pheme Perkins sees the report of Mary as having 'a crucial role in the process of 'community founding' which followed the shattering events of Good Friday'.[20] The message brought by her served to gather together the disciples in readiness for Jesus' appearances at a time when it was feasible that the whole group could quickly disperse.

Jesus Encounters the Disciples

Mary's message ensures that the disciples are prepared for their own encounter with Jesus, which happens later on that day. The text states that the doors were shut for fear of the Jews (21.19). Mary's news has done nothing to dispel the anxiety of the disciples, who have gone into hiding, locking the doors perhaps to prevent the entrance of police sent by the Jewish authorities.[21] They expect the victimization promised by

16. It is not necessary to debate the exact meaning of οὔπω γὰρ ἀναβέβηκα πρὸς τὸν πατέρα. See the commentaries, particularly Brown, *Gospel According to John*, II, pp. 1011-17; and Schnackenburg, *Gospel According to St John*, III, pp. 317-20 for full discussion.

17. Interestingly, Luise Schottroff states that although Mary has the first encounter with the risen Jesus and carries out the 'order of proclamation', she is not *commissioned* at the tomb (*Let the Oppressed Go Free: Feminist Perspectives on the New Testament* (Louisville, KY: Westminster/John Knox, 1991), p. 102.

18. Matera, 'John 20.1-18', p. 402.

19. Schneiders, 'Women in the Fourth Gospel', p. 44.

20. Perkins, 'I Have Seen the Lord', p. 41.

21. A suggestion of Brown (*Gospel According to John*, II, p. 1020). W.R. Clark

their dead leader. Jesus comes to them in this state with no word of rebuke, no 'upbraiding',[22] but instead with words of comfort: 'Peace be with you' (Εἰρήνη ὑμῖν). Although this was an ordinary greeting in normal circumstances,[23] it has a fuller meaning in this context. Brown notes that it is 'a statement of fact, not a wish'.[24] Peace, here is an antidote to fear, as indeed Jesus indicated it was in 14.27 with his words:

> Peace I leave with you;
> my peace I give to you;
> not as the world gives do I give to you—
> Let not your hearts be troubled, neither let them be afraid.

Jesus does not just have a word for the disciples, but also provides them with (unrequested) evidence that he has risen by showing them the site of his wounds. This reminds the reader of the physical suffering of Jesus. Resurrection has not erased the evidence of the violence that led to his death. The fear of the disciples is transformed to joy (ἐχάρησαν) when they see him, but Jesus has more than this for them. He has a gift and a commission. His gift is the Holy Spirit which he breathes onto them (20.22). This, according to Dodd, is 'the ultimate climax of the personal relations between Jesus and His disciples.'[25] The last 'intimate' act we saw Jesus undertaking for them was the footwashing, which, it was argued, was an act of humiliation undertaken by 'Jesus as slave', commensurate with his identity as a victim. Now we see him carrying out an act of empowerment. His gift to the disciples is the Spirit that

---

notes that Jesus' ability to pass through the doors is not solely a feature of his post-resurrection state—he has already walked across the sea in Jn 6. Also, it should not be seen as a feat unique to Jesus. Clark claims that it is no more spectacular than Lazarus, bound hand and foot, walking out of the tomb ('Jesus, Lazarus, and Others: Resuscitation or Resurrection?', *RL* 49.2 [1980], pp. 230-41 [234]).

22. Contrast Mk 16.14.

23. See Barrett, *Gospel According to St John*, p. 568.

24. Brown, 'Resurrection in John 20', p. 202. He adds that in biblical Hebrew the shalom greeting tends to be confined to solemn, often revelatory moments. The fact that he repeats the words also indicate it is more than a greeting. J.M. Ford notes that Jesus does not greet his disciples with this salutation prior to the resurrection and that the concept of 'peace' must be seen in the context of Jesus' suffering: '*Shalom* is irrefrangibly bound up with Jesus' passion, for in this Gospel... peace comes through the agency of the defeated one, not the defeating one (the vanquished, not the victor)' ('Shalom in the Johannine Corpus', *HBT* 6.2 [1984], pp. 67-89 [81]).

25. Dodd, *Interpretation*, p. 227.

liberates, bringing about a rebirth to enable them to continue Jesus' work.[26]

There are four actions associated with their commission: sending, receiving, forgiving and retaining. The first two require passivity on the part of the disciples—they will be sent, they are to receive; the second two indicate an active role within the community with authority in spiritual matters. The pericope ends abruptly and, as with Mary's encounter, we do not know where or how Jesus has gone. We know, however, that the fearful disciples have experienced the resurrected Jesus by hearing his voice, seeing his body and feeling his breath and that their fear has become joy.

Jesus Encounters Thomas

The third resurrection appearance of Jesus seems to be entirely for the benefit of a disciple who had missed him on his previous visit. Verse 25 describes the response of Thomas to the testimony of the other disciples: unless he can satisfy his need for physical proof of Jesus' risen body, he refuses to believe. We are not told why Thomas was not with the disciples on the first night, but the evangelist notes that he was one of the twelve, and hence was part of the inner circle of Jesus' followers. It is not difficult to envisage his state of mind when the other disciples tell him that they have seen Jesus. Sorrow and bitter disappointment at missing Jesus perhaps fuelled his inability to believe, hardening it into unwillingness. By the end of v. 25 Thomas has talked himself into a

26. Davies notes that Jesus' action recalls the account of the creation of Adam in Gen. 2.7, where God breathes life into Adam's nostrils. She continues, '[t]he Fourth Gospel replaces the Septuagint πνοή (breath) with 'the Holy Spirit' because it depicts not creation but re-creation. Jesus' departure has brought about the possibility of the disciples' re-creation or rebirth' (*Rhetoric and Reference*, p. 149). G.M. Burge discusses the significance of this verse in detail, exploring whether it is should be interpreted symbolically, as a pre-Pentecost anointing, or as the Johannine Pentecost. He concludes the latter, arguing that in Jn 20 the disciples were experiencing the eschatological Spirit predicted in Jn 1.33. He attributes a theological motive to the evangelist: the coming of the Spirit is a result of the sacrifice of the cross, and death, resurrection, ascension, and anointing are all components of this 'single event of glorification'. He too sees the 'insufflation' as the climax of Jesus' relation with his disciples. It is their time of new birth and the advent of the Paraclete (*The Anointed Community: The Holy Spirit in the Johannine Tradition* [Grand Rapids: Eerdmans, 1987], pp. 148-49).

corner. He *cannot* participate in the faith shared by the other disciples, but has made the possibility of belief for him conditional on a repeat appearance by Jesus. And not just an appearance, but a thorough examination: 'unless I *see* the print... and *put* my finger in... and *put* my hand in...'[27] It is surely surprising then to learn in v. 26 that eight days have passed and Thomas is still keeping company with the disciples. After eight days spent as an outsider whose friends are all 'in the know', Thomas must be feeling pretty alienated, yet he has not deserted the cause. This does not just tell us that he is a loyal follower, but it indicates that, beneath the protestation of unbelief, there is a man desperate to believe.

The evangelist tells us that the disciples, including Thomas, were again gathered in the house with the doors shut (although not for fear this time), when Jesus came again to them. Apart from his initial words, his attention is focused solely on Thomas, who appears to be the primary reason for his visit. Jesus invites Thomas to carry out his examination: '*put* your finger... and *see*... and *bring* your hand... and *place* it in... ' He finishes with a liberating command: 'Do not be faithless, but believing' (καὶ μὴ γίνου ἄπιστος ἀλλὰ πιστός, v. 27). Thomas does not need to carry out his examination, but is immediately freed to proclaim his belief in and confirm his personal allegiance to Jesus through his proclamation 'my Lord and my God!'. Jesus affirms Thomas's faith, but states that seeing should not be a pre-requisite for believing. It is clear, however, that Jesus has responded to Thomas's need and has met him entirely on Thomas's terms. The impetus for this meeting is Jesus' love for Thomas and concern for his wholeness. It is not an opportunity for recrimination.[28] His grace and tenderness has brought about a healing in Thomas which enables him to join the community of faith.

27. Bultmann states: 'Thomas demanded no other proof than Jesus had freely offered the others', all of whom only believed when they saw (*Gospel of John*, p. 696). That the others did not *demand* proof at all is surely the point.

28. Brown sees Jesus' words containing a touch of sarcasm. Thomas is to be reprimanded both for refusing to accept the word of the other disciples and for attempting to establish the miraculous aspect of Jesus' appearance (*Gospel According to John*, II, pp. 1045-46). Beasley-Murray sees it as half-rebuke, half-appeal (*John*, p. 384). Calvin sees Jesus blaming Thomas for being so slow to believe and needing to be 'drawn violently to faith by the experience of his senses' (*Gospel According to St John*, II, p. 211).

Jesus Encounters Peter

The final appearance of the resurrected Jesus is focused around the character of Peter. There is unfinished business between Peter and Jesus and this pericope seeks to remedy the situation, resulting in a healing for Peter. The following structure will be used to discuss the text:

1. 21.1-3   The scene is set; 'I am going fishing'
2. 21.4-14   Miracle takes place; 'It is the Lord'
              Reaction of Peter: 'Bring some of the fish'
3. 21.15-23   Discussion with Peter: 'Tend my sheep'

In the first section Peter appears restless and announces his intention to go fishing. The response of the other six disciples with him indicates that they too wish for something practical to do. Peter does not invite them—'Let's go fishing'—but states that this is what he is going to do, and the others join him.[29] Several scholars have suggested that Peter's decision indicates a denial of the commission received from Jesus in 20.21, and an intention to return to his former occupation as a fisherman.[30] Although this is disputed by some commentators, who see the scene as neutral,[31] Timothy Wiarda argues that this is a difficult position to sustain:

> It must be observed that a contrast, an implied tension, is set up by describing Peter and the others as being disciples on the one hand and as engaging in the fishing trade on the other. There is something unexpected about this juxtaposition. It causes the reader to ask questions. How

---

29. S.M. Schneiders sees him as the leader of the expedition, the one who takes the initiative ('John 21.1-14', *Int* 43 [1989], pp. 70-75 [72]).

30. Harrington states; 'Peter and the other disciples have returned to their jobs as fisherman and show no special effect from the Jerusalem appearances' (*John's Thought and Theology*, p. 111). Likewise Brown: 'Disciples who came to believe in Jesus in Jn 20 are now engaged in ordinary activity without a sign of transformation' ('The Resurrection in John 21: Missionary and Pastoral Directives for the Church', *Worship* 64.5 [1990], pp. 433-45 [435]). See also Stibbe, *John*, p. 210. Hoskyns sees it as a scene of 'complete apostasy' (*Fourth Gospel*, p. 552).

31. Barrett exclaims: 'That Peter and his brother disciples should contemplate a return to their former occupation after the events of ch. 20 is unthinkable' (*Gospel According to St John*, p. 579). See also Beasley-Murray for another strong denial (*John*, p. 399).

does this fishing activity relate to the calling of Peter and the others with him have received to be Jesus' disciples?[32]

By the end of the first three verses the scene has been set; the disciples have engaged in a fruitless fishing trip, about which the reader feels a little uncomfortable.

In v. 4 Jesus arrives on the scene, although the disciples do not know that it is he. The exchange between them is short and functional, with the aim being the execution of a miracle resulting in the recognition of Jesus. It is not, however, without emotion.[33] Jesus' first word, παιδία (children), indicates that his feeling toward them is one of tenderness.[34] They have been sitting miserably in the middle of a lake all night and have caught nothing. Jesus' method of handling the situation is not to reproach them for neglecting their calling as disciples, but instead to confront them with his generosity. Heeding his word results in a larger catch than they could have dreamed of.

The recognition of Jesus by the beloved disciple results in immediate action by Peter: he pulls on his clothes and springs into the sea (v. 7). Peter's emotions at this point are generally viewed as falling into one of two categories: joy[35] or shame.[36] The difficulty caused by the juxtaposition of Peter's actions—dressing and then jumping in the sea—is also variously explained,[37] but whatever the reason, it seems clear that

32. T. Wiarda, 'John 21.1-23: Narrative Unity and its Implications', *JSNT* 46 (1992), pp. 53-71 (58).

33. Contra S.S. Smalley, who sees the exchange between them as 'factual, almost laconic and certainly unemotional' ('The Sign in John XXI', *NTS* 20 [1974], pp. 275-88 [282]).

34. Stibbe: 'a term of affectionate endearment' (*John*, p. 211); BAGD, 'fatherly intimacy' (p. 604).

35. Carston Thiede sees an 'exuberance' in his action (*Simon Peter: From Galilee to Rome* [Exeter: Paternoster Press, 1986], p. 93). Brown claims 'the Johannine scene portrays Peter's spontaneity and love of the Lord' ('The Resurrection in John 21', p. 437). Schuyler Brown's comment implicitly sees Peter's actions in a positive light: 'For Peter, the man of action, faith is *ex auditu*: When he hears from the Beloved Disciple that 'it is the Lord,' he springs into the water (v. 7) and swims to shore.' ('The Beloved Disciple', p. 373).

36. The shame being caused by guilt over the courtyard denials.

37. Barrett notes that to offer greeting was a religious act and could not be performed without clothing. Peter therefore puts on a garment in readiness to greet Jesus (*Gospel According to John*, pp. 580-81). Brown claims that Peter does not put on additional clothes, but merely tucks in the fisherman's smock he was already wearing (*Gospel According to John*, II, p. 1072). Thiede simply sees Peter making a 'polite

Peter's intention is to reach Jesus quickly and before the other disciples.[38] Perhaps this is indicative of Peter's overwhelming desire for reconciliation with Jesus, preferring to greet him in privacy before the others arrive on the scene. If this is the case, then his desire for privacy is granted as there is no mention in the text of the reunion between the two men, nor any indication of its tone. Further indication that Peter desires reconciliation is provided by the fact that, although Jesus' request to bring some of the fish for cooking is addressed to the disciples in general (v. 10), it is Peter who responds immediately. As was the case with Thomas, he is a man desperate for wholeness and here is a practical step he can easily take. Perhaps his willingness to carry out this task is an indication that he is now emotionally ready for Jesus to carry out his healing work.

Breakfast, which passes without further discussion, has a decidedly eucharistic feel about it.[39] But this is not the eucharist of violence, as was encountered in John 6, but a meal of fellowship used to facilitate wholeness. The *sparagmos* is over, the victim has been devoured and this meal is presided over by the transformed Jesus, whose concern is to bring transformation and wholeness to those he loves.

On finishing the meal, Jesus turns to Peter and asks him an explicit and deeply serious question. The time for Peter to face his guilt has come and Jesus does not prevaricate. On reading the whole passage, it

gesture' towards Jesus, adding, 'one realizes that even in a hurry, Peter is conscious of the reverence due to the Lord' (*Simon Peter*, p. 93).

38. Stibbe sees Peter throwing himself towards Jesus and swimming to the shore ahead of the other disciples (*John*, p. 211). Thiede comments: 'to try to reach Jesus faster than with the boat by swimming and wading such a distance [90 meters] fully clad, demonstrates Peter's completely restored eagerness of discipleship' (*Simon Peter*, p. 93). Similarly Hawkin states: 'Peter reacts quickly and jumps into the sea in his desire to reach Jesus' ('Function of the Beloved Disciple Motif', p. 147). D.H. Gee has an alternative interpretation of the event. He sees Peter's motivation as being fear and guilt and suggests that, having jumped into the water, Peter remains there, hiding behind the boat while it runs into shore. His plan is to swim to another point on the beach and sneak off when the boat nears land, avoiding Jesus altogether. In the end, however, Peter cannot see this through and is unable to leave without encountering Jesus. This story line is certainly creative, if not wholly convincing ('Why Did Peter Spring into the Sea?', *JTS* 40 (1989), pp. 481-89).

39. Schneiders claims: 'the evangelist deliberately evokes the Eucharistically freighted account of chapter 6.9-12 by saying that Jesus "*took* the bread and *gave* it to them and so with the fish"' ('John 21.1-14', p. 72, emphasis original). See also Bultmann, *Gospel of John*, p. 710; and Brown, *Gospel According to John*, II, p. 1099.

becomes obvious that Jesus has a healing strategy which begins by requiring Peter to clarify his priorities and ends with an warning of the cost of discipleship.[40] The repetition of his question 'Do you love me...?'[41] serves not only to mirror the threefold denial of Peter, but also to emphasize the solemnity of the situation, penetrating beneath Peter's initial knee-jerk response of 'Yes, Lord...' It is only at the third time of asking that Peter has an emotional response to this question, and the reader feels that his words come from the heart. It also becomes obvious that Jesus' question is not just an inquiry as to how fond of him Peter is, and that the command to feed his sheep should not be taken at face value. These are issues about which Jesus wants Peter's carefully considered answer and full commitment, the reason being that Peter's life is at stake.[42] The commission of following Jesus and feeding his sheep will result in him sharing a similar fate to the good shepherd.

Rehabilitation in a man as impulsive as Peter is not easily wrought and he reacts to this news in a manner that undermines the commitment he has just made to Jesus. Hearing his destiny, he turns away from Jesus to inquire about the destiny of another—arguably his rival in the Gospel. This requires firm treatment by Jesus. Peter must understand and be committed to his own commission and not concern himself with that of another. There is no further response from Peter and the reader can assume that the message has finally sunk in. Jesus' work with him is over. He has helped him to face the shame of the past, as well as preparing him for the challenge of the future. This has been the most lengthy and complex account of healing by the resurrected Jesus, although this is unsurprising when the role played by Peter among the disciples is considered.

40. Barrett claims that rehabilitation is *not* the primary focus in this passage, but rather Peter's later role in the church (*Gospel According to John*, p. 583). This seems untenable: without proper rehabilitation, there would be no later role for Peter.

41. On the meaning of the first question: ἀγαπᾷς με πλέον τούτων; see Wiarda, who argues for 'Do you love me more than these things?' on the basis that the immediate context is the tension between discipleship and fishing. The phrase could also mean 'Do you love me more than these do?', implying a comparison with the other disciples, or 'Do you love me more than you love these others?', which is self-explanatory ('John 21.1-23', pp. 60-64).

42. Windisch comments: 'the Johannine Christ... stirs and heals the conscience with a tenderness that is scarcely any longer human' ('John's Narrative Style', p. 58).

Concluding Comment: The Other Side of Death

Having discussed the text, we are now in a position to return to the questions raised at the beginning of this chapter concerning Jesus' identity. It will have become evident during the last few pages that the argument of this study is that the resurrected Jesus no longer perceives himself to be a victim. It should be noted that to claim *his* perception has changed does not mean he cannot be perceived by *others* as a victim—that is a matter for the reader to decide. But the Johannine Jesus no longer gives an indication of victimal behaviour in these last scenes. His actions are characterized by a deep concern for others and a desire to relieve their pain, rather than a preoccupation with his own pain. In the resurrection encounters we see him bringing each disciple to a new state of wholeness as he responds to their particular need. These are four narratives of emotional healing,[43] which show him assuaging grief, fear, unbelief and guilt in a manner that is thoughtful and compassionate.

From the material available in the narrative itself it is possible to explore this change in Jesus' behaviour further and to suggest the reasons for it. It would seem that Jesus himself as undergone a healing of sorts. Moreover, it is death that has been the cause of this healing in him.[44] Not because it has been conquered but because it has been encountered and finally escaped. Gone is the continual anticipation of the violence of the hour. The violence has been embraced, the *sparagmos* has taken place and the hour has now passed. This liberation can be seen in his character—a peace of mind which is now used to mediate peace to others. Gone is the fear, anger and impotence of the Jesus who failed to communicate with his disciples on their last evening together. The resurrected Jesus perceives how best to speak to each follower according to their need. For Mary it is her name; for the disciples a word of peace; for Thomas an invitation to believe; and for Peter a searching question.

43. Although these are obviously not healings in the strict physical sense, they are Jesus' therapeutic response to the emotional needs of his disciples. This type of healing is less frequently recognized by scholars. For example, J.T. Carroll in his article 'Sickness and Healing in the New Testament Gospels' sees only seven (physical) healings in John, finishing with the resurrection of Lazarus (*Int* 49 [1995], pp. 130-42 [136]).

44. I do not mean here that it was death which wrought the healing in him, but that it was the event of his death that was the occasion of healing.

Signs that a change has taken place in Jesus are discernible in the transformation of two images from the past that reappear in John 21. As discussed in Chapter 6, both the 'bread of life' and 'good shepherd' discourses were significant moments in the public ministry of Jesus. These were moments of crisis when he struggled with the inevitability of a brutal death. Now these images are used by Jesus in the context of life. The bread that Jesus takes and gives to the disciples does not call forth the literal figure of mutilation. There is no link made with his flesh or any mention of it being 'given' for them. Jesus' only words are an invitation—'come and breakfast'—and his offer meets their need in a practical manner. There are no demons here. Likewise, Jesus uses the metaphor which caused him anguish in John 10, revealing that laying down his life will mean surrendering to a savage fate, to invoke anguish in Peter. This time there is no mention of the death of Jesus; the context is the death of Peter. The role of shepherd is conjoined with the role of victim. Jesus no longer understands this as his role; it now belongs to Peter and the other disciples. Perhaps this is the key to understanding the change that has taken place in the resurrected Jesus. He has escaped from the victim-cognizance which characterized his life before 'the hour'. The evidence of his victimization remains—one need look no further than the scars on his body—but there has been a shift in his self-understanding, revealing his own liberation from grief and fear.

11

The Disconcerting Outcome

The starting point for this book was the recognition that there is 'something disconcerting' about the Fourth Gospel, and that this can be traced to its protagonist. The source of unease, it has been suggested, lies in the dynamics of violence within the narrative: the nature of the interplay between the victim and victimizers is complex and is related in part to the victim's self-understanding. In drawing this study to a close, the main arguments and insights which have been introduced during the course of the discussion will be summarized and some conclusions and suggestions for further study put forward.

Some considerable effort was expended in setting the context for this study during the first four chapters. The aim of this was not solely to establish the ground rules for investigation, but to use the theological, historical and literary reviews to advance ideas which could be used to add weight to the main body of exegesis. These ideas are interlinked but not interdependent, thus if one is felt to be unsustainable the validity of the rest of the investigation is not automatically jeopardized. Supported cumulatively, however, they add to the overall strength of the argument. This is, of course, important when pursuing an approach which could be viewed as inadmissable by some areas of scholarship. The line of thought is as follows:

1. *True Liberation is from Below*

An effective and credible liberator must be closely identified with the oppressed and be seen to share their experiences. Within a theological framework, suffering communities adopt or create appropriate christological models that are relevant to their circumstances.

2. *Key to Understanding a Text is Understanding its Context*

The themes of violence and victimization pervade John's Gospel and could have been exegeted without reference to the historical origin of the text. Nevertheless, it has been argued that it is preferable to try to anchor the text within a social context, however tenuous this might be. This way, one gains some clue as to what the motivation and 'point' of the story is.

3. *The Text's Context Was One of Violence*
The historical context of the Gospel of John was that of a community in crisis, experiencing persecution and alienation from both Jewish and Roman sources. This resulted in the group developing a sectarian attitude, with victimization being both a frequent experience and a contributing factor to shaping its identity.

4. *The Contents of the Text Reflect the Context*
The ancient oppressed community has created in the Johannine Jesus a liberator with whom they can identify—one whose experience is akin to their own. The 'personality' of the Johannine Jesus therefore reflects the nature of the group which created it. The community has created its liberator in its own image.

5. *The Text's Content Is Violent*
There is a substantial amount of material relating to the victimization of Jesus throughout the Fourth Gospel. Over 50 separate references to direct and indirect opposition can be documented and there is a higher level of violence present in the John's narrative than is found in the other gospels.

6. *Violence Shapes the Liberator's Identity*
The text's protagonist perceives his own identity and role to be that of a victim. This understanding permeates his character and influences his response to key events which happen in the narrative. This includes behaviour that could be seen to incite violence and some instances where he appears to collude with his oppressors.

This is essentially the line of thought that has been pursued throughout the entire narrative. There are obvious limitations to an approach which attempts the formidable task of tracing a theme through a whole Gospel. The volume of published work on John is immense, making exhaustive consideration of the material for each section impossible. Choosing specific parts of the Gospel and focusing on them in more detail would have been one way round this, but probably would have weakened the overall argument. What is notable about John's Gospel is the *prevalence* of the theme. It can be found in every chapter. Each episode of the narrative can be convincingly read from the perspective of Jesus as a victim, and, I would contend, frequently the reading is more convincing and explains the events more naturally than traditional interpretations.

Doubtless many scholars would not have difficulty in conceding that Jesus is a victim in the loosest sense of the term; after all he is an innocent man who is executed for religious and political reasons. This study goes much further, exploring the nature and extent of Jesus' victimization through extensive exegesis and showing that 'victim' is not just another loose label for the Johannine Jesus; it is, in fact, a fairly snug fit. Where, then, do these conclusions lead us? This work throws up several lines of inquiry that could be further pursued by scholars. Perhaps most significant is the issue of complicity. I have been clear that my discussion is confined to the literary dimension, relating to the behaviour of a character within a narrative. However, if this discussion is found to be convincing, then there are clearly theological avenues to be explored, such as the christological implications of a saviour who colludes with his oppressors, courting betrayal. In beginning to address such questions a number of problems arise. On the one hand there are matters of the allocation of blame. Are we, as readers, really surprised that Jesus ends up on the cross, given his behaviour, and does this impact on the level of sympathy we extend to him and the judgments we make about him? To what extent was Jesus 'asking for it', and where have we heard that phrase before? On the other hand, for those bold enough to think the theologically unthinkable, there is a more sinister angle that can be pursued. To what extent can Jesus be seen as an accomplice in his own murder? The bottom line is that both Jesus and his enemies will the same end—his death—and in achieving this there are instances of covert and overt collusion on his part. The question that inevitably follows is how his complicity interracts with his innocence. Is he not culpable, or at least tainted in some way and what does it mean that the evangelist asserts his innocence nonetheless? I have already mentioned the 'nefarious symbiosis', a kind of codependence, between victim and victimizer and again, what does this mean in the context of a 'sovereign' liberator?

These questions can be used to explore a theology of victimage, the seeds of which will inform a whole range of liberation theologies which have the oppression of the individual at their centre. Girard has done much to advance our understanding of victims from a cultic perspective, but there is further to go in terms of integrating theology not solely with anthropology but also with psychology and criminology, particularly if a therapeutic approach is desired. However, the results may be difficult for more conservative theologies to bear. I have not, in this study, sought to mitigate the more unpalatable aspects of the Johannine Jesus' behaviour, but to expose them, defining them in terms of an overall theme. If, having explored this theme, the reader finds the Johannine Jesus even *more* unappealing, perhaps it is because his mission requires him not simply to endure violence, but to embrace it. His escape into wholeness is mediated through this embrace. Suffering *in extremis* is the disconcerting example we are confronted with. The concept of Jesus as some kind of 'servant–king' who is subjected to a shameful death is not difficult to accept while the soft-focus filter is firmly in place: A scene of raw brutality can readily be transformed into that 'Italian primitive painting'.[1] I have attempted to remove that filter and to expose a story where exaltation must be understood in terms of degradation and sovereignty means the abnegation of power; where kingship means servitude and service means a debasement so embarrassing that loved ones shy away from it. Jesus the victim may be more of a suffering servant than we bargained for, but perhaps we have begun to penetrate his heart of darkness.

Martin Hengel begins *The Johannine Question* with the comment by David Friedrich Strauss that the Fourth Gospel can be compared to 'Christ's seamless robe'. 'Nowadays', adds Hengel, 'even a conservative theologian would no longer dare to say anything like that; 'Christ's seamless robe' has long become a "patchwork coat of many colours"'.[2] Whether seamless robe or patchwork coat, the predominant colours that have been seen in John's garment are the lustrous golds and silvers of the majestic and exalted Christ. That there are colours of a darker hue and more menacing nature present in the garment is now clear; the colours of violence, of *sparagmos*, of death.

1. Lindars, *Gospel of John*, p. 573.
2. Hengel, *Johannine Question*, p. 1.

BIBLIOGRAPHY

Abrams, M.H., *A Glossary of Literary Terms* (Fort Worth: Holt, Rinehart & Winston, 5th edn, 1988).

Alfaro, J., 'The Mariology of the Fourth Gospel: Mary and the Struggles for Liberation', *BTB* 10 (1980), pp. 3-16.

Allen, E.L., 'The Jewish Christian Church in the Fourth Gospel', *JBL* 74 (1955), pp. 88-92.

Alter, R., *The Art of Biblical Narrative* (London: George Allen & Unwin, 1981).

Ashby, G., *Sacrifice: Its Nature and Purpose* (London: SCM Press, 1988).

Ashton, J., *Understanding the Fourth Gospel* (Oxford: Clarendon Press, 1991).

Ashton, J. (ed.), *The Interpretation of John* (Philadelphia: Fortress Press, 1986).

Aune, D.E., *The Cultic Setting of Realized Eschatology in Early Christianity* (NovTSup, 28; Leiden: E.J. Brill, 1972).

Bailey, L.R., *Biblical Perspectives on Death* (Overtures to Biblical Theology; Philadelphia: Fortress Press, 1981).

Barrett, C.K., *The Gospel According to St John: An Introduction with Commentary and Notes on the Greek Text* (London: SPCK, 2nd edn, 1978).

—*Essays on John* (London: SPCK, 1982).

—'The Lamb of God', *NTS* 1 (1954), pp. 210-18.

Barton, S., 'The Believer, the Historian and the Fourth Gospel', *Theology* 96 (1993), pp. 289-302.

Bauer, W., *Das Johannesevangelium* (HNT, 6; Tübingen: J.C.B. Mohr [Paul Siebeck], 3rd edn, 1933).

Beasley-Murray, G.R., *John* (WBC, 36; Waco, TX: Word Books, 1987).

—*Gospel of Life: Theology in the Fourth Gospel* (Peabody, MA: Hendrickson, 1991).

Beattie, J.H.M., 'On Understanding Sacrifice', in M.F.C. Bourdillon and M. Fottes (eds.), *Sacrifice* (London: Academic Press, 1980), pp. 29-44.

Behm, J., 'αἷμα', *TDNT,* I, pp. 172-76.

Benko, S., *Pagan Rome and the Early Christians* (London: B.T. Batsford, 1984).

Berkowitz, L., *Aggression: Its Causes, Consequences, and Control* (New York: McGraw–Hill, 1993).

Bernard, J.H., *A Critical and Exegetical Commentary on the Gospel According to St John* (ed. A.H. McNeile; ICC; 2 vols.; repr.; Edinburgh: T. & T. Clark, 1942 [1928]).

Bertram, G., 'ὑψόω', *TDNT*, VIII, pp. 606-13.

Beutler, J., 'Two Ways of Gathering: The Plot to Kill Jesus in John 11.47-53', *NTS* 40 (1994), pp. 399-406.

Beutler, J., and R.T. Fortna (eds.), *The Shepherd Discourse of John 10 and its Context: Studies by Members of the Johannine Writings Seminar* (Cambridge: Cambridge University Press, 1991).

Bishop, E.F.F., '"He that Eateth Bread with me Hath Lifted Up his Heel Against me" Jn 13.18 (Ps. 41.9)', *ExpTim* 70 (1958–59), pp. 331-33.

Blass, F., and A. Debrunner, *A Greek Grammar of the New Testament and other Early Christian Literature* (ed. R.W. Funk; Cambridge: Cambridge University Press, 1961).

Boer, M.C. de, 'Narrative Criticism, Historical Criticism, and the Gospel of John', *JSNT* 47 (1992), pp. 35-48.

Boer, M.C. de (ed.), *From Jesus to John: Essays on Jesus and New Testament Christology in Honour of Marinus de Jonge* (JSNTSup, 84; Sheffield: JSOT Press, 1993).

Boff, L., *Jesus Christ, Liberator: A Critical Christology for our Time* (trans. P. Hughes; Maryknoll, NY: Orbis Books, 1978).

Bonhoeffer, D., *Letters and Papers from Prison* (ed. E. Bethge; trans. R. Fuller *et al*; London: SCM Press, 1967).

Bonino, J.M. (ed.), *Faces of Jesus: Latin American Christologies* (trans. R.R. Barr; Maryknoll, NY: Orbis Books, 1977).

Borgen, P., *Bread from Heaven: An Exegetical Study of the Concept of Manna in the Gospel of John and the Writings of Philo* (NovTSup, 10; Leiden: E.J. Brill, 1965).

Brodie, T.L., *The Gospel According to John: A Literary and Theological Commentary* (Oxford: Oxford University Press, 1993).

Brooks, O.S., 'The Johannine Eucharist: Another Interpretation', *JBL* 82 (1963), pp. 293-300.

Brown, C. (ed.), *New International Dictionary of New Testament Theology* (3 vols.; Exeter: Paternoster Press, 1976).

Brown, R.E., *The Gospel According to John* (AB, 29, 29A; 2 vols.; repr.; Garden City, NY: Doubleday, 1972 [1966]).

—The Resurrection in John 21: Missionary and Pastoral Directives for the Church', *Worship* 64.5 (1990), pp. 433-45.

—'The Resurrection in John 20: A Series of Diverse Reactions', *Worship* 64.3 (1990), pp. 194-206.

—*The Community of the Beloved Disciple* (London: Geoffrey Chapman, 1979).

—'The "Mother of Jesus" in the Fourth Gospel', in de Jonge (ed.), *L'Evangile de Jean*, pp. 307-10.

—'Johannine Ecclesiology: The Community's Origins', *Int* 31 (1977), pp. 379-93.

—*New Testament Essays* (London: Geoffrey Chapman, 1965).

Brown, R.E., K.P. Donfried and J. Reumann (eds.), *Peter in the New Testament: A Collaborative Assessment by Protestant and Roman Catholic Scholars* (London: Geoffrey Chapman, rev. edn, 1974).

Brown, S., 'The Beloved Disciple: A Jungian View', in Fortna and Gaventa (eds.), *The Conversation Continues*, pp. 366-77.

Bruce, F.F., *The Gospel of John* (Basingstoke: Pickering & Inglis, 1983).

Bruns, J.E., review of *John's Gospel in New Perspective: Christology and the Realities of Roman Power*, by Richard Cassidy, in *CBQ* 56 (1994), pp. 134-35.

Bultmann, R., *Jesus and the Word* (trans. L.P. Smith and E.H. Lantero; New York: Charles Scribner's Sons, rev. edn, 1958).

—*Theology of the New Testament*, II (trans. K. Grobel; London: SCM Press, 1983) (originally published as *Theologie des Neuen Testaments* [Tübingen: J.C.B. Mohr [Paul Siebeck], 1948]).

—*The Gospel of John: A Commentary* (trans. G.R. Beasley-Murray; Oxford: Basil Blackwell, 1971) (originally published as *Das Evangelium des Johannes* [Göttingen: Vandenhoeck & Ruprecht, 1964]).

Burge, G.M., *The Anointed Community: The Holy Spirit in the Johannine Tradition* (Grand Rapids: Eerdmans, 1987).

Burkett, D., 'Two Accounts of Lazarus' Resurrection in John 11', *NovT* 36 (1994), pp. 209-32.

Calvin, J., *The Gospel According to St John* (ed. D.W. and T.F. Torrance; trans. T.H.L. Parker; 2 vols.; Calvin's Commentaries; Edinburgh: Oliver & Boyd, 1959, 1961).

Cardenal, E., *Love in Practice: The Gospel in Solentiname* (trans. D.D. Walsh; London: Search Press, 1977).

Carroll, J.T., 'Sickness and Healing in the New Testament Gospels', *Int* 49 (1995), pp. 130-42.

Carson, D.A., *The Gospel According to John* (Leicester: IVP, 1991).

—*The Farewell Discourse and Final Prayer of Jesus: An Exposition of John 14–17* (Grand Rapids: Baker Book House, 1980).

Carter, W., 'The Prologue and John's Gospel: Function, Symbol and the Definitive Word', *JSNT* 39 (1990), pp. 35-58.

Casalis, G., 'Jesus: Neither Abject Lord nor Heavenly Monarch', in Bonino (ed.), *Faces of Jesus*, pp. 72-76.

Cassidy, R.J., *John's Gospel in New Perspective: Christology and the Realities of Roman Power* (Maryknoll, NY: Orbis Books, 1992).

Chambers, R., *Story and Situation: Narrative Seduction and the Power of Fiction* (Theory and History of Literature, 12; Minneapolis: University of Minnesota Press; Manchester: Manchester University Press, 1984).

Chatman, S., *Story and Discourse: Narrative Structure in Fiction and Film* (repr; Ithaca, NY: Cornell University Press, 1989 [1978]).

Chilton, B.D., *The Temple of Jesus: His Sacrificial Program Within a Cultural History of Sacrifice* (Pennsylvania: Pennsylvania State University Press, 1992).

Chopp, R.S., *The Praxis of Suffering: An Interpretation of Liberation and Political Theologies* (Maryknoll, NY: Orbis Books, 1986).

Clancy, J.P., *The Earliest Welsh Poetry* (London: Macmillan, 1970).

Clark, W.R., 'Jesus, Lazarus, and Others: Resuscitation or Resurrection?', *RL* 49.2 (1980), pp. 230-41.

Clines, D.J.A., *I, He, We, and They: A Literary Approach to Isaiah 53* (JSOTSup, 1; Sheffield: JSOT Press, 1976).

Collins, A.Y., 'New Testament Perspectives: The Gospel of John', *JSOT* 22 (1982), pp. 47-53.

Collins, R.F., *These Things Have Been Written: Studies on the Fourth Gospel* (Leuven: Peeters, 1990).

Collins, S., 'A Feminist Reading of History', in Kee (ed.), *The Scope of Political Theology*, pp. 79-83.

Corsini, R.J. (ed.), *Encyclopaedia of Psychology* (4 vols.; New York: John Wiley & Sons, 2nd edn, 1994).

Cullmann, O., *Peter: Disciple, Apostle, Martyr* (trans. F.V. Filson; London: SCM Press, 2nd edn, 1962).

—*The Christology of the New Testament* (trans. S.C. Guthrie and C.A.M. Hall; London: SCM Press, 1959).

Culpepper, R.A., 'The Johannine *Hypodeigma*: A Reading of John 13', *Semeia* 53 (1991), pp. 133-52.

—*Anatomy of the Fourth Gospel: A Study in Literary Design* (Philadelphia: Fortress Press, 1983).

Culpepper, R.A., and F.F Segovia (eds.), *The Fourth Gospel from a Literary Perspective* (Semeia, 53; Atlanta: Scholars Press, 1991).

Dahl, N.A., *The Crucified Messiah and other Essays* (Minneapolis: Augsburg, 1974).

Danby, H. (ed.), *The Mishnah: Translated from the Hebrew with Introduction and Brief Explanatory Notes* (Oxford: Oxford University Press, 1933).

D'Angelo, M.R., 'A Critical Note: John 20.17 and the Apocalypse of Moses 31', *JTS* 41 (1990), pp. 529-36.

Davies, M., *Rhetoric and Reference in the Fourth Gospel* (JSNTSup, 69; Sheffield: JSOT Press, 1992).

Davies, P.R. and B.D. Chilton, 'The Aqedah: A Revised Tradition History', *CBQ* 40 (1978), pp. 514-46.

Derrett, J.M.D., *Law in the New Testament* (London: Darton, Longman & Todd, 1970).

Detienne, M., *Dionysos Slain* (trans. M. Muellner and L. Muellner; Baltimore: The Johns Hopkins University Press, 1977).

Dias de Araújo, J., 'Images of Jesus in the Culture of the Brazilian People', in Bonino (ed.), *Faces of Jesus*, pp. 30-38.

Dixon, R., *Management Theory and Practice* (Oxford: Butterworth–Heinemann, 1991).

Dodd, C.H., 'The Portrait of Jesus in John and in the Synoptics', in W.R. Farmer, C.F.D. Moule and R.R. Niebuhr (eds.), *Christian History and Interpretation: Studies Presented to John Knox* (Cambridge: Cambridge University Press, 1967), pp. 183-98.

—*Historical Tradition in the Fourth Gospel* (repr.; Cambridge: Cambridge University Press, 1979 [1963]).

—*The Interpretation of the Fourth Gospel* (Cambridge: Cambridge University Press, 1953).

Domeris, W.R., 'Christology and Community: A Study of the Social Matrix of the Fourth Gospel', *JTheolSA* 64 (1988), pp. 49-56.

Droge, A.J., 'The Status of Peter in the Fourth Gospel: A Note on John 18.10-11', *JBL* 109 (1990), pp. 307-11.

Duke, P., *Irony in the Fourth Gospel* (Atlanta: John Knox Press, 1985).

Dunn, J.D.G., 'The Question of Anti-Semitism in the New Testament Writings of the Period', in Dunn (ed.), *Jews and Christians*, pp. 177-211.

—*The Partings of the Ways: Between Christianity and Judaism and their Significance for the Character of Christianity* (London: SCM Press, 1991).

—'Let John be John: A Gospel for its Time', in P. Stuhlmacher (ed.), *The Gospel and the Gospels* (Grand Rapids: Eerdmans, 1991), pp. 293-322 (originally published as *Das Evangelium und die Evangelien: Vorträge vom Tübingen Symposium 1982* [WUNT, 28; Tübingen: J.C.B Mohr [Paul Siebeck], 1983]).

—*The Evidence for Jesus: The Impact of Scholarship on our Understanding of how Christianity Began* (London: SCM Press, 1985).

—*Christology in the Making: An Inquiry into the Origins of the Doctrine of the Incarnation* (London: SCM Press, 1980).

—'John VI: A Eucharistic Discourse?', *NTS* 17 (1971), pp. 328-38.

—'The Washing of the Disciples' Feet in Jn 13.1-20', *ZNW* 61 (1970), pp. 247-52.

Dunn, J.D.G. (ed.), *Jesus and Christians: The Parting of the Ways A.D. 70 to 135* (WUNT, 66; Tübingen: J.C.B. Mohr [Paul Siebeck], 1992).

Dyer, G., Critique of Norman Sherrin's biography of Graham Greene, *The Guardian*, 30 August 1994, p. 13.

Ebel, G., 'Persecution, Tribulation, Affliction', *NIDNTT*, II, p. 806.

Edwards, R.A., *The Gospel According to St John: Its Criticism and Interpretation* (London: Eyre & Spottiswoode, 1954).

Edwards, R.B., 'The Christological Basis of the Johannine Footwashing', in J.B. Green and M. Turner (eds.), *Jesus of Nazareth, Lord and Christ: Essays on the Historical Jesus and New Testament Christology* (Carlisle: Paternoster Press, 1994), pp. 367-83.

Elias, R., *The Politics of Victimization: Victims, Victimology and Human Rights* (Oxford: Oxford University Press, 1986).

Ellis, P.F., *The Genius of John: A Composition-Critical Commentary on the Fourth Gospel* (Collegeville, MN: Liturgical Press, 1984).

Evans, C.A., 'Obduracy and the Lord's Servant: Some Observations on the Use of the Old Testament in the Fourth Gospel', in C.A. Evans and W.F. Stinespring (eds.), *Early Jewish and Christian Exegesis: Studies in Memory of William Hugh Brownlee* (Atlanta: Scholars Press, 1987), pp. 221-36.

—'Jesus' Self-Understanding', in *idem, Life of Jesus Research: An Annotated Bibliography* (Leiden: E.J. Brill, 1989), pp. 128-38.

Evans, C.A., and W.R. Stegner (eds.), *The Gospels and the Scriptures of Israel* (JSNTSup, 104; Sheffield: Sheffield Academic Press, 1994).

Evans, C.F., 'The Passion of John' in *Explorations in Theology,* II (9 vols.; London: SCM Press, 1977), pp. 50-66.

Exum, J.C., *Tragedy and Biblical Narrative: Arrows of the Almighty* (Cambridge: Cambridge University Press, 1992).

Fee, G.D., 'John 14.8-17', *Int* 43 (1989), pp. 170-74.

Flusser, D., 'What Was the Original Meaning of *Ecce Homo*?', *Immanuel* 19 (1994–95), pp. 30-40.

Ford, J.M., 'Shalom in the Johannine Corpus', *HBT* 6.2 (1984), pp. 67-89.

Forestell, J.T., *The Word of the Cross: Salvation as Revelation in the Fourth Gospel* (AnBib, 57; Rome: Biblical Institute Press, 1974).

Forster, E.M., *Aspects of the Novel* (ed. O. Stallybrass; repr.; Harmondsworth: Penguin Books, 1985 [1927]).

Fortna, R.T., *The Fourth Gospel and its Predecessor* (Edinburgh: T. & T. Clark, 1989).

—'Christology in the Fourth Gospel: Redaction-Critical Perspectives', *NTS* 21 (1975), pp. 489-504.

Fortna, R.T., and B.R. Gaventa (eds.), *The Conversation Continues: Studies in Paul and John. In Honor of J. Louis Martyn* (Nashville: Abingdon Press, 1990).

Frankl, V.E., *Man's Search for Meaning: An Introduction to Logotherapy* (trans. I. Lasch; London: Hodder & Stoughton, 1964).

Freed, E.D., *Old Testament Quotations in the Gospel of John* (NovTSup, 11; Leiden: E.J. Brill, 1965).

Frei, H.W., *The Eclipse of Biblical Narrative: A Study in Eighteenth and Nineteenth Century Hermeneutics* (New Haven: Yale University Press, 1974).

Frend, W.H.C., *Martyrdom and Persecution in the Early Church: A Study of a Conflict from the Maccabees to Donatus* (Oxford: Basil Blackwell, 1965).

Frye, N., *Anatomy of Criticism: Four Essays* (London: Penguin Books, rev. edn, 1990 [1957]).

Fuller, R.H., 'The Passion, Death and Resurrection of Jesus According to St John', *ChS* 25 (1986), pp. 51-63.

Gee, D.H., 'Why Did Peter Spring into the Sea?', *JTS* 40 (1989), pp. 481-89.

Gerstenberger, E.S., and W. Schrage, *Suffering* (trans. J.E. Steely; Nashville: Abingdon Press, 1980).

Giblin, C.H., 'The Tripartite Narrative Structure of John's Gospel', *Bib* 71 (1990), pp. 449-68.

Girard, M., 'La composition structurelle des sept "signes" dans le quatrième évangile', *SR* 9.3 (1980), pp. 315-24.

Girard, R., *Things Hidden since the Foundation of the World* (trans. S. Bann and M. Metteer; London: Athlone Press, 1987).

—*Job the Victim of his People* (trans. Y. Freccero; London: Athlone Press, 1987) (originally published as *La route antique des hommes pervers* [Paris: Editions Grasset & Fasquelle, 1985]).

—*The Scapegoat* (trans. Y. Freccero; Baltimore: The Johns Hopkins University Press, 1986) (originally published as *Le Bouc émissaire* [Paris: Editions Grasset & Fasquelle, 1982]).

—*Violence and the Sacred* (trans. P. Gregory; Baltimore: The Johns Hopkins University Press, 1977) (originally published as *La Violence et la sacré* [Paris: Éditions Bernard Grasset, 1972]).

Golsan, R.J., *René Girard and Myth: An Introduction* (New York: Garland Publishing, 1993).

Goulder, M., 'Nicodemus', *SJT* 44 (1991), pp. 153-68.

Grassi, J.A., 'Eating Jesus' Flesh and Drinking his Blood: The Centrality and Meaning of John 6.51-58', *BTB* 17 (1987), pp. 24-30.

Grenier, B., 'Jesus and Women', *St Mark's Review* 119 (1984), pp. 13-21.

Grossouw, W.K., 'A Note on John XIII 1-3', *NovT* 8 (1966), pp. 124-31.

Haenchen, E., 'History and Interpretation in the Johannine Passion Narrative', *Int* 24 (1970), pp. 198-219.

—*John* (trans. R.W. Funk; Hermeneia Commentaries; 2 vols.; Philadelphia: Fortress Press, 1984).

Hamerton-Kelly, R.G., *Sacred Violence: Paul's Hermeneutic of the Cross* (Philadelphia: Fortress Press, 1992).

Hanson, A.T., 'John's Use of Scripture', in Evans and Stegner (eds.), *The Gospels and the Scriptures of Israel*, pp. 358-79.

—*The Prophetic Gospel: A Study of John and the Old Testament* (Edinburgh: T. & T. Clark, 1991).

Hardison, O.B., *Christian Rite and Christian Drama in the Middle Ages: Essays in the Origin and Early History of Modern Drama* (Baltimore: The Johns Hopkins University Press, 1965).

Harrington, D.J., *John's Thought and Theology: An Introduction* (Good News Studies, 33; Wilmington, DE: Michael Glazier, 1990).

Hartman, L., and B. Olsson (eds.), *Aspects on the Johannine Literature: Papers Presented at a Conference of Scandinavian New Testament Exegetes at Uppsala, June 16-19, 1986.* (ConBNT, 18; Uppsala: Almqvist & Wiksell, 1987).

Harvey, A.E., *Jesus on Trial: A Study in the Fourth Gospel* (London: SPCK, 1976).

Hatch, E., and H.A. Redpath, *A Concordance to the Septuagint and the other Greek Versions of the Old Testament* (2 vols.; Oxford: Clarendon Press, 1897).

Hawkin, D.J., 'The Function of the Beloved Disciple Motif in the Johannine Redaction', *LTP* 33.2 (1977), pp. 135-50.

Hellig, J., 'The Negative Image of the Jew and its New Testament Roots', *JTheolSA* 64 (1988), pp. 39-48.

Hengel, M., 'The Old Testament in the Fourth Gospel', in Evans and Stegner (eds.), *The Gospels and the Scriptures of Israel*, pp. 380-95.

—*The Johannine Question* (trans. J. Bowden; London: SCM Press, 1989).

Hentig, H. von, *The Criminal and his Victim: Studies in the Sociobiology of Crime* (New Haven: Yale University Press, 1948).

Hesselink, I.J., 'John 14.23-29', *Int* 43 (1989), pp. 174-77.

Hickling, C.J.A., 'Attitudes to Judaism in the Fourth Gospel', in de Jonge (ed.), *L'Evangile de Jean*, pp. 347-54.

Higgins, A.J.B., *The Lord's Supper in the New Testament* (London: SCM Press, 1952).

Hooker, M.D., *Jesus and the Servant: The Influence of the Servant Concept of Deutero-Isaiah in the New Testament* (London: SPCK, 1959).

Hoskyns, E.C., *The Fourth Gospel* (ed. F.N. Davey; London: Faber & Faber, 2nd edn, 1947).

Hubbard, D.A., 'John 19.17-30', *Int* 43 (1989), pp. 397-401.

Hultgren, A.J., 'The Gospel of John', in *New Testament Christology: A Critical Assessment and Annotated Bibliography* (New York: Greenwood Press, 1988), pp. 267-95.

Jeremias, J., 'παῖς θεοῦ', *TDNT*, V, pp. 654-717.

Johnson, E.A., *Consider Jesus: Waves of Renewal in Christology* (New York: Crossroad, 1990).

Jones, W.H.S. (trans.), *Pausanias: Description of Greece Books VI-VIII* (LCL; 4 vols.; repr.; London: Heinemann, 1966 [1933]).

Jonge, M. de, *Jesus, the Servant–Messiah* (New Haven: Yale University Press, 1991).

—*Jesus, Stranger from Heaven and Son of God: Jesus Christ and the Christians in Johannine Perspective* (trans. J.E. Steely; Missoula, MT: Scholars Press, 1977).

Jonge, M. de, (ed.), *L'évangile de Jean: Sources, rédaction, théologie* (BETL, 44; Leuven: Leuven University Press/Uitgeverij Peeters, 1977).

Karris, R.J., *The Marginalized in John's Gospel* (Zacchaeus Studies, New Testament; Collegeville, MN: Liturgical Press, 1990).

Käsemann, E., *The Testament of Jesus: A Study of the Gospel of John in the Light of Chapter 17* (trans. G. Krodel; Philadelphia: Fortress Press, 1968) (originally published as *Jesu letzter Wille nach Johannes 17* [Tübingen: J. C. B. Mohr, 1966]).

Katz, S.T., 'Issues in the Separation of Judaism and Christianity after 70 CE: A Reconsideration', *JBL* 103 (1984), pp. 43-76.

Kee, A. (ed.), *The Scope of Political Theology* (London: SCM Press, 1978).

Kermode, F., 'John', in R. Alter and F. Kermode (eds.), *The Literary Guide to the Bible* (London: Collins, 1987), pp. 440-66.

Kirk, G.S., *The Bacchae of Euripides: Translated with an Introduction and Commentary* (Cambridge: Cambridge University Press, 1979).

Knight, G.A.F., *Deutero-Isaiah: A Theological Commentary on Isaiah 40–55* (New York: Abingdon Press, 1965).

Kott, J., *The Eating of the Gods: An Interpretation of Greek Tragedy* (trans. B. Taborski and E.J. Czerwinski; London: Eyre Methuen, 1974).

Krieger, M., *A Window to Criticism: Shakespeare's Sonnets and Modern Poetics* (Princeton, NJ: Princeton University Press, 1964).

Kutash, I.L., 'Victimology', in Corsini (ed.), *Encyclopaedia of Psychology*, III, pp. 564-66.

Kysar, R., 'Anti-Semitism and the Gospel of John', in C.A. Evans and D.A. Hagner (eds.), *Anti-Semitism and Early Christianity: Issues of Polemic and Faith* (Philadelphia: Fortress Press, 1993), pp. 113-27.

—'Johannine Metaphor—Meaning and Function: A Literary Case Study of John 10.1-8', *Semeia* 53 (1991), pp. 81-111.

—*John* (Augsburg Commentary on the New Testament; Minneapolis: Augsburg, 1986).

—'The Gospel of John in Current Research', *RSR* 9 (1983), pp. 314-23.

—'Community and Gospel: Vectors in Fourth Gospel Criticism', *Int* 31 (1977), pp. 355-66.

—*John: The Maverick Gospel* (Atlanta: John Knox Press, 1976).

—*The Fourth Evangelist and his Gospel: An Examination of Contemporary Scholarship* (Minneapolis: Augsburg, 1975).

Lagrange, M.-J, *Evangile selon Saint Jean* (Paris: J. Gabalda, 7th edn, 1948).

Lamb, M.L., *Solidarity with Victims: Toward a Theology of Social Transformation* (New York: Crossroad, 1982).

Lee, D.A., *The Symbolic Narratives of the Fourth Gospel: The Interplay of Form and Meaning* (JSNTSup, 95; Sheffield: JSOT Press, 1994).

Le Guin, U., 'It Was a Dark and Stormy Night; or, Why Are we Huddling about the Campfire?', *Critical Inquiry* 7.1 (1980), pp. 191-99.

Lieu, J.M., review of *The Partings of the Ways*, by J.D.G. Dunn, in *JTS* 44 (1993), pp. 668-70.

—*The Second and Third Epistles of John* (SNTW; Edinburgh: T. & T. Clark, 1986).

Lightfoot, R.H., *St John's Gospel: A Commentary* (ed. C.F. Evans; Oxford: Clarendon Press, 1956).

Lilburne, G.R., 'Christology: In Dialogue with Feminism', *Horizons* 11 (1984), pp. 7-27.

Lincoln, A.T., 'Trials, Plots and the Narrative of the Fourth Gospel', *JSNT* 56 (1994), pp. 3-30.

Lindars, B., 'The Persecution of Christians in John 15.18-16.4a', in W. Horbury and B. McNeil (eds.), *Suffering and Martyrdom in the New Testament: Studies Presented to G.M. Styler by the Cambridge New Testament Seminar* (Cambridge: Cambridge University Press, 1981), pp. 48-69.

—'Traditions behind the Fourth Gospel', in de Jonge (ed.), *L'Evangile de Jean*, pp. 107-24.

—*The Gospel of John* (NCB; London: Oliphants, 1972).

Loades, A., *Searching for Lost Coins: Explorations in Christianity and Feminism* (London: SPCK, 1987).

Loades, A., (ed.), *Feminist Theology: A Reader* (London: SPCK, 1990).

Loisy, A., *Le Quatrième Evangile* (Paris, Alphonse Picard et Fils, 1903).

Lohse, E., *History of the Suffering and Death of Jesus Christ* (Philadelphia: Fortress Press, 1967).

MacGregor, G.H.C., 'The Eucharist in the Fourth Gospel', *NTS* 9 (1962–63), pp. 111-19.

McHugh. J., 'In Him was Life', in Dunn (ed.), *Jews and Christians*, pp. 123-158.

McKenna, A.J. (ed.), *René Girard and Biblical Studies* (Semeia, 33; Atlanta: Scholars Press, 1985).

McKenzie, J.L., *Second Isaiah* (AB; New York: Doubleday, 1983).

McKnight, S., *Interpreting the Synoptic Gospels* (Grand Rapids: Baker Book House, 1988).

Malatesta, E., *St. John's Gospel 1920–1965* (Rome: Pontifical Biblical Institute, 1967).

Malatesta, E., 'The Literary Structure of John 17', *Bib* 52 (1971), pp. 190-214.

Malbon, E.S., and E.V. McKnight (eds.), *The New Literary Criticism and the New Testament* (JSNTSup, 109; Sheffield: Sheffield Academic Press, 1994).

Malbon, E.S., and A. Berlin (eds.), *Characterization in Biblical Literature* (Semeia, 63; Atlanta Scholars Press, 1993).

Malina, B.J., *Christian Origins and Cultural Anthropology: Practical Models for Biblical Interpretation* (Atlanta: John Knox Press, 1986).

—'The Gospel of John in Sociolinguistic Perspective', in H.C. Waetjen (ed.), *Protocol of the Forty Eighth Colloquy, 11 March 1984: Centre for Hermeneutical Studies in Hellenistic and Modern Culture, Graduate Theological Union and University of California, Berkeley* (Berkeley, CA: The Centre for Hermeneutical Studies, 1985).

—'Jesus as Charismatic Leader?', *BTB* 14 (1984), pp. 55-62.

Marshall, I.H., *The Gospel of Luke: A Commentary on the Greek Text* (NIGTC; Exeter: Paternoster Press, 1978).

Martin, L.H., *The Hellenistic Religions: An Introduction* (Oxford: Oxford University Press, 1987).

Martyn, J.L., *History and Theology in the Fourth Gospel* (Nashville: Abingdon Press, 2nd edn, 1979).

—*The Gospel of John in Christian History: Essays for Interpreters* (New York: Paulist Press, 1979).

—'Glimpses into the History of the Johannine Community', in de Jonge (ed.), *L'Evangile de Jean*, pp. 150-75.

Matera, F.J., 'John 20.1-18', *Int* 43 (1989), pp. 402-406.

Maynard, A.H., 'The Role of Peter in the Fourth Gospel', *NTS* 30 (1984), pp. 531-48.

Meeks, W.A., 'Asking Back to Jesus' Identity', in de Boer (ed.), *From Jesus to John*, pp. 38-50.

—'Breaking Away: Three New Testament Pictures of Christianity's Separation from the Jewish Communities', in J. Neusner and E.S. Frerichs (eds.), *To See ourselves as others See us: Christians, Jews, 'Others' in Late Antiquity* (Chico, CA: Scholars Press, 1985), pp. 93-115.

—'The Man from Heaven in Johannine Sectarianism', *JBL* 91 (1972), pp. 144-72.

—Review of *The Testament of Jesus*, by Ernst Käsemann, in *USQR* 24 (1969), pp. 414-20.

Menken, M.J.J., 'John 6.51c-58: Eucharist or Christology?', *Bib* 74 (1993), pp. 1-26.

—'The Christology of the Fourth Gospel: A Survey of Recent Research', in de Boer (ed.), *From Jesus to John*, pp. 292-320.

—'The Translation of Psalm 41.10 in John 13.18', *JSNT* 40 (1990), pp. 61-79.

Michaels, J.R., 'Betrayal and the Betrayer: The Uses of Scripture in John 13.18-19', in Evans and Stegner (eds.), *The Gospels and the Scriptures of Israel*, pp. 459-74.

—*John* (San Francisco: Harper & Row, 1984).

Miller, D.G., 'Tribulation but...', *Int* 18 (1964), pp. 165-70.

Minear, P.S., *John: The Martyr's Gospel* (New York: Pilgrim Press, 1984).

—'The Audience of the Fourth Evangelist', *Int* 31 (1977), pp. 339-54.

—'The Beloved Disciple in the Gospel of John: Some Clues and Conjectures', *NovT* 19 (1977), pp. 105-23.

Minor, M., 'John', in *Literary Critical Approaches to the Bible: An Annotated Bibliography* (West Cornwall, CT: Locust Hill Press, 1992), pp. 434-50.

Miranda, J.P., *Being and the Messiah: The Message of St John* (trans. J. Eagleson; Maryknoll, NY: Orbis Books, 1977).

Mlakuzhyil, G., *The Christocentric Literary Structure of the Fourth Gospel* (AnBib, 117; Rome: Pontificio Istituto Biblico, 1987).

Moloney, F.J., 'A Sacramental Reading of John 13.1-38', *CBQ* 53 (1991), pp. 237-56.

—'The Structure and Message of Jn 15.1–16.3', *AusBR* 35 (1987), pp. 35-49.

—*Woman: First among the Faithful* (London: Darton, Longman & Todd, 1984).

Moltmann-Wendel, E., *The Women around Jesus* (London: SCM Press, 1982).

Moore, S.D., 'How Jesus' Risen Body Became a Cadaver', in Malbon and McKnight (eds.), *The New Literary Criticism and the New Testament*, pp. 269-82.

—'Are There Impurities in the Living Water that the Johannine Jesus Dispenses? Deconstruction, Feminism and the Samaritan Woman', *BibInt* 1.2 (1993), pp. 207-27.

Morris, L., *The Gospel According to John: The English Text with Introduction, Exposition and Notes* (Grand Rapids: Eerdmans, 1971).

Munzer, K., 'Head', *NIDNTT*, II, pp. 156-63.

Neirynck, F., 'John 21', *NTS* 36 (1990), pp. 321-36.

Neusner, J., *Judaism: The Evidence of the Mishnah* (Chicago: University of Chicago Press, 1981).

Newbigin, L., *The Light Has Come: An Exposition of the Fourth Gospel* (Edinburgh: Handsel Press, 1982).

Neyrey J.H., 'What's Wrong with this Picture? John 4, Cultural Stereotypes of Women and Public and Private Space', *BTB* 24 (1994), pp. 77-91.

—*An Ideology of Revolt: John's Christology in Social-Science Perspective* (Philadelphia: Fortress Press, 1988).

Nicholson, G.C., *Death as Departure: The Johannine Descent–Ascent Schema* (SBLDS, 63; Chico, CA: Scholars Press, 1983.

O'Connor, F., *Mystery and Manners* (ed. S. Fitzgerald and R. Fitzgerald; London: Faber & Faber, 1972).

Oepke, A., 'διώκω', *TDNT*, II, pp. 229-30.

O'Grady, J.F., 'The Human Jesus in the Fourth Gospel', *BTB* 14 (1984), pp. 63-66.

Okure T., *The Johannine Approach to Mission: A Contextual Study of John 4.1-42* (WUNT, 2.31; Tübingen: J.C.B. Mohr, 1988).

Olsson, B., 'The History of the Johannine Movement', in Hartman and Olsson (eds.), *Aspects on the Johannine Literature*, pp. 27-43.

Orlinsky, H.M., *Studies on the Second Part of the Book of Isaiah: The So-Called 'Servant of the Lord' and 'Suffering Servant' in Second Isaiah* (VTSup, 14; Leiden: E.J. Brill, 1967).

Osborne, G.R., *The Hermeneutical Spiral: A Comprehensive Introduction to Biblical Interpretation* (Downers Grove, IL: IVP, 1991).

Painter, J., *The Quest for the Messiah: The History, Literature and Theology of the Johannine Community* (Edinburgh: T. & T. Clark, 2nd edn, 1993).

—'Tradition, History and Interpretation in John 10', in Beutler and Fortna (eds.), *The Shepherd Discourse of John 10 and its Context*, pp. 53-74.

—'Quest and Rejection Stories in John', *JSNT* 36 (1989), pp. 17-46.

—'The Farewell Discourses and the History of Johannine Christianity', *NTS* 27 (1981), pp. 525-43.

—*John, Witness and Theologian* (London: Darton, Longman & Todd, 1975).

Pallis, A., *Notes on St John and the Apocalypse* (Oxford: Oxford University Press, undated).

Parr, J., 'Jesus and the Liberation of the Poor: Biblical Interpretation in the Writings of Some Latin American Theologians of Liberation' (Unpublished thesis, University of Sheffield, 1989).

Perkins, P., '"I have seen the Lord" (John 20.18): Women Witnesses to the Resurrection', *Int* 46 (1992), pp. 31-41.

Petzger, J.H., and P.J. Hartin (eds.), *A South African Perspective on the New Testament: Essays by South African New Testament Scholars Presented to Bruce Manning Metzger during his Visit to South Africa in 1985* (Leiden: E.J. Brill, 1986).

Pfitzner, V.C., 'The Coronation of the King: The Passion in the Gospel of John', *CurTM* 4 (1977), pp. 10-21.

Pixley, G.V., *God's Kingdom* (trans. D.E. Walsh; London: SCM Press, 1981).

Plessis, P.J. du, 'The Lamb of God in the Fourth Gospel', in Petzger and Hartin (eds.), *A South African Perspective on the New Testament*, pp. 136-48.

Poland, L.M., *Literary Criticism and Biblical Hermeneutics: A Critique of Formalist Approaches* (AAR Academy Series, 48; Chico, CA: Scholars Press, 1985).

Potterie, I. de la, 'Jésus, roi et juge d'après Jn 19.13', *Bib* 41 (1960), pp. 217-47.

Powell, M.A., 'The Gospel of John', in *The Bible and Modern Literary Criticism: A Critical Assessment and Annotated Bibliography* (Bibliographies and Indexes in Religious Studies 22, London: Greenwood Press, 1992), pp. 324-38.

Pryor, J.W., *John, Evangelist of the Covenant People: The Narrative and Themes of the Fourth Gospel* (Downers Grove, IL: InterVarsity Press, 1992).

Quast, K., *Peter and the Beloved Disciple: Figures for a Community in Crisis* (JSNTSup, 32; Sheffield: JSOT Press, 1989).

—'Re-examining the Johannine Community', *TJT* 5 (1989), pp. 293-95.

Rahner, K., 'Dogmatic Reflections on the Knowledge and Self-Consciousness of Christ', in *idem, Theological Investigations*. V. *Later Writings* (trans. K.H. Kruger; 20 vols.; London: Darton, Longman & Todd, 1969), pp. 193-215.

Rand, J.A. du, 'Plot and Point of View in the Gospel of John', in JPetzger and Hartin (eds.), *A South African Perspective on the New Testament*, pp. 149-69.

—'The Characterization of Jesus as Depicted in the Narrative of the Fourth Gospel', *Neot* 19 (1985), pp. 18-36.

Reese, J.M., 'Literary Structure of Jn 13.31–14.31; 16.5-6, 16-33', *CBQ* 34 (1972), pp. 321-31.

Reinhartz, A., 'Jesus as Prophet: Predictive Prolepses in the Fourth Gospel', *JSNT* 36 (1989), pp. 3-16.

Reiser, W.E., 'The Case of the Tidy Tomb: The Place of the Napkins of John 11.44 and 20.7', *HeyJ* 14.1 (1973), pp. 47-57.

Rensberger, D.K., *Overcoming the World: Politics and Community in the Gospel of John* (London: SPCK, 1989) (first published as *Johannine Faith and Liberating Community* [Philadelphia: Westminster Press, 1988]).

Riley, W., 'Situating Biblical Narrative: Poetics and the Transmission of Community Values', *Proceedings of the Irish Biblical Association* 9 (1985), pp. 38-52.

Rissi, M., 'Der Aufbau des vierten Evangeliums', *NTS* 29 (1983), pp. 48-54.

Roberts, A., and J. Donaldson (eds.), *The Ante-Nicene Christian Library*. V. *Irenæus* (Edinburgh: T. & T. Clark, 1884).

—*The Ante-Nicene Christian Library: The Writings of Origen* (2 vols.; Edinburgh: T. & T.. Clark, 1894-95).

Robinson, J.A.T., *The Priority of John* (ed. J.F. Coakley; London: SCM Press, 1985).

—'The Last Tabu? The Self Conciousness of Jesus', in *idem, Twelve More New Testament Studies* (London: SCM Press, 1984), pp. 155-70.

Robinson, J.M., 'The Johannine Trajectory', in J.M. Robinson and H. Koester (eds.), *Trajectories through Early Christianity* (Philadelphia: Fortress Press, 1971), pp. 232-68.

Rose, H.J., *A Handbook of Greek Mythology: Including its Extension to Rome* (London: Methuen, 6th edn, 1972).

Ruether, R.R., *To Change the World: Christology and Cultural Criticism* (London: SCM Press, 1981).

Russell, L. (ed.), *Feminist Interpretation of the Bible* (Oxford: Basil Blackwell, 1985).

Ryken, L., *Words of Delight: A Literary Introduction to the Bible* (Grand Rapids: Baker Book House, 1987).

Sabbe, M., 'The Arrest of Jesus in Jn 18.1-11 and its Relation to the Synoptic Gospels', in de Jonge (ed.), *L'évangile de Jean*, pp. 203-34.

Salinger, J.D., *Franny and Zooey* (repr.; New York: Penguin Books, 1980 [1964]).

Sanders, E.P., *Jesus and Judaism* (London: SCM Press, 1985).

Sanders, J.N., *A Commentary on the Gospel According to St John* (ed. B.A. Mastin; London: A. & C. Black, 1968).

Sandmel, S., *Anti-Semitism in the New Testament?* (Philadelphia: Fortress Press, 1978).

Schafer, S., *The Victim and his Criminal: A Study in Functional Responsibility* (New York: Random House, 1968).

Schaff, P. (ed.), *A Select Library of the Nicene and Post-Nicene Fathers of the Christian Church. XIV. Saint Chrysostom* (New York: The Christian Literature Company, 1890).

—*A Select Library of the Nicene and Post-Nicene Fathers of the Christian Church. VII. Saint Augustine* (New York: The Christian Literature Company, 1888).

Schiffmann, L., 'At the Crossroads: Tannaitic Perspectives on the Jewish–Christian Schism', in E.P. Sanders (ed.) with A.I. Baumgarten and A. Mendelson, *Jewish and Christian Self-Definition*, II (2 vols.; London: SCM Press, 1981), pp. 115-56.

Schnackenburg, R., *The Gospel According to St John* (trans. C. Hastings, *et al.*; HTKNT; 3 vols.; repr.; London: Burns & Oates, 1988 [1982]) (originally published as *Das Johannesevangelium* [Freiburg: Herder, 1968]).

Schneiders, S.M., 'John 21.1-14', *Int* 43 (1989), pp. 70-75.

—'Women in the Fourth Gospel and the Role of Women in the Contemporary Church', *BTB* 12 (1982), pp. 35-45.

—'The Foot Washing (John 13.1-20): An Experiment in Hermeneutics', *CBQ* 43 (1981), pp. 76-92.

—'History and Symbolism in the Fourth Gospel', in de Jonge (ed.), *L'Evangile de Jean*, pp. 371-76.

Scholes, R., and R. Kellogg, *The Nature of Narrative* (Oxford: Oxford University Press, 1966).

Schottroff, L., *Let the Oppressed Go Free: Feminist Perspectives on the New Testament* (Louisville, KY: Westminster/John Knox, 1991).

Schüssler Fiorenza, E., *But She Said: Feminist Practices of Biblical Interpretation* (Boston: Beacon Press, 1992).

—*In Memory of Her: A Feminist Theological Reconstruction of Christian Origins* (London: SCM Press, 1983).

Scroggs, R., *Christology in Paul and John* (Proclamation Commentaries; Philadelphia: Fortress Press, 1988).

—'The Earliest Christian Communities as Sectarian Movement', in J. Neusner (ed.), *Christianity, Judaism and other Graeco-Roman Cults: Studies for Morton Smith at Sixty* (SJLA, 12; 2 vols.; Leiden: E.J. Brill, 1975), pp. 1-23.

Segovia, F.F., *The Farewell of the Word: The Johannine Call to Abide* (Minneapolis: Fortress Press, 1991).

—'John 13.1-20: The Footwashing in the Johannine Tradition', *ZNW* 73 (1982), pp. 31-51.

—'The Love and Hatred of Jesus in Johannine Sectarianism', *CBQ* 43 (1981), pp. 258-72.

Segundo, J.L., *Jesus of Nazareth Yesterday and Today*. II. *The Historical Jesus of the Synoptics* (trans. J. Drury; Maryknoll, NY: Orbis Books, London: Sheed & Ward, 1985).

Seim, T.K., 'Roles of Women in the Gospel of John', in Hartman and Olsson (eds.), *Aspects on the Johannine Literature*, pp. 56-73.

Shachter, J., H. Freedman, and I. Epstein (eds.), *Hebrew–English Edition of the Babylonian Talmud: Tractate Sanhedrin* (London: Soncino Press, 1969).

Sherwin-White, A.N., *The Letters of Pliny: A Historical and Social Commentary* (Oxford: Clarendon Press, 1966).

Shuchter, S.R., and S. Zisook, 'The Course of Normal Grief', in M.S. Stroebe, W. Stroebe, and R.O. Hansson (eds.), *Handbook of Bereavement: Theory, Research and Intervention* (Cambridge: Cambridge University Press, 1993), pp. 23-43.

Sloyan, G.S., *What Are they Saying about John?* (New York: Paulist Press, 1991).

—*John* (Interpretation; Atlanta: John Knox Press, 1988).

Smalley, S.S., *John: Evangelist and Interpreter* (Exeter: Paternoster Press, 1978).

—'The Sign in John XXI', *NTS* 20 (1974), pp. 275-88.

Smith, D.M., *John among the Gospels: The Relationship in Twentieth-Century Research* (Minneapolis: Fortress Press, 1992).

—'The Life Setting of the Gospel of John', *RevExp* 85 (1988), pp. 433-44.

—*John* (Proclamation Commentaries; Philadelphia: Fortress Press, 1986).

—*Johannine Christianity: Essays on its Setting, Sources and Theology* (Columbia: University of South Carolina Press, 1984).

—'The Presentation of Jesus in the Fourth Gospel', *Int* 31 (1977), pp. 367-78.

Smith, J.B., *Greek–English Concordance to the New Testament* (Eastbourne: Kingsway, 1955).

Snyder, G.F., 'John 13.16 and the Anti-Petrinism of the Johannine Tradition', *BibRes* 16 (1971), pp. 5-15.

Snyder, M.H., *The Christology of Rosemary Radford Ruether: A Critical Introduction* (Mystic, CT: Twenty-Third Publications, 1988).

Sobrino, J., *Christology at the Crossroads: A Latin American Approach* (trans. J. Drury; London: SCM Press, 1978).

Spicq, C., 'Τρώγειν: Est-il synonyme de φαγεῖν et d'ἐσθίειν dans le Nouveau Testament?', *NTS* 26 (1979–80), pp. 414-19.

Staley, J.L., 'Subversive Narrative/Victimized Reader: A Reader Response Assessment of a Text Critical Problem, John 18.12-24', *JSNT* 51 (1993), pp. 79-98.

—'Stumbling in the Dark, Reaching for the Light: Reading Character in John 5 and 9', *Semeia* 53 (1991), pp. 55-80.

—*The Print's First Kiss: A Rhetorical Investigation of the Implied Reader in the Fourth Gospel* (SBLDS, 82; Atlanta: Scholars Press, 1988).

Stibbe, M.W.G., 'A Tomb with a View: John 11.1-44 in Narrative-Critical Perspective', *NTS* 40 (1994), pp. 38-54.

—*John* (Readings; Sheffield: JSOT Press, 1993).

—'"Return to Sender": A Structuralist Approach to John's Gospel', *BibInt* 1 (1993), pp. 189-206.

—*John as Storyteller: Narrative Criticism and the Fourth Gospel* (Cambridge: Cambridge University Press, 1992).

—'The Elusive Christ: A New Reading of the Fourth Gospel', *JSNT* 44 (1991), pp. 19-38.

—'Literary Criticism in John's Gospel', Unpublished paper presented in the Department of Biblical Studies, University of Sheffield, 1985.

Stibbe, M.W.G., (ed.), *The Gospel of John as Literature: An Anthology of Twentieth-Century Perspectives* (NTTS, 17; Leiden: E.J. Brill, 1993).

Story, C.I.K., 'The Mental Attitude of Jesus at Bethany: John 11.33, 38', *NTS* 37 (1991), pp. 51-66.

Strack, H.L. and Billerbeck, P., *Kommentar zum Neuen Testament aus Talmud und Midrasch*, II (4 vols.; Munich: C.H. Becksche Verlagsbuchhandlung/ Oskar Beck, 1924).

Suggit, J.N., 'John 13.1-30: The Mystery of the Incarnation and of the Eucharist', *Neot* 19 (1985), pp. 64-70.

Swidler, L., 'Jesus Was a Feminist', *Catholic World* 212 (1971), pp. 177-83.

Talbert, C.H., *Reading John: A Literary and Theological Commentary on the Fourth Gospel and the Johannine Epistles* (New York: Crossroad, 1992).

Tartt, D., *The Secret History* (London: Penguin Books, 1992).

Tate, W.R., *Biblical Interpretation: An Integrated Approach* (Peabody, MA: Hendrickson, 1991).

Taylor, V., *The Atonement in New Testament Teaching* (repr.; London: Epworth Press, 3rd edn, 1963 [1958]).

Thiede, C.P., *Simon Peter: From Galilee to Rome* (Exeter: Paternoster Press, 1986).

Thomas, J.C., *Footwashing in John 13 and the Johannine Community* (JSNTSup, 61; Sheffield: JSOT Press, 1991).

Thompson, M.M., *The Humanity of Jesus in the Fourth Gospel* (Philadelphia: Fortress Press, 1988).

Tompkins, J.P., (ed.), *Reader-Response Criticism: From Formalism to Post-Structuralism* (Baltimore: The Johns Hopkins University Press, 1980).

Trible, P., *Texts of Terror: Literary-Feminist Readings of Biblical Narratives* (Overtures to Biblical Theology; Philadelphia: Fortress Press, 1984).

Trumbower, J.A., *Born from Above: The Anthropology of the Gospel of John* (HUT, 29; Tübingen: J.C.B. Mohr, 1992).

Turner, M., 'Atonement and the Death of Jesus in John: Some Questions to Bultmann and Forestell', *EvQ* 62.2 (1990), pp. 99-122.

Van Belle, G., *Johannine Bibliography 1966–1985: A Cumulative Bibliography on the Fourth Gospel* (BETL, 82; Leuven: Leuven University Press/Uitgeverij Peeters, 1988).

Wagner, G., *An Exegetical Bibliography of the New Testament: John and 1, 2, 3 John* (Macon, GA: Mercer University Press, 1987).

Wahlde, U.C. von, 'The Johannine Jews: A Critical Survey', *NTS* 28 (1982), pp. 33-60.

Warren, W.F., 'Christology, Culture and Reconciliation in Latin America', *TE* 44 (1991), pp. 5-14.

Watts, J.D.W., *Isaiah 34–66* (WBC, 25; Waco, TX: Word Books, 1987).

Weber, H.R., *The Cross: Tradition and Interpretation* (trans. E. Jessett; London: SPCK, 1979).

Weiser, T., 'Community: Its Unity, Diversity and Universality', *Semeia* 33 (1985), pp. 83-95.

Westcott, B.F., *The Gospel According to St John* (London: John Murray, 1898).

Westermann, C., *Isaiah 40–66: A Commentary* (trans. D.M.G. Stalker; London: SCM Press, 1969).

Whitacre, R.A., *Johannine Polemic: The Role of Tradition and Theology* (SBLDS, 67; Chico, CA: Scholars Press, 1982).

Whybray, R.N., *Thanksgiving for a Liberated Prophet: An Interpretation of Isaiah 53* (JSOTSup, 4; Sheffield: JSOT Press, 1978).

Wiarda, T., 'John 21.1-23: Narrative Unity and its Implications', *JSNT* 46 (1992), pp. 53-71.

Williams, J.G., *The Bible, Violence, and the Sacred: Liberation from the Myth of Sanctioned Violence* (New York: HarperCollins, 1991).

Wilson, B.R., *Magic and the Millennium: A Sociological Study of Religious Movements of Protest among Tribal and Third-World Peoples* (London: Heinemann, 1973).

Windisch, H., 'John's Narrative Style', in Stibbe (ed.), *The Gospel of John as Literature*, pp. 25-64.

Wipfler, W.L., 'Identifying Jesus the Victim in the Victims of Oppression', *Tugon* 11.2 (1991), pp. 259-68.

Witherington, B., *Women in the Ministry of Jesus* (Cambridge: Cambridge University Press, 1984).

Woll, B.D., 'The Departure of "the Way": The First Farewell Discourse in the Gospel of John', *JBL* 99 (1980), pp. 225-39.

Woods, D., *Biko* (London: Penguin Books, rev. edn, 1987).

Wuellner, W., 'Putting Life Back into the Lazarus Story and its Reading: The Narrative Rhetoric of John 11 as the Narration of Faith', *Semeia* 53 (1991), pp. 113-32.

Wyatt, N., '"Supposing him to Be the Gardener" (John 20.15): A Study of the Paradise Motif in John', *ZNW* 81 (1990), pp. 21-38.

Yalom, I.D., *Love's Executioner and other Tales of Psychotherapy* (London: Penguin Books, 1989.

Young, F.M., *Sacrifice and the Death of Christ* (London: SPCK, 1975).

Young, F.W., 'A Study of the Relation of Isaiah to the Fourth Gospel', *ZNW* 46 (1955), pp. 215-33.

INDEXES

INDEX OF REFERENCES

OLD TESTAMENT

JOURNAL FOR THE STUDY OF THE NEW TESTAMENT
SUPPLEMENT SERIES